D1117246

Making Competition Work in electricity

Founded in 1807, John Wiley & Sons is the oldest independent publishing company in the United States. With offices in North America, Europe, Australia, and Asia, Wiley is globally committed to developing and marketing print and electronic products and services for our customers' professional and personal knowledge and understanding.

The Wiley Finance series contains books written specifically for finance and investment professionals as well as sophisticated individual investors and their financial advisors. Book topics range from portfolio management to e-commerce, risk management, financial engineering, valuation and financial instrument analysis, as well as much more.

For a list of available titles, please visit our Web site at www.WileyFinance.com.

Making Competition Work
in electricity

SALLY HUNT

John Wiley & Sons, Inc.

This book is printed on acid-free paper. ♾

Published by John Wiley & Sons, Inc., New York.
Published simultaneously in Canada.

ISBN 0-471-22098-1

Printed in the United States of America.

10 9 8 7 6 5 4 3 2 1

foreword

Here is the book I've been looking for to guide me through the devilishly complicated experience of electric industry deregulation, drawing on the author's direct involvement in this process in several of the countries that have undergone it—none of which, significantly, has seriously considered reversing the process.

Some of its judgments are wondrously pithy.

California allowed itself to get into the dreadful position of designing its trading arrangements so as to rely on demand response, and then having customer prices frozen. There was no transition: it went cold turkey into a world of no installed reserve requirement, no demand response, no intelligent price caps, no anything.

Equally, some of its recommendations:

FERC should just hire Bill Hogan to set out the coherent set of trading arrangements that he has been advocating indefatigably for a decade, and drop all the paraphernalia of wheeling.

More important, she explains why.

Most valuable of all, she presents a clear, explanatory road map, a detailed exposition of the order in which to proceed, step-by-step, which steps are essential, which optional, which worth taking whether or not we proceed to the next one, which not. Some of the essential steps, such as pricing transmission services efficiently, are elegantly described; some, such as the overwhelming importance of instituting efficient pricing, amazingly simple.

An admirable and indispensable guide; detailed, annotated and authoritative.

Alfred E. Kahn
Former Chairman, New York State Public Service Commission
Former Chairman, Civil Aeronautics Board
Professor Emeritus, Cornell University

preface

I wanted to write this book. It seemed a fitting way to begin retirement, allowing me the luxury of concentrating on one thing, discussing complex issues with many really smart people, pulling together everything I have learned about the electric industry for nearly 30 years, and expanding it to develop a workable solution to the current impasse in the United States. It has been more difficult than anything I have ever done, but I have enjoyed it immensely.

The Edison Electric Institute (EEI), at the behest of its then chairman, John Rowe, requested the book and partially supported the writing of it, but this is not an industry position paper. The members knew my views on the issues, which I had expressed in speeches and in a previous book. No EEI member was ever going to agree with everything I would say, and they do not; but the feeling was that the country needed a coherent intellectual framework to work from, and no one but the industry was going to take on the task of providing one.

There are so many people to thank for their knowledge, their detailed attention, and their prose. Paul Joskow, who has been a demanding and generous colleague for a quarter century, read two of the early drafts and commented extensively. His intellectual contribution to the book is so great that it dwarfs all others. It was he who suggested dividing it into two parts, which made it a much better book although it killed three weeks. Alfred Kahn, everyone's favorite guru, and mine, lent his time to reason with me about the federal/state question. Graham Shuttleworth of NERA London, the coauthor of my previous book, and now sadly too far away for continued collaboration, read and improved it; he also provided information for the U.K. appendices.

Among my NERA U.S. colleagues, the most special thanks must go to Hamish Fraser who worked with me constantly during the writing of the book. I no longer know which paragraphs he wrote and which I did. He has done a sterling job of keeping me honest, cutting the waffle, also drafting the trading arrangements and transmission sections. (Hamish's training ground was in the New Zealand and the New York trading arrangements—two success stories; while I participated in the design of old U.K. Pool, now regrettably demised, and in the contorted California process, which nearly demised me.) Hethie Parmesano drafted the retail sections and, as always, returned comments and provided examples each time I changed my mind about what I thought. Jeff Makholm explained gas deregulation, which was a turning point in the analysis. Carolyn Berry and Kristina Sepetys provided information on California. Jonathan Falk is my source for analogies, and also for market power and environmental issues. Gene Meehan, Kurt Strunk, Karl McDermott, Oscar Arnedillo, Chantral LaCasse, and Andy Joskow helped with the thinking, and Veronica Irastorza, Willis Geffert, and Veronica Lambrechts filled in many of the details. Stephanie Godkin did the graphics, David Tabak taught me about liquid and efficient markets, Bill Taylor about telephone, Lou Guth about alcohol, and Fred Dunbar about roads. Dick Rapp, the president of NERA, originally suggested writing the book and has provided moral support, office space, and the time of the NERA staff.

David Owens of EEI offered valuable assistance and provided Mathew Morey and Ken Linder as readers. They discussed it with me chapter by endless chapter, but they never tried to censor. Elizabeth Moler, the former Chair of FERC, provided detailed and illuminating comments; Tom Rose and Mike McCall filled me in on Texas.

In these restructuring matters, working with clients on real problems has always been my major source of learning. Since 1996 when my last book was published, I have collaborated principally, and over long periods, in New Jersey with the two Franks—Cassidy and Delany—at PSE&G, in Mexico with the Energy Ministry under Luis Tellez, and in China with Noureddine Berrah for the World Bank.

Thanks also to Robert Marritz, Charles Stalon, Laura Manz, Tony Robinson, Jose-Luis Aburto, Larry Ruff, Fiona Woolf, Jim Barker, and Daniel Fessler. My son, Mark Streiter, acted as a target reader on the early drafts, forcing me to greater clarity. And finally, sincere acknowledgments to Bill Hogan, who has made his thinking available to all of us, both on his Web site and in person, and has shaped so much of the progress in this area. Thank you all very much.

SALLY HUNT

contents

CHAPTER 1

Introduction

This was to have been a book about the electric industry in the United States. Ten years after federal legislation began the process in 1992, the United States is stuck in the middle, with some states regulated and some deregulated. There is still no clear policy at the national level for where we are trying to get to, and no road map for getting there. The aim of the book was to return to the fundamentals, to set out a consistent framework for national policy, and proposals for achieving it, so that any interested person could understand it.

But books have a way of going off in their own direction. It turned out that it was impossible to explain even where we are now, let alone what went wrong in California and where we should be headed, without extensive footnotes explaining the concepts, which then turned into text boxes, and eventually into whole chapters. Finally, a wise reviewer suggested dividing the book into two parts—the general story of how to make competition work in electricity, which can apply to any country, and a policy framework for the United States. And that is what we did. It is as simple as I could make it.

Although the book has a single author and reflects in the end a personal prescription, colleagues at NERA have contributed substantially to the drafting and have reviewed every chapter. We (the collegial "we" who pontificate throughout the book) have been involved in virtually every electricity restructuring around the globe and in the United States. By now there is little disagreement between us—we think we know what works and what does not, and which issues are not yet settled. There is even substantial agreement among the few consulting firms who have specialized in these matters. But to my knowledge, this is the first attempt at gathering it all together and applying it to U.S. policy issues.

The restructuring of the electric industry in the United States has had a short but bumpy history. The 1992 federal legislation required open access to the transmission network for some transactions, and removed some roadblocks to independent generators. Since 1994, the states have been deregulating one by one. Most state plans were stalled by the debacle in California,[1] which cost the citizens of that state, as taxpayers and as customers, billions of dollars out of pocket, 40 percent rate increases, and the first set of rolling blackouts in the memory of most citizens of the United States. Deregulation is widely viewed as a failed experiment, competition as a rip-off. Countries as far away as China and as close as Mexico put their plans on hold because of the risks exposed by California.

This does not have to be the case. The industry is technically complex and also institutionally complicated, but there is by now, after a decade of international experience, a "standard prescription" to deal with the complexities: a checklist of what is required for this industry to become competitive. The technical complexity can be solved: The institutional issues are at the root of the problem in the United States.

The basic problem is the split of regulation between the federal government and the states. It is a thoroughly interstate industry, but no one has overall authority to decide what needs to be done. This has resulted in a plethora of incompatible initiatives. What is required is to develop the conceptual framework, make a plan, and to implement the institutional changes necessary to make it happen.

THE ELECTRIC INDUSTRY

Electric systems around the world are physically and operationally very similar. The physical functions of the industry are generation (production), system operations, transmission, and distribution. The merchant functions are wholesaling and retailing. Transmission and distribution are transport functions—the transmission wires are networked and serve large areas; the distribution wires are local. The typical organization of the industry prior to deregulation was *vertically integrated companies*, incorporating all these functions.

These companies built their own generating plants and coordinated the planning of generation with the planning of transmission. In real time their system operators coordinated the generating plants, telling them when to run and when to back off so as not to overload the transmission network. The customers received a bill that had all these functions "bundled" into a single tariff—the vertically integrated company was the retailer as well as

[1] Appendix C reviews the California crisis of 2000–2001. Texas did go ahead with its long-planned deregulation on January 1, 2002.

the producer. The vertically integrated companies had monopolies in their own areas, and because of this, prices were regulated—in the United States mostly by regulators at the state level, in other countries by the central government. The integrated companies built to serve their own customers, and had to build enough to serve them all, at all times.

Competition in the electric industry generally means competition only in the production (generation) of electricity and in the commercial functions of wholesaling and retailing. These are the functions that would be deregulated—their prices would be set in competitive markets and not by regulators. The transportation functions (transmission and distribution) cannot be competitive—they are natural monopolies. It doesn't make economic (or environmental or esthetic) sense to build multiple sets of competing transmission systems; everyone has to use the same wires.[2] They have to serve everyone, and they have to be regulated. System operations also has to be a monopoly, since the system operator has to control all the plants in a control area, or the system will not function. The worry is that in restructuring, the competitive parts need to be separated from the regulated parts, and the coordination that was working well in the integrated companies under regulation may be lost. Institutions have to be designed to replace the previous internal coordination without losing its important efficiencies. This has been done successfully in parts of America, and also abroad, but it is still the major challenge.

THE CASE FOR COMPETITION

The major theme of this book is simple: The need in the United States is to *refocus* on introducing competition into the production markets, because this is where most of the long-term benefits of restructuring will accrue. Competition in the retail markets will not produce low prices if the production markets are not competitive. It was in the production end that the problems of the old U.S. system were mainly observed[3]—a highly politicized process of investment, inefficiencies in choice of technology, construction, and maintenance, and difficulties in regulation and pricing, that led to a desire to reorganize the industry. Since these are the places that competition can help, introducing competition in production makes sense for the United States.

---

[2] This is in contrast to telephone, where competition in long distance provision did involve competing methods of transmission (such as microwave transmission and fiber-optic cables) owned by different providers.

[3] Paul Joskow, *Deregulation and Regulatory Reform in the U.S. Electric Power Sector,* MIT Department of Economics, Working Paper, February 17, 2000.

Competition is the basis upon which the U.S. economy was built. It is not an end in itself. It is generally supposed to bring a whole bundle of good things that we as a society value—efficiency and technical progress among them. The U.S. Supreme Court has called the Sherman Act of 1890:

> *. . . a comprehensive charter of economic liberty aimed at preserving free and unfettered competition as the rule of trade, resting on the premise that the unrestrained interaction of competitive forces will yield the best allocation of our economic resources, the lowest prices, the highest quality and the greatest material progress, while at the same time providing an environment conducive to the preservation of our democratic political and social institutions.*[4]

The Court was enunciating the economic case for competition—the best allocation of our economic resources, the lowest prices, the highest quality, and the greatest material progress.

In general, a monopoly held in check by regulation is considered a poor substitute for a competitive market and is only to be adopted where, for reasons of natural monopoly or some overriding public interest, competition is not feasible or performs poorly without government controls. We now know from experience elsewhere and in parts of the United States that competition in electricity production is feasible. We know that many of the reasons the industry was organized as regulated monopolies for so long no longer apply. So competition is the standard to beat. Competition is what benefits consumers. And in the final analysis, benefiting consumers should be what public policy is all about.

Consumers want, and should expect to have:

- Low prices (although they know they have to pay enough to keep suppliers in business);
- Reliable service;
- Fairly predictable bills; and
- The opportunity to benefit from value-added services that may come available.

So far, except in the notorious case of California, competition has managed to provide these things where it has been introduced in electric industries around the world. Many other countries, and some jurisdictions in the United States, have successfully introduced competition in production and open access to transmission. There is by now a decade of international

[4]U.S. Supreme Court: *Northern Pacific Railway Co. v. United States,* 356 U.S. 1, 4 (1958).

experience good and not so good, but not one of the countries that introduced competition has gone back to the old monopoly ways. This, in its own way, is a ringing testimonial to the benefits of competition.[5]

However, there are certain technical details that have to be attended to for competition to be able to produce these results. There are cogent reasons why electricity was a monopoly for so long—electricity is indeed different from other commodities. It cannot be stored; it is transported at the speed of light, following laws of physics unique to this commodity, over a fragile and interactive transmission network. The instant you flip the switch, something happens at a generating plant somewhere, and the electricity gets to you in a millisecond. The network requires the constant vigilant control of a system operator; the penalty for inattention is to black out the whole area, as has happened twice on the East Coast of the United States.

But the technical complexity exists everywhere there is electricity. We know what to do, and we know what we don't know. We also know that restructuring this industry is harder than most people think. Airline, gas, banking, and telecommunications industries have been made competitive, with considerable success. They were a piece of cake in comparison to electricity. One thing has been made clear from experience both at home and abroad: You cannot simply cease to regulate the industry and walk away from it expecting a competitive market to rush in and work its magic. The introduction of competition poses some really difficult problems, and rational solutions depend upon understanding these complexities and designing ways to account for them.

Part One of this book is the "Standard Prescription"—the issues that need to be addressed, explanations of the controversial points, and proposals for the most resilient solutions, derived both from economic theory and from years of practical experience in the field. The institutional changes must, in the end, permit competitive markets in electricity to meet the ordinary requirements of commerce. Many buyers and many sellers must be able to access each other easily; they must be able to make contracts in advance and at spot prices; and they must be able to transport the electricity with a high degree of certainty as to the price and availability of the transmission network.

Efficiency is the goal; competition is the means; *open access, restructuring,* and *deregulation* are terms sometimes used to describe the reforms, but they are the tools to achieve it. We now turn to what these terms mean.

---

[5]The United Kingdom (actually England and Wales—Scotland and Northern Ireland work under different systems) was an early adopter of competition and has a decade of experience with it. It has made mistakes, but the overall result has been positive. Appendix A reviews the downward course of prices, the introduction of new technology, and the reduction in complaints in the United Kingdom.

Open Access

Competition in production requires *open access* to the transmission and distribution wires so that any competing producer can use them. Transmission is an *essential facility*—everyone has to use it. Open access means that everyone gets the same deal, with no discrimination in the opportunity to use the wires or in the cost to use them. But making this happen requires major institutional changes, which are discussed in detail in Part One.

First, real-time coordination of generation with transmission is a necessity. In the old vertically integrated industry, they were coordinated internally by the companies; in the competitive industry new *trading arrangements* have to be set up to ensure real-time coordination in a disaggregated world, because if coordination fails, we will all be literally in the dark. The design of trading arrangements for open access takes up much of this book, not only because it is complex in theory, but also because of the complicated industry and regulatory structure in the United States.

When potential competitors (the old monopolies who owned both transmission and production facilities) own the transmission wires, it is important to ensure that the real-time coordination does not favor the sale of power by the transmission owner at the expense of sales by other competitors. This has been accomplished in most of the world by complete separation of system operations into an independent organization, and by trading arrangements that do not give priority to the transmission owner.

In addition to short-term coordination, open access requires arrangements for long-term control of the transmission—the transmission business model. Before deregulation, the utilities built for themselves, and never had to set prices for use. Who will plan and build for competition? What are the right prices? What rights do those who built the transmission for their own use retain in the new world? If transmission expansion is in the hands of competing generators, there are issues of discrimination; if it is in too many hands, there are issues of coordination. These are the main areas where even internationally there is no standard institutional design.

Retail access,[6] or more accurately, "customer choice" refers to the opportunity for individual consumers to choose from among competitive electricity suppliers. Traditionally, customers have been able to purchase electricity from just one supplier (i.e., their local, vertically integrated

[6] Retail access is a term used more in the United States than anywhere else; it is a holdover from the terminology used in the disputes of the 1980s over whether municipal utilities and cooperatives should be given access to the transmission wires to purchase competitively—this was called "wholesale access" to distinguish it from permitting final customers to choose their suppliers, which was called "retail access."

monopoly). Under deregulation they are given the opportunity to choose their supplier, and "retail access" refers to the ability of suppliers to reach customers over local distribution wires. This (unlike transmission) is not a technically complex matter, but can run into many political complications, such as how much protection to afford the smaller consumers.

Restructuring

Restructuring is about changing existing companies—separating some functions and combining others, and sometimes creating new companies. The aim is to prevent discriminatory behavior, or to create more competitors, or to consolidate transmission over a wide region. The theory is fairly simple. Some functions must be separated; some should be kept together, while for some there is room for significant policy choices. There are various degrees of and approaches to separation. There may also be questions of regional consolidation, both separating and combining companies as part of a restructuring. The offset to dividing up the functions is the loss of the economies inherent in the traditional monopoly structure, and the cost of all the lawyers needed to set up new companies.

Restructuring is time-consuming, even when the government owns the company and the legislature wants competition. Dividing physical and financial assets between new companies is often the major element on the critical path for restructuring, even when everything else is agreed. (The normal time is about two years.) But the decisions about restructuring are complicated in the extreme where, as in the United States, many companies are privately owned, and one third of the industry is in the ownership of thousands of different government bodies, from the federal government to municipalities. It is not exactly clear who has or should have the authority to order necessary restructuring. The U.S. telephone monopoly was restructured as the result of a massive antitrust case, but we are not talking antitrust cases here. What has been done so far in the United States is that state regulators have offered carrots and brandished sticks to encourage voluntary restructuring, and some state legislatures have acted, although so far without their actions being tested in the courts.

Deregulation

Deregulation means ceasing to regulate. Regulation is about controlling prices of monopoly suppliers and restricting entry to the markets, so the standard definition of deregulation is to remove controls on prices and entry of competing suppliers. This would be simply disastrous for consumers in the electric industry, if it were done without necessary safeguards or supportive market conditions. Just declaring the industry deregulated and providing open access to the transmission system cannot produce competitive markets in electricity.[7] The existing suppliers are local monopolies with 100 percent of a local area both at the production and at the retail level. It would hardly be surprising if they were dominant suppliers after such a "deregulation." So something else has to happen for deregulation to produce competition. In fact, for competition to work in the electric industry, there is a long list of conditions that ought to be in place before deregulating. That is what Part One of this book is about. At the end of Part One there is a checklist—the standard prescription—of the changes that are needed. In this Introduction we will not attempt to do more than summarize the conclusions—the material is quite difficult and will not fit into a thimble, but the text explains each point in detail.

The five major changes required are:

1. *Demand side:* Hourly metering for most of the consumption (this does not mean most of the customers), and pricing plans that expose customers to the spot price for some of their consumption.
2. *Trading arrangements:* System operations separated from traders and regionally consolidated. Trading arrangements based on an integrated model, with central dispatch and locational energy prices.
3. *Transmission business model:* Control of transmission separate from traders; pricing and expansion arrangements; our preference is for regional profit-making regulated Transcos incorporating the system operator.
4. *Supply side:* Remove barriers to entry. Buy out of the old regime by valuing assets. Expand market areas by improving transmission. If necessary for market power control, divest utility generation into smaller parcels.
5. *Retail access:* When production markets are working, choice for all customers. This needs an extensive settlement mechanism and customer education, and decisions about default provision.

This is a standard prescription, and it is never quite like this; as any doctor can tell you, the standard prescription may not apply if there are complicating

[7] In the best case, nothing happens at all. The United Kingdom had a law on the books permitting competitive entry and requiring open access from 1984 onwards; but since it did not provide the "trading arrangements" for access to the transmission that we mention above, there were no takers at all until the industry was totally restructured in 1990.

factors. All those years in medical school teach you to understand not only the straightforward case and the best treatment, but also the underlying anatomy and physiology so that you can treat the complications that arise in real cases. In this book we look at the underlying issues that need to be addressed in electricity, and try to explain the rationale, so that if the prescription must be adjusted, it does not kill the patient.

Each country has its own preexisting conditions or political necessities, and most of them have to muddle through in some way or another. It is certainly much easier to start from a situation where the government owns the industry and also has the legal power to change things, generally in the run-up to privatization. This at least assures a fairly consistent plan, and a unitary design that can hold up under stress. All plans involve winners and losers, and when the government can accept being the short-term loser, because it has the longer view of the benefits of change, everyone else can be kept happy. In the long run, as Keynes did not say, we are all dead except the government.

THE UNITED STATES

In Part Two we consider in detail the situation in the United States, why it got to where it is, and how it could get out of it.

The United States is enormous—it contains one-quarter of all the electric capacity in the world. One of its strengths is that for two centuries it has managed to walk the line between the benefits of national standardization and state and local autonomy. The electric industry began locally, and federal legislation from the 1930s actually kept it fragmented. But today it is so fragmented that—even leaving aside competition—efficiency is suffering. Two hundred or more private companies submit to divided and sometimes contradictory regulatory jurisdiction. Each of the fifty states and the District of Columbia has its own plan to deregulate, or not. The rest of the industry includes three thousand or so entities that operate, uncoordinated, at federal, state, and municipal level. These entities are not subject to most of the state or federal regulation applied to the private entities. Transmission is owned by over two hundred public and private entities. There are one hundred and forty or so local system operators.

All these complications bring their own problems for implementation of reforms. Private ownership complicates restructuring of companies; fragmented operational control inhibits efficient trading arrangements; fragmented transmission ownership permits states (or companies) to hold up expansions that would benefit neighboring states (or competing generators). Public ownership can stand in the way of regional consolidation of the network. There has never been a national policy or regional framework other than a vague desire on the part of Congress and the federal regulators to see the industry competitive. There are no regional bodies to coordinate over wide areas.

It is hardly surprising then that reforms have so far been confined to the big states and states with preexisting regional agreements. California, New York, and Texas were big enough to go it alone, and Texas has the distinct advantage of unitary regulation. Texas is not electrically interconnected with the rest of the United States and therefore is not regulated by Federal Energy Regulatory Commission (FERC). In two other cases in the Northeast,[8] preexisting interstate agreements (the "tight pools") have been the springboard for coordinated actions by states. These states can be considered to have created the basis for more or less competitive markets, but these are the low-hanging fruit, and even these would not meet our checklist in all respects.

In the rest of the country, natural market areas clearly cover more than one state, but there are no national or regional plans. If there were, there would be no authority to impose them. The rest of the country is at an impasse; *markets are bigger than a single state and states cannot go it alone.* Any further developments are stymied, and probably would be even without the well-publicized problems in California.

The central problem for the rest of the country is that jurisdiction over the industry is divided between federal and state governments in a way that was established in 1935, when the industry was mainly a local industry. Now the transmission networks have expanded and interconnected so much that electricity is clearly in interstate commerce, but the 1935 jurisdictional split remains. Referring to our five big issues on the checklist:

- The first (metering and tariff design) and the last (retail access) are in the jurisdiction of the individual states.
- The second and third (the trading arrangements and the transmission business model) are mostly in federal jurisdiction, but FERC has insufficient authority to require the changes it says it wants.[9] The metering necessary to get competitive wholesale markets working well is in the hands of the states.

---

[8] The New England states, through NEPOOL and its offspring, and the Pennsylvania–New Jersey–Maryland Interconnection (PJM).

[9] The extent of FERC's actual authority in these matters is still being tested in the courts. (See p. 296.)

- The supply side is divided. Only the states can deregulate; no one can expand transmission over wide areas to create larger and more competitive markets; no one can require divestiture if it is needed to control market power. The states control siting of generation and transmission.

The centerpiece of competition—ensuring competitive production markets—is in no one's jurisdiction. The states alone can deregulate production and free customers to choose; but they cannot put all the underpinnings in place to make sure the markets are competitive. They cannot control market power over wide areas; they cannot require other states to install metering; they cannot implement trading arrangements or require consolidation of transmission.

The situation in the United States is a complicated muddle. Implementation has gotten far ahead of policy. Professor Paul Joskow of MIT, a longtime and respected observer of the industry, puts it this way:

> *I do not believe that . . . the electric power sector can exist and prosper with a checkerboard of competitive and non-competitive states taking power from the same transmission networks, or even with a large number of competitive states which have adopted a wide array of different rules and institutions for wholesale and retail competition.*[10]

It is a fair question, and often asked: Why bother when it is so complicated? What was wrong with the old system? Under regulation, the U.S. electric industry had a good history, by international standards of the time, of innovation, low prices, and reliable service. The vertically integrated monopolies had reasonably good arrangements for short-term coordination of system operations with production; and good arrangements for expanding transmission, that took into account the trade-offs between transmission and generation.

But while it might be instructive to consider the problems of regulation and how competition will improve them, that is no longer the issue. We cannot ignore the fact that some changes are already well underway. Open access was ordered in 1992, but a decade later the trading arrangements have not been resolved; regional organizations have not been put in place; metering and rate design have not been attended to; transmission investment has mostly ground to a halt; detection and mitigation of market

[10] Paul Josko, *Deregulation and Regulatory Reform in the U.S. Electric Power Sector,* MIT Department of Economics, Working Paper, February 17, 2000.

power is rudimentary. We do not have the option of going back a decade—the appropriate comparison is what is happening now, which in many cases is not as good as it was pre-1992. We have taken the industry apart and have put nothing comprehensive in its place.

The reason to resolve this impasse speedily is that the customers are at risk. If they are let loose, given "retail access" and told to choose, without the production markets being truly competitive, or even tolerably competitive, they are at great risk of being ripped off. This may be why state regulators have intuitively built in so many protections for small consumers, which they would not need if the production markets were competitive. Competition at the production level is what protects consumers. But the states cannot create competitive markets by themselves. Natural market areas are bigger than single states. The answer lies with broader regional solutions and clear cohesive national policies.

The changes since 1992 have forever changed FERC's role. States that deregulate find that in doing so they cede much of their jurisdiction to the federal authorities since under deregulation, all sales from generating plants and all transmission pricing fall to federal jurisdiction. FERC also has to determine whether the new trading arrangements are efficient, and whether the markets are competitive before approving the resulting wholesale prices as "just and reasonable." In addition, for reasons we explain later, some generating plants fall into federal jurisdiction even in states that have not deregulated.

The result has been, paradoxically, that the federal regulators, with a limited legislative mandate, have had more and more responsibility thrust upon them. FERC now has much more responsibility for the industry than it ever had, but however much authority it has acquired, it still does not have the role of national leader in these matters. It has enunciated a vision of competition, but it has no authority to implement it. Key parts of the private industry are under divided jurisdiction; key players like municipal utilities and cooperatives are outside FERC's control. FERC may need more staff (staff has been reduced from 1,500 to 1,200) and it may need different skills, particularly more engineers and economists, than it currently has. Clearly, it needs more sophisticated experienced players than it now has.

What should be done? At the end of Part Two we examine the options for jurisdictional change. The conclusion is that there is a strong case for federal legislation to give the federal regulator (or some successor body[11]) authority to get ahead with metering, trading arrangements, and

[11] Robert Marritz has suggested to me that there is room in the constitution for federal-state compacts. (See p. 353.)

the transmission business model (the first three of our five essential items on the checklist). These items are valuable for their own sake if only because they would resolve the current confused situation. These changes would make it feasible to get to competition. They are needed to underpin competition in market areas that are wider than the single state. They would improve the efficiency of the current industry even if nothing further were ever done about introducing competition. For the metering and tariff design issues, there is further precedent in the 1978 federal legislation PURPA, which mandated the states to take certain actions, based on a national need to conserve energy.

In addition we believe the legislation should give the federal regulator jurisdiction over the entire supply side, and not just the ad hoc portion that has fallen there haphazardly: This would allow the federal regulator to order generating companies to dispatch their plants into a regional system. It would consolidate jurisdiction over the changes that are necessary to get to competition, while leaving the decision about retail access for small customers in the hands of the states. These are fairly radical solutions, but it is hard to see how to get out of the impasse without them. The United States needs to complete the tasks it has started. It has permitted open access; it has encouraged independent generators. But it has not completed the essential underpinnings for competitive generating markets, which the states cannot do alone.

Ideally the United States should take three bold steps:

1. It should adopt a coherent national model of what it is trying to do; it needs an overall framework, a national model of trading arrangements, and a full checklist of requirements for competition.
2. It should accept the need for, and legislate to require, restructuring of privately owned companies, and for including the government-owned entities in the national plan.
3. It should revise the line between federal and state jurisdiction so that coherent regional decisions can be made and wholesale trading arrangements established, permitting generation to be deregulated at the wholesale level with some confidence that competition would be robust.

PART one

The Standard Prescription

CHAPTER 2

The Essential Aspects of Electricity

FUNCTIONS OF THE ELECTRIC INDUSTRY

How does the electricity industry function in simple terms? There are the traditional physical functions: generation (production), transmission, system operations, distribution (Figure 2.1); and there are merchant functions such as retailing to final customers and wholesale power procurement. Traditionally, the entire industry has had its prices set for it by governments or by independent regulators appointed by the government. In the worldwide move to competition, some of these functions are being deregulated, but others will continue to have prices set by regulators or governments.

Generation (Production)

Generation (production) accounts for about 35 percent to 50 percent[1] of the final cost of delivered electricity. The production of electricity has been described as the opposite of the oil industry. Whereas the oil industry uses crude oil to produce multiple products such as gasoline, heating oil, and kerosene, the electric industry takes in multiple fuels and turns them all into exactly the same product. It is totally standardized—it has to be or electric appliances would not run properly.

Electricity is produced commercially in thousands of generating plants all over the world. Wires turning in a magnetic field produce the electricity. The wire is turned by a *motive force* acting against a fan or *turbine*. The motive force is generally steam, but it can also be falling water, turning windmills, tidal energy, or in some cases by direct combustion of a fuel, as

[1] The relative cost of the various functions of the electricity industry varies widely from place to place, and the percentages are given as a general indication only.

FIGURE 2.1 Physical functions of electricity.

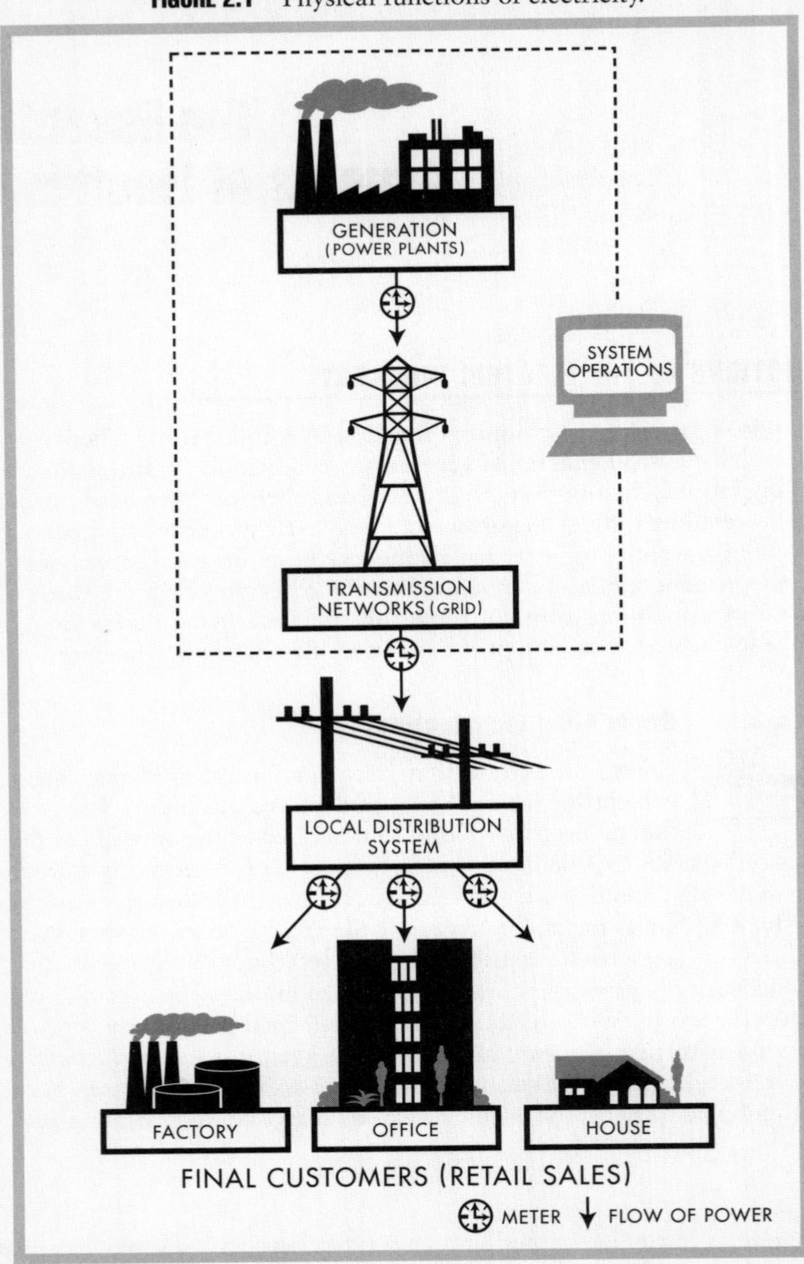

in a jet engine.[2] The motive force of the vast majority of the commercial plants is steam, which in turn is produced by a variety of fuels. Coal is the major fuel, but there are also substantial amounts of oil, natural gas, and uranium (nuclear power[3]). Virtually all plants use only one fuel, but any one company may use a variety of fuels in different plants.

The various fuels have different prices, which affect the cost of a plant's output. The efficiency of plants also varies, but they all have their place in production. The plants that burn fuel less efficiently cost less to build and are used only occasionally for "peaking" purposes, while the efficient ones are used full-time as baseload units. (Appendix E describes how decisions are made to build different types of plants.) Before the late 1980s, efficiency typically varied from about 18 percent to 36 percent, and there were economies of scale—the bigger plants were more efficient. Because of the scale factors, plants got larger and larger; they took years to plan and build.

Then a technological advance in the 1980s, which combined the steam generators with direct fuel combustion, increased the maximum efficiency of new plants to 60 percent or 65 percent. These new plants, called *combined cycle gas turbines* (CCGTs) use natural gas as a fuel, and are today the technology of choice. They also come in much smaller packages, are cleaner in operation, and are easier to build than the old models. This technological advance is one of the forces shaping the worldwide industry, because it made it clear that economies of scale were not an inevitable part of electricity production, and opened the door to competition in generation.[4] In fact, generation and the associated merchant functions that we discuss later are the only parts of the industry that are real candidates for full competition.

Blackouts due to lack of generating capacity were virtually unknown in the United States until 2000–2001, when five episodes of rolling blackouts in California, after restructuring, hit the front pages of the national press for months. In poorer countries, blackouts are not rare at all.

---

[2] There are some technologies, such as the fuel cell, that produce electricity chemically; this technology works (it powered the space capsules), but it has not yet become economic for large scale commercial applications.

[3] Nuclear plants simply boil water to make steam.

[4] It was not only the technical advances of CCGTs that opened the door to competition, but they are a major factor. Some other type of smaller plants were economic before the 1990s.

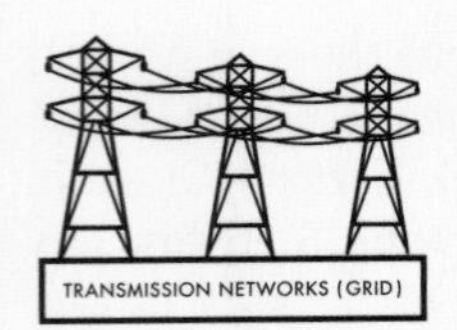

Transmission

Transmission accounts for about 5 percent to 15 percent of the final cost of electricity. Electricity is transported over a network of copper or aluminum wires called the transmission system, on poles or towers, or sometimes underground or underwater; and the electricity is delivered to local distribution systems, and thence to customers. This is not a switched network like railroad or telephone networks—the electricity flows freely on an alternating current (AC)[5] network according to laws of physics known as Kirchoffs' laws. The transmission system is quite fragile—if it overloads it becomes unstable and can cause widespread blackouts, such as the famous 1965 blackout of the Northeast United States. Flows have to be managed on a continuous, real-time basis—no traffic jams, no busy signals. For this reason, which we examine in more detail a little later, the transmission system requires the constant attention of a *system operator* to integrate the operation of the generating plants with the transmission system on a second by second basis.

System Operations

System operations is the function that coordinates the generating plants with the *load* (the sum of all customers' instantaneous usage) to maintain a stable transmission system. The instant the electricity is produced, it leaves the generating plant, travels at the speed of light (about 186,000 miles per second), and is consumed within a millisecond. The moment a customer throws a switch, something happens in a generating plant somewhere. Since customers do not have to call up and ask for power, and their usage is not controlled, it is the generating plants that have to be controlled to meet the load at all times.[6]

This is the job of the system operator and his staff, which is peculiar to electricity, and a major focus of this book. They sit in a control room, following the changes in load and ordering plants to start and stop generating—*dispatching* the system in real time. They also schedule the plants in advance—how far in advance depends on how long it takes the slow plants

[5] The alternative, DC or direct current, is not widely used because it is less efficient, but it can be controlled more easily.

[6] On some systems, the system operator can directly control a few large industrial customers. This is not done routinely; it is reserved for emergency purposes. We return to this in the discussion of the demand side of the industry later.

to start up. Hydro plants need only minutes. In contrast, a nuclear plant needs a day or more.

These days most control rooms are heavily computerized, but it was not always so, and even today there is a lot of judgment involved. Especially when the job had (or in some cases still has) to be done with slide rules, diagrams, and intuition, the best engineers were assigned to this function, since it is so critical. The system operator's job includes holding plants in reserve, ready to run, and calling for special outputs known as *ancillary services*. (More about this later.) The system operator has the extremely complex task of managing the system in real time and ensuring that no transmission lines get overloaded. Each line has a maximum it can safely take. When it has reached this maximum, it is considered *congested*. Beyond that, it is considered *overloaded* and a threat to system stability. The operator plans in advance to avoid overloads. In real time he instructs (*dispatches*) plants in order to manage congestion. The system operator also has to coordinate with the system operators of neighboring systems.

There is one system operator per system, although there may be additional satellite area control rooms, under the general control of the system operator, but with local responsibilities. In some cases, a system is virtually an entire country (France, England and Wales, New Zealand, Argentina, Mexico); in others, it is organized at the provincial or regional level (Australia, China). In still others (United States and Canada), a system has generally been a single company. There were, for example, about 140 system operators in the United States in 2000. Companies can combine their systems for operational purposes and put several companies under the control of a single operator in a *tight pool*. In the United States, historically, there were three such tight pools (New York, New England, and Pennsylvania–New Jersey–Maryland or PJM). Each one combined the systems of all the companies in the area, putting all the plants in the area under the control of a single system operator.

Distribution

The distribution function accounts for about 30 percent to 50 percent of the final cost of electricity. Its basic job is "the wires business"—transporting electricity from the transmission system to customers. But distribution is not really a single function, because it is the local end of the business, and is usually associated with the customer service operation, with metering and billing and retail sales. Transmission and distribution together are the transport system (they both have wires and poles, and are fully connected with each other) but we generally think of them

FIGURE 2.2 Network and radial flows.

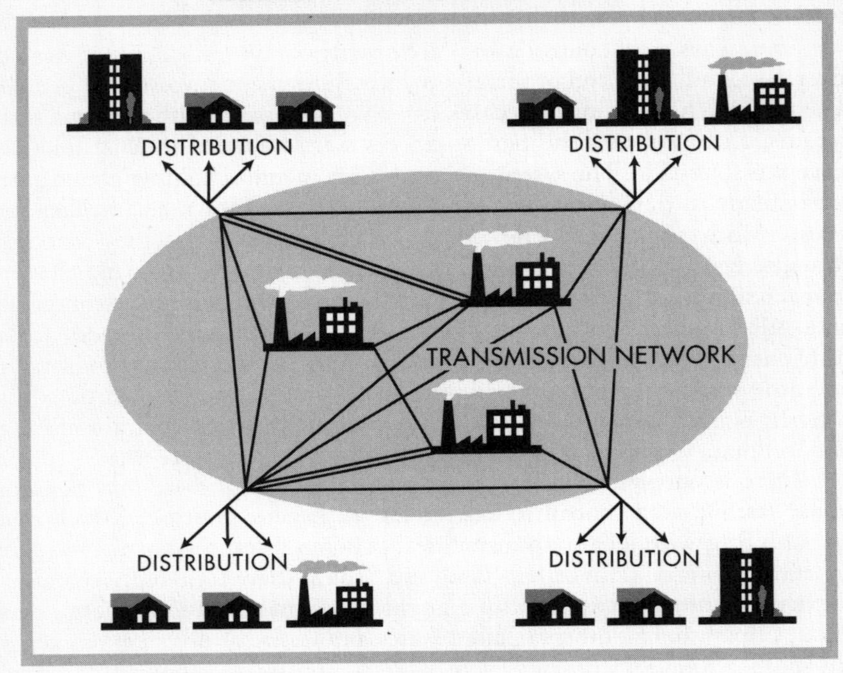

separately, and they are always organized separately. Transmission works with generation (through the system operator); distribution works with the customer.

As far as the transport element of distribution, transmission is like major highways while distribution is like local roads. Transmission operates at higher *voltages* than distribution (which means packing power in tighter); transmission is networked, and the flows can reverse, whereas distribution is usually radial and the flows are one-way (to the customer). (See Figure 2.2.)

The theoretical difference between transmission and distribution wires is not always clear-cut, since there is a wide range of voltages, and some distribution systems are networked. There are some cases where high voltage lines, especially in big cities, are really part of the distribution system.[7]

[7]In the United States, FERC set out criteria in its Order No. 888 to make the distinction between transmission and distribution for regulatory purposes.

By the time electricity reaches the distribution wires it is too late to control the generating plants. The electricity simply flows over the wires to the customers. No one "takes delivery" except the final customer—electricity just flows, and meters record how much has flowed. The distribution people do not receive, store, and send it out—they just read the meters and send the bills. The big physical task of the distribution function is to keep the local wires in good shape, replacing poles and wires after storms or, if they are underground, protecting them from salt on the streets, and adding new ones as the population moves or as the load grows. The wires heat up as the load rises, and this can cause overloads and local blackouts if the installation is not large enough for the load. The vast majority of all consumer outages are local, and caused by storms, malfunctions, or overloads on the distribution system.[8]

Retailing

Generation, system operations, transmission, and distribution are physical functions. Retailing and wholesaling are merchant functions. Retailing is sales to final consumers and involves a series of commercial functions—procuring, pricing, and selling electricity, and also metering its use, billing for it, and collecting payment. In the typical organization of the industry up to the 1990s, no one even thought of retailing as a separate function. It was always part of the distribution function.

Wholesale Power Procurement

Wholesale power procurement is only a separable function where someone in the company makes decisions about which producer to buy from. In companies that produce all their own power, there is no wholesale power procurement. But as trading increases, wholesale procurement becomes a bigger function.

[8] The vast majority of outages affecting final customers arise from the distribution system, but customers tolerate them as part of the vicissitudes of life. For instance, during the period in 2001 when four-hour rolling blackouts due to lack of generating capacity in California were hitting the national headlines, a four-day distribution outage in Georgetown, DC, which is home to many of the influential in Washington, barely made the newspapers.

WHOLESALE: In ordinary language the term *wholesale* is loosely defined. It may mean "sales by a producer" or "sales to a reseller"; it is ambiguous. We will use the convention that a *wholesale sale* is a technical term meaning "sales to a reseller"—(not "any sale by a producer"). This is in line with the U.S. convention.

In the United States, wholesale sales in the electric industry is a regulatory term of art, and specifically means "sales for resale"—a sale is only a wholesale sale if it is not a sale to a final customer. This is an important distinction in the United States, where the federal government regulates sales for resale, and sales to final customers are regulated by the states. In the United States, also, as a matter of regulatory convention, sales from one affiliate to another affiliate of the same holding company are wholesale sales, whereas if the company is not set up as a holding company, transfers between divisions are internal transactions and not wholesale sales. We return to this point later.

However, the looser term *wholesale markets* does not necessarily imply that the buyers are all resellers. Wholesale markets are where producers sell their wares. In our terminology, it would not be a contradiction in terms to say that some final customers purchase power in the wholesale markets. (Sorry about that—it is confusing! Please don't ask whether a producer selling to a final customer in a wholesale market has made a "wholesale sale"—he has just made a "sale." We will let the lawyers decide who has jurisdiction.)

TRADITIONAL ORGANIZATION OF THE INDUSTRY

For 100 years after electricity was commercialized in 1878, a single company in each area typically produced, transported, and retailed the product and operated the system. This *vertical integration* of functions was always the typical organization of the industry throughout the world. The vertical integration was almost always accompanied by a legal monopoly within a *service area*—only one company could provide electricity to customers in that area.

The only important exceptions to complete vertical integration and legal monopoly in the first hundred years were in instances where a large generation/transmission company sold to a series of smaller distribution companies. Virtually everywhere these distribution companies were umbilically attached to a single supplier, who provided them with all their power on contracts or by tariff. This was in effect vertical integration by contract, a variation, but not an exception, to the rule of vertical integration.

The actual mechanism of establishing the monopoly is generally to limit customers' choice of supplier by legislation rather than by prohibiting independent generators, although in some cases both are in place. It may seem to come to the same thing, but in most places self-generation is permitted, for a person's or a factory's own use. (The precise mechanism of regulation also makes a technical difference to the process of deregulation: Legislation is generally required to free up the customers to choose suppliers; sometimes legislation may also be required to permit new independent generators to sell.)

Sometimes, in fact in most countries, the government or a government-owned company had the monopoly (in Mexico it is written into the constitution). In other countries (the United States, Spain, and Germany are the main examples), private companies dominated the industry.

Reasons for Vertical Integration and Monopoly

No one ever thought it could be done any other way, but in retrospect, the reasons for vertical integration and the monopoly were due to *transactions costs* as well as to the characteristics that made some functions *natural monopolies.*

The elements relevant to the 100-year history of the industry as a monopoly were these:

1. The natural monopoly aspects of distribution—only one set of wires would run along a street, a public right of way. This was both for reasons of space and visual appearance, and also because there are serious economies of scale in distribution, which makes competing distribution functions uneconomic.
2. The natural monopoly aspects of transmission, not only its scale economies and siting requirements but also its network characteristics. Only one set of transmission wires could economically serve any area.

But these two things alone would have led to monopolies only on the wires businesses; they did not demand vertical integration. The main reasons for vertical integration were:

3. The technical challenges of coordinating the generation with the transmission demanded such complex integration of generation and transmission (via the system operator) that it was considered impossible to separate them. The transactions costs were too high. The managers of the generating plants had to obey the system operator, and the best way to do that at the time was to have them in the same company. So, if only

TRANSACTIONS COSTS: Transactions costs are the costs associated with making contracts to replace command and control. It is always theoretically possible to replace command and control relationships (within a firm) with *contractual* relationships (between firms). Contractual relationships in this context may mean any agreement about the terms on which the transactions take place between the separate firms. However, it is sometimes difficult to specify all the necessary terms of the contract so that all possible situations are covered, and so expensive to negotiate, execute, and litigate such a contract that it is not worth attempting. It is more efficient to keep the activities with a single firm where one manager manages both activities. The technical term for the costs of negotiating, executing, and litigating the required contracting mechanisms is *transactions costs.*

NATURAL MONOPOLIES: Economies of scale over the entire range of output are one of the major reasons for considering a product a *natural monopoly.* This is because, if competitors start out equal, one will gain the advantage of size and hence have lower average costs and will be able to get all the customers. This is considered wasteful competition in a static sense, unless competition is leading to dynamic improvements in technology.

a single transmission entity could serve a particular distribution system, then the system operator and the generating plants had to come along with it.

4. The long-term planning of transmission and generation also benefitted from the vertical integration of generation with transmission.
5. Finally the economies of scale in generation, during the period when bigger and bigger plants produced lower and lower prices, added to the conventional wisdom that generation also was a natural monopoly.

Of these five factors, the first two remain—distribution and transmission are still considered natural monopolies. However, in most places the scale economies in generation are no longer considered sufficient to warrant monopolies—the optimum size of a CCGT is 250 to 400 Megawatts (MW) against a nuclear plant optimum of 900 to 1,000 MW or coal plant optimum of 500 to 600 MW. The plants are smaller, and the markets are larger, through growth over many years and because of additional transmission, so it no longer requires a monopoly to deliver the minimum cost plant in any particular market. (However, in small countries, or in those with low demand and/or inadequate transmission networks, the economies of scale might well indicate continued monopoly.)

The complexities of short-term coordination of generation with transmission have been solved in many places, although long-term coordination still poses many problems. These two issues are central themes of this book.

Economic Regulation of Monopolies

The implication of the legal monopoly was that prices had to be controlled to protect consumers. When the government owned the monopoly, which was what happened in most countries, the government set the prices. When private companies owned the monopoly, there had to be some form of economic regulation so that they could not exercise their monopoly power. The basic job of regulation is to set prices—to limit prices to the cost, somehow defined. But by extension, it also has to monitor costs, ensure that quality of service is not degraded, and offer incentives to be efficient.

The standard way to do this is for the government to appoint an independent regulator whose job is to enforce the laws relating to the economic regulation of the industry. When countries are privatizing, they need to set up independent regulators to set prices.[9]

In vertically integrated monopolies, the prices (or rates) are generally bundled—set without separating the various functional components. In restructuring, since some of the functions continue to be monopolies, they need to be unbundled, and decisions need to be made about the form of economic regulation. There are two basic models: the U.S. model and the U.K. model. Each has some good and some bad aspects.

The United States, with its extensive private industry, has the most comprehensive history in the world of economic regulation of private suppliers. Rate-of-return regulation as developed in the U.S. electric industry allows companies the chance to earn a reasonable rate of return on their assets, in addition to recovery of expenses. But this is done in advance—so prices (*rates*) are set in advance and fixed until the next *rate case,* which happens irregularly, usually at the request of the company. This provides some incentives for efficient operation—the companies are at risk between rate cases—

[9] In many countries, the notion of an independent regulator appointed by the government appears to be a contradiction in terms. However, many people are happy to have a regulatory authority that is independent of the *industry.*

and gives the companies a chance, but not a guarantee, of earning a market return on their assets.

When the United Kingdom privatized its utilities, it pioneered a different form of regulation—RPI – X—in which average prices are set for a specified period, and allowed to rise each year at the rate of inflation (Retail Price Index or RPI) less the rate (X) by which the regulator believes the companies should be able to increase efficiency year on year.

Both these forms of regulation are workable since they both do two important things: they base prices generally on cost, but also unhook the prices from the actual costs for some period of time, which provides incentives for efficient operations.

In many ways the U.K. and U.S. methods are similar to each other but quite different from the practice in those countries where the price of electricity is determined mainly by political considerations, such as the impact of a price increase on overall inflation. This latter, and unfortunately ubiquitous, form of ratemaking generally keeps prices below cost, leading to continuous deficits. It cannot continue in a competitive environment, unless the government is prepared to fund explicit subsidies. Countries where the tariffs are not remunerative should concentrate on revising tariffs and eliminating or explicitly funding subsidies before considering competition.

Performance of the Traditional Structure

Each country needs to make an assessment of the performance of its industry before deciding whether to make changes. In the U.S. industry it is fairly clear that the major problems with the old structure lay in the generation part of the industry—the efficiency of the investment decision, its regulation, and the tendency for decisions on generation to become politicized. Since generation is the major candidate for competition in the industry, the assessment meshes well with the possibilities for improvement.

However we should warn that in other countries, this might not be the case. In some places the performance of the existing system may be such that it is important to get the accounting systems working, and metering and billing operational, to remove subsidies and get tariffs up to remunerative levels, to expand transmission, and to improve the physical efficiency of distribution systems. These changes might take first place in reform agendas before ultimately deciding that competition in generation is the answer.

Why Competition?

What are the benefits of competition? *The major difference between regulation and competition has to do with who takes responsibility for various risks.* The placement of the risks is what provides the incentive to improve.

The main relevant risks are:

- Market demand and prices;
- Technological change rendering plants economically obsolete, or at least uncompetitive;
- Management decisions about maintenance, manning, and investment; and
- Credit risk.

Under regulation, *the customers take most of the risks,* and also take most of the rewards, with the regulators doing their best to oversee the big expenditure decisions, sometimes fining companies after the event for bad management decisions. Under regulation, if new technology is invented, the customers continue to pay (more) for the old technology, whereas under competition the old-technology producers find their assets are worth less. Under regulation, if demand turns out to be less than anticipated, prices have to rise to cover the cost of excess capacity, whereas under competition, excess capacity causes prices to fall.

Under competition, these *risks are initially with the owners of the plants*—they will pay for mistakes or profit from good decisions and management.[10] Under competition, the generators also take the risk of changes in technology, so they have strong incentives to choose the best technology and not get sidetracked into costly mistakes. They also take the risk of changes in market demand and prices, so they need to be flexible in their building plans, and watch the market constantly. They need to adjust their maintenance schedules to get plants back on line when prices are high (which is just when they are needed). The profit incentive works everywhere else to make producers sharpen their pencils, and it has had this effect elsewhere in the world when competition has been instituted in electricity.

KEY FACTORS SPECIFIC TO THE ELECTRIC INDUSTRY

There are key technical factors specific to the industry that may not be obvious to the lay reader. They dictate the complexities of the short-term

[10] Under competition, risks are only initially with the owners of the plants because producers will try to contract away at least some of the market risk, by making contracts with customers who have an equal and opposite desire to avoid extremes of prices. They may also be able to shift risk through insurance and hedging.

trading arrangements, mapping almost one-to-one to the critical design features that we examine later.

Four Technical Truths

- *Truth 1: Electricity cannot be stored.* Or rather, it cannot be economically stored. Battery technology has not advanced to the point where electricity can be bought in periods of low demand and stored at home for periods of high demand. All electricity has to be generated when it is needed.[11] The implication of this is that when demand varies over the course of a day, production has to vary at exactly the same time. Some people hear the word *pool* in connection with electricity and think of it as a big lake where electricity is stored—but nothing could be further from the truth.

  In addition, demand (usage) is highly variable over the day and the year. Use is low at night, and rises in the morning, usually reaching a peak in the afternoon, especially on hot days when air conditioning is in full use. In hot areas, summer is the peak season. (See Figure 2.3.) In cold areas, winter brings heating and lighting demands and is often the peak season.

  The result? As in other industries with peak demands and no storage (airlines, vacations, hotels) the wholesale price of electricity varies tremendously with the demand/supply balance. Wholesale hourly electric prices in competitive markets commonly vary by about 2 : 1 over the course of a day in the off-season and by as much as 10 : 1 between the peak in the high season and the overall low (with some spikes above this as well). (See Figure 2.4 on page 32.)
- *Truth 2: Electricity takes the path of least resistance* (literally—that is where the expression comes from). *Resistance* is a technical word in electricity, which means roughly what it sounds like—low resistance means it is easy to pass, and high resistance means it is difficult. A big thick transmission line is an easy path with low resistance and electricity will flow there rather than over a skinny line elsewhere in the network. It

[11] Hydroelectric plants with dams are sometimes thought of as a form of storage, since they store water that can be saved for peak uses; but this is not really storage—to be used, the water must pass through a turbine-generator to create electricity, so in many ways it is the same as having a coal pile and considering it "stored electricity" except that the hydro responds much faster. There are a few hydro plants that are actually filled by pumping water into them, using cheaper electricity at night to do the pumping, but they also have to generate power on demand.

FIGURE 2.3 Daily load curves for New York state.

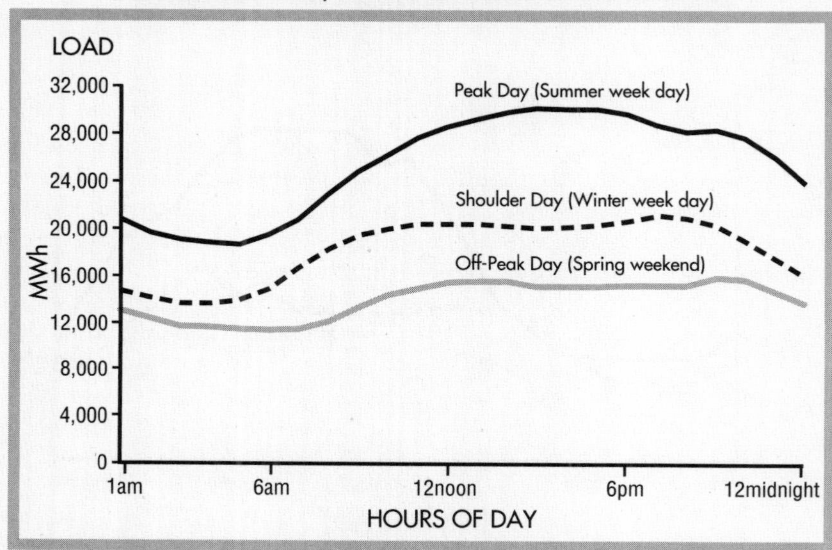

Source: New York Independent System Operator, New York state load on March 22, 2001, May 27, 2001, and August 7, 2001. www.nyiso.com.

is virtually impossible to command electricity to take a particular path—it flows where it will over the network, according to the laws of physics.

One implication of this is that there is no such thing as a defined path for delivery: Final customers simply get whatever electricity happens to be flowing by them at the time. The secret of dispatch is to arrange the inflow of generation and the configuration of the network so that electricity "chooses" to flow to the customers who want it. Another implication is that the addition of a new line to a network may radically change flows elsewhere, and can actually destroy useful capacity on a network.

- *Truth 3: The transmission of power over the network is subject to a complex series of physical interactions,* so that what happens on one part of the system affects conditions on the network many miles away—in some cases many hundreds of miles away. Many things can potentially destabilize the network, including changes in customers' use, reactions from certain electrical equipment, and sudden loss of output at a generating plant. And a single plant can produce multidimensional outputs (such as fast response and products called reactive power, and

FIGURE 2.4 Daily price curves for New York City.

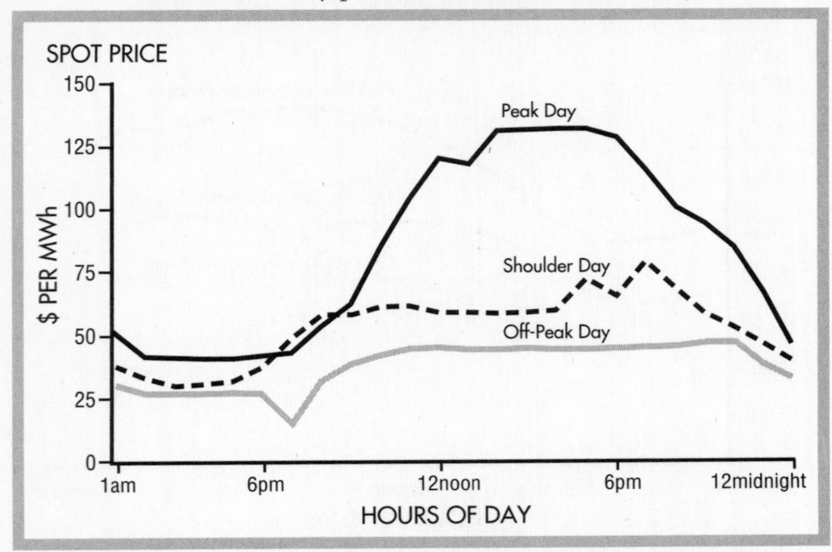

Source: New York Independent System Operator, day-ahead market zonal LBMP for New York City on March 22, 2001, May 27, 2001, and August 7, 2001. www.nyiso.com.

other ancillary services that are essential to electric system operations), but often one output is an alternative to another.

As a consequence, those responsible for trading arrangements have to be concerned with pricing these various outputs so that the system operator gets what he needs when he needs it.

- *Truth 4: Electricity travels at the speed of light.* Each second, output has to be precisely matched to use. If it is not, the *frequency* falls, clocks go slower, more sophisticated appliances can fail, and if the situation is serious enough, so many loads fail that it can set off a chain of events leading to a blackout. It is critical that the system not become unstable in this way, so the system operator has to be able to call on some generators to raise or lower output to meet load changes within seconds. Further, transmission lines cannot be allowed to overload, and plans have to be made in advance to prevent them from doing so.

The implication is that it requires advance planning and split-second control by the system operator to coordinate everything. The system operator turns out to be the major player in the technical side of this book.

Implications for System Control

Electricity really is different from other commodities in its need for short-term coordination. (Short-term coordination here means day-ahead, on-the-day, and real-time coordination.) The system operator has to be able to control the plants. The nearest analogy is the air traffic controller. His job certainly has lives at stake rather than just risking a blackout of the whole East Coast, but the air traffic controller can tell planes to circle for an hour, whereas the system operator has to respond in seconds to get plants to change their output if an overload threatens.

In the first 100+ years of electric industry history, these factors dictated that system operations were always integrated with generation—the system operator's relation to generation was that of command and control. For a long time it was believed that it was an inevitable technological truth that system operations could not be unbundled from generation. *But the real difficulty was designing new institutions—trading arrangements—that replicated the results of command and control when the system operator is separated from the folks running the generating plants. Without this competition is not possible.* However, this has been done in every place that has introduced competition in generation, including several areas in the United States.

Whatever changes are made, the system operator still has to be in charge of the system and has to tell plants when to run, when to increase or reduce output, and when to stop. Sometimes directly, via computer; sometimes by telephone. He or she has to make sure the load is met at all times, relieve congestion on the transmission system, and call for reserves and use them when necessary. Replacing command and control with a system of rules and incentives that accomplish the same thing involves understanding exactly what the system operator does, and trying to make sure that the rules not only replicate the traditional set-up, but also are *incentive-compatible* so that everyone who uses the system will *want* to obey the system operator.

The system operator must first try to accommodate what the competing generators tell him they want to do. If they *cannot simultaneously* do what they would prefer, the system operator will ask them to do something different. The rules must be set up in advance so that the generators (1) have incentives to offer the system operator useful information and (2) want to obey the system operator when he tells them to change their plans, otherwise they will find reasons not to do it.

Some of the changes the system operator requires (ramping up or ramping down generation) are potentially very costly to the generators. Whereas before, under command and control, the generators said, "Yes sir," now under competition they effectively say, "What are you prepared to pay to

INCENTIVE-COMPATIBLE: This term will come up quite often, since it is the key to defining good rules. An incentive-compatible rule is one that makes the people who have to obey it do so voluntarily because it is in their own interest to do so. It is a cheat-proof rule. A good example of an incentive-compatible rule is driving on the right side of the road. People do it voluntarily because it is in their own best interests. By contrast, speed limits are not incentive-compatible. They may be in the general interest, but each individual wants to go faster, so highway patrols are required. The idea is to set up the rules so that the need for highway patrols is minimized. The design of the rules is a complicated job for technical specialists, and generally involves using prices to do the work of providing incentives.

compensate me for doing this?" But there is no time to negotiate about a price—*they must obey immediately knowing it is in their economic interest to do so;* they must know that they and the system operator are working under the same clear incentive-compatible rules that determine how they will be paid.

The series of special factors just laid out is unique to electricity; they are the reason, and the only reason, that wholesale market institutions (trading arrangements) have to be "designed" in electricity—to enable short-term coordination of generating plants with transmission. Delivery has to be coordinated by the system operator—there is no other way to do it. And this involves unique arrangements that are found in no other industry. Electricity has special attributes that require certain market design decisions be made centrally and in turn require the design of fair and incentive-compatible wholesale trading arrangements.

We describe the issues of designing trading arrangements in Chapters 7 and 8.

Implications for Retail Access

The critical thing to understand about retail access is that *physically,* there is no difference between the old integrated systems and those where customers have a choice of supplier—*retail access* or *customer choice.* There are no duplicated poles and lines. The same lines as before carry the same electricity, just as they always have. The electricity flows over them, and when the customer flips the switch, the lights go on, just as they always have.

There is no conceivable way that the power generated by a customer's supplier could actually flow to that customer—it is all mixed up in delivery. There are no green electrons for *green power*[12] or nuclear electrons for nuclear power. They are all the same. The entire job of deciding who sold what to whom is done by metering, contracts, and an extensive accounting (settlement) system.

Even the contracts between customers and retailers are essentially financial contracts—they do not themselves ensure delivery. If the baker is out of bread, you go elsewhere. If your electric supplier is out of power, the *system operator* goes elsewhere, within seconds, and charges your supplier, not you, for the additional power. Almost no one has seriously proposed trying to physically match the customer's use to the supplier's output.[13] If for some reason the supplier does not have enough power for his customers (the plant is out for repairs, or the supplier oversold), then someone else will supply, and *the customer will never know.*

You cannot buy different grades of power—it is not like gasoline, it is all the same, the most homogeneous product imaginable, because the system operator controls the frequency within strict limits.[14] This means that the *quality* of electricity you get is in no way dependent on how good a generator, or what type of generator, serves you or your retailer. The alternate service offerings are differentiated by price, by the efficiency of the billing, and by other value-added services that may be available, but not by the grade of electricity.

The reliability of your service is not even affected by who serves you and how reliable his plant is. If his plant malfunctions, you are served anyway. You may be able to agree to be cut off in the event of an overall shortage of power and to pay less for your contract if you do. This is called *interruptible service*. But individual customers are not cut off according to

---

[12] Environmentally benign power from windmills, solar energy, and similar is commonly known as *green power.*

[13] KEGOC (Kazakhstan) used to cut off customers whose load exceeded their contract amount.

[14] Power is sold at different voltages but it is the same power; some buildings install heavier lines and special gadgets so that brief interruptions do not upset computers, but the electricity is still the same. The system operator keeps quality within strict limits. The quality of delivered power depends on the system operator (and the quality of the distribution network), not on a customer's contract with his supplier.

whether they have a contract with someone who is actually generating—cutoffs are done, as they have always been done, by area, with rolling blackouts for a few hours at a time.

So from the point of view of the physical system, there are no changes under retail access. The power flows just as it always did. *All that changes is who gets paid and how much.*

CHAPTER 3

Reforming the Industry

In this chapter, we set out the standard prescription for reform of the electric sector—the issues that need to be dealt with, no matter which country and no matter what the initial conditions are.

We first see which functions can be competitive and which have to remain (regulated) monopolies. Then we describe four models showing in broad terms the structural options for introducing competition into the electric industry. These models are *defined* in terms of the degree of monopoly retained in the sector. But the models *imply* different requirements for restructuring the industry—breaking up existing companies and developing new coordinating institutions to replace the internal coordination that formerly existed. They also imply different roles for regulators.

CANDIDATES FOR COMPETITION

The *generation function* is the major candidate for being made competitive. The old arguments from economies of scale no longer hold; and the problems of coordination of generation and transmission have been eased but not entirely solved by the advent of high-speed computers. However, it is the design of trading arrangements that have actually worked in practice to replace internal coordination, which has made generating competition possible.

The *retail function* can be competitive as far as procuring, pricing, and selling electricity. There is some dispute over the metering, billing, and collection functions, because of some peculiarities of electricity, which we leave to Chapter 10 to discuss in detail.

The *system operations function* cannot be competitive—one system operator is required per system.

The *transmission network* is a natural monopoly, although there are a few cases, mainly of isolated lines (peripheral to the network), where an investor might make a transmission investment and charge for it. This is not really competition in transmission but rather competition to build additions to the transmission network.

The *distribution wires function* is still considered to be a natural monopoly everywhere, insofar as competing for the same territory. This does not preclude competition for franchises, but we will not cover this possibility in this book.[1] For covering new territory there could also be competition for a franchise, but again we ignore these issues, and consider distribution a natural monopoly.

These last three functions (system operations, transmission, and distribution) remain monopolies because no one could economically provide competing service. But all competitors require access to them—they are "essential facilities"—and without nondiscriminatory access for generators to reach their customers, there will be no competition. Therefore, as monopolies they will remain regulated under any of the four models we introduce; and as essential facilities there will have to be ways of assuring open and nondiscriminatory access to them in the competitive models.

The general problems are:

- To eliminate as far as possible any conflict of interest between the competitive entities (generators and retailers) and the providers of the essential facilities (transmission, system operations, and distribution). This includes eliminating opportunities to discriminate, as well as cross subsidies between regulated and unregulated activities.
- To ensure coordination between competitive entities and essential facilities—coordination that was previously provided by the integrated company—is replaced by new institutions, and new agreements and rules.
- To ensure that the market prices that replace regulated prices are set in a market that is truly competitive. This is the critical issue that ought to be central to policy.

OTHER OBJECTIVES AND CONSTRAINTS

Competition in production has to be the major objective, but there are many constraints on the process of reform. Constraints always act to increase the cost and time required for restructuring, but some constraints are fairly easy to accommodate while others are like handcuffs. Too many

[1] The main problems in competition for distribution franchises are the incentives for investment in the waning years of a franchise. Some regimes (e.g., Australia and Spain) have also considered competition between distribution companies for the consumers at the boundaries of their existing service territories, but such competition is usually hamstrung by regulatory constraints on pricing.

> **STRANDED COSTS:** The difference between the *market value* of an electric company and the value at which the assets are carried on the regulatory accounting books (the *book value*). The net present value of the future stream of profits determines the market value of any assets. Regulation sets the price of electricity so as to earn a reasonable profit on the book value of assets, so the market value of assets, under regulation, should be close to the book value. But when the price of electricity is determined in a market, if the market price is lower than the regulated price, the market value of the underlying assets will fall.

constraints and the system becomes unworkable. The two that present the major issues are buying out of the old regime and ensuring the reliability of the system.

Buying out of the Old Regime

All countries need to buy out of the old regime. Issues such as pensions, employment rights, fuel contracts, and so on are part of the general problem, but we will not go into them in this book. For countries where the ownership is initially private, the biggest problem is the *stranded costs.*

In countries where the government owns the electric sector, stranded costs are not a front-burner issue. If the market price of the sector when privatized is lower than the value on the account books, the government takes the hit in terms of the lost value.[2] But in the United States and other countries where companies are private and regulated, buying out of the old regime has proven quite complex.

Market prices of electricity would naturally vary across the country according to natural endowments and environmental costs. This should be a good thing, encouraging increased production where costs are lower; but like international trade, it provokes opposition from producers in high-cost regions and consumers in low-cost regions. If this were the main issue, the debate over deregulation would be a "free trade" argument—we are all better off in the end when the low-cost producers do the producing.

Unfortunately, the United States has not only the classic free trade problem, but also the historic (accounting) cost problem, and the historic cost problem is much greater. In some states, for a variety of reasons, the

---

[2] Quite often the retail prices for electricity were never set to bring a market return on the book value in the first place, so the book value may be meaningless as a guide to the hit the government takes.

regulated prices were well above the potential market price. Market prices would have exposed the utilities to losses, sometimes greater than their equity in the company.

In principle this problem has been solved in the United States—the companies are allowed to collect their stranded costs from consumers. Selling the generating plant to establish an asset value to compare to the book value is the cleanest way to do this—the difference is amortized and charged in distribution charges. In practice, it has proved complicated, because companies and/or their regulators have been unwilling to divest, and have tried to solve the problem with top-down pricing. We look at the problems of top-down pricing in Part Two.

In other states, the regulated prices are below market prices. The states in this fortunate position have been the least likely to embrace reforms and, after California, are even more unlikely to do so. Nevertheless, there are ways to introduce competition to low-cost states, and to keep some of the existing benefits at home. This can be done in a way that does not render the markets impotent to do their job.

Preserve the Reliability of the System

Reliability has three main aspects—short-term system stability, adequate investment in production plant, and adequate investment in transmission.

System stability is a major concern of the engineers who understand how complex and fragile the transmission system is, and how remarkable it is that widespread blackouts (the penalty for inattention to this matter) have been so infrequent. The two big examples in the United States, on the East Coast in 1965 and 1977, are folklore in the industry and of course on the East Coast. The trading arrangements under competition have to be developed so as not to compromise short-term transmission stability.

However, the engineers and the regulators may need to restrain themselves and forgo their traditional role of overseeing adequate generating capacity. Competitive markets largely replace this oversight role by decentralizing this planning function. Market participants make investment decisions, not central planners. The signal of where, when, what, and whether to build is the market price. Everything about the market price is, therefore, crucial: the way it is set; the factors that influence it; its ability or inability to be manipulated; uncertainties surrounding it; the influence the regulator has over it—such as the ability to cap it; and so on and so on. Properly constructed competitive markets should provide adequate generating plant in the long run, and even in the short run, and excessive interference to make sure there is enough capacity can simply destroy the markets. These points are elaborated further in Chapter 8 and Appendix E.

The adequacy of transmission in the long term is a real problem. Congestion on the transmission is what makes markets too small; and competition will bring increased use and increased congestion. The business model for transmission companies is important—who has to build and who has to pay (discussed in Chapter 9). Using the existing transmission efficiently is discussed in Chapter 7.

FOUR MODELS FOR INDUSTRY STRUCTURE

We consider four models,[3] differentiated by how much monopoly is retained. All of the models assume continued monopoly over transmission, distribution wires, and system operations. The defining question is: If there are to be competitive generators, whom can they sell to? Or alternatively, who are the buyers—who has the choice of supplier? The four models provide progressively more choice, and progressively reduce the scope of monopoly. These models are all in operation somewhere in the world; they each have their merits and difficulties.

Model 1: Vertically Integrated Monopoly

Model 1 is a vertically integrated monopoly of the kind we have just described. There are no competitive generators because no one is permitted to buy from them. All functions in the industry are bundled together, and regulated (see Figure 3.1). This model served the industry well for 100 years, and is still the model in existence in most places. In this section, we will give more attention to the alternative models.

Model 2: Single Buyer

This is the model first adopted[4] (perhaps inadvertently) in 1978 by the United States, when under the Public Utility Regulatory Policies Act (PURPA) utilities were required to purchase power from some types of small generators. Thereafter many utilities chose to buy on long-term contracts from Independent Power Producers (IPPs). In a single-buyer model, only the existing integrated monopoly in any area is permitted to buy from

---

[3] These models are set out in much greater detail in a previous book: Sally Hunt and Graham Shuttleworth, *Competition and Choice in Electricity,* John Wiley & Sons, 1996.

[4] The aim of PURPA in the United States was not to introduce competition, but to encourage environmentally benign generation sources.

FIGURE 3.1 Model 1—monopoly.

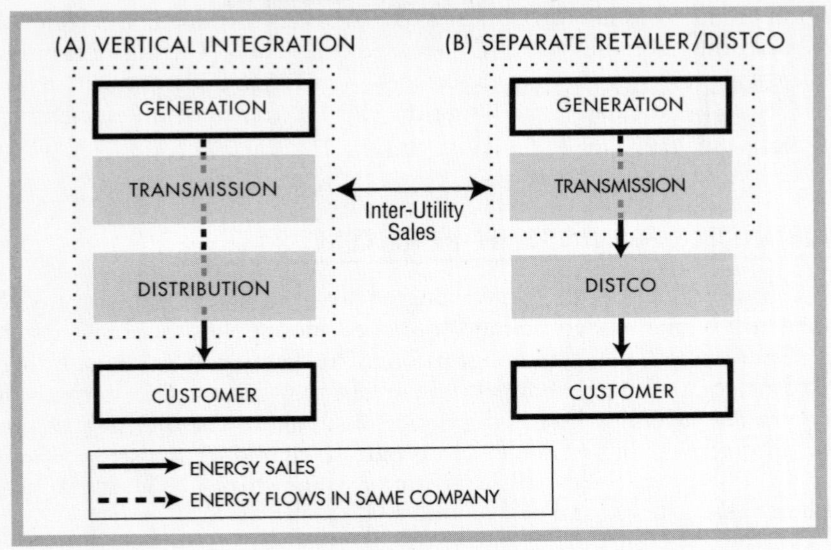

the competing generators (see Figure 3.2). This model is being followed in many countries, in Asia particularly, as a first step to liberalization and as a way of attracting much needed investment by private capital. The defining feature is that independent generators may only sell to the existing utilities, which still have a complete monopoly over all final customers.

The prices at which the IPPs sell to the utilities are regulated, but not at their own cost of service[5]—generally some form of auction is held to determine the lowest cost offering, and the utility signs long-term life-of-plant contracts with the IPPs when the regulator has approved the process of the auction and the results. These contract prices are then passed on to the final customers as part of the bundled tariffs. (This, or sometimes Model 1, is the current model in places that have not moved to competition.)

The single-buyer model is a limited form of competition. *A market structure based on long-term contracts, like the IPP markets under regulation, transfers market risk, technology risk, and most of the credit risk back to customers because the IPP contracts shelter the IPPs from market prices and improved technologies,* and the utilities are generally good credit risks. This

[5]Under PURPA, the utilities were required to purchase, from any facilities that qualified under the Act's requirements, at the utility's "avoided cost," which proved quite hard to determine.

FIGURE 3.2 Model 2—single buyer.

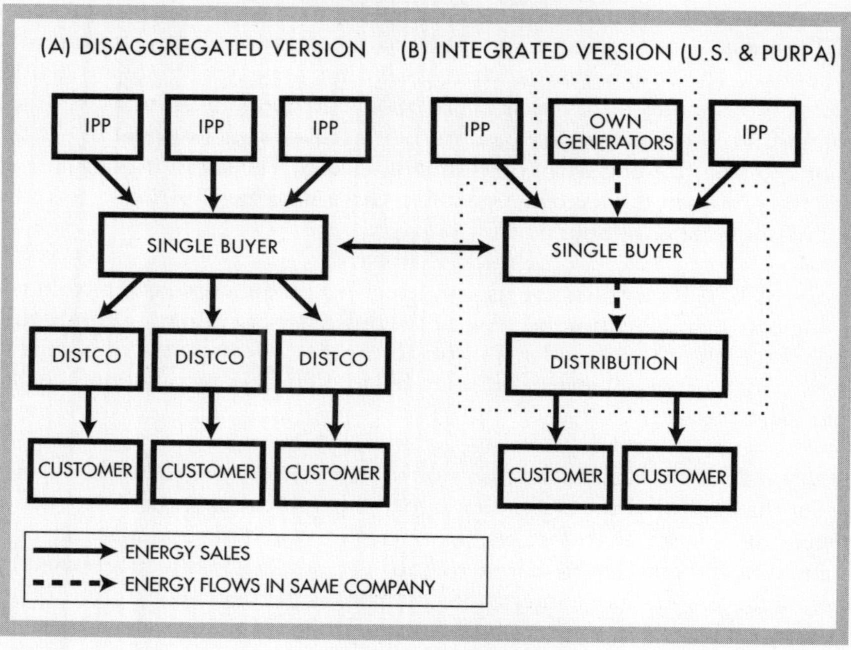

is the attraction for the Asian countries, because they are perceived as fairly risky anyway—the long-term contract takes away some of the risk of investing in these countries.[6] The competition in the single-buyer model is only competition to build plants and operate them.

The single-buyer model requires long-term (life-of-plant) contracts because there are not enough buyers for full competition. Without a contract, a would-be generator is reluctant to sink large amounts of capital in a plant if he runs the risk of being beaten back to his running costs in price negotiations with the single buyer after the plant is completed. *Sellers need either many potential buyers or life-of-plant contracts.*

The design of these IPP contracts is the major conceptual problem in the single-buyer model. The issues here are quite different from the design

[6] But where most of the investment would be from foreign sources, the investors usually insist on the host country denominating the contract in dollars. This puts the countries at tremendous risk from the exchange rate, and also uses up a lot of their international credit, since the contract payments are considered to be part of external debt. For this reason, the Mexican government in 1999 proposed a Model 3-type reform, where the exchange rate risk would be transferred to investors.

of contracts in the later models. The IPP contracts are almost invariably two-part contracts that pay a fixed annual fee to cover the IPP's fixed costs, and amounts designed to cover the variable costs for each unit of power generated. The design issue is where the profits are earned: How to get the plants to run at all if they have been paid their profits up front in the fixed charges; or, if the profits are paid in the variable payments, how to get the plants to stop running when they are not needed. The solution is usually to pay the profits in the fixed charge and to have penalties for failing to run a minimum number of hours.

Problem 1: IPP contracts are usually specified by the purchaser as to technology, fuel, and location because of the difficulty of evaluating competing bids if the choices are wider. But this limits the effectiveness of competition, which often achieves efficiency by finding new technologies, fuels, and locations.

Problem 2: IPP contracts have very often been made *nondispatchable*—not under the control of the system operator. This was because the independent generators feared that the system operator would discriminate against them. The IPP plants were competing for dispatch against plants owned by the purchaser—the same integrated company as the system operator. If they were not dispatched, they would lose any profits in the variable payments and might not meet the target running hours—hence, under nondispatchable contracts, they just told the system operator when they wanted to run.

Nondispatchable contracts can only work for a few relatively small plants, or the system operator will lose control of the system. The system operators should really be separated in single-buyer systems to avoid these conflicts, but seldom are, because it would require the new trading arrangements needed for Model 3 and Model 4. However, if Model 2 is to be a step on the way to the later models, the new trading arrangements can be set up at this stage, and transmission separated from generation, as has been proposed in China.[7]

[7] This proposal is, as a transitional stage, setting up new regional or provincial trading arrangements, separating generation from transmission, and continuing with the current single-buyer regime in order to: (1) achieve economic dispatch; (2) strengthen incentives for generators to maximize efficiency; and (3) provide public information on spot market prices, volatility, and risk. "Stage 1 must be viewed as a transitional stage during which market skills and supporting regulatory and supervisory institutions are developed before wholesale competition is allowed." See Noureddine Berrah, Ranjit Lamech, and Jainping Zhao, *Fostering Competition in China's Power Markets*. World Bank Discussion Paper No. 416, March 2001, p. 23.

This is all we will say about Model 2 structural issues. Models 3 and 4 are where the action is. *It is, however, worth remembering that the new trading arrangements can be developed and put into operation before Models 3 and 4 are actually introduced. Transmission and system operations can be separated from generation and new trading arrangements instituted before any deregulation takes place or any competitors enter the market.* In the United States, this would be somewhat similar to the operation of the old tight pools, where (for many years, and well before the introduction of competition) the final price to customers was regulated but the dispatch and transmission were coordinated over a wide area, and the pricing rules for wholesale sales between companies were approved by FERC. This should not be taken as a proposal that the rules of the old tight pools should be adopted in the United States. However, the rules we do propose for trading arrangements later in the text could be adopted in modified form even before wholesale competition is introduced.

Model 3: Wholesale Competition

Model 3 as we define it here has a fully competitive generating sector. There is no cost-of-service regulated generation. Distribution companies (now

FIGURE 3.3 Model 3—wholesale competition.

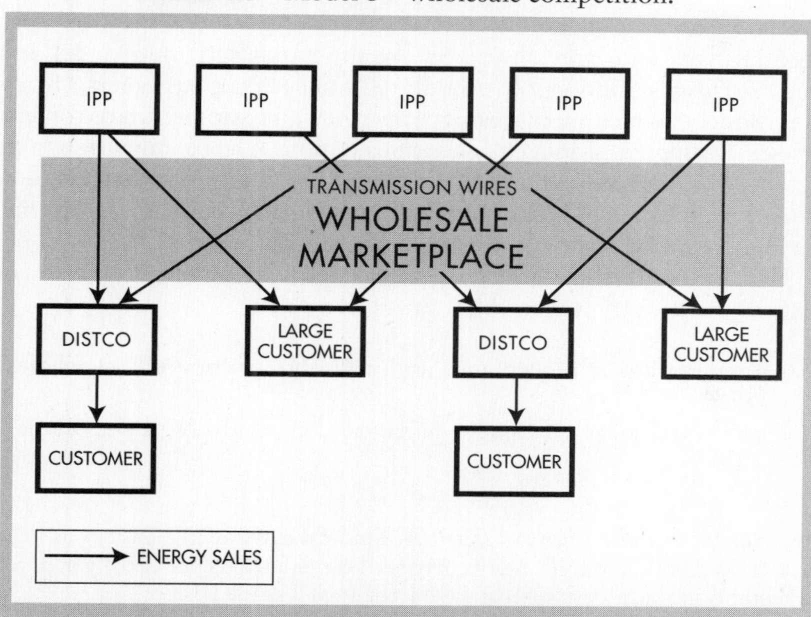

NOTE ON TERMINOLOGY: What the United States calls *wholesale competition* under the 1992 Act is not what we mean by Model 3. The wholesale market was (and in some places still is) a marginal or fringe market where regulated utilities sell power to one another. Utilities can also purchase from independent generators for incremental load, or when they close old generating plants. In the United States, there is an additional purchasing sector, the municipal utilities and cooperatives that own no generation. Independent generators and utilities are permitted to sell to them. But there is not much of a market in selling to vertically integrated utilities that have their own generation, plus a few municipals. This is hardly vibrant production competition—most of the sector is still regulated; the number of potential unmarried suitors for an independent generator is minimal. This may be called wholesale competition, but it should really be called marginal or fringe competition. Nowhere in the United States has a Model 3 approach with competitive generation been considered—the approach of making generation fully competitive but keeping the number of deregulated final buyers much smaller. If deregulation comes, it always comes as full retail competition—straight to Model 4.

called Distcos) and large customers are the purchasers, but Model 3 still gives the Distcos a monopoly over all the smaller final customers. (By contrast, Model 4, which we discuss later, permits all customers, large or small, a choice of supplier.) Model 3 is a serious option. It has competition in production, which is where most of the benefits are, it has many buyers to pull through the benefits of lower prices, and it avoids the costs and problems of providing retail access for all the small customers.

Here is the form of Model 3 that we would recommend (have recommended) if a country is working from a clean slate:[8]

1. All generation is deregulated and sells into a competitive wholesale market.
2. Distcos and large customers purchase competitively in the wholesale market.

[8] In *Competition and Choice in Electricity,* Model 3 had only the Distcos as buyers. Markets need enough buyers, just as they need enough sellers and usually in practice this requires the large customers to be buyers as well as the Distcos.

3. Retailers, aggregators, brokers, and marketers are permitted.
4. No default option for the large customers other than the spot market price.
5. Distcos provide for the small customers by making contracts with generators or aggregators. The tariff for small customers is the recommended fixed-plus-variable type that we discuss in detail later, in Chapter 4.

Model 3 is designed to produce the competitive wholesale markets that are supposed to bring the benefits of competition. It requires all the features we review in more detail next—short-term trading arrangements and a long-term business model for transmission, many buyers and sellers, supply and demand responsiveness. It is a major step. It is only simple in that it does not require the whole new consumer-oriented billing, settlement, and information infrastructure needed for retail access in Model 4. We return to the question of whether Model 4 is a better option later.

Why the Large Customers? The large customers are included as purchasers, but not the small customers. Markets need many buyers as well as many sellers—too few buyers lead back to Model 2, the single buyer, where sellers require long-term contracts to persuade them to enter. An alternative version of Model 3 might allow only the Distcos to purchase. The Distco would be like a distribution-only municipal utility in the United States, purchasing at wholesale and selling to all customers in its territory. But depending on the initial conditions, this could leave too few purchasers in the market, or even if there are many purchasers, some of them may be too large to enable competition to develop. One alternative would be to break up the distribution to provide enough buyers. If a single distribution company, or just two or three, covers most of a market area, that would not provide enough buyers. Permitting the large customers to purchase in the competitive markets adds buyers, thus reducing and probably removing any necessity to break up the Distcos. In the United States, for example, industrial companies account for one-third of consumption but much less than 1 percent of customers (see Figure 3.4). Making arrangements for metering, billing, and settlement for them is much less onerous than for all the millions of residential customers.

Model 3, with large users also permitted to purchase in the market, is the model of the U.S. gas industry, where large customers can purchase directly from producers, but small customers in most states still purchase from the local distribution company. It was also the first step of the U.K. restructuring in 1990.

FIGURE 3.4 U.S. electricity consumption and percentage of customers by type of customer, 1999.

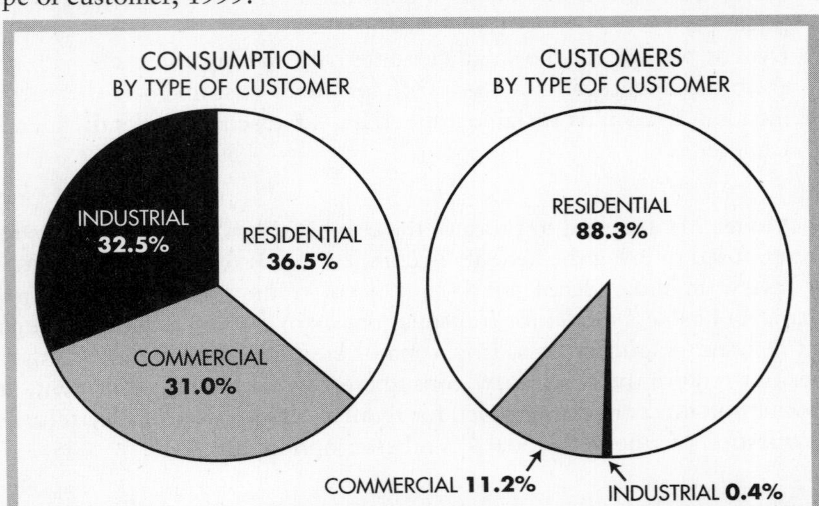

Source: Department of Energy, Energy Information Administration, Electricity Revenue, Sales, and Price by State and Utility (Tables 14–17).

As can be seen from the U.K. data (Table 3.1), there are plenty of buyers even in just the very large customer group, which is, however, a tiny percentage of total customers.

However, allowing only customers above a certain size to purchase competitively can create boundary problems. The U.K. regulator spent a full year issuing definitions of eligibility when that country was in its Model 3 phase. Customers with demand over 1 megawatt (MW) were allowed choice—could 1 MW include two meters at the same site? Could the "site" include two buildings across the street from each other? If so, why not all the sites owned by a single company? Or, why not all the sites served by the same aggregator? There is no logical stopping point, and much effort was wasted in trying to define one, and in gaming the rules.

This boundary problem mainly arises, or is much more acute, when those customers who are given freedom of choice also avoid paying "stranded costs" and are therefore really paying a lot less than the captive customers. (This happened both in the U.K. electric liberalization and in the U.S. gas industry.) If the stranded cost issue is solved before the wholesale markets are set up, then this boundary problem is not such a big issue. The

TABLE 3.1 England and Wales Customers Eligible for Direct Access

Phase	Minimum Size	Number of Customers Eligible for Direct Access	Customers Electing Direct Access in First Year
1990	1 MW	4,347	28%
1994	100 kW	50,716	25
1998/1999	none	24,060,000	11

Source: A Review of the Development in Industrial and Commercial Electricity Supply, OFGEM, December 2000; Electricity and gas competition review: Research study conducted for OFGEM, January 2000; and the U.K. electricity supply and distribution business development, MBD, 2000.

Distco is buying in the same wholesale market as the large customers, so the small customers should not be disadvantaged. Small customers in the United States who lobbied hard for retail access for all may well have been protesting the possibility of being saddled with paying the entire stranded cost obligation.

Should the Distco Be Required to Offer Default Service? Default service means the Distco is required to offer service at regulated prices to the deregulated customers. It can be a real nuisance. It means that the customers with choice of supplier have an additional choice—to return to the Distco whenever they wish and purchase at the tariff rate. Evidently, they will wish to come back when the Distco's offering is below market (because it made good contracts earlier) and will leave in droves if the Distco's contracts are above market. Someone pays for the Distco's extra cost of buying more at market prices, or for the cost of the contracts the Distco is left holding. That someone is either the utility's stockholders or the utility's small customers. This is not a risk the Distco or their small customers should have to take. There are various possible solutions:

- Do not offer default service to the large customers. They are big boys, with purchasing managers. They buy everything else on the market—why offer them protection? Let them go. But what happens if a retail supplier of a large customer goes out of business? The customer will get power anyway, and someone has to be deemed to have supplied it. That will be the Distco. There has to be a tariff at least for this eventuality.

- Let the large customers make a once-and-for-all choice as to whether they leave the utility, with no option to return. Once and for all seems like a long time; if they mostly decide to stay where they are, this could nullify the benefits of having many buyers in a competitive market.
- Offer Distco default service on a yearly contract, using the contract form we recommend for competition (see Chapter 4) with a fixed price for a fixed component and the rest at spot prices. This enables the utility to purchase enough and not too much for the default service. However, this option still may remove too much of the independent purchasing power from the competitive market.
- Offer a standard default service at spot market prices (*virtual direct access* as it is sometimes called) and let the large customers choose to go find a contract with another retailer if they prefer. Buyers who know what they are doing will cover themselves with a contract for at least some of their usage—normally contracts cover about 80 percent of the competitive markets. The large customers should be assumed to know what they are doing. This is the simple default option for large customers. (We mention here, so as not to be misinterpreted, that for small customers we do not recommend virtual direct access as a default option, because the small customers are not so savvy, the regulators want to give them more protection, and political risks of exposing them to the spot price are in our view too great.)

How Does the Distco Procure Power for Small Customers? The major problem with Model 3 is the problem of contracting. How does the Distco purchase power for its small customers?

One possibility is that the Distco does not contract at all, but simply passes through the wholesale spot price to small customers, as in the default option for large consumers. This is not a good option when so much of the load is still regulated. The small customers in Model 3 do not have the choice of finding another supplier and making contracts. The Distco is acting as the purchaser for the small customers, and must be able to offer a (more or less) fixed price.

Furthermore, the wholesale spot markets need a good proportion of contracts to control market power. (See Chapter 5 for a fuller explanation.) If most of the power is sold forward, on contracts, as it has been in most of the competitive markets in the world, this acts to limit market power in the spot sale markets. We believe that the markets, when they are fully competitive, should be left alone so that market participants collectively through their actions decide what proportion of spot and contract sales they want. But if half the load is still regulated, the regulator's choice should lean in the direction of contracts rather than spot purchases.

This, however, leads to another set of problems—getting the incentives right for the Distco to purchase at the lowest cost; and ensuring the Distco against capricious regulatory disallowances of contracts made in good faith. The Distco is not a final consumer, but rather is buying on behalf of its customers. It must be able to anticipate passing on the costs to the customers when it has purchased in good faith, but it must also expect its decisions to be reviewed by the regulator.[9] The virtual direct access solution avoids the risk for the Distco, but it does not offer predictable prices for the customers, and it does not provide the contract cover for the spot markets.

Perhaps the Distco should simply go out and buy the best contracts available, for, say, 80 percent to 90 percent of its expected load, and purchase the rest at spot prices. But these contracts are really hard for the regulator to monitor and evaluate. Contracts for the purchase of electricity need to specify time-slices, contract duration, indexing provisions, and other things that make contracts very hard to compare with each other. When the regulator looks at the purchasing strategy of the Distco, with hindsight there would always have been a better way. The Distco is at risk of having good faith efforts disallowed. Or, in places where corruption is an issue, the contracting process is a place where corruption can creep in since it is so hard to monitor.

Perhaps under Model 3, the Distco could own its own generation, and sell to the small customers at regulated prices, based on the cost of service of its own generators. The regulated prices would simply act as if they were a contract between the generator and the Distco—a regulated transfer price. This may be the way to navigate a transition (see the next paragraph) but it will not work in the long haul. This would be a two-market system—a regulated market for small customers and a competitive market for large customers. It only takes a thought experiment to see that this is not a viable solution. While initially the prices can be set at the old regulated rates, what happens as time goes on? Which assets enter the rate base of the regulated part, and which sell their output at competitive prices? How are the regulated prices set? Can the regulated assets be disposed of? Can the Distco build new plants? No one will be satisfied with the result, unless by absolute chance the regulated prices were exactly the same as the market prices. If they are not, the big customers will lobby for re-regulation, or the small customers will seek deregulation. Then next year the positions will be reversed. It is far preferable to buy out of the old regime and start anew.

---

[9] The idea that the regulator could set a fixed price in advance, and hope the Distco could purchase later in competitive markets without losing its shirt, is so bizarre that we would not mention it, except that it has happened.

Even the small customers should be paying market prices, and they will if the Distco in Model 3 buys in the competitive market.

There can be transition mechanisms, generally called *vesting contracts,*[10] set at the old prices, that stabilize prices for the first few years while the production markets settle down. Actually, this is what most countries have done. When the plants are divested or deregulated, they go to the competitive market with a suite of contracts to sell to the Distcos. This sets the generators' revenues and the customers' prices and gradually phases in the market prices. After the transition, the generating plants live or die by their performance in the competitive markets. Even in the transition, while the vesting contracts are in place, the generating companies are not regulated—they choose whether to open and close plants, they are penalized at market prices by having to purchase in the spot markets to meet their contracts if their plants did not work; they gain additional profits from increasing efficiency. They are subject to all the pressures of competition except that of having to make contracts in the real markets, which they do after the vesting contracts run out. But the vesting contracts are artificial—they are not determined by market prices as the result of arm's-length transactions—they are a holding action. What happens when these vesting contracts run out? Then we are back to the original problem of how the Distco should contract.

Another solution is an auction with public bids for a specified form of contract (indexing provisions, time-slices, etc.) so that the bids are comparable. This is probably the best available alternative, although it may prevent the Distco from making useful contracts in different forms as needed, and leads to inefficient contracting. Setting up the auction is expensive and time consuming—a perfect example of transaction costs. As yet not many places have tried it, so perhaps the costs are not continuing transaction costs so much as one-time start-up costs. Once the wrinkles are ironed out, auctions for contracts may well become the preferred way of doing business.

However, if an auction is to be held, we do suggest that it not be for *full requirements,* the traditional form of tariffs, but rather for fixed amounts, with the rest bought at spot, consistent with the tariff form that we believe should be the basis for improved efficiency in regulated markets, and the best tariff for default or other provision in deregulated markets (see Chapter 4).

None of these traditional regulatory solutions is really efficient, although each has some merits. A better scheme, in the United States at least, would be to encourage Distcos to contract on the private forward markets, and for the regulators to permit pass-through of arm's-length transactions

[10] These are called *vesting contacts* because Distcos are endowed or *vested* with the contracts at the time of the changes in structure.

completed there. This depends on the forward markets being liquid and efficient (see Chapter 6). Requiring all the Distcos in a market to use the forward markets would certainly encourage their growth, and also their liquidity and efficiency. A mixture of a transition mechanism of vesting contracts, expiring over, say, a three-year period, and new contracts completed on the forward markets, would work—the regulator could specify the percentage of the sales that should be contracted.[11] However, at present these markets do not exist at all in many places, and when they do, they do not extend more than about six months into the future.

This problem of the Distco contracting is the main reason for preferring eventual migration to the full-blown Model 4, where the problem goes away because the final customers, not the Distco, get the choice of provider. The Distco does not have to provide tariff service so there is no need for regulators to decide how well they contracted to do so. But in most jurisdictions, the same problem resurfaces in Model 4. Even with choice for all consumers, the Distco is often required to sell default service at regulated rates. Then all these issues come back. We reserve further discussion of this to Chapter 10 on retail competition, where we conclude that default provision should be at most only a transition stage.

The three big problems with Model 3 are with boundaries, the need for contracts, and the difficulties of making these contracts. The contract question is really quite difficult, and is a good reason for going to Model 4, retail competition. The main advantage of Model 3 in our view is as a transition—to allow the new wholesale trading arrangements to get set up and working well before imposing the additional, potentially enormous, number of transactions that come with Model 4. However, Model 4 is not a panacea. If it involves substantial transactions costs there may be a trade-off, the inefficiency of contracting against the costs of Model 4, and in some places, Model 3 might be a reasonable end point.

Model 4: Retail Competition

Model 4 (Figure 3.5) permits all customers to choose their suppliers, so a competing generator can sell to anyone, although small customers usually buy through aggregators or retailers. Model 4 is known in the United States as "retail access" or "customer choice." It is the model now in place, or

[11] The Enron debacle, still unfolding as we go to press, may yet reveal fraud in the forward electricity markets themselves, where Enron was easily the largest player. But so far the revelations have not touched the actual transactions in these markets—only the way they were accounted for.

FIGURE 3.5 Model 4—retail competition.

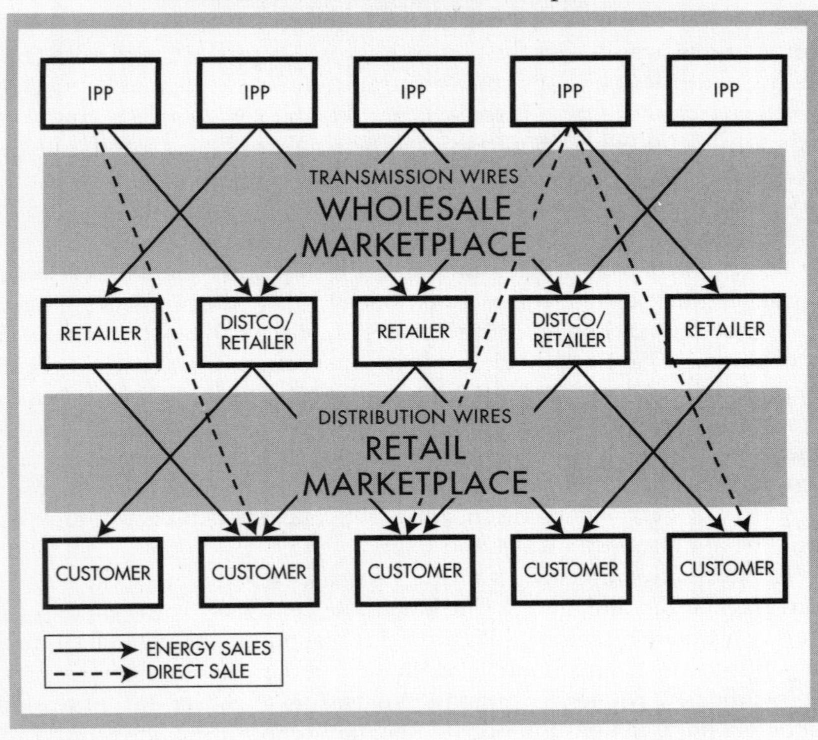

being put in place, in the United Kingdom, New Zealand, Australia, Argentina, Norway, Sweden, Spain, Alberta, and many states of the United States. Retail access pulls through the benefits of a competitive wholesale market by allowing many competing retailers (and not just the Distcos) to pressure generators into better prices, and to offer deeper and more liquid markets for financing new plants.

Model 4 requires the new wholesale trading arrangements, and competitive wholesale markets, as did Model 3. The main additional requirements in Model 4 are the settlement process, meter reading, and billing, which are greatly expanded from Model 3, and the education of millions of customers. We address these problems in more detail in Chapter 10; they are real, and argue for gradual implementation of Model 4. Gradual implementation also leaves time for the new institutions on the wholesale markets to be fine-tuned.

Model 4 works best where regulators trust the competitive markets to produce the best deal for the customers, and do not waste time trying to

FIGURE 3.6 The switching rate over time was similar in the United Kingdom.

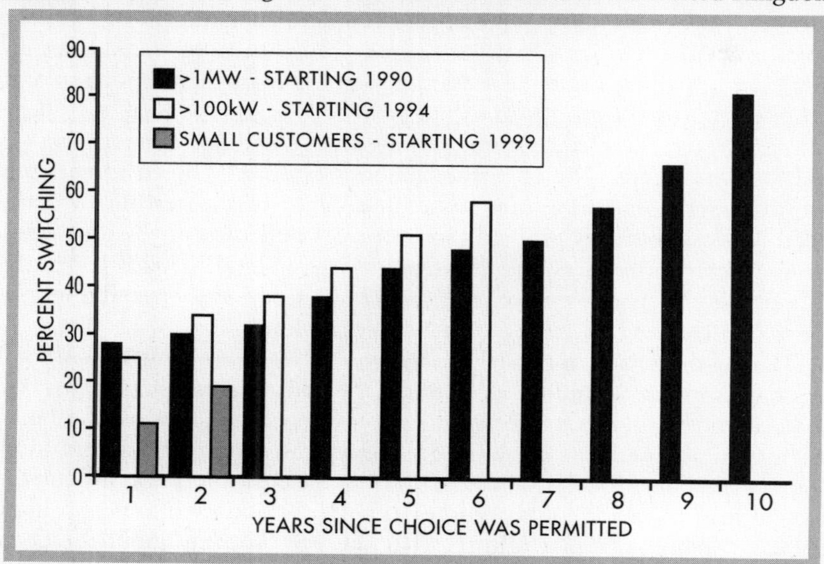

Source: A Review of the Development in Industrial and Commercial Electricity Supply, OFGEM, December 2000.

retain old-style regulatory protections. However, this presumes that the wholesale markets are in fact competitive and working to keep costs and prices down. Model 4 suffers from the instinctive desire of regulators to continue to protect small customers, by regulating prices, which leads back to some of the Model 3 problems. If the wholesale markets in Model 3 are working well, competition should be controlling prices, and regulators should be reassured.

The advantage of Model 4 is that it gives all customers choice, which they have in the rest of the economy; they seem to want it, and when they have it, they seem to like it. For example, in the United Kingdom, which phased in retail access in three tranches, in 1990, 1994, and 1999, while requiring the Distco to provide regulated default service, quite a large proportion of customers do choose, and the number grows as time goes on. The United Kingdom made no special incentives in the early years for switching, and (correctly) did not consider customer switching a goal of reform.[12] So Figure 3.6 shows customer preferences for competing retailers as compared

[12] Although it sometimes used the switching figures to support arguments that reforms were working.

to the regulated Distco default option. The horizontal axis is the number of years since the customer group had retail choice. The patterns of increasing choice in the first two groups are the same. Competitive retailers penetrated the markets at about the same rates and after six years the proportion of the two larger customer groups that had switched supplier was about 60 percent. (However, the verdict is not yet in on the small customers, who were the last to be offered choice in the United Kingdom.) The customers must have preferred something; that something might be clearer bills or value-added services, but it is probably lower prices pulled through from wholesale markets by more competition at the retail level. This does suggest (although it clearly does not prove) that competition at the retail level is effective in increasing efficiency at the wholesale level.

The big drawback of Model 4 is the cost of the settlement system for all the small consumers, and the need to get the consumers educated. Just how big the incremental investment has to be may depend on how much of it can be consolidated with the software needed for the new metering and billing arrangements for Model 3. The education of the customers is a difficult task and can lead to much confusion. For example, a conscientious and highly educated Texan consumer told me that she was worried about the choice she had to make, because she did not want to be blacked out, without power, if her supplier was unreliable. She was astounded when I told her this could not happen and it was all about price.

In addition, it can be argued that the costs of retail competition are wasted on small customers. Large customers have purchasing managers, who spend full time on buying supplies, but small customers do not have the time or energy to do this, and if middlemen or retailers do it for them it pushes up the cost. Some people believe that small customers would be satisfied with a small menu of default options provided by the Distco, and that retailers would be happy to concentrate on larger customers to whom profitable value-added services are more likely to be of interest. And this is essentially Model 3—what we would propose for the medium term. If a jurisdiction can install sufficient hourly metering to get the wholesale markets working, and give customers a real choice of time-of-use pricing options, such as those we describe in Chapter 4, then it will have made a big step forward. But this takes time.

Furthermore, retailing electricity is not a particularly profitable business. Retailing in other products generally is much more complicated than just reselling the product, but that is most of what it is about in electricity. If customers believe they are getting "better electricity" or "more reliable service," they are misinformed. Electricity is just a commodity. It is exactly the same everywhere. In other industries, a retailer (think Macy's) performs value-added functions such as:

- Displaying goods in a store;
- Making preliminary style and quality choices among different manufacturers;
- Taking risks on unsold amounts and on price changes;
- Checking the quality of merchandise delivered by manufacturers;
- Unbundling large shipments for sale as smaller bundles; and
- Providing other value-added services such as advice on purchases, a crèche for children while you shop, delivery, and other services.

These are functions that earn the retailer an often-handsome return. In electricity, the retailer's role is probably much more limited. The only real roles that have emerged are risk-taking and repackaging—buying or producing electricity to sell under a form of contract that suits the customers' needs. Retailers may be able to offer value-added services, although the innovations that were immediately apparent in the telephone industry after competition was introduced have not yet appeared in any of the liberalized electricity markets.

In general, we believe that *reselling* is not a particularly attractive stand-alone (merchant) business. In the United Kingdom, stand-alone retailers came and went quite fast; the major retailers are the competitive affiliates of other Distcos (who own their own generation) and Centrica, the gas company that owns fuel used for generation. The other major retailers in the United Kingdom are the generating companies themselves, through a retail affiliate.

In the United States, the take-up on retail choice for small consumers has so far been quite minimal, despite sometimes-excessive incentives. This may mean that relatively few retailers will enter the market for small consumers, leaving the competitive retail affiliate of the Distco with a very large de facto share of the market. This in turn will attract regulatory attention, as it has in Texas, where the utility affiliates are required to sell at prices set by the regulator until competitors have taken 40 percent of the retail market. This could take forever—a sort of limbo default service at regulated rates.

But despite our reservations as to the value of full retail access, if it is not inordinately expensive to offer it, and customers want it, it does have the distinct advantage of getting out of the contracting problems in Model 3. Or does it?

The problems we are left with in Model 4 are ones of inertia: What to do with the couch potatoes—those who would rather not be bothered; and the customers nobody really wants to serve? Regulators and politicians are more inclined to require default service for small customers, even if they are willing to let the large customers fend for themselves. This then raises the same issue we discussed earlier—the problems of the Distco making contracts, and how to avoid the risks of customers trying to return to the utility if the market price is high, and leaving when the market price is low.

We return to these questions in Chapter 10.

Which Model?

To summarize the models:

- Model 1 was the standard for 100 years, the model everyone is familiar with.
- Model 2—single buyer—allows independent generators to sell to a single (utility) buyer in each area on long-term life-of-plant contracts.
- Model 3—wholesale competition—makes the Distcos and the large industrial customers the buyers from competitive generators.
- Model 4—retail competition—gives choice of supplier to all customers.

The choice of model is up to the policy makers, but in deciding they need to understand the implications for structural change, the need for new institutions, and the complications, given the existing arrangements, of getting from here to there. The different models need different amounts of structural change and rearrangement of functions in the industry, new institutions especially for wholesale markets, and new roles for regulation (Figure 3.7).

If the goal is competition in production, most of this can be achieved through Model 3, wholesale competition. Model 3 requires most of the structural and institutional changes at the wholesale level needed for Model 4, if it is to be real competition, and not just letting in a few competitors on the edges while retaining 90 percent of the system in the hands of the incumbents. Model 3 requires changes in the structure of the industry, in trading arrangements, and also in metering at the customer level, so that customers can be responsive to price, an aspect we review in more detail later.

FIGURE 3.7 Changes needed for wholesale and retail competition.

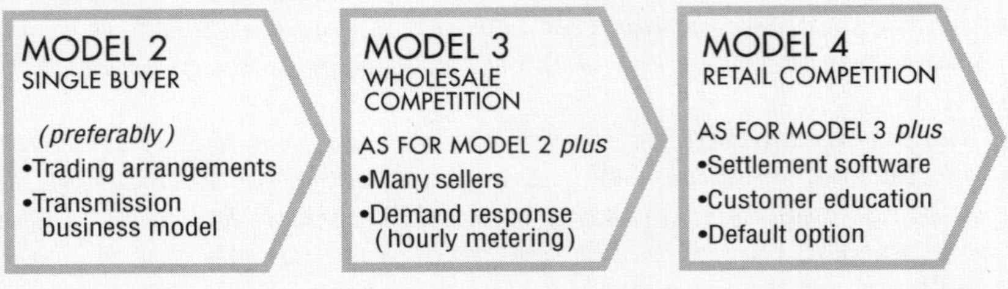

MODEL 2
SINGLE BUYER
(preferably)
•Trading arrangements
•Transmission business model

MODEL 3
WHOLESALE COMPETITION
AS FOR MODEL 2 *plus*
•Many sellers
•Demand response (hourly metering)

MODEL 4
RETAIL COMPETITION
AS FOR MODEL 3 *plus*
•Settlement software
•Customer education
•Default option

The problems of Model 3 are problems of boundaries and contracting. The problems of Model 4 are the transaction costs of having so many customers participating in a huge new settlement system, and understanding what is going on; and if default service is required, it does not avoid the Model 3 problems.

Full retail competition is a logical end point to these reforms, because Model 4 avoids the potential conflicts and inefficiencies of Model 3. It gets the regulators out of the competitive market. The pressures for increased efficiency come directly from the customers, not from regulated Distcos. Also, many customers, particularly the larger and medium-size ones, seem to want choice and there is no particular reason, other than cost, for them not to have it. Our recommendation (not, however, as strong a preference as some of our other recommendations, and depending on the infrastructure cost) is to go to Model 3 and then proceed step by step with liberalization of the retail markets, gradually reducing the size of the customers who are offered choice, with the aim of eventually offering choice to everyone, and getting the Distco out of the business of selling electricity.

RESTRUCTURING EXISTING COMPANIES

When competition is introduced, the structure of existing companies has to change. Rearranging a whole industry is much easier to do when the government owns the whole thing than when companies are already private. Most countries start from a government monopoly, and the government imposes solutions, usually (but not always) as a prelude to privatization. Changes that involve redistribution of stockholder values in private companies are much harder to implement. Nonetheless, the principles are the same, the potential conflicts are the same, and the requirements for new institutions are the same. The questions of what to do if the first best solution is unattainable because of existing constraints is left to Part Two where we consider the situation in the United States.

Some functions have to be unbundled because of potential conflicts of interest. The main potential conflict problems of joint ownership are those where owners of essential facilities are also competitors for using that facility:

- Transmission and system operations with generation.
- Distribution with retailing.

There are also problems of potential cross-subsidy. When competitive and regulated activities are in the same company (or affiliated companies) the concern is cross-subsidization of the competitive activity by the regulated activity.

The broad options for unbundling integrated functions, in order of severity, are:

- *Accounting separation:* Unbundle the accounts of different functions and price them separately; this is always a necessary first step.
- *Functional separation:* Separate the functions within the company and impose restrictions on activities—some combination of physical separation of people; separation of information that competitors may need, to be made equally available to all; services to other functions priced at market levels and available to all; codes of conduct to limit anticompetitive behavior.
- *Functional separation into an affiliate:* Separate the functions into different companies (affiliates) under a holding company, with similar restrictions.
- *Corporate separation:* Divest (sell) the function completely so that it is no longer part of the company. This always solves the conflict and cross-subsidy problems, but may be overkill.

The choice of which remedy to use depends on how severe the problem is and how difficult it is to police; but also, on the other side, what benefits there are to keeping functions together—what economies of scope benefit consumers? Every country, whether the industry is initially government owned or private, has to face these issues.

The first step always has to be unbundling the accounts of the various functions. This invariably leads to problems about *allocating* the overhead functions of the company (human resources, purchasing, legal, and so on). The bigger problems arise when it is a question of further separation, and possible *duplication* of the functions with loss of efficiency (several human resources departments, several purchasing departments). It is a fine judgment to weigh the scope for cross-subsidy against the duplication involved from separation; but some of the issues of conflict of interest that we review next are so serious as to settle the matter of separation for at least some functions, and in these cases the cross-subsidy issue solves itself.

Natural Allies—Generation and Retailing

There is one pairing where there is not only no conflict, but positive benefit in keeping functions together: Generation and retailing.

Stand-alone competitive retailers who do not own generation are at much more risk than retailers who do own generation. In Model 4, a retailer who agrees to provide final customers with power at fixed prices needs to hedge the risk—he cannot rely on buying at the volatile spot market price to sell contracts at fixed prices. This situation was a major problem in the 2000 to 2001 California crisis (see Appendix C). He must back those sales contracts up with a purchase contract to hedge the risk, or he needs to have a generating plant. The make-or-buy decision is complicated: Ownership of assets has its own risks and involves long-term commitments. But there are transaction costs to contracting. For instance, if the market price rises and the supplier defaults on a fixed price contract, the retailer has to buy elsewhere at the higher prices; he has a long legal battle to recoup his costs, and meanwhile he has to serve the customers, or default and perhaps go out of business. A generating plant is the natural hedge for a competitive retailer against changes in market prices, and cross-ownership of generation by retailers should not be prohibited.

Distco with Affiliated Generation

If the Distco has to retail to small customers at a fixed price in Model 3, or as a default option in Model 4, should the Distco or an affiliate be permitted, or even encouraged, to own generation to hedge its risks? Is it like all other retailers, for whom generation is a natural hedge? Owning generation presents a conflict of interest if the Distco can contract with its own affiliate. The contracting problems of the previous section are really magnified. Some places (New Zealand, Maine) have simply prohibited Distcos from owning or being affiliated with any generation. But on the other hand, as we have seen, retailing and generation are natural allies—a plant may be better than a wholesale contract as a hedge on commitments to a fixed retail price.

However, the Distco that is required to be a retailer only needs to own generation to hedge its risk *if it is indeed at risk*. If it can pass through to customers all the cost of all the contracts it makes, it has no risk and therefore it does not need a generating plant to hedge the risk. In Chapter 4 we discussed the tariff form that we believe further limits the Distcos' risk. But if, as in California, the Distco is required to sell at an absolutely fixed price, with no provision for adjustments if the wholesale price changes, and no contracts, then it must have generating plants to hedge the risk of changes in market prices, and fuel price hedges to offset the risk of fuel price changes, or it must be evaluated for rate of return purposes as a much riskier company.

If the Distco owns generation and is permitted to contract with itself, there can be a serious problem of self-dealing, which is very hard to detect under some regulatory schemes. So there is a problem with the Distco owning generation in Model 3 (and also in Model 4 if the Distco is required to retail at regulated rates) unless there is some way to ensure that any contracts are indeed at market prices. The auction method does this, as does a requirement for the Distco to purchase, and the affiliated generator to sell, in the forward markets. In the auction, the generating affiliate simply bids along with other bidders, and if it wins the auction it gets the contract.

If the Distco has no regulated retail obligations, there is no intrinsic problem with it owning generation other than the potential for cross-subsidy. In the United Kingdom, for instance, the Distcos were initially severely limited in the amount of generation they could own; nonetheless there were allegations of self-dealing through purchases of power from partnerships the Distcos had invested in. In the end, the Distcos were permitted to own generation, and almost all of them do, and were released from their statutory responsibility to provide default service.

Conflicts of Interest—Transmission and Operations with Generation

Transmission and system operations are "essential facilities." Open and nondiscriminatory access to them is essential for competition. The problem here is the severe conflict of interest in having these two functions owned by a competing generator, against the undeniable need for close coordination among generation, system operations, and transmission expansion. The only sustainable resolution to these is well-designed trading arrangements, and even then the arrangements for transmission expansion will inevitably be something of a compromise.

The major locus of conflict of interest in the short term is the system operator. As we have stated before, the system operator has to have complete control over the short-term operations of the generating plant and interface with the transmission system. He has a hundred subtle ways of influencing access to transmission, which are hard to police, because the system operator's judgment is relied on at very short notice to resolve problems on the transmission system *by telling generators what to do*. If he is employed by a company that also owns generation, he is not independent, he is a competitor: no one will trust him. *In a competitive world, the system operator needs to be independent of all generators, and indeed all traders, buyers, and sellers. Everyone agrees on this and independence of the system operator is always a central objective of restructuring.*

A second source of conflict is the responsibility for expanding the transmission system—the short-term problem of transmission access translated into the long term. If a competing generating company or utility owns the transmission system and has responsibility for maintaining and expanding it, there are many subtle ways in which it can thwart competitors by being dilatory about construction and maintenance of the transmission assets. This is not so immediately apparent, since any bad results are longer term, not day by day, as with the system operator. Competitive generators also complain about delays and costs involved in connection of their generators to a transmission system that is under the control of a competitive company.

Most countries have dealt with these two issues by complete corporate separation of both functions from any other function in the industry. We would absolutely recommend this separation, preferably including divestiture of transmission.[13] This is fundamental. The system operator may be in a separate organization (the independent system operator or ISO) from the transmission owners, or together in one organization. While we prefer the latter—consolidated transmission and system operations (Transcos)—the more important concept is that neither of them be owned or controlled in any way by the competitive companies they serve. The pros and cons of ISOs, Transcos, and other alternatives we leave to Chapter 9 on the transmission business model.

Conflict of Interest—Distco with Retailing in Model 4

Another issue to be resolved is whether the Distco can use its monopoly on low voltage wires to discriminate against competing retailers. This is only an issue in Model 4 where there are competing retailers and the Distco's affiliate is competing for customers. In one way, it is like the conflict between transmission and generation, but the control of the transmission wires is much more central to the profitability of the generators than the control of the distribution wires is to the profits of the retailers. The distribution wires are essentially passive—the Distco does not control them in a minute-by-minute sense.

Let us distinguish between the situation where the Distco is required to make *regulated* sales, and the full-blown Model 4, when the Distco makes *no regulated* retail sales. This section refers to Model 4, retail competition, where if the Distco also produces power, it is competitively sold. In the full-blown Model 4, the Distco is just one of many competitive retailers; as a retailer, it will probably wish to retain its own generation, for reasons we already discussed. But this should not be too much of a problem since the

[13] In the United States, there are three sets of laws that make this difficult: the tax law, and two laws applying to publicly owned facilities—the public use doctrine and the two-county doctrine—see Part Two.

customers are free to choose: If the offering is not as good as the competitor's, the customers will go elsewhere. The regulator does not need to watch the price of contracts—the market is supposed to do that for him.

The problem is with three more subtle types of potentially unfair anticompetitive behavior on the part of the Distco:

1. *Favoring affiliates through consumer confusion:* Customers may take suggestions from a trusted source rather than investigate conditions on their own. Thus, if they complain to their distribution company about the high price of electricity, the staff at the distribution company answering the phone may inappropriately steer the customer to its own retail offerings.
2. *Favoring affiliates through differential service:* When lines break in an ice storm, trucks owned by the distribution company must go out and repair the damage. The Distco might favor its own retail customers (say, by fixing their lines first) rather than following a plan that minimizes the Distco's costs. It might also rewire an area to avoid overloading and blackouts more quickly when its own retail sales are at stake.
3. *Favoring affiliates through information sharing:* A distribution utility, particularly if it carries out the billing and metering functions, may gather data on customers that is quite valuable commercially. This data might be used to illegitimately leverage the monopoly's position as collector of such data to reap profits for its own retail subsidiary.

These problems argue for some sort of separation of the Distco from any retailer. On the other hand, the needs of the customers should be what matters here. If they have had good service from their integrated company, they may very well prefer to stay with them, as a positive preference and not just because they are confused. Actually prohibiting the Distco from being affiliated with a retailer is (in our view) removing some real customer benefits. There are also employees to consider. A very large proportion of employees of an integrated company are in the distribution/customer service end of the business and most of the rest of them are in generation. In an integrated company, they can change jobs and retain pension rights. Making the companies much smaller, for no good public policy reason, changes employees' career opportunities.

The typical regulatory response to the conflict of the Distco is to require a functional separation, preferably into a retail affiliate, and create a code of conduct regulating the relationship between the retail subsidiary and the Distco. Information from the regulated business should be made available to all competitors, including the competitive affiliate, on the same terms, and customer service personnel should not be allowed to steer customers to the affiliate. The retail affiliate should perhaps be in a different building. The regulator, who needs to set up reporting requirements directed at this issue, should carefully police any favoritism in maintenance or reinforcements.[14] If this code of conduct is abused, then divestiture of the retailing affiliate may be necessary, or the affiliate can be prohibited from retailing in its own territory.

But note that this recommendation only holds for countries with a history of strong economic regulation. In other countries, and particularly where corruption is a major issue, the decision to separate retailing completely from the Distco is sometimes taken from the start. Or, if Distcos wish to have a retail subsidiary, they may not retail in their own distribution territory.

Generation Divestiture for Market Power Reasons

Finally, at the end of this long list of structural changes, is the question of whether generation has to be divested, not because of internal conflicts, but because of two other reasons—to mitigate market power, and to establish the value of the generating plants as they are moved from a regulated to a competitive situation.

In countries that are working from a relatively clean slate, with, for example, a single government-owned monopoly and enough generating plant to support competition, the government divides the plant into enough companies to ensure a competitive generating market. Even this is not quite as simple as it seems, since there can be small areas where transmission is not adequate, and where there may be too few competitors, or only one. And there may well be a history of regional organization of generating divisions and powerful labor unions that make reorganization every bit as complex as creating competition in a country with a history of local privately owned monopolies.

But in countries with this history of local monopolies, the starting situation is difficult. Just moving the generating plant into a single generating

---

[14] However, some observers and regulators insist that utility retailing affiliates should not be allowed to use the utility logo or brand name, hire the utility's employees, and so on. Such rules deny consumers the savings from economies of scale and scope available to the utility and deny employees the right to change jobs freely. These rules also hide information from consumers and make it difficult for them to make use of their own experience regarding service quality and other aspects of the utility's reputation to make an informed choice of supplier. We think this impedes efficiency.

affiliate might well mean that the affiliate has much too much market share for the market to be competitive. Divesting it to a single unaffiliated company would not change the problem at all. When a single company has too big a share of the market initially, it has to be broken into smaller slices. If the company has life-of-plant contracts with IPPs, as in Model 2, then perhaps the IPP contracts can be bought out to create more competitors. If not, the clean way to create small enough companies is by divestiture. Whether this is necessary depends on the size of the underlying market. If there are good transmission connections with other areas, there may be no need for existing companies to divest for market power reasons. But it clearly needs to be investigated.

There may be cases where competition is simply not feasible, either because the market is very small, or because legal constraints restrict divestiture. The very best solution to market power problems is to have enough competing generators to begin with, and in some cases there are no alternatives to full divestiture (sale) of existing generation into smaller groups of plants to create enough competitors. In these cases, divestiture is not simply an option, but a necessity.

Generation Divestiture for Valuation

The second reason to divest by selling generating plant is to establish the value of the generating plants in the new competitive regime. Divestiture to different owners creates a clean cut—the value is established, the allocation of any surplus or deficit can be decided, and the matter is out of the way. Otherwise these issues have a way of dragging on and impeding other changes that need to be made.

The other solutions to valuation involve estimations, negotiations with the regulator, or an intermediate solution of top-down pricing. (See Part Two, this is mainly a U.S. problem.) While they are plausible, and attractive to utility management and regulators who understandably want least-change options, divestiture has proven to be the most resilient solution to valuation for all concerned. If divestiture is not required for market power reasons, the utility can be a bidder itself. If it wins, it can take the plant back into a subsidiary and sell power in the market. The distribution company then handles the surplus or deficit.

If the tax code needs to be adjusted for the specific purpose of enabling asset sales to be made for valuation purposes without triggering major tax consequences that would not otherwise have occurred (and maybe for other purposes in the restructuring process), it is worthwhile to seek legislation to get the process going.

So to summarize divestiture of generation:

- If the markets are too small or the utility too big, there is no escaping divestiture to other owners to break up the company that is too big for the market. However, there are some small-area market power problems that cannot be solved by divestiture. (Simply divesting a too-big company to other owners just exacerbates the market power problem by removing it from regulation.)
- Divestiture is recommended if there are issues of determining value for stranded cost recovery. Unless there are market power reasons for divesting, the utility should be able to bid for its own plant.
- Model 3, if it is to be permanent, may require divestiture of generation to avoid problems of self-dealing. But for short-term transitions, public bidding on standardized contracts can avoid conflict of the Distco with its own generation.

ENSURING COMPETITIVE MARKETS

In Models 3 and 4, the critical element is competitive wholesale markets for electricity. This is the main message of this book: *The need is to refocus on introducing competition into production markets.*

Markets and Marketplaces

A word on terminology: competition implies markets. *Market* is a word with many meanings. When economists talk about markets, they usually mean *the entire set of conditions* surrounding production, transport, and distribution of a product. The everyday sense of the word markets (as on the evening news programs) means *the real or virtual place for buying and selling and coming to a price.*

Since they are both known as markets, to make the distinction, we call the buying and selling market a *marketplace,* and the entire set of conditions a *market.* The trading arrangements are the rules of the marketplace.

Just to be clear about this terminology—the market for cornflakes includes Kellogg's and Post and you and me, and the corn producers, and the railroads and the trucks that transport the inputs and the final product, and all the supermarkets that sell it. The (retail) marketplace is just the supermarket. The trading arrangements of the supermarket are: they open from 8 A.M. to 11 P.M.; you can come any time; no smoking; you pick out your own items; you pay at the checkout; you pay what they ask; delivery is optional on payment of a fee; wholesale deliveries must be at a prespecified time; wholesale price is negotiated in advance; payment is 30 days or immediate.

The size of a *market* is naturally determined by geography, transport, and by taste and cost—the market for cement is local, because of the transport costs. By contrast, the size of a *marketplace* is determined by the number of entities trading under the same rules. The stock markets are national marketplaces. In electricity, we could have a national marketplace with the same rules throughout, but we would still have many local markets unless transmission were expanded, and more buyers and sellers could reach each other physically.

The ambiguity of the word *markets* has led to untold confusion in discussion of electricity restructuring. Competitive markets need efficient marketplaces. But efficient marketplaces are not all they need—efficient marketplaces are a necessary but not a sufficient condition for competitive markets. Nor do big marketplaces necessarily create big markets. If the United States were to establish regional transmission organizations (RTOs) and consistent rules, then there would be big marketplaces, with everyone following the same rules;[15] but if there are transmission constraints within the marketplaces, there will still be fragmented markets. Nonetheless, big marketplaces are probably the first step—fragmented marketplaces can limit the size of the real markets.

Markets can work to the benefit of consumers, if the market has been structured to be competitive and the marketplace is efficient. Then politicians should leave the markets and the marketplaces to do their job of setting the price, eliciting the supply at minimum cost, and making sure it goes to those who most value it.

But when markets are not competitive, or the marketplaces are not efficient, they do not work to give the cheapest and the best results for consumers. In fact, they can fleece consumers and leave producers very rich. State regulators in the United States perhaps have a built-in suspicion of this, which may be why they have been unwilling to release the customers in their jurisdictions from the very price controls that end up (ironically) impeding the development of competitive markets.

Competitive Markets—a Checklist

What is needed for competitive markets? Economists routinely hold up the standard of perfect competition to evaluate actual competitive results.

[15] FERC's Standard Market Design initiative is poised to do this as we write.

Anything called "perfect" immediately scares politicians and regulators, who are used to compromises. So we hasten to add that neither electric markets nor any other market will ever reach the ideal of perfect competition. As there are no perfect parents, and good-enough parenting is what we strive to do, good-enough markets are what we live with. That said, in *designing* a competitive market, we should have more comfort that the market will perform well if it is designed to mimic features of perfectly competitive markets, as far as possible. Then at least we have a conceptually sound framework against which to evaluate the compromises.

The elements that need to be in place for the *markets* to be competitive and work properly are:

- Many buyers and many sellers—lack of market power on both sides of the market;
- Demand and supply responsiveness to price;
- Liquid and efficient marketplaces;
- Equal access to any essential facilities (in this case transmission and distribution wires); and
- Treatment of subsidies and environmental controls so that they do not interfere with the workings of the market.

Achieving this in electricity is quite a substantial design job. Yet after so many years of experience, and some really bad experiences, people still say, "Markets do not need to be designed—they just happen. After all, no one designed the coal markets or the cornflakes market." We have explained the need for design of trading arrangements, and how electricity is different. But in electricity there is also a long and continuing history of regulation, resulting in concentrations of local production, fixed and averaged final prices to consumers and no way easily to de-average them, and delivery over a transmission system designed for maintaining local reliability and not broad, regional trading of electricity. Something has to happen before these markets are competitive. *For virtually all dimensions of markets, the preexisting situation does not provide underpinnings that would lead to competitive markets if the regulators simply went away and did nothing. This is especially true in the United States, where every aspect of the competitive market requires some sort of institutional, structural, or regulatory change.*

In Part Two we return, as promised, to the U.S. situation, but first we set out the basic requirements and our preferred solutions in more detail. At the end of Part One we sketch out a "theory of muddling through"—what substitutions can be made to work and what is essential.

CHAPTER 4

Requirements for Competition: Demand Side

A requirement for a competitive market is to have *many buyers*, and in particular, *many buyers who are responsive to price*. We discussed the importance of many buyers in Chapter 3 of Models 2 and 3 and we have mentioned the importance of price response several times before. *There is no single thing more important to the markets as they currently stand than to get demand responsiveness into them.* With competitive generating markets (and not just when there is retail access), it is important for a substantial proportion of the load to have usage tracked hourly and to pay prices that vary hourly with system conditions.

THE ROLE OF DEMAND IN MARKETS

Figures 4.1 and 4.2 show the traditional graphs of price determination in a competitive market. The customers, just as much as the producers, set the price. In all competitive markets the price settles at:

- The price offered by the last (highest cost) supplier who supplies, when there is plenty of capacity. This is also the value to the last (lowest value) consumer who purchases.
- The value to the last consumer who purchases, if the capacity is limited. This is called the *rationing price*—it is the price that rations available capacity to the demand when supplies are tight.

In other words, the customers get a very good deal. They pay much less than the product is worth to them most of the time. Even when capacity is scarce, and the price rises to the rationing price, those who continue consuming are paying less (by definition) than it is worth to them. The very last

FIGURE 4.1 Normal supply and demand.

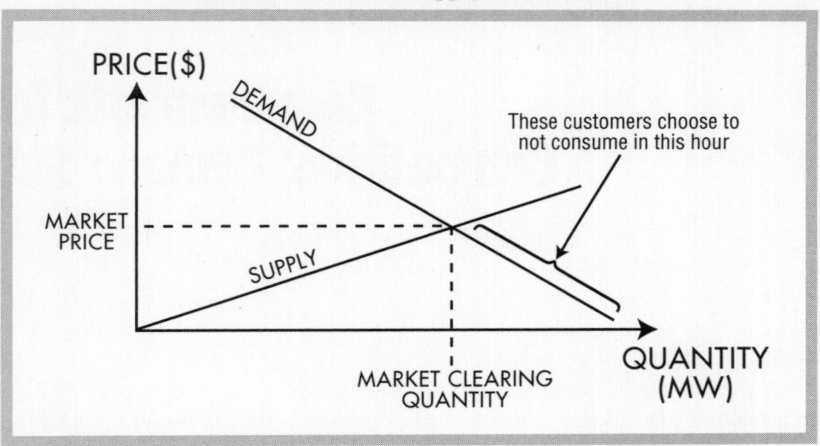

consumer (the marginal buyer) pays exactly what it is worth to him and sets the price.

Those buyers who decide it is not worth it, and refuse to buy, are constraining the price. *Buyers always therefore "participate" in markets, even when they don't buy, by refusing to pay more than a product is worth to them.* Even an unconstrained monopolist—who is often said to be able to set the price wherever he likes—still cannot set it higher than buyers are willing to pay.

FIGURE 4.2 Price rises and consumers respond to supply shortage.

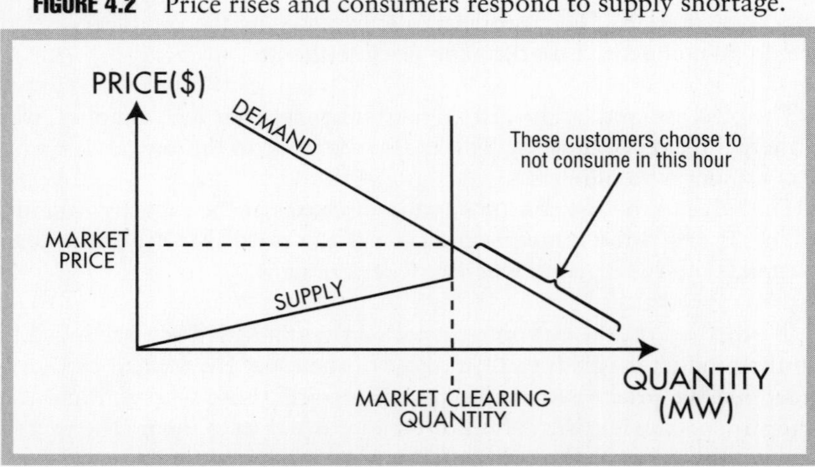

This buyer participation is especially important at times of tight supply. At peak times, it is the marginal buyers who should set the price, and it is important that they should have not only *incentives to respond,* but also a *means to respond,* so that they can have control over the price that they pay.

Lack of Incentives to Respond

In most places where electricity is sold, retail buyers don't have an incentive to respond *because they never face the short-term movements in the wholesale price. They pay a retail price that is averaged over time,* despite the fact that an electricity transaction trades at the wholesale and retail level at the same instant, because of the speed of light and lack of storability factors. This is a problem because the wholesale price does, necessarily, fluctuate greatly in the short term. It is much higher at peak times than at off-peak times. (Sometimes the prices go up because supply falls, rather than because demand rises, but demand is the major fluctuating factor.) The prices vary by up to a factor of 10 between the peak times and the lowest times. The peak times occur generally on a weekday afternoon after several days of high heat, when everyone is using air conditioning (except in northern regions where they occur in deepest winter evenings).

Peak electricity and off-peak electricity are different products, with very different prices. It is hard to think of any other industry where products whose price varies so widely are bundled together for sale, so that the customer who uses relatively little on peak is forced to subsidize those who use a lot. In electricity, we bundle the expensive peak hours with the cheap off-peak hours and sell them at one average price. This long-standing custom makes no sense except for the savings on the cost of using more expensive meters required to record hourly usage. But these metering costs have come down fast.

For example, the choice of an expensive Armani suit or cheap Gap jeans is left to the customers. If we did with clothing what we do in electricity (charged the average of the Armani and the Gap prices for clothing), there would be a big migration to Armani and a drop-off in demand for Gap. What we have always done in electricity is the equivalent of saying: Buy any mixture you want of Armani and Gap, and your regulated clothing supplier will simply produce more Armani—the extra costs will be rolled in and will increase the average price, but no matter—you just buy what you want. Those who need jeans would be subsidizing those who prefer Armani. But everyone likes to think he is getting a bargain and does not want to have to pay more for Armani—forgetting that he is overpaying greatly for the vast bulk of his use—the jeans.

This sort of cross-subsidy can only continue if there is a regulated clothing supplier who keeps building Armani factories and who is able to roll in the extra cost. It cannot survive deregulation, or if it does, deregulation will not survive. Regulators can make temporary fixes, but Gap will try to get out of them, leaving someone to pick up Armani's costs.

Competitive markets should have the prices of Armani and the Gap unbundled; customers should pay more for the peak and less for the off peak. In fact, as in the clothing markets, they need a whole suite of price points, and a choice of how much they are willing to pay at all times—peak, off-peak, and everything in between.

Electric prices have always been bundled—you pay by the quantity, but not by when you use it. There were moves toward time of use pricing with 2- or 3-part tariffs, and at least a few utilities have had some form of real-time pricing for years, but it never caught on. First, there was no real-time price determined by markets—the utility would have to decide what the price was each hour, and someone would have to police the calculation for cheating. Second, the real-time price, when there is a market, is very volatile, and many people prefer fixed prices. Third, hourly meters used to be expensive. And fourth, there was always a regulated utility that would build the extra capacity and roll in the costs.

Lack of a Means to Respond

Added to this is the problem that customers lack a *means* to respond to changing electricity prices. The actual mechanism by which buyers in other industries participate varies from marketplace to marketplace. In an auction, a form of marketplace that is often used when supply is limited to what has already been produced and is sitting waiting to be sold, there is no additional short-term cost of production and the demand side clearly sets the price. (If the price does not cover the sunk costs of producers, they lose money; they have no way to influence the price once the product is at the market.) In apparent contrast, in the supermarket, the sellers "set the price"; but if the customers refuse to pay, the price goes down.

In electricity markets, consumers buy electricity whenever they turn on a light switch. They have never needed to check the price first, or negotiate a price in advance, so there are no methods in place for them to do so now.

DEMAND RESPONSIVENESS

The lack of attention to the demand side in the electricity business probably occurred because in most other industries the demand side works and can safely be ignored. Thousands of individuals choose what they want to buy, and how much they are willing to pay in every competitive market. But in electricity, although in some places there is customer choice, there has not been sufficient attention paid to getting direct participation of buyers in setting the market prices, or an adequate temporary substitute.

In the design of electric markets, all the emphasis has been on the supply side, with the implicit assumption that the customers will just take what they want and pay. But it is vital to pay attention to the customer response, because that is what will make the markets work. Academic and trade journals are beginning to converge in agreement on this matter,[1] but demand response has been virtually ignored, or, indeed, treated as positively deleterious in restructuring plans to date. The first step in any restructuring plan is often a price freeze, on the grounds that this is required to achieve the acquiescence of voters to the concept of competition. Consumers, it is asserted, should be shielded from volatile electric prices.

As the California debacle makes clear, such plans can destroy a functioning market when the supply/demand balance becomes tight. If California had installed hourly metering and pricing there would have been no crisis.[2] Even with tight capacity, the wholesale prices would never have risen so high; even if the utilities had been purchasing at spot prices, they would not have been hemorrhaging money; there would have been no credit crisis and associated withholding—there would have been no blackouts. In fact, just raising the overall customer price reduced demand by so much that the crisis that had been predicted for the summer of 2001 simply went away, and the spot prices fell back. This was after retail prices were raised 40 percent on average. Think what could have been saved by hourly metering and appropriate tariff design in the first place.

Role of Demand Response in Reliability

In well-functioning markets for other commodities, customers choose whether to consume or not at the market price. The choice is always theirs, not a system operator's or some other third party's. *Well-functioning mar-*

---

[1] Steven Braithwait and Ahmad Faruqui, "The Choice Not to Buy: Energy $avings and Policy Alternatives for Demand Response," *Public Utilities Fortnightly,* March 15, 2001, pp. 48–60; James Bushnell and Erin Mansur, The Impact of Retail Rate Deregulation on Electricity Consumption in San Diego, Berkeley Power Conference, March 2001; Hamish Fraser, "The Importance of an Active Demand Side in the Electricity Industry," *Electricity Journal,* November 2001; and Eric Hirst and Brendan Kirby, Retail-Load Participation in Competitive Wholesale Electricity Markets, Prepared for the EEI, January 2001.

[2] Refer to Appendix C. We argue that any one of three things would have averted the crisis—hourly metering and pricing; not prohibiting contracting; not fixing prices so that changes in factor prices were not passed through.

kets are always reliable because the lights only go out if a customer wants them to, given the price.

Put another way, *markets always clear.* Or rather, markets where buyers actually participate always clear. There are no shortages—the price acts to make supply and demand match. Customer response limits price rises, and also increases reliability.

If there is no customer response, when supplies get tight there have to be involuntary curtailments, by exhortations to conserve or by rolling blackouts. An unreliable market is one where customers are willing to pay the posted price, but are denied service. But if customers see a high price and refuse to buy, there is no need for involuntary curtailments—customers will voluntarily curtail themselves, and the price will drop. They will do this if they are in fact paying the high price, if they know what it is, and if they save money by not buying. The electricity industry has tried every form of conservation from exhortation to subsidy—every form, that is, except the one used in all other markets—price. Conservation by price means that customers reduce their demand when the price is high, which is just when the system needs it most—the price is high when supply is tight. *Price response is conservation in the most practical way.*

Unless customers are able to respond to prices at the peak, through hourly metering and hourly pricing, the generators have a distinct advantage over the customers. They can bid up the peak price as high as they like unless there are customers who can say "play this hand without me."

It is only in electricity markets that we somehow manage to put demand response last on the list of desirable things to do, with a shrug as if to say it would be nice to have instead of what it is—an absolute necessity. Demand response is critical at peak times, when a few percentage points of demand can make the difference between a reliable system and rolling blackouts—California had to institute rolling blackouts with a shortage of only 300 MW in a system of 50,000 MW, so only a tiny proportion of total demand in that case needed to stop using for four hours to avoid the blackouts.

The lack of customer response is the reason for worries about reliability. Adequate attention to demand response would remove the need for capacity markets, installed capacity requirements, price caps, and other holdovers from regulation. (See Chapter 7 on Trading Arrangements for more on this.)

Demand Response and Contracts

We are accustomed to paying for electricity on a specific form of contract—a *full requirements tariff.* All electricity we use is at the same fixed price, or at most it varies seasonally, or by two or three blocks of time. But these tariffs, by their nature, cannot elicit demand response when it is needed—when the spot (i.e., real-time) price is high.

It is not necessary for consumers to pay spot prices for all energy consumed; in fact, it would be a very bad idea. Contracts are necessary, because:

- Contracts stabilize the prices that consumers pay.
- They make it financially possible for generators to enter the market.
- They are also necessary for control of market power in the generation market (see Chapter 5).

There should be a mix of spot and contract sales. When the markets are fully competitive, no one should be forcing anyone to decide how much to contract and how much to take at spot prices—the choice should be up to the customer. During a transition period when the Distco is providing customers with power, either as the retailer to smaller customers under Model 3, or as the default service provider under the transition to Model 4, companies and regulators should not be tempted to do away with contracts and just go with the spot price.

But there are many forms of contract. In retail access (Model 4), retailers will no doubt think up many different forms of contract for final customers, including perhaps "no-hassle 10 cents an hour." But if they have contracts with generators, they themselves are probably paying wholesale prices that are time-differentiated; and if they are themselves generators, they will have opportunity costs that vary by the hour. So it would be natural to have prices that vary at least by some sort of time-variable block. Hourly metering on consumers will make unregulated retailers responsible for their customers' consumption in high-cost periods and give them incentives to price accordingly or install load management devices—one of the value-added services that might indeed add value.

There could, for example, be a fixed price for a nominated block of power, and customers could pay (or receive a credit) for additional energy (energy below the block) at the spot price. This provides price stability and preserves the incentive to respond to market prices. It has been done for years in optional real-time pricing tariffs for large customers at Georgia Power and at Niagara Mohawk.[3] It requires, however, that consumption be

[3] The real-time pricing programs in place for more than 10 years at utilities such as Georgia Power and Niagara Mohawk work on this principle. Customers establish a baseline usage level, which is priced at the standard rate, and purchase (or are credited) for additional (reduced) usage at a "market price" estimated a day ahead or an hour ahead.

metered hourly. The most efficient plan would involve a fixed price for a fixed block of energy, and the spot price charged (or credited) for energy used above (or below) the contracted block size. This block could be based on some percentage of historic consumption, or an amount chosen by the customer. The utility might offer a menu of pricing options with various levels of price insurance. An example of this proposed pricing design is illustrated in Figure 4.3. In this example, the customer's actual consumption is less "peaky" than the contracted block. The customer consumes 500 kWh less in peak hours and 500 kWh more in off-peak hours, but is better off because peak prices are higher than off-peak prices.

Creating Incentives to Respond

The inefficient pricing cannot be fixed without new (hourly) metering. Just because a customer is metered by the hour does not mean he has to be charged by the hour; but if he is not metered that way, he cannot possibly be charged by the hour.

What do we mean by "charged by the hour"? First, we mean that the meters must *record* usage by the hour. Most meters now record total use only and are read once a month, although some large customers have "interval" meters that can record usage every hour.[4] Hourly metering does not mean that the information necessarily has to *be transmitted by the hour* to the billing system—to do this can be expensive—but there are cheap methods of recording the data and transmitting it periodically. Metering data can be transmitted, for example, over regular telephone lines, over cellular telephone networks, by radio telephone to roving vans, and by other methods. Or it can be collected by traditional meter readers. Hourly meters often include telecommunications equipment to send the hourly usage information to the system/market operator as well; usually this is done monthly. Some of the meters can provide data to the customer in real time to facilitate the customer's response to hourly market price variations. But for a start we could record hourly and collect it monthly, if real-time data transmission is expensive.

Second, the bill should show an hourly price, multiplied by the amount used, for each hour of the month. The hourly price does not have to be the spot price in the wholesale market; customers can get contracts from retailers that will give them a fixed price. But the retailer will obviously want the contract price to be higher when the wholesale price is likely to be higher.

[4] Some meters record usage by sub-periods within the billing period (for time-of-use rates), and some record both total energy use and monthly peak demand (actually maximum average energy use over a short period such as 15 minutes).

FIGURE 4.3 Illustration of pricing reform.

This simplified example (which groups hours of the month) illustrates how the bill is computed for a consumer who has nominated a block of power in each hour at fixed prices, and consumes either more or less than the nomination in each given hour.

	kWh per Month			Cents per kWh		Charge for Month	
Hours	Fixed Block	Actual Usage	Difference	Contract Price	Spot Price	Charge for Block	Charge (Credit) for Difference
a	b	c	d=c-a	e	f	g=bxe/100	h=fxd/100
0-4	200	250	50	3.5	1.5	$7.00	$0.75
4-8	300	400	100	3.5	2.0	$10.50	$2.00
8-12	450	650	200	3.5	3.5	$15.75	$7.00
12-16	1000	750	-250	3.5	4.5	$35.00	($11.25)
16-20	1100	850	-250	3.5	4.0	$38.50	($10.00)
20-24	350	500	150	3.5	1.5	$12.25	$2.25
Total	3400	3400	0			$119.00	($9.25)

Bill for fixed price block:		$119.00
Charge for extra use:	$12.00	
Credit for reduced use:	($21.25)	
Net charge (credit) for different use:		($9.25)
Total Bill:		$109.80

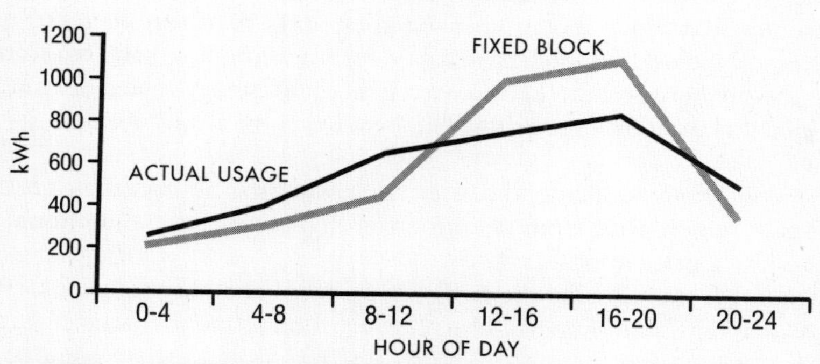

Note: For clarity this illustration uses a set of spot prices that would have resulted in the same charge of $119, if actual usage had not deviated from the nominated blocks. This is to demonstrate that the $9.25 saving is from the modified usage, and not from systematically lower spot prices.

Or he may say "up to 3,400 kWh per month at the contract price—differences from that at the spot price," as was illustrated in Figure 4.3.

Third, the customer should have information about the price he will be paying. If he has a contract, he will know the price. If he is paying an hourly spot price there has to be some way for him to find out what it is. It could be the TV or the Web. And since most of the peaks occur after three days of especially hot weather, it will probably be obvious when prices are high. Some customers may prefer to install computerized equipment that actually cuts off some of the usage when prices get high (the refrigerator, a big electricity user in the home, can manage for an hour or two if no one is opening it; air conditioning can be cycled) but we would argue that this is not the essential requirement—it is just essential that customers have metering that reads consumption by the hour, and the rest will follow—someone will provide the online controls if the customers want them. (We do not recommend that the basic metering function be left to the retailers, for reasons specific to electricity that are detailed in Chapter 10 on retailing.)

How Much Hourly Metering?

What is the trade-off between hourly metering and averaged prices?[5] And therefore, what is the right mix of hourly metering and averaged prices? First, many large customers already have sophisticated metering, so for them it is only a question of getting the prices right. If there were no cost differences between using hourly meters and using averaged prices, it would be efficient to put all retail access customers on hourly meters. Hourly meters are not that much more expensive these days than regular meters, but *replacing* all the existing meters that last for 40 years, is expensive. So there is a trade-off between the extra cost of the new hourly metering, and the extra benefits of hourly metering. The benefits come from two places:

1. Benefits from reducing the societal losses (the so-called *deadweight losses*) which arise from charging too high a price in some hours and too low a price in others; and
2. Benefits from reducing the cost of socialized reliability solutions. (Refer to Chapter 8 and, in particular, capacity obligation methods.)

We can say upfront that there is virtually no doubt that hourly metering for large customers is beneficial—the costs are minimal compared with their bills. But for small customers the benefits can be determined using standard cost analysis, as illustrated in a simplified way in Figure 4.4. Given a customer's demand curves for electricity, it is possible to determine the

[5] One way of averaging prices is *load profiling,* which is discussed in more detail in Chapter 10 on retailing. But a load profile still delivers an average price to consumers.

FIGURE 4.4 Benefits of metering electricity.

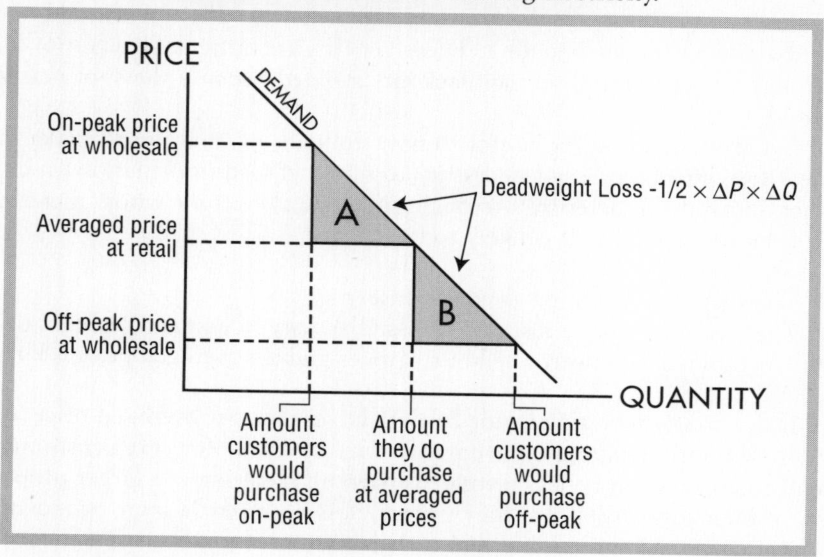

societal losses. These losses are the shaded triangles labeled *deadweight loss.*[6] If the deadweight losses exceed the incremental cost of hourly metering, the customer should be required to have an hourly meter. Triangle A is the extra cost of producing peak power minus its value to consumers. Triangle B is the value to consumers of energy they did not use off peak, minus its cost. If the demand curve is approximated as a straight line, the area of each triangle is $\frac{1}{2} \times \Delta P \times \Delta Q$, where ΔP is the (vertical) difference between the averaged retail price and ΔQ is the (horizontal) difference in consumption between what it is at averaged prices and what it would be at de-averaged prices. This deadweight loss triangle applies to each customer. The size of ΔQ depends on the size of the customer and the responsiveness of his demand to changes in price. For any given situation the value of metering depends on how distorted the averaged pricing is, on the absolute size of customers, and on how responsive their demand is.

[6] Returning to the clothing analogy: Triangle A is the wasted cost of producing more Armani than is really needed; Triangle B is the loss to consumers of not buying as much Gap as they would like because it is overpriced.

The second benefit of hourly meters increases the number of hourly meters that should be installed beyond those that are already justified on a stand-alone basis from benefit 1. These benefits are difficult to quantify, but the place to start would be the blackouts avoided because the spot market cleared.

But while it would be useful to have enough information to make detailed assessments, it is not necessary to have detailed information on customer demand characteristics to begin to define classes for whom metering might be cost effective. It is likely to be the case if:

- The customer is a large electricity user;[7]
- The customer's price responsiveness (elasticity of demand) is high; or
- The difference between the hourly prices and the averaged price is large.

If the hourly metering is not cost effective, then the averaged price will have to do until metering costs come down, especially for small customers. Small customers can be less price-sensitive and metering is a larger proportion of their total costs. But they nevertheless represent a large proportion of total usage. Meter reading and data communication costs benefit from economies of scale; they have a low cost per customer when applied to many customers, so if the smaller customers are considered as add-ons to a large system, it may still pay to meter them.

The price of simple meters that read hourly but do not transmit the data electronically has come down to about $100. This amounts to about $1 per month, installed and amortized. Since the benefits are shared by all, it is probably wise for the distribution company simply to install them where they are cost-beneficial, and charge the costs to all users.

Customer Response: U.K. Example The best-documented example of customer response is shown in Figure 4.5. In February 1996, the U.K. was severely short of generating capacity because of gas supply problems, and blackouts were a possibility. But in fact they did not happen—the price rose to $1 for one hour on Monday; to 80 cents for one hour on Tuesday; to 50 cents for an hour on Wednesday, and then began to fall back into its normal pattern. No customer was cut off and there were no rolling blackouts.

The U.K. has compulsory hourly metering for all consumers with a peak demand above 100 kW. (Some consumers below that level also have hourly metering.)

---

[7] Remember that less than half a percent of customers—the industrial customers—consume one-third of the electricity in the United States.

FIGURE 4.5 United Kingdom price spikes in 1996.

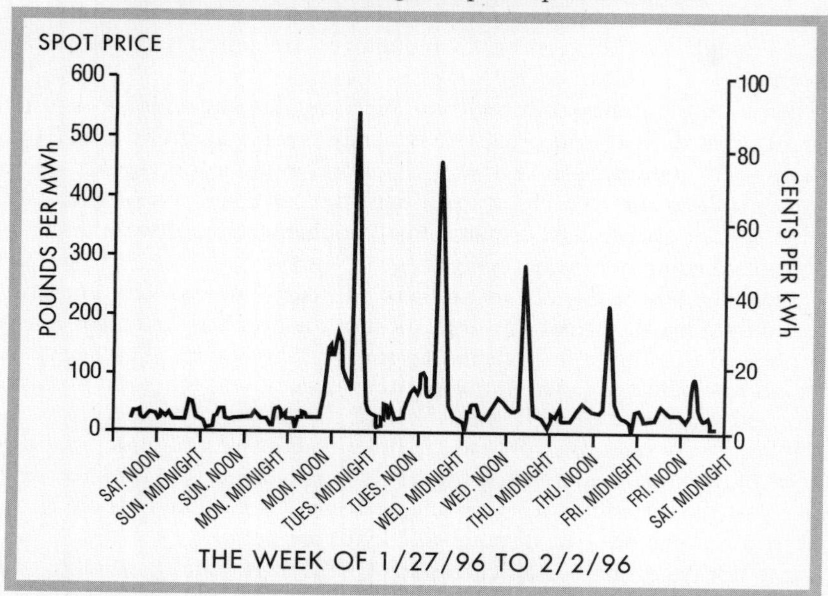

Creating the Means to Respond

It is desirable that retailers (and some large consumers who buy directly from wholesale markets) make bids to the market specifying the quantities they are prepared to buy and the reservation prices they are prepared to pay. Furthermore it is desirable that the market is capable of processing this information and accepting or rejecting bids, in a timely manner. It is also desirable that the bids are actually used in the price-setting mechanisms in the spot markets. This is taken up in more detail later, in Chapter 8.

With day-ahead markets[8] it is relatively straightforward: buyers submit demand schedules. The market operator can then evaluate the demand bids against the day-ahead generator offers and can produce a set of prices and scheduled production and consumption quantities consistent with all the bids and offers. Depending on whether bids are accepted or not, a buyer can plan consumption for the following day. The day-ahead

[8] The discussion in the next few paragraphs presupposes some familiarity with concepts discussed in more detail in Chapter 8.

purchase is a contract—if the amount purchased a day ahead is not fully used, imbalances are sold back at the real-time price, and conversely if not enough has been ordered, imbalances are purchased at the real-time price.

For energy purchased in real-time markets, demand bidding is not so straightforward. Real-time prices are typically calculated after the fact, once actual system conditions are known. Therefore, in order for a system operator to be able to curtail a bid in real time based on a reservation price (i.e., for the system operator to dispatch load) sophisticated software and real-time control equipment is necessary.

Typically, where day-ahead markets and real-time markets both have demand bidding, the prices converge; most of the power is sold a day ahead, and the real-time price only cleans up small discrepancies. The day-ahead price is known before consumption actually occurs, and is a good predictor of the real-time price.

If large MW quantities of load are price-responsive and under real-time control of the system operator (dispatchable loads) it adds to the short-term security of the system; as reserves fall, prices rise and some bids are consequently not accepted—the dispatchable loads are cut off.

It is not necessary for all customers to bid; it is equally valuable from a system security point of view if customers find alternative means to respond to rising prices. It is not necessary to rely on price-responsive load being dispatchable and bid into spot markets. If buyers even anticipate high prices, for example, because it is hot or expected to be hot, and have the ability to respond by not consuming in real time, then they will also contribute to a market-based solution to the longer-term reliability issue.

Finally there are interruptible customers—customers who agree to be cut off sometimes in the event of a shortage, near shortage, or for short-term system stability reasons, in return for lower prices or an explicit payment. Interruptible customers have existed for decades, although they were seldom interrupted. There are some examples of radio-controlled cutoffs for residential users, for example, to control water heaters or air conditioners. The Distco, as retailer, has generally been the conduit for interruptions, although there is no reason the retailer should not use interruptibility as part of a price offer to large users.

With competitive generating markets and a spot price, hourly metering should, itself, provide sufficient demand response that the rolling blackout plan will not be necessary. But until the metering is in place, much the same effect can be achieved by encouraging retailers to offer interruptible rates. A customer would agree to have a whole wiring circuit that could be tripped by the retailer when the market price exceeded a certain level. For this the customer would get a better price the rest of the time. The retailer would save the cost of purchasing the power (or could sell it in the spot market).

INELASTIC DEMAND AND PRICE CAPS

For products that are necessities, the demand response is said to be inelastic—people cannot respond by reducing consumption, and therefore will pay whatever it takes to get the necessity. But this does not mean that prices of necessities have to be high, if production costs are low—oxygen is a necessity, but the creator provided immense quantities at no cost; food and clothing are necessities, but the markets have provided sufficient quantities at very reasonable cost. If the market is competitive the producers will compete to provide even the necessities. It is only when supplies are limited that prices are bid up to what customers are prepared to pay. And if customers will pay *any* price to get it, then prices can go very high, producers can get very rich, customers are "gouged," and politicians are outraged and impose price caps.

Price caps and competitive markets do not mesh well. Under a price cap there will be customers who would have wanted to purchase at the capped price, but who cannot; therefore, there must be some other form of rationing. (In the electric industry rationing is generally done by selective blackouts.) *But price caps and rationing are only necessary when price cannot, or in natural justice should not, rise to the rationing price.* Any proposal to impose a price cap should first explain why supply response and demand response are not sufficient to clear the markets. If the answer is that there is a war on and supplies are so limited that poor people would not be able to afford clothes and food, then price caps and rationing may be a better response than rationing by price. If there is a temporary crisis of supply (natural disasters), then temporary price caps may be necessary for essential goods whose purchase cannot be postponed. But the imposition of price caps and rationing is always an indication that something is wrong with the markets; and in the case of electricity the culprit is usually quite clear—there is no *mechanism for demand response.* Customers in the electric industry have long been assumed to be more or less unresponsive to prices. But *there is no product for which the demand is completely unresponsive to price,* and price response in electricity has been shown to exist so many times that it is a wonder that the assumption has survived, but it survives in many subtle ways.

For example, the overbuilding in the United States in the 1970s and 1980s was a direct result of ignoring the evidence that increases in price following the oil crisis of 1973 would limit the demand growth of the utilities.[9] There is also short-run demand response. In competitive markets, many factories compute how much they are willing to pay, at a maximum, and shut down for a few hours when the price reaches this level.

It is well established that when people are charged more, they use less. In New York City, where some apartment buildings continue with the mad practice of including electricity in the rent (so that any particular use is "free") it has been found that simply metering consumption apartment by apartment reduces consumption by 15 percent to 30 percent, according to the New York State watchdogs.[10] This is because when it is free, folks leave the air-conditioner on all day to come home to a cool apartment. When they are charged for what they use (even at ordinary averaged rates) they turn it off and spend a few uncomfortable minutes while the place cools down after they get home.

It is the faulty design of marketplaces rather than the intrinsic nature of electricity that have induced the more egregious price spikes[11] *and made price caps necessary.* Electricity may, by now, be something of a necessity, just as food and clothing are, but not every use at every moment is a necessity, in the technical sense that consumers in the aggregate will pay any price for it. *The problem is not that customers will not respond to high prices by rationing their demand, but rather that markets have been designed with no mechanism for them to do so.*

Some wholesale marketplaces have been established where the demand side cannot respond adequately:

- In some markets the buyers are distribution companies that have an *obligation to supply* any final use[12] when the final customer flips a switch; in these "markets" the buyers are under obligation to purchase no matter what the price.

---

[9] It did—demand growth dropped from 7 percent per year to 2 percent per year, and although some of this was due to the slowing of the economy, it has never returned to the previous levels.

[10] Energy Smart Program: Submetering in Multi-Family Buildings, a program administered by the New York State Energy Research and Development Authority, www.submeteronline.com.

[11] Not every price spike is egregious—the lack of storage makes electricity prices intrinsically volatile. Lack of demand response makes them egregious—the price can rise to virtually any level.

[12] California 2000–2001 and the bulk supply markets in the United States; in the United Kingdom the distribution companies are not required to purchase if the spot price reaches a predetermined level set by the regulator.

- Or, the buyers are retailers who have no means to charge more for the peak hours, and physically cannot cut off their customers.
- Or, the buyer is the system operator, buying for the imbalance market.

None of these buyers is a final consumer; this is why the response is inelastic. In the end, it is the final consumers who need to be able to respond:

- The final customers are not paying the high peak prices because their prices are averaged over all hours. (Or, worse yet, the prices are fixed. A fixed price is just a bad form of averaged price.)
- They cannot be charged the high peak prices because there is no way to de-average the peak from the lower prices off peak. To do this requires hourly metering.

The three prerequisites for demand to take an active part in the electricity markets are that wholesale marketplaces should have mechanisms for incorporating demand, that hourly metering be installed on a significant percentage of the load, and that final prices should be unbundled so that high cost hours are charged at more than low cost hours. We recommend that eventually all customers, except perhaps the very smallest, have hourly meters and be exposed (at least for some of their consumption) to the wholesale prices so that they can decide when to use and how much.

CHAPTER 5

Requirements for Competition: Supply Side

The flip side to the demand side requirements is that a competitive market needs to have *many sellers who are responsive to price.*

MANY SELLERS

A competitive market needs many sellers. In a perfectly competitive market, with many, many sellers, every seller is a price taker, and cannot affect the market price. If they try to charge more, customers will go elsewhere.

By contrast, a monopoly (a single seller) has the ability to drive up the price without fear that other sellers would undercut his price; he will produce less than a perfectly competitive market will produce, and at a higher price that is well above costs, and make more profits. By restricting output, the monopolist diverts resources from their highest value use;[1] and the high prices transfer money to the monopolist at the expense of the consumers.

In reality, all real-world markets are somewhere in between pure monopoly and perfect competition, but if a market has only a few large players, they act more like a monopoly, and can set the market price to some extent. If a seller is not a price taker, and recognizes that by reducing the output supplied to the market he can raise the market price and do so *profitably,* we say that he has *market power.* (*Market power* is a general term that applies in any market and to either buyers or sellers. It is particularly confusing in electricity because we are talking about *markets for power*—electricity—or *power markets.*)

Not all high prices are due to market power. For example, although prices in a competitive market should settle at marginal generation costs

[1] This is the *dead weight loss* from monopoly.

much of the time, even in a perfectly competitive market, prices *should* rise above marginal cost when capacity is tight, to the level the last customer left buying is willing to pay. (Refer to Chapter 8 for more on this.) This is not market power, but rather a *scarcity rent.* Providing there is demand response, as discussed in the previous chapter, so that the price can only rise to what the last person consumer is willing to pay, scarcity rents are a necessary feature of electricity markets.

Market power is always characterized by withholding of capacity from the market. However, looking for withholding by a supplier of his own output as a test for market power comes up against other reasons for withholding—the plant broke down, for instance. And while it is clear (as we demonstrate later) that deliberate withholding of your own capacity is the classic way to exercise market power, it is not the only way—there are subtle ways to prevent your competitors from getting their product on the market, that have the same effect of reducing overall supply and raising prices.

The term *market power* is also used in a legal context, in connection with antitrust laws. Here, market power is what the law or the regulator says it is; economists try to help judges figure out how to measure market power, and how to evaluate in particular cases whether the results are bad for competition. All real markets have some market power at some times. The questions are usually: How much of it is bad and is it worth devoting resources to control it?

HOW DOES MARKET POWER WORK?

The classic method of exercising market power is to withdraw your own capacity. Of course you take a loss on the capacity you unilaterally withdraw. If there is freedom of entry, a competitor can replace your capacity and make your behavior unprofitable, but this may take a while. In markets where entry takes time, the secret of successfully exercising market power is to have enough other units that the increased price for your other units' output more than makes up for the loss on the withdrawn capacity. *To make this work, in general you have to be big, compared with the size of the market.*

Example of Unilateral Market Power by a Dominant Firm The example that follows shows how market power can be exercised in electricity spot markets—but it can also of course be exercised in electricity contract markets, or any other market, in an analogous way. Figure 5.1 is a more specific form of the general supply and demand curves of Figure 4.1, in which each individual generating unit is shown as a step in the supply curve. There are 16 generating units. Each one has capacity of 100 MW. They are listed in *merit*

FIGURE 5.1 Merit order.

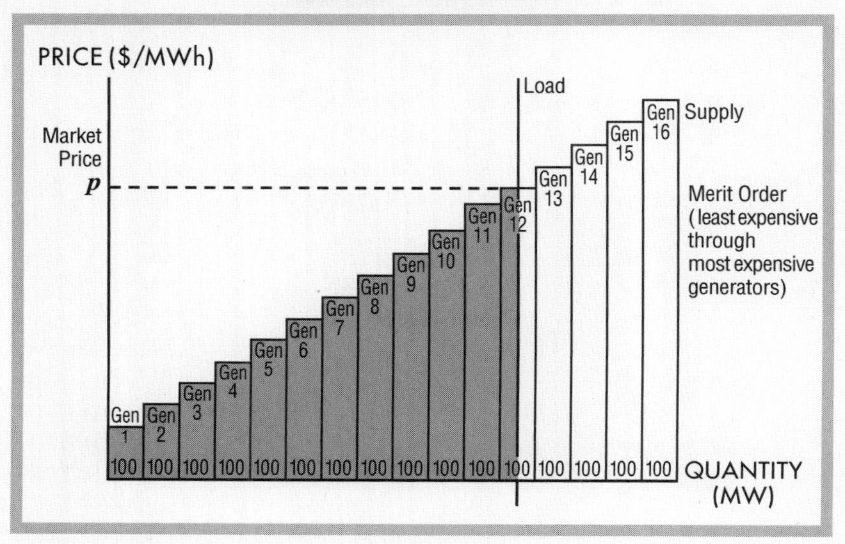

order [i.e., from least expensive (Gen 1) to most expensive (Gen 16)]. For simplicity, load is shown at a fixed level, somewhere between 1,100 MW and 1,200 MW. (Of course, this is a very simplified situation—most electric systems are much larger and have many more generating units—we are keeping it small to keep the point simple.) If this were a perfectly competitive market, not in a state of scarcity, the market price would equal the offered price of the marginal unit; that is, the price of Gen 12.

Assume now that a single company owns Gens 2, 4, 5, 7, and 11. The darkest shaded area in Figure 5.2 shows the profit—or more correctly, the contribution to fixed costs—of this company.

What if there is market power? Imagine that the company deliberately and temporarily closes Gen 11. (It is always better to withdraw the highest cost plant—the one on which there are fewer profits.) Gens 12 through 16 now move to the left on the supply curve. Gen 13 now must be used in order to meet load, and it sets the new market price. The price therefore rises. From the point of view of the company owning Gens 2, 4, 5, 7, and 11, it no longer makes any profit from Gen 11. But the profit from Gens 2, 4, 5, and 7 have increased, and in this example, the increase more than offsets the lost profit from Gen 11. The company is better off (see Figure 5.3).

Note that it doesn't matter if Gen 11 is withdrawn from the market, or simply offered at a high price. The effect is the same. Either way it is

FIGURE 5.2 Profit when price is competitive.

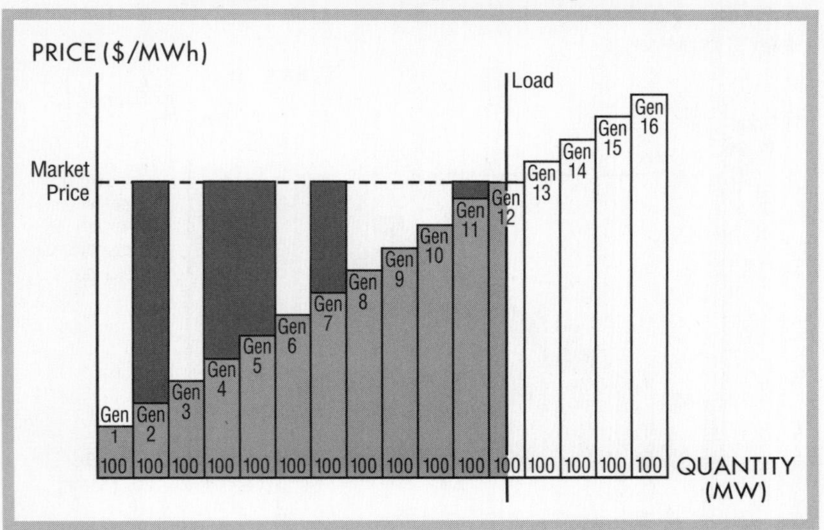

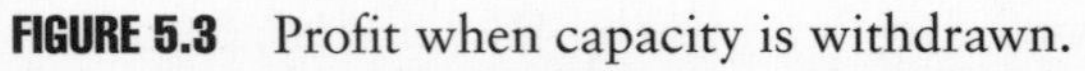
FIGURE 5.3 Profit when capacity is withdrawn.

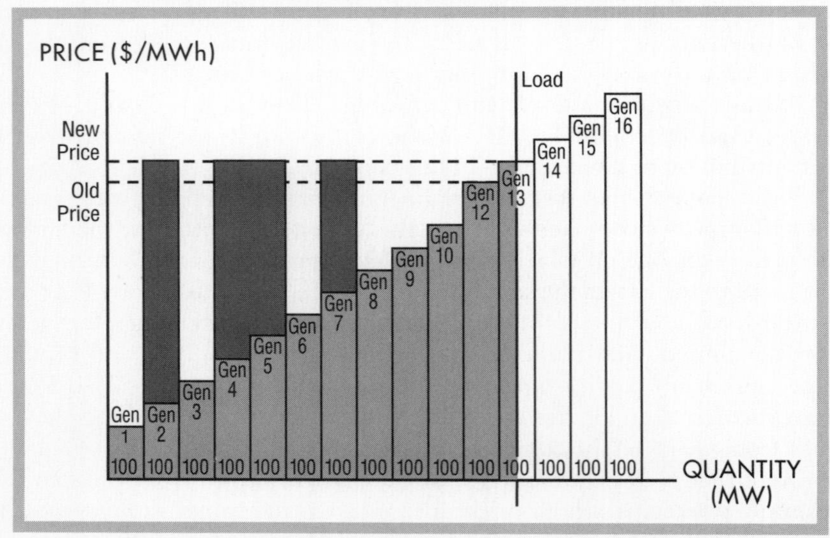

FIGURE 5.4 Profit when offered price is increased.

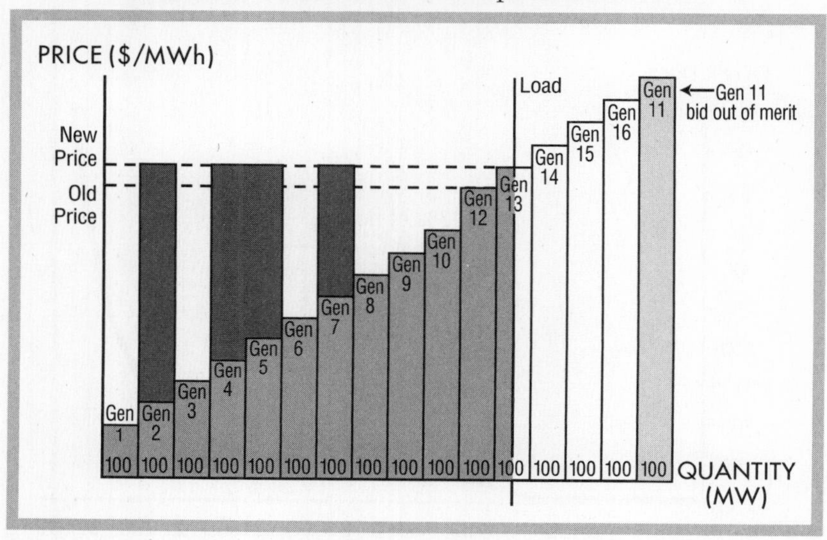

economically withdrawn but it is more difficult to detect an inflated bid price than a plant that does not bid at all. Figure 5.4 shows the situation when the offered price of Gen 11 is increased to a very high level.[2]

In real-world situations, the shape of the supply curve is important. The steeper it is, the more likely it is that economic withdrawal is profitable. Figure 5.5 shows a typical curve for the industry (that of New York State). The curve is relatively flat for most levels of load when plants have

---

[2] Does any profitable bidding up of offer prices constitute *market power*? What about if higher prices are offered, but the merit order stays the same? Sometimes a generator can increase its offered price by a small amount, so that it does not prevent itself from being selected by the system operator to run, but does increase the market price and thus its profits. For example Gen 12 could profitably lift its offered price to just under that of Gen 13s.

This is not normally regarded as market power—it is simply an effect of discontinuities in the supply function. Capacity has not been economically withdrawn, and Gen 13 restricted the price that Gen 12 could bid up to. "Bidding up" to just under the nearest competitor is normal in competitive markets. It should not make the market inefficient. (In fact, some auctions are designed so that the first offer not accepted sets the price, rather than the last offer that is accepted.) In any event, it is not normally much of an issue in practice because the supply curve is continuous (lacking in steps) and also its precise shape can be difficult for competitors to guess.

FIGURE 5.5 Supply curve for New York state (August 15, 2000, 2 P.M.).

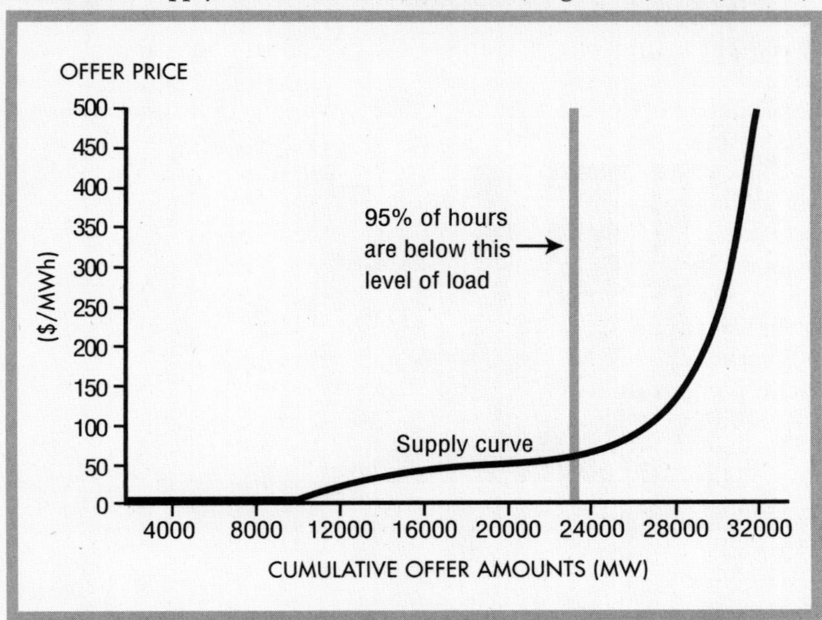

Source: New York ISO Annual Assessment of New York Electric Markets, 2000.

relatively similar costs. It starts to become quite steep after 95 percent of hours when the high cost plants have to be used.

How else can you profitably raise prices? You can do it by forming a cartel and explicitly colluding to reduce output, which is what OPEC does; but this is illegal between companies in the United States, and in most other countries.[3] You may not even meet and discuss price with your competitors. However, there are many subtle ways to signal your intentions to other players, and there is no doubt that players try to guess the

[3] OPEC is a cartel of countries that colludes on oil prices. (There are few ways to prevent *countries* doing this, but within a country it is normal to have laws to prevent *companies* from doing it.) Oil ministers from OPEC countries meet regularly and agree to restrict output. Each country has a quota, and so long as they all stick to the agreed levels they are all better off. As with other cartels, individual OPEC members have incentives to renege on agreed output restrictions, and make more money by exceeding their quotas. This is why cartels often break down, unless one supplier is so big that it can take most of the output restriction and still increase profits.

intentions of others and plot their strategy accordingly. This is known as "tacit collusion." Here again, it is more difficult to signal if there are more players. The four members of a string quartet listen to one another's music and read each other's subtle signals—a string quartet does not need a conductor, but an orchestra does. It is more difficult to signal effectively when there are more players.

You can also profitably raise prices by preventing your competitors from getting output to market—by tying up the transmission system with reservations you do not intend to use, or tying up the approval process for new plant in a regulatory maze. While the antitrust laws prohibit this sort of thing in principle, in practice it can be hard to pin down in a highly complex system like electricity.

In general, while the ideal state of perfect competition is unrealistic, the general proposition holds that the more sellers, the better. Argentina sold each generating plant individually when it privatized. The United Kingdom, by contrast, broke the existing national generator into only three companies, and had endless problems with market power until the regulator forced them to divest some of the plants to other owners. There is really no doubt that *the best solution to supplier market power in the energy markets is to have enough suppliers to begin with, to have a demand side that works, and to police subsequent mergers carefully.*

NEWLY DEREGULATED MARKETS

The ownership structure prior to deregulation is typically geographically concentrated in existing companies. For example, the preexisting regulated structure in virtually every part of the United States gave the monopoly utility a 100 percent share of generation capacity in its service territory either from plants that it owned or from independent plants with life-of-plant contracts. So it would not be surprising to find that after deregulation it also had 100 percent of the market share in its territory.

However, because transmission was expanded in the United States after the 1965 blackouts, geographic markets are generally bigger than a utility's territory, so in most cases *some* other electricity can get to any area. The question is how much? Where transmission systems are particularly robust, competition is possible even where the incumbent generator holds a high market share within his own local area. Supply can come from as far away as the transmission system and physics of transmission losses will allow. *It is congestion on the transmission that limits the natural geographic markets for electricity, and hence increases market power within the transmission constraints.*

Since transmission systems have limits, the extent of geographic competition for any generator for nearby loads will depend on both the level and location of loads and generation. Thus, although we *say,* "utility X has 20 percent of the New England market," this is not really accurate. It is impossible to speak generally of "the number of generators in the market"—it is more complicated than that. Market definitions change depending on the demand level and the transmission constraints that are active—you can only specify the number of generators that can reach a particular location under some set of transmission system conditions and load conditions. In any given geographic area the market size could change several times a day. But however often they change, we can say with confidence that congestion on the transmission makes markets smaller. (See Chapters 7 and 8 for more on congestion.)

MARKET POWER SOLUTIONS

There are several methods for ensuring *enough competitors* in a market:

- Encourage entry;
- Expand the geographic area by relieving transmission constraints;
- Buy out existing IPP contracts to free capacity to compete in the markets;
- Divest existing utility capacity into tranches that are resold to new entities; and
- Ensuring appropriate exit conditions is also important.[4]

The additional methods for controlling market power in the structure of electric markets are:

- Ensuring that the demand side of the market works. Having even modest amounts of load responsive to increases in price will serve to make most of the problem disappear.
- Ensuring sufficient contract cover so that relatively little energy is traded through the spot markets. This limits market power in spot markets, but not necessarily in the forward contract markets unless the contracts are long term.

---

[4] New competitive markets, wherever they have been set up, often have some existing plants that are uneconomic—too costly to run even if the sunk costs are disregarded—because they burn fuel inefficiently or are constantly breaking down. These plants should be closed, but sometimes regulators step in and keep them open to ensure reliability. This prevents new entrants offering cheaper power and increasing diversity of ownership.

If all else fails, there are regulatory remedies: price caps, bidding restrictions, and profit controls.

Entry Is Too Slow to Do the Job

One strand of the theory of market power holds that market power will solve itself by entry of competitors, who will rush in to take advantage of the creamy profits being earned by the big boys, thus pushing the market price back to the competitive level. But this has not worked in practice, and we should be very careful of just deregulating markets where there is an existing dominant supplier, and hoping entry will solve the problem for us.

A dominant supplier can set the price in the market. If he sets it too high, entrants will come in to take market share. The dominant supplier has two choices of strategy—keep prices high and lose market share fast; or lower them, scare off the competition and lose share slowly. We might imagine that if the dominant supplier chooses to keep prices high, entrants would just rush in, building energetically, and forcing the dominant supplier to lower his prices to the costs of the entrants. But in the real world this does not happen overnight, if it happens at all.

If the dominant supplier follows the high price strategy, a few entrants will initially come in and price a bit below, under the umbrella of the incumbent. This does not reduce prices to the competitive level. These entrants (especially in a slow-growing market) displace some of the incumbent's market share, leaving the incumbent and the market with unused capacity. Other would-be entrants know quite well that the dominant supplier has already sunk his investment, and if pushed can allow market prices to fall below the entrants costs. So they tend to tread warily. The lesson from the United Kingdom is clear—insufficient competition between suppliers does not result in massive entry—it results in too-high prices. Stephen Littlechild, the first electricity regulator after the privatization when competition was introduced, says:

> *National Power ended up with just under half the total output, PowerGen 30 percent, and Nuclear Electric 15 percent. So the largest two companies had nearly 80 percent and the largest three had 94 percent. Interconnectors and others provided the remaining 6 percent. By today's standards, the degree of concentration of output in two or three incumbent companies would be unacceptable. The implicit assumption was that customers would be protected by the ability of other generators to enter the market and construct new plant if these three incumbents were able and willing to exercise market power. In the event, entry took place on a larger scale than anyone had foreseen. Nevertheless, this was not*

sufficient to prevent the incumbents from increasing prices above the new entry level. As regulator, I had to take steps to require the two largest incumbents to divest some price-setting mid-merit plant to a new competitor. Since then there has been further divestment, partly in the context of merger clearance and partly on a more voluntary basis. Now, the largest company, which is neither of the two former duopolists, has less than 20 percent of total output. PowerGen and the successor to National Power each have less than 10 percent. It is now generally agreed that three successor companies were by no means enough.[5]

With slow growth, in a market that has few major suppliers, or only one, diversification of ownership will take too long if we rely only on entry. U.S. demand growth is expected to be about 2 percent per year over the next decade. If new entrants simply met all the load growth in the United States, it would still take 35 years for them to gain 50 percent of the market (Figure 5.6). So before doing the politically and legally complicated step of breaking up companies, it makes sense to try to reduce transmission constraints, and introduce demand response.

Expand the Market by Relieving Transmission Constraints

The larger the market, the less the need to restructure and break up existing generating companies. Transmission constraints cause congestion, which reduces the effective size of markets (although entry in the United States is projected to be greater than demand growth, as old plants will close, and will almost certainly close faster under deregulation). Electric systems follow the laws of physics and attributes of the transmission system often sharply limit the choice of generators from which an incremental MW can be generated. In this situation, the possibilities for market power replicate themselves on smaller scales. As NERC points out:

with the recent industry restructuring and the development of regional wholesale markets, the utilization of the transmission grid has drastically changed to try to accommodate a large volume of energy transactions over very long distances.[6]

---

[5] Stephen Littlechild, *The Beesley Lectures on Regulation Series XI,* London, England, October 9, 2001.
[6] North American Reliability Council Reliability Assessment 2000–2009.

FIGURE 5.6 Years for entrants to have an effect.

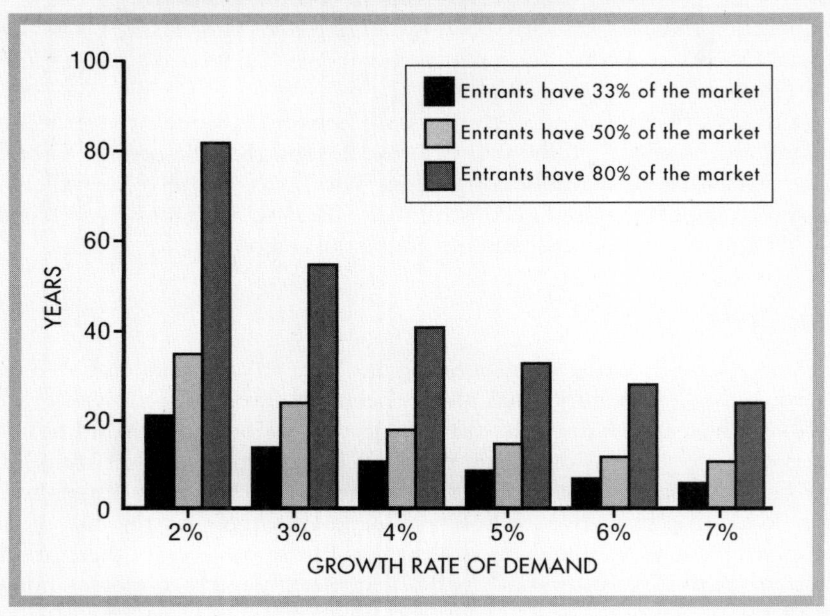

The system of allocating physical transmission rights used in much of the United States can exacerbate market power in two ways.[7] First, it reduces the effective available transmission capacity below the maximum efficient level, because it defines and allocates it on criteria that are not related to the most efficient use; and second, the very nature of physical transmission rights makes it possible to withhold them, reducing energy supplies to the market and raising the market price of electricity.[8]

Lack of transmission, transmission constraints, and physical transmission rights, reduce market size and exacerbate market power problems. *The trading arrangements we propose in the following chapters make the best*

[7]The discussion in this and the following two paragraphs presupposes some familiarity with material that is presented later, in Part One, Chapter 7 on trading arrangements, and in Part Two on trading arrangements in the United States.

[8]Refer to "Transmission Rights and Market Power on Electric Power Networks I: Financial Rights," Paul Joskow and Jean Tirole, *The Rand Journal of Economics,* Vol. 31, No. 3, pp. 450–487, Autumn 2000.

possible use of existing transmission, and reduce market power problems to the maximum extent feasible short of building new transmission. They use efficient short-term congestion management rules, congestion pricing rules, and Financial Transmission Rights.

Efficient management of the existing network, through the proposed trading arrangements, is the first priority. Beyond that the need is to build more transmission to relieve congestion. The Texas plan involves relieving the three major transmission constraints in Texas so as to make a statewide market and sharing the cost equally among all customers.

Divestiture

Separating and divesting the generation has been an emotional as well as an economic issue. Generation has always been the jewel in the crown of utilities—the most interesting and difficult part of the business. A utility with assets of many billions of dollars does not like to think of itself shrunk to one-third that size and having to contemplate life as "simply a distributor." Nor do the top executives, whose pay depends largely on the size of the company, want to see the company shrunk. But in some cases there are no alternatives to divestiture into smaller generating parcels to create enough competitors.

Contract Cover

The ability to profit from withdrawing capacity in spot markets is severely limited if that power has been sold forward. Most electricity markets end up with about 80 percent contract cover. The remaining 20 percent that passes in the spot markets is all that can be affected by withdrawing capacity, and any participant who has sold most of his output forward will not be able to gain by withdrawing from the spot market.

Going back to the example in Figure 5.3, the company withdrawing Gen 11 made more profits because it gained from the increased spot prices for Gens 2, 4, 5, and 7. But supposing 80 percent of its capacity had been sold forward, in contracts. Then, when Gen 11 is withdrawn, the spot market price will increase, but none of this company's portfolio is selling at spot—Gens 2, 4, 5, and 7 have been contracted. So it will not be worth losing the profits of Gen 11 by withholding it. This is how contracts limit market power—by reducing the profits that can be made from withholding capacity.

But note: The generator with market power in the spot market will probably want to avoid signing contracts and limiting its own ability to exercise its market power in this way. And even if it is forced to contract as a requirement imposed by a regulator, he will be able to exercise market power in the contract market. Short-term contracts will simply reflect the anticipated market power price. Some of the contracts should therefore be for a period sufficiently far enough ahead that other generators, who enter the market in time to compete, can also bid for the contracts and undercut the prices in the contract market. However, even short-term contracts can prevent the use of market power in unanticipated problems in the spot market, such as a breakdown of plant.

Contracts should preferably be made freely, and the proportion contracted should depend on the risk preference of participants. It makes no sense at all to prohibit contracting; the only question is whether it should ever be required. For example, contracting may have to be required in Model 3 (production competition where the Distco is the purchaser), or Model 4 (retail competition) where the Distco has to provide default service.[9] The presumption should be in favor of about 80 percent contracting, despite the conflict problems. At least some of the contracts should be set up to allow new entrants to bid on them (with a start date that permits new construction) so that any market power problems do not just get transferred to the contract markets.

PRICE CAPS, BIDDING RESTRICTIONS, AND PROFIT CONTROLS

The additional solutions to market power, if the structure is wrong to start with, are solutions related to conduct (bidding caps, contracting requirements) and solutions related to outcomes (profit limitations, price caps). These secondary solutions are less desirable compared to getting the structure right to start with. Having to institute these secondary measures post-restructuring is a confession that the structure is wrong. Sometimes they are necessary and cannot be avoided, and they may have to be used as transitional measures, but they should be avoided if possible.

Many solutions to market power in electric spot markets revolve around reducing market power by capping the market price, capping potential offer prices (bids) of generators, and/or capping profits. Sensible implementation revolves around the questions of how these caps should be set. There are several possibilities, including:

- *Bid caps based on the marginal cost of the most expensive unit.* Such caps are predicated on the notion that if each unit bid its marginal cost, price could never rise higher than the cost of the marginal unit. The

[9] One way to avoid conflict of interest when the Distco also owns generation is to pass through the spot price (virtual direct access); but this artificially restricts contracting, with bad effects on the spot market if market power is a possibility.

problem here is calculating the marginal costs (see the section on detecting market power). If the cap is set too low, suppliers will simply not offer their output.

- *Bid caps based on the marginal cost of the most expensive unit, with exceptions allowed with explanations for higher bids.* This is the so-called FERC soft cap. The problem comes from the fact that explanations can readily be constructed in hindsight to justify virtually any bid.
- *Bid caps based on previous bidding behavior.* Rules are put in place to restrict a unit's bids under certain conditions of tight supply, to be no higher in price than some average of previous bids, plus some fixed amount.[10]
- *Price caps based on the value of lost load (VOLL).* This is a way of making a price cap a proxy for demand response. The price cap is set at the *value of lost load* or the estimate of customer valuation, and applied only when load is actually shed. Estimates of this value vary, but are in the order of $2,000/MWh to $5,000/MWh.
- *Intelligent price caps.* A variation of the previous method is to cap the price at progressively higher prices depending on the *loss of load probability* (LOLP). A proxy for LOLP is the level of reserve generation.
- *Profit controls.* Profit controls are essentially a last resort, and as we have said earlier, an admission that procompetitive reforms have failed and that regulation must be reinstated.

SMALL MARKETS, BIG PLANTS, AND ANCILLARY SERVICES

The previous discussion was about the energy markets. In electricity, there are also products that we come to later, called *ancillary services,* that need to be provided locally, and in some cases only a single generating plant can provide them at all. This is sometimes also true in energy markets, that a single plant is dominant in an area. Here, divestiture will not solve the problem—whoever owns the plant will have market power. So what can be done?

Sometimes expanding the transmission will help; sometimes (for ancillary services), there are alternative ways to provide them.[11] If a large generating plant really dominates an area, one way to control the inevitable market

[10] Refer, for example, to New York's Automated Mitigation Plan implemented in 2001. www.nyiso.com.

[11] Reactive power can be provided by capacitors as well as by generating plants; reserve can be provided by dispatchable customers as well as by generating plants.

power is to require it to contract pieces of its output in an auction, to many buyers, who can then resell it. Selling rights to schedule the output of "strips" of the plant to different buyers is one method that has been tried with hydro plants; in thermal plants however it creates issues about who has to pay the overhead costs of the plant.

Another option is to designate the plants as *reliability must run* (RMR) plants. California did this. An RMR plant is a plant whose output is often required—whether because it has local market power in the supply of energy under certain congestion conditions, or because it is otherwise needed to keep the transmission system in operation (e.g., to provide necessary voltage support services). RMR plants may simply be barred from participating in the competitive scheme and be operated on a traditional cost-of-service basis. The problem with such schemes is that the incentives to substitute cheaper generators for these generators is then muted, as are (perhaps) inexpensive alterations to the transmission system which would nullify the obligatory output of these units. Moreover, RMR plants can be withheld from the market just like any other plant. When such plants are withheld the system operator may be forced to call on other units at their bid price, even if it is out of merit.

Another problem may arise if energy and ancillary service markets are run separately. Errors in prediction of the clearing prices in other markets can lead to de facto "withdrawal" of a plant because it bid into the wrong market, which can appear to be the exertion of market power. This can be averted under a merged energy and ancillary services market. (Refer to Chapter 7 and the integrated trading model.) Some markets (New York and Ontario, for example) have already created simultaneous clearing markets for reserves and energy.

PREDICTING AND DETECTING MARKET POWER

How can we tell in advance whether there is likely to be market power in an electricity market? The first line of attack is to look at market concentration, generally using measures such as the Herfindahl Index, which is the sum of the squares of percentage market shares in a market. (Ten equal sized competitors would each have 10 percent: the Herfindahl Index would be $10^2 \times 10$, or 1,000; five equal competitors would give a Herfindahl Index of $20^2 \times 5$ or 2,000. Two big players with 40 percent and ten with 2 percent would give an index of $2 \times 40^2 + 10 \times 2^2$ or 3,240. The maximum is 100^2 or 10,000.) There is no universal agreement about how much concentration is too much, although somewhere between 1,500 and 2,500 is often used as a screen.

But concentration measures are static. They do not take the tightness of supply into account. They do not take account of how people really behave in competitive situations—they do not predict the results of the real world where competitors learn the other competitors' strategies and adjust their strategies accordingly. Nor do they take into account the complexities of electric markets—transmission constraints, demand response, and so on. So analysts have concentrated on observing how markets actually work.

Studies in the United Kingdom and the United States to detect market power in the actual markets have generally worked on the premise that if the market were completely competitive, the prices would be set at marginal cost. Determining what the marginal cost is, and whether the prices were in fact set at marginal cost, proves to be a complicated exercise. How, for example, do you deal with opportunity costs of hydro plants, or plants that can sell into other markets?

How do you know whether a plant that is not running at all is out of service for physical reasons, or being withheld deliberately to raise the price? This is a question of intention, and unless there is a string of e-mails saying "forget about maintaining the sucker" there may be no way to tell. Even if this is not a problem, there are major data problems and issues of interpretation. The theory is good, and can lead to analyses that at least raise some real issues—but we are not there yet.

OPPORTUNITY COST: The "what if" value of using the resource at some other time or some other place. The direct cost of studying for a degree is the tuition cost and room and board; the opportunity cost is what the candidate might have made in the job market during those years. In electricity, one important example is hydro power: using water to generate power literally has no direct cost, but it has high opportunity costs. Hydro is different from plants using other fuels in that its annual output is fuel limited, not capacity limited. Most plants can get as much fuel as they need, and what stops them at any particular time is that the plant is running at full capacity. Hydro plants with dams can use their limited water when it is most valuable—which is usually at peak times—and if they do not use it they can "save it for another day." The real difference with hydro is that the "cost" of using it is not what the supplier paid for the fuel (which is nothing), but the "opportunity cost" of not selling it some other time. The same is also true of oil if there is an oil shortage, and of all power if there are other markets to sell into.

The best solution to market power is to reduce the need for police and monitors by having enough competitors in the first place, by making entry easier, by divestiture, by relieving transmission constraints, and by allowing uneconomic plants to close, together with a price-responsive demand side. The second best solution is contract cover (particularly during the transition to competitive markets). The third best solution (in fact the last resort) is to rely on forms of partial regulation such as price caps, bidding restrictions, and profit controls. But monitoring will always be necessary.

SUPPLY RESPONSIVENESS

Until now in this chapter, we have been talking about the importance of having many sellers and big markets. As on the demand side, competitive markets need an active price-responsive supply side. We tend to take this for granted. The market price must signal for supply to respond by producing more output when it is needed, and to shut off expansion, and even close plants when demand falls off.

Long-Run Response—Entry

Ease of entry, both in the short run and long run, is critical to the maintenance of effective competition. One thing that is critical to entry may seem obvious—new generators have to have the expectation (not necessarily the guarantee) that they will be able to cover their costs. For this it is critical that the spot price be determined so as to include a scarcity rent when supplies get tight. The tightrope we are walking is that, in competitive markets, prices should sometimes rise above marginal costs in order to yield scarcity rents, but not so high as to constitute market power. The correct premium is the customers' valuation (i.e., what the last customer would pay rather than not use). No theorist would disagree about this. The question is how to do it. We have argued earlier for the hourly metering and pricing of customers, so as to provide them the chance to participate actively in setting the market price. But there are also second-best solutions, which in the absence of adequate demand response have been widely adopted in wholesale markets. We discuss these in Chapter 8.

Short-Term Response—Availability

Supply response in the short term includes getting plants back from maintenance, even if it means working around the clock; or manning an old plant that is normally not operating. If prices are high, then more and more expensive units can now provide power and still make a profit. Consumers who install emergency generators can watch the price and generate only at peak times.

Availability that responds to price will prove more efficient than league tables of availability that encourage plant managers to be available at all times. As an example, one of the major impacts on generating plant managers in the United Kingdom was adjusting their plants to be able to stop running overnight. It had always been assumed that it was uneconomic to shut the large plants overnight. The spot market price actually hit zero one night, and showed that it paid to make the adjustments to be able to close down; there was no longer excess supply at night. The trading arrangements should be designed to let the spot price go negative, to give incentives to get off if too many generators want to stay on line.

Barriers to Entry

Regulators have to learn that to protect customers they now have the opposite role to the one they used to have—easing construction rather than limiting it.

In a regulated setting, limiting capacity reduces prices to consumers as the fixed costs are spread over more units; and excess capacity raises prices because the customers pay all the costs. This is why regulators controlled construction so carefully.

But in a competitive regime, *it is the other way around*—market prices will rise dramatically through the suppression of easy entry, while if many competitors choose to enter, the price will be reduced. The consumers can only benefit from easier entry of competing generators.

There are several important barriers to entry, which can thwart the goal of free entry into the electricity generating business, including:

- A critical barrier to entry is from state siting boards and their allies NIMBY (Not in my backyard!). In the old regulated paradigm, utilities were often required at the state level to demonstrate a need for power before they would be allowed to build new facilities. The California Energy Commission was quite dilatory in approving new power plants until the crisis hit.
- In many states, the utilities have powers of eminent domain for siting new plant, which independent generators, and unregulated subsidiaries, do not have. More pertinent perhaps is the inventory of existing approved sites, which may be concentrated in few hands.
- In addition, environmental boards require demonstrations that the proposed plant will not be unduly detrimental to the environment. Of

course, no state should endanger environmental quality just to allow a competitive generation sector. But the trade-offs in siting flexibility and the performance of deregulated markets are real.

Ease of entry is a prerequisite for a well-functioning competitive market, and much more important than it is in a regulated setting.

ENVIRONMENTAL ISSUES

An additional requirement for competition on the supply side of the industry is to solve environmental issues. The production of electricity has colossal environmental consequences, mainly the emissions from burning fossil fuels.[12] Regulations have been developed over decades to dictate how vertically integrated utilities must respect the environment. How do these rules relate to competition? What new rules are required before competition takes place? Environmental protection is entirely compatible with a competitive electricity market, but the specific rules of the market and of the environmental regulations may have radical implications for prices.

Two major issues present themselves:

1. What does a restructured electricity market imply about the best forms of emission regulation to implement?
2. Can environmentally friendly plant (like windmills) compete? How will these be paid for in a world in which costs cannot be simply passed along to the consumer?

Under traditional regulation, utilities passed along to consumers the costs of complying with whatever environmental rules they were forced to follow. There is no explicit mechanism like this in restructured markets to recover environmental costs. Under competition, environmental costs are just like any other costs: they subtract from net income for the producers. For those environmental costs that are fixed, prospective operating profits from generation must be sufficient to cover prospective environmental costs, or the plant will shut down rather than make capital investments for environmental improvements. However, the spot price for electricity will normally include the marginal environmental costs of the marginal generator, one way or another. It works differently under different control methods.

[12] Environmental consequences also arise from the need for cooling water and visually displeasing transmission towers and generating plants, but fuel burning is the major issue.

Methods of Control

There are three main methods of environmental controls that are used to regulate emissions: best available control technology (BACT), output limitation, and cap-and-trade.

Under BACT, the environmental regulator imposes a specific pollution control technology. The generator either installs the technology or not. Almost all costs are fixed, and they reduce generator profits. If prospective market prices are not sufficient to support the BACT costs, the unit will shut down rather than make the investment. The effect on the market price of electricity arises solely from the fact that units that cannot afford these improvements will inevitably shut down, reducing supply and increasing price.

This method is simple to apply but inefficient, because it relies on some regulator deciding what the best technology is. Under regulation, at least the generator got to recover his costs. In competitive electric markets, since there is no link between the cost of control and the market price of electricity, and there is no other method of recovering the cost of pollution control equipment, there is a real risk that too much plant would close. Moreover, if the generator expects that the government will later change the rules, and impose a different technology, he may not be willing to make the initial investment even if it is itself cost effective, for fear of having to spend more to change it again later.

Under *output limitations,* the total emissions for each plant over some period (say, a year) are limited. The generator can put in pollution control equipment of his own choice to meet the limitation, but once a plant has used up the emission limit, it has to stop running. Therefore the decision as to whether to install equipment to control emissions depends on how much profit the plant stands to lose by closing down when it has run out of its limitation. In other words there is an *opportunity cost* to generating at any time, which is the profits forgone by having to shut the plant down later in the year. It is this opportunity cost that has to be compared to the cost of control technology. But how do you know what it is? The plant operator must decide when to generate; this becomes an exercise in guessing when the highest prices will occur, or making computer models to predict the prices in advance. A wrong guess leaves the unit with additional output it might have generated, or having to shut down at the end of the year because it ran out of emissions permits.

The opportunity cost of temporary closure is a legitimate element of the electricity market price, although its precise value is a mystery both to the generator and to anyone watching for market power. This method is not so simple to apply, although it is less inefficient than the BACT, since choice of what equipment and when to install it is left to the market participants.

Under *cap-and-trade,* some aggregate capacity of emissions is established (which may be regional or seasonal) and translated into permits to produce emissions up to that level. Initial endowments of permits are allocated which can then be freely traded. You have to have a permit for an emission to be allowed to generate and produce that emission. The choice is to install equipment and not need a permit, or to buy a permit. The benefit of this method is supposed to be that those who can most economically reduce emissions do so, otherwise they pay for the permits. The market price of permits is a marginal cost that would normally appear in the market price of electricity, so the cost of the permit should be covered, while those who do not pollute gain additional revenues to cover the cost of the control equipment.

Cap-and-trade plans often include plans to gradually reduce the number of permits, thus improving the air, which generally increases the price of permits, and hence the marginal cost of generating, and hence the market price of electricity. Tightening of caps will raise the value of the permits already purchased and thus partially alleviate the costs associated with compliance. The initial allocation of permits can be critical to achieving a fair balance of the costs of control. Initial allocations can be used to alleviate effects on particular sectors of the economy.

The cap-and-trade mechanism is the preferred method of economists, since it prices clean air and makes polluters pay for dirty air by purchasing permits. The cost of the permits is a marginal cost of generating, and as such, it goes directly into the market price of electricity, rather than indirectly through temporary or permanent closures of generating plant. This reduces risk and makes compliance, rather than closure, more likely.

Cap-and-Trade Programs in the United States

Sulfur dioxide is subject to a nationwide cap-and-trade program in the United States. At the margin, every plant that emits sulfur dioxide can lower its output of the pollutant by generating less energy. Since every pound emitted requires a permit, then the decision to generate creates an incremental cost of sulfur dioxide permits. Similar programs apply in certain seasons of the year in ozone non-attainment for nitrogen oxides (NO_X).

These costs can serve to sharply increase the market price of power. Nitrogen oxide trading prices alone raised the market-clearing spot price in California in August 2000 by almost 70 percent.[13] Since there was very little

[13] Paul Joskow and Edward Kahn, "A Quantitative Analysis of Pricing Behavior in California's Wholesale Electricity Market during Summer 2000." MIT Department of Economics, Working Paper, January 15, 2001.

contract cover in the California markets, and the utilities were purchasing at spot prices, this increase applied to the price paid for all power from all units, so the aggregate cost to consumers was much higher than the cost of the permits themselves.

Some number of units (the extent to which this occurred is not yet clear) may have chosen simply not to generate rather than purchase emission credits in California's Summer 2000 crisis. This raises an additional question as to whether cap-and-trade programs, if too tightly drawn, limit supply availability; or if they can serve as a mask for market power, a unit which a generator wishes to withdraw from services uses the "unavailability" of permits as an excuse not to operate.

Joskow and Kahn sharply criticize the fact that the NO_X requirements of a fairly small number of units caused huge transfers from buyers to sellers. Indeed, by their calculations, buyers could have saved a large amount of money by joining together to make capital improvements in the affected plants. In theory, a coalition of electricity buyers and polluting generators could have made side deals under which both were better off. They did not do so, of course, either because they did not know, or because there was no vehicle for them to do so.

Critically, the phenomenon in which the aggregate transfers greatly exceed the social cost can occur only when capacity is quite tight; otherwise, the affected generators will simply not be running. When units with very high costs are called on to run, it should serve as a signal that by backing off consumption by a small amount, large amounts of money could be saved. *This is another example of the need for demand response in the short run.* Environmental marginal costs are no different than any other marginal costs, in that demand response is critical in getting an adequate performance. In the longer run, of course, if the aggregate costs exceed the price of entry (including the necessary credits) those affected plants will simply be driven from the market.

Green Power and the Markets

Finally, how can environmentally friendly (green) power compete? (*Green power* is the name given to power from renewable resources; power from windmills, solar cells, and so on.) Green power is often expensive to produce because of the high capital cost involved, but there has always been a big political constituency for it. Some technologies such as photovoltaic cells and fuel cells have been promising for 20 years (they went to the moon in 1969) but have not yet achieved widespread commercial applications. This is due to the cost. Green power sources account for less than 2 percent of U.S. commercial production.

Competitive markets certainly make it easier for any technology that holds the promise of competitive costs to gain a foothold in the market. The design of the trading arrangements is important. We will argue later that a transparent spot price is important for many reasons, but it is especially important for renewables, such as wind and solar. A transparent spot price for backup (when the wind does not blow or the sun does not shine) would be imperative for these technologies. But if renewables cannot produce power at less than the cost of other incremental supplies, then there are still options.

First, each of the three methods of control above has the effect of raising the price of electricity and increasing the cost of emission-producing alternatives. Thus, these three methods all shift the playing field in favor of green power: market revenues are raised and competitors' costs are raised, which makes green power more competitive.

If renewables still cannot produce power at less than the cost of other incremental supplies, and someone is prepared to pay the difference to build renewable plants so that overall emissions are reduced, then there are various options for structuring subsidies so that they do not interfere with market mechanisms.

- *A utility subsidy.* Such plans can still exist under competition in the form of non-bypassable customer charges to customers of the distribution utility if it still has default responsibility. The utility contracts for power at above market prices and passes the above-market portion through in the distribution charge.
- *A government subsidy.* Such subsidies must be designed to be compatible with the restructured markets. One way to do this is for the government to purchase green power on above-market contracts and resell into the spot markets. The loss the government takes is the subsidy.
- *A direct consumer purchase of green power.* Customers pay a premium to have their power supplied from renewable resources.

If a cap-and-trade program is in place and someone—government or otherwise—is prepared to pay a premium so that overall emissions are reduced, the alternative to subsidizing green power is to purchase permits directly. To purchase a permit and then not use it to produce emissions is literally to purchase fresh air, and the cost can be directly compared to subsidizing green power.

To summarize on environmental issues: The best form of emission regulation to implement in a restructured electricity market for major environmental programs is the cap-and-trade method. (For very specific situations or locations with unique environmental rules, it may be simpler to require a specific pollution control technology—BACT.)

The aim with green power sources should be to make it easy for them to enter competitive markets, whenever they are economic, and if they are to be subsidized in the interim, to subsidize in a way that does not impact the mechanisms that make the markets competitive. All emission regulations directly or indirectly encourage green power, but the cap-and-trade method allows a market price for reduced emissions against which a subsidy for green power can be explicitly compared.

CHAPTER 6

Liquid, Efficient, and Complete Marketplaces

In the previous chapters, we discussed some of the requirements for competitive markets—the demand side and the supply side. Another major requirement for competitive markets is efficient, liquid, and complete marketplaces, and now we turn to what this means, before we apply the general formulation to the electricity marketplaces. (Although the following discussion is about marketplaces, we will sometimes call them markets, for short, when the meaning is not in doubt.)

THE RULES THAT GOVERN A MARKETPLACE

All marketplaces have trading rules. Some trading rules are developed by custom; some are prescribed in detail by groups of traders; some are prescribed by law. The rules cover the method of setting the price, arrangements for delivery, settlement terms, and the obligations of the buyers, sellers, and the organization (if there is one) running the marketplace, to one another. How is the price set? How is payment made? How is delivery made? What happens if a party to a transaction defaults?

Competitive industries depend, in ways that in the western world are taken for granted, on a national substructure of property rights, contract law, and mechanisms for ensuring payment. Specific marketplaces like financial markets and commodity markets, and public auctions also have specific rules that traders have to sign up to and follow—and so will electric markets.

The trading arrangements for each marketplace are different. The central function of a marketplace is to set the price and there are many different methods of arriving at the price:

- At the supermarket, the rules are you pay what they ask.
- In a bazaar, you haggle over the price.
- The NY stock exchange market is a form of continuous auction, while the NASDAQ uses market makers to match buyers and sellers.
- Sotheby's runs auctions known technically as "English auctions."
- The real estate market is a series of decentralized bilateral transactions (haggling over the price!).

Note that in these marketplaces the buyer is always an integral part of the price-setting mechanism—even in the supermarket, where the prices appear to be set, if no one buys, the price goes down or the product goes unsold.

LIQUID MARKETS

We say the marketplaces are *liquid* if there are many buyers and sellers who can access each other easily and have access to information about the market prices. In liquid markets, the price settles down quite fast to a *market price.* A defining feature of a liquid market is that it can generally absorb the addition or loss of a buyer or seller without a noticeable change in the market price. *If there is good information, and the ability to resell, a competitive market comes to a single price for a specific product at a specific time and place.*[1] The flower auction in Aalsmeer, Holland, disposes of millions of flowers daily in a series of Dutch auctions where virtually every bunch is sold individually. In the 13 auction rooms, each transaction takes less than a second, and everyone in the auction room knows the price. Within seconds, the price of "24 red tulips on Tuesday" reaches an equilibrium and stays there—all subsequent transactions are at virtually the same price. This is known colloquially as *the law of one price*—for the same product, same time, same place, there will be one price if the market is liquid.

The bond markets, in contrast, are sometimes not very liquid. It is hard to find a buyer, and not always clear what the market price is. The market in fine art is not very liquid—there are relatively few buyers and even Sotheby's cannot tell what price it will get for a Picasso masterpiece. In these markets, the addition or subtraction of a single buyer could easily have a large effect on the market price.

[1] Sellers would like to be able to discriminate, and charge more to those who value the product more, selling off the rest at prices that just cover the marginal costs to those who are more "price sensitive." But they can only do this is the product cannot be resold—which is one reason the airlines, who have perfected this method of charging, don't allow you to transfer your ticket, and always ask for ID.

A liquid market allows an additional buyer or seller to enter the market and not affect the price. Note that an electricity market might appear liquid to a small buyer but may not appear liquid to an investor considering building a power plant.

EFFICIENT MARKETS

Another characteristic of a good marketplace is that it is *efficient*. Economists typically say a *market is efficient if participants cannot predict which way prices will move.*[2] Intuitively, the market as a whole should not be able to predict price movements; if everyone knows that a stock is trading at $5 today but will trade for $10 tomorrow, today's sellers are either desperate for cash today or are incredibly stupid. Arbitrageurs perform a useful function by buying and selling until the small differences between prices for the same product in different markets are "arbitraged away." Arbitrageurs make a lot more money in inefficient markets where there is little information.

An illiquid market can still be efficient if the price *movements* cannot be predicted (i.e., if all the available information is included in the current price). The market for fine art is probably efficient: If market participants knew that an investor was willing to pay $1 million for a certain Picasso in the near future, the Picasso would only sell for $1 million today (less some interest and transaction costs).

COMPLETE MARKETS

Fully competitive markets require *complete markets* (marketplaces), that is, *a full set of forward and spot markets (marketplaces) and risk-management tools, for each specific product/time/place.* A complete market for electricity would allow you to buy or sell electricity for delivery at any time or place, including here and now.

---

[2] There are actually three forms of market efficiency, which depend on what information could help participants predict which way prices will move. In the weak form of market efficiency, access to past prices would not help one predict future price movements. In the semi-strong form, no public information (including past prices) could help predict future price movements. In the strong form, no information (whether public or private) would help predict future price movements.

Economists generally believe that many public markets are efficient in the weak and semi-strong form senses, but not in the strong form. (Hence the need for laws against insider trading, which would only be profitable if private information gave someone an ability to buy before a price rises and/or sell before the price falls.)

A market is characterized by the underlying product, the time, and the place of delivery. So "Pork bellies for September delivery in Chicago" is a different product and therefore a different market than "Pork bellies for October delivery in Chicago." But different markets can also exist for a particular product/time/place ("Pork bellies for October delivery in Chicago") where the product can be bought and sold at *different points in time in advance of its delivery*. Complete markets include:

- Spot markets;
- Forward markets;
- Futures markets; and
- Risk-management tools.

Spot markets are those markets for immediate delivery. The spot markets for October delivery in Chicago has to take place in October (but not necessarily in Chicago). *Forward markets* are the markets where delivery is at some point in the future. Forward contracts are traded in forwards markets; these contracts are promises to deliver a product at some time in the future. Each contract can be quite idiosyncratic and negotiated bilaterally between buyer and seller. A *futures market* is one type of forward market that takes place on an organized exchange. It relies on standardized contract terms—the only item that can vary is price—so that the market for that forward contract is liquid and facilitates trading. *Risk-management tools* include contracts, insurance, hedges, and options.

Forward contracts and markets are useful for buyers and sellers because they fix the price in advance, reduce price risks to both buyers and sellers, and may provide liquidity, which helps to underpin the costs of expansion. Different markets develop different mixes of contract and spot sales, depending on the participants' appetite for risk, and the underlying nature of the product, for example:

- Output that is not sold ahead on the forward market will eventually be sold on the related spot market. It is the same product, whether sold forward or at spot, and the value of a forward contract tends to converge to the spot price as the date of delivery approaches. In some markets (retail supermarkets, restaurants) everything is sold at spot.
- In real estate, there is only a tiny spot market (the foreclosure auctions on the courthouse steps)—it is all done with forward contracts. Property developers especially like to sell far ahead, because that way they can finance their construction, and not run the risk that they sell at a

bad time—they pass on the risk to the buyer. There is a small discount to the buyer for the time value of money and for taking the price risk.[3]

A liquid market in forward contracts increases competition further by providing funds from people who have no wish to take delivery, but who have money they are prepared to put at risk. The most obvious examples of this are the organized commodity markets. If you trade pork bellies, you may never want to take delivery (and would be horrified to have a truck turn up at your door). You sell the contract before delivery. But someone wants those pork bellies (the bacon factory?). The whole point of commodity markets is to provide liquidity to enable the original producer of the pork bellies to "sell them forward" before the hogs are slaughtered. If the bacon factory does not want to put up the money months in advance, the commodity markets provide risk-takers who bet on the eventual price and buy and sell the pork belly "futures." But in the end the pork bellies are delivered to some bacon factory—*all commodity markets are markets for delivery.* Electric forward markets are commodity markets and are for eventual delivery. If you don't want to take delivery, you cash out by selling the contract. If the farmer does not want to deliver (the hogs got sick and died) than he has to buy back the contracts at the prevailing price. The existence of a liquid forward market and a visible forward price is what allows you to trade out of your position or "book out the contract," which reduces your risk of being stuck with a bad deal.

All forward contracts are in some sense a hedge against the spot price. The pork farmer wants to lock in a price for his pork bellies in advance of raising the hogs, so as to not be at risk to whatever the going price happens to be the day they are delivered to the bacon factory. Similarly, the property developer uses forward contracts to finance construction, to lock in a price in advance of purchasing all the building materials. The same principles hold for financing electricity projects.

ELECTRICITY MARKETPLACES

The lack of storage in electricity has some important implications for forward markets. Note that for *storable products* like oil there is a clear relationship between prices for delivery in adjacent periods—it is the cost of storing the

[3] This discount is taken for granted—it always happens—and is not an exception to the rule that efficient markets are ones where the future price is not predictable.

product from one month to the next. In the stock markets, the cost of "storage" is the interest rate. The whole theory of options pricing rests on the storability of the product—a share in IBM is inherently storable. If an arbitrageur discovers a price difference between the price for September delivery and the price for July delivery that exceeds the cost of storage, he sells one and buys the other, thus bringing them into line.

But by contrast, the price of electricity for July delivery will not tell you much about the price for September delivery. There is no cost of storage, because there is no storage. So in some ways, the markets in a storable product are automatically more liquid and efficient than markets in a product that cannot be stored, *because there are more buyers and sellers and more information—the market implicitly subsumes the whole phalanx of buyers in all future periods*. But electricity is not storable, so electricity markets are intrinsically less liquid and efficient than other markets.

Furthermore, electricity cannot easily be moved from place to place. The price of oil varies from place to place by the cost of transport. But the cost of transport in the case of oil is competitively determined, and can be locked in, and oil can be transported anywhere. In electricity, price differences between areas may change from day to day and cannot be locked in, and there is no transport between many places. The price of oil for delivery in Chicago will be quite easy to derive from the price for delivery in Rotterdam (by the cost of transport). But the price of electricity in Rotterdam will tell you nothing at all about the price in Chicago. In fact, even the price in New York will tell you almost nothing about the price in Chicago.

In electricity, to make good estimates of future prices at each time and in each place, you really need a computer model, and much information about hydro availability, plans for maintenance of the generating plant and the transmission, fuel prices, and demand levels. This is a costly and time consuming exercise, features that benefit from scale economies—the bigger the trader the more money he can make.

We can make a strong conclusion that electricity marketplaces will be inherently less efficient and liquid than markets in storable products:

- Because each forward market in each time and place is effectively separate, there are inevitably fewer buyers and sellers (i.e., the markets will be less liquid).
- Because the prediction of future prices in electricity will be better or worse depending on the information available to traders, some people will predict better than others, so the forward markets will be inherently less efficient.

In restructuring the industry, nothing much can be done about the inherent unstorability of the product. But just because of that, it would pay to make strenuous efforts to expand the marketplaces, and expand the transport to increase the underlying markets, to increase liquidity. The markets need to be large, with transmission constraints removed, and trading arrangements that can cover wide areas. In addition, since time-adjacent markets will not give much information about future prices, there is an enormous premium on information—about which plants are available, who is building, how much fuel prices are moving around—and on the models that use this information to predict prices.

Electricity marketplaces will be illiquid and inefficient if the information that allows the markets to come quickly to a single price is in the hands of very few traders, or if the trading arrangements are so complex and irrational that only a few people can understand them. Forward markets will be illiquid unless spot markets provide a transparent price for eventual settlement.

In the 1990s, electricity marketplaces have expanded significantly in the United States and around the world as competition has expanded. There are spot markets, forward markets, bilateral markets, futures markets, and options/insurance and other derivatives markets. All the markets are either markets for *delivery,* or are based on markets for delivery. However, delivery of electricity is constrained by the physical transmission network, which complicates the full development of efficient liquid markets in electricity. The arrangements for delivery have to be coordinated with the system operator; the rules he has to use are called the trading arrangements, to which we now turn.

CHAPTER 7

Trading Arrangements

Where there is competition in production, the right of access to the transmission, which is an essential facility, has to be legislated. But the detailed rules for assuring access—the trading arrangements—have to take into account the problems of delivery. The arrangements for delivery of the power are the fulcrum of the production markets, the bridge between buyers and sellers. No other product, and no other market, has these problems, which are both technical and institutional. *Electricity is a one of a kind market.*

The trading arrangements are legal agreements covering all aspects of the traders' relation to the system operator and to the transmission owner. The short-term arrangements, which are the focus of this chapter, determine what happens in or close to real time (say, up to a day ahead); how the forward contracts are delivered; and how spot sales are made and delivered. *The trading arrangements have to be integrated with the short-term operational concerns of the system operator.*

The longer term arrangements that ensure the transmission is available are covered in Chapter 9.

This chapter describes the four pillars of the short-term trading arrangements, and how they relate to the specific ways in which electricity is different; we set out the preferred trading model—including a spot market integrated with operations and run by the system operator—and why it is preferred; and we compare the preferred trading model to two others, *wheeling* and a decentralized model.

COMPONENTS OF THE TRADING ARRANGEMENTS

The collective term *trading arrangements* denotes legal agreements between traders and the system operator and/or the transmission owners. The discussion of trading arrangements has been plagued by the use of the terms *voluntary* and *compulsory*—as in *voluntary pool* or *compulsory trading*. In these discussions, *voluntary* is always a term of approbation, and *compulsory*

FIGURE 7.1 Short-term and long-term trading arrangements.

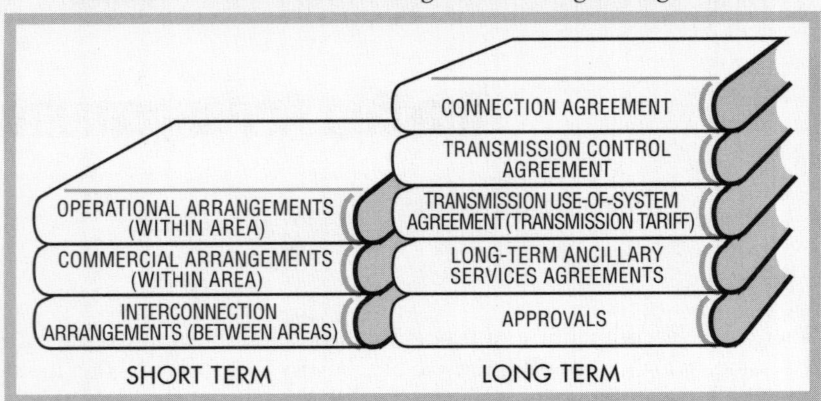

a term of disapproval. There is one element of any trading arrangement that has to be compulsory—to use the network at all, traders must sign agreements to obey the rules. The rules are the trading arrangements. It is never voluntary to obey the rules for using the transmission network. The trading arrangements are about the operational integration of generation with system operations and transmission in the short term and in the long term—the things that were done internally by command and control under the old system—and about the commercial arrangements for the traders to pay each other (Figure 7.1).

Short-term trading arrangements consist of three parts:

1. *Operational arrangements* that cover access and short-term operations within an area (outside the United States this is sometimes known as an *Operating Code*);
2. *Commercial arrangements* that cover the buying and selling of power within an area (outside the United States this is sometimes known as a *Power Exchange Code* or *Settlement Agreement*); and
3. *Interconnection arrangements* that cover operational and commercial arrangements between areas.

These trading arrangements define the day-to-day responsibilities of the system operator and of market participants.[1] There has to be one set of

[1] For the system operator, the operational arrangements have to do with things like the scheduling and dispatch of generation, emergency procedures, transmission maintenance scheduling, planning procedures, safety coordination, information exchange,

operational and commercial agreements per area, and one interconnection agreement between each pair of areas. Evidently, with a large number of areas the required number of agreements grows exponentially. Electricity marketplaces also require long-term rules; we are only going to touch on them here, and then return to them in the chapter on transmission. The long-term rules include:

- A *connection agreement* between the system operator/transmission owner and a market participant to ensure that a generator who builds a plant that will last for many years will be able to stay connected to the transmission system, at terms that are fair to the parties involved and efficient.
- A *transmission control agreement* is needed, if transmission operations are separated from transmission ownership, to set out the relationship between the system operator and the transmission owner.
- The terms and charges for using the transmission system. (This is sometimes known as the *transmission use-of-system agreement* or the *transmission tariff*.)
- Arrangements for purchase by the system operator of certain ancillary services from market participants under long-term *ancillary services agreements*.
- *Approvals* (or sometimes *authorizations* or *licenses*) defining the responsibilities of the various parties, and tying the other agreements and arrangements together.

WHY ELECTRICITY IS DIFFERENT

Some people have argued that trading arrangements do not need to be made specific for electricity. In particular, they have argued that electricity-specific commercial rules be minimized, and that normal commercial laws that apply to the rest of the economy should apply to electricity, without the need for special arrangements.

But they are wrong—electricity is physically different from all other commodities. We described earlier the four special conditions that apply to

---

metering, demand forecasting, load control, interconnector management, monitoring, testing, and so on. For market participants, they have to do with things such as the need to follow system operator instructions, the way that market participants communicate with the system operator, and so on. The commercial arrangements have to do with how spot electricity prices are determined, and how settlement, meter reading, billing, creditworthiness provisions, and other arrangements are conducted.

electricity. These special features of electricity map fairly precisely to the special features of short-term trading arrangements (Table 7.1). All alternative designs for trading arrangements have to (and in fact do, in different ways) accommodate these features.

No Storage → Imbalances

Forward contracts between buyers and sellers make up the bulk of deliveries in virtually all electricity markets where traders have a choice. Because of the complications of the production and delivery system, it is certain that at all times and for all contracts there will be a difference between the amounts contracted and the amounts actually sent out by the supplier and consumed by the customer in real time. This difference is called an *imbalance*.

The system operator stands ready to make up any shortfalls or absorb any excesses, regardless of their reason. This has to happen—the system operator has to be able to deal with the imbalances quickly and efficiently by adjusting production (or occasionally, consumption). It is impossible to design a delivery system that does not make provision for imbalances, because the system operator is working with seconds to spare—he cannot wait for you to call your supplier, find he has just had a malfunction, and find another supplier before you get your toast from your electric toaster—the system would collapse. In all trading systems, the system operator buys and sells imbalances. The questions are: from whom, to whom, and at what price?

Law of Physics → Congestion Management

Electricity is transported on transmission wires networked in a complex grid. It travels according to laws of physics that apply only to electricity. And any

TABLE 7.1 Features of Electricity That Constrain Trading Arrangements

Feature	Problem	Design Issues
No storage	Contract amounts will not match usage or output	Imbalances
Path of least resistance	Possible overloading	Congestion management
Network interactions	Plants need to produce several outputs and stand as reserve	Ancillary services
Speed of light	System operator needs to be in charge	Scheduling and dispatch

one transaction of electricity over the transmission system can affect any or all others.

Unfortunately, *you cannot tell electricity where to go*—you can't even tell it not to overload a route and melt down the line. The system operator has to make sure that total electricity flows will not overload any line. He uses complex computer predictions of the consequences of virtually any instantaneous and unexpected event, and develops contingency strategies that deliberately underutilize capacity in the day-to-day operation of the network, so as to be safe.

Whenever any line reaches its capacity, the system operator tells some producers they have to back down and others that they have to generate instead because of the limits of transmission capacity. This is called *congestion management*. The questions are who does he tell, and how does he get generators to agree to back down or bring up their plants?

Interdependencies → Ancillary Services

There are also interdependencies between the production of energy and the production of other services—*ancillary services*—necessary to make the transmission system work, such as operating reserves, reactive power, and other items that we look at in more detail later. Mostly, ancillary services are produced by generating plant.

The problem is that production of ancillary services is dependent on also producing energy, which is normally only produced and sold when the energy price is high enough. This complicates things because a single generator can be simultaneously needed to produce multiple outputs, or to produce an ancillary service rather than energy. The questions are: How does the system operator procure these ancillary services? What does he pay? What does he charge the users?

Speed of Light → Scheduling and Dispatch

Finally, electricity travels at the speed of light and it cannot respond to busy signals or traffic jams. Despite the fact that traders schedule forward contracts with each other, energy is mingled together in real time as it instantaneously travels over the transmission and distribution wires. The system operator has to be in charge of the fluctuating needs, the imbalances, the congestion, and the complex interdependencies. He has to tell generators when to start up, when to increase and decrease output, and when to stop. This is called *scheduling* (in advance) and *dispatching* (in real time). There is no escaping this—the system operator has to schedule and dispatch. The question is how this indubitable fact should be reflected in the rules of the electricity marketplaces. How does the system operator decide who should generate at any time? How are forward contracts tied to scheduling? How should financial settlements be tied to physical operations?

These issues used to be decided internally in the electric company—the trading arrangements have to replace command and control with incentive-compatible rules, using prices to do the job of traffic cop as far as possible.

The Four Pillars of Market Design

The trading rules that deal with the four features of electricity just mentioned are the four pillars of good electricity market design (see Figure 7.2). All other aspects of market design become quite straightforward once these are in place:

1. Imbalances;
2. Congestion management;
3. Ancillary services; and
4. Scheduling and dispatch.

All of these pieces must work together. Design of trading arrangements really is a technical issue, in which economists and engineers are the experts. If you want to build a bridge, you ask an architect/engineering firm. You can have a covered bridge, a Roman arch, and a suspension bridge. Or whatever. But don't have half of one and half of another! One of the biggest problems in setting up trading arrangements arises if they are designed through a piecemeal process of litigation or negotiation—processes typical in the United States. Trading arrangements are, after all legal agreements and computer

FIGURE 7.2 The four pillars of market design.

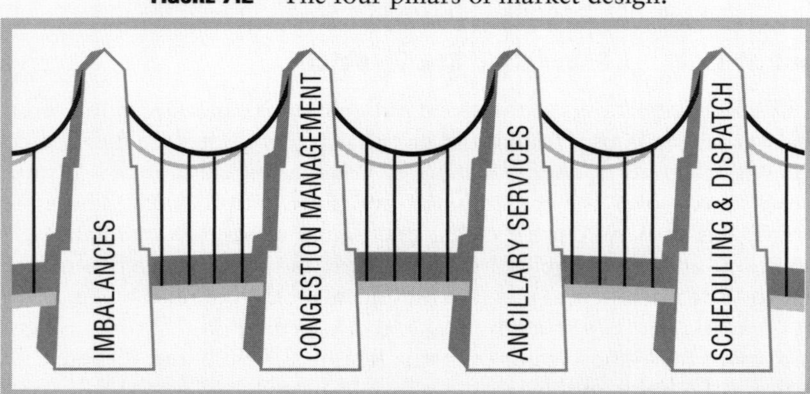

A Bad Process in California

In California, the design of the initial trading arrangements came out of a lengthy and contentious process including all the stakeholders, and the legislature, and reflect compromises between warring parties—those who wanted integration and those who wanted decentralization—both within the state regulatory agency (CPUC) and outside it. In the end it reflected incompatible and truly awful elements. (Building a bridge by voting where the girders should go!) The California Power Exchange, or spot market, one of the areas of contention, went bankrupt and closed its doors in January 2001. (For more on the design of the California markets, see Appendix C.)

programs, but problems arise if lawyers and programmers design them. *The right process is for economists and engineers to set out clearly what is supposed to happen, for the lawyers to write this into detailed documents, and for the programmers to turn this into operational software.*

THREE MODELS OF TRADING ARRANGEMENTS

The design of short-term trading arrangements has been controversial. There are many different opinions as to how to deal with the unique problems that electricity competition presents.

The subject is also plagued by jargon used in an attempt to categorize different types of trading models: "California is a *bilateral* market," "New York is a *pool,*" "the Midwest uses the *wheeling* model," and so on. There are certainly similarities between some trading models, but the fact of the matter is that most of the existing geographic marketplaces are actually quite different from each other and defy being pigeonholed. The terminology is causing much of the confusion, and is preventing policy makers from finding common ground.

In our view, the best way to categorize alternative trading models is on the *degree to which operational arrangements and commercial arrangements for scheduling, imbalances, congestion, and ancillary services are integrated with spot markets.* So for purposes of clarity in this book, we use some new terminology for trading models, based on this categorization. We describe three models of trading arrangements: integrated, wheeling, and decentralized (see Figure 7.3).

The *integrated* model, as its name suggests, is highly integrated. The *wheeling* model has a low level of integration. The *decentralized* model is in

FIGURE 7.3 Trading models.

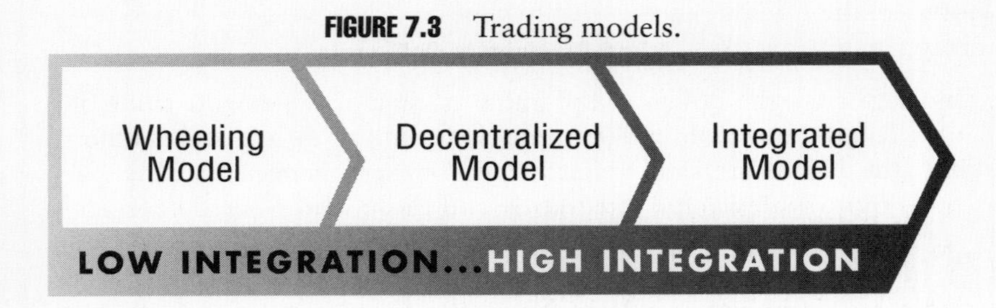

between. The basic difference is in how the models deal with the four pillars of market design.

Integrated

Under integrated models, which are used in three regions of the United States, and also in most markets abroad, the system operator schedules forward contracts at the request of traders, but also *takes bids from traders to modify scheduled contracts* and to provide imbalances, congestion management, and ancillary services. The system operator runs the spot market using a large computer optimization program (of which more will be said later), and by doing so, the system operator minimizes the overall cost of these services.

Wheeling

Under wheeling (the type of model used in much of the rest of the United States, in those areas that have not gone fully to competition) an integrated utility with its own generation runs the transmission and system operations; it provides access to the transmission by scheduling contracts at the request of traders, after it has scheduled its own resources for its own load. *The utility provides imbalances and manages congestion and ancillary services using its own generation resources.* These services are priced at regulated rates. There is no formal spot market.

Decentralized

Under decentralized models (California and Texas in the United States are partially decentralized, and the new NETA in the United Kingdom is the main example elsewhere), the system operator also schedules traders' contracts, but the aim is to get the system operator out of the spot markets. *The system operator has to administer arrangements for imbalances.* As far as possible, the traders run the spot market and manage congestion; separate arrangements are set up for ancillary services.

We go into these models in more detail later.

Why the Controversy?

Why is there all this controversy over the trading arrangements? There is substantial agreement that wheeling impedes competition; but why the controversy between *integration* and *decentralization?* In many ways it is because there are two groups of people coming at it from different directions—the utility engineers, whose concern is the stability of the transmission system, and who know little about markets, and tend to favor integration; and the young MBAs, the marketers, and traders, who know how other markets work and tend to favor decentralization, figuring the engineers will sort out the details.

The *integration* people have sometimes forgotten that markets require demand and supply to meet and set a price. They concentrate on what they know best—controlling the generators for short-term stability; and sometimes they carry over too much of the old agreements that were based on command and control. The folks who favor *decentralization* have been remiss in thinking that markets can operate without being integrated with the complexities of system operations—in their version they think they can just tell the system operator to schedule their contracts. They do not like giving the system operator so much authority.

But it is critical to get both elements into the new markets—complete, efficient, liquid marketplaces for trading, and reliable short-term system operations. This is the secret of a good market design—that it combines both aspects. The system operator has to have a lot of authority anyway—it is better to concentrate on making what he does transparent and fair, rather than trying to stop him from doing it at all.

The sheer complexity of the laws of electricity physics and the vast geographic scope of electricity networks means that to run the system efficiently, some of the world's most sophisticated optimization software, computer equipment, and communications equipment is needed to direct operations from second to second. And this equipment is already installed in many systems—it does not have to be invented, it just has to be factored into the solution.

A PREFERRED MODEL

Despite the controversy over trading models, *we believe that a clear winner has now emerged.* For those who have followed this dispute for years, we show our hand here. Then, we will go back and explain the details throughout this chapter.

- That clear winner has a high level of integration between operational and commercial arrangements, especially in the areas of congestion management and imbalances. We have referred to it as the *integrated model.*
- The clear winner is, at the risk of pigeonholing, broadly similar to the trading arrangements in PJM, New York, and New Zealand.

It would be fair to say that your authors are biased in respect of the question of what works. We have been involved in perhaps 20 designs for trading arrangements over the last decade, on every continent, and in all the new markets in the United States, and by now we know what we would recommend with a clean slate—in fact have recommended. There is very little disagreement among international experts on the essentials for trading arrangements, and how they work, or do not work. We believe the benefits of a high level of integration have been proved. The United Kingdom originally had a fairly rudimentary integrated model and has recently (2001) gone to a decentralized model—NETA—New Electric Trading Arrangements. Later in this chapter and in Appendix A we discuss why we do not think NETA is an improvement.

The integrated trading model that we recommend first schedules contracts at the traders' request. It recognizes that the system operator has to adjust these schedules to deal with imbalances, congestion, and ancillary services, and so the system operator takes bids from traders for *reservation prices*—the prices at which traders are willing to buy or sell more or less than they have scheduled. It also recognizes that the system operator might find mutually beneficial deals between traders, that the traders might not have been able to find themselves due to the four special complications of electricity. Using the same reservation prices, traders are able to indicate their willingness for the system operator to make such deals, and in doing so, to lower cost.

In the integrated model, the system operator uses a computerized optimization process to convert the information from traders about their willingness to buy and sell into a least-cost feasible plan that everyone will be happy with, issuing dispatch instructions every few seconds. To some people this does not sound like a market (no haggling over the price). But auctions of this sort are a perfectly respectable form of market and computers make it much simpler to deal with imbalances, transmission constraints, and ancillary services. Think eBay. The electricity sector merely predated Internet trading. In the United States, at least, the big-picture thinking is actually converging, albeit at a snail's pace, and FERC seems, at the time of writing, to be moving towards a model similar to this.

For those who are familiar with the terminology, the following is a summary of the main features of the integrated model. For those who are not familiar with the terminology—you are not alone. This is a knotty subject area. We begin a less condensed explanation in the next section.

- A system operator-run spot market, which also serves as the imbalance market. This is the most efficient mechanism for dealing with the complex operational problems of delivery. As we will explain, the system operator has to run a system for imbalances anyway, under any trading model. The incentive-compatible price for imbalances is the market price. Energy traded in the spot market is the same product, time, and place as imbalance energy—the prices will converge. There is no reason to try to keep them separate.
- Supply and demand bidding of "reservation" prices, with the spot price set at the highest generator bid or the lowest demand bid that clears the market. Market clearing done by optimization, calculated by security-constrained dispatch software.
- Day-ahead markets in addition to spot markets.
- Locational prices for energy. These give good signals for location of new generation, for expansion of transmission, and for congestion management.
- Operating reserves, including regulation reserves, integrated with energy markets and priced as options. Reserves are options to call for supply of energy. It is inefficient to try to separate the energy and reserve markets—it increases prices and contributes to shortages.
- Congestion management integrated with the system operator optimization process and the locational prices, with bottleneck fees for scheduled contracts. This is the only workable way to deal with real-time congestion on a large and complex network with many traders. It is efficient and incentive-compatible. It has the additional virtue of giving a good picture of where expansion is needed.
- The treatment of transmission losses integrated with the security-constrained optimization and with the determination of locational spot prices.
- Contracts scheduled with the system operator; net quantities (spot price transactions) settled financially. This system of scheduling and settling contracts is simple and efficient.
- Trading arrangements that enable ownership of the transmission wires by an independent, regulated regional Transco. The Transco is not permitted to own generation in its own marketplace in any way.

- Long-term financial transmission rights, issued by a Transco. These permit traders to hedge against bottleneck fees. They also have several additional useful properties—they can be used to compensate those who pay for new construction of transmission; and they can be used to provide incentives to the Transco to maintain the transmission system properly.
- Hourly (or more frequent) settlement intervals, together with the required hourly metering for final customers we have recommended earlier, so as to enable meaningful demand response.[2] Retail prices that incorporate the spot price at the margin.
- We would not include capacity obligations that are being used in PJM and New York in the long term, as we believe them to be unnecessary and potentially detrimental to market development. Capacity obligations can be useful in the interim *only* if hourly metering, hourly pricing, and demand response (see above) are woefully inadequate. The other interim alternative is some form of capacity payment based on value of lost load to consumers. But one of these must be in place in the interim if demand bidding cannot be implemented expeditiously.

The integrated trading model is known to work. Most competitive markets throughout the world have adopted some form of this model, yet no marketplace yet has all the features listed.[3]

The integrated trading model works smoothly, incorporating the necessary complexities of the transmission system and providing incentive-compatible rules. A major benefit is that *independent generators can find an outlet for their power without having to find specific customers* and can purchase any extra energy they need automatically. This provides liquidity to underpin real competition in the production markets. The major downside is, paradoxically, the transparent price, which is a magnet for *price caps,* with predictably bad results. (Nevertheless, some price caps may be necessary in the interim if demand response is limited or absent.)

Some people believe that transparency of spot markets and a high level of integration between operational and commercial arrangements encourage collusion and the use of market power. To the contrary, we believe that

---

[2] While all final customers should be metered to unbundle "Gap and Armani," response from half the load or perhaps even less would be sufficient to control wholesale prices. In many places, large industrial customers *are* half the load.

[3] New York and PJM, in particular, have many of the required features and others are awaiting implementation. In a way, this shows that changes can be implemented a step at a time, providing the steps are the right steps—the designs in place in New York and PJM were produced from a committee process, and reflect some compromises.

INTEGRATED VS. DECENTRALIZED MODELS: The essential difference between integration and decentralization is whether or not the system operator administers a spot market integrated with the pricing of imbalances, congestion management, and the ancillary services.

The integrated model says the system operator should run the spot market, integrated with imbalances, and the others, because he will anyway be doing something very similar, and we might as well accept this and make it work efficiently. The decentralized model attempts to keep the spot market separate from the system operator, to be organized off-line by traders, as in the wheeling model.

The basic problem of the decentralized model is that it ends up requiring not only private markets for *regular* energy, but also markets for congestion energy, markets for imbalance energy, and markets for ancillary services. All of these markets deal in the same energy, at the same time, in the same place—in other words the same product. In a liquid and efficient market all these *separate* products will be exchanged at the same price, time, and place.

Our view (which we explain in detail in the rest of this chapter) is that the decentralized model does not ensure that the prices of all these different products converge, and creates complexity, bureaucracy, and inefficiency. The integrated model avoids all this and pulls everything together—all the energy for imbalances, congestion, reserves, and spot sales are bought and sold at the spot price determined by the system operator.

transparency and integration helps detect market power problems if they occur, and by underpinning smaller generators, actually militates against market power abuse.

In the remainder of this chapter, we describe the preferred model in more detail and why it is a clear winner. We explain how the way electricity systems must be operated lends itself directly to an integrated set of commercial trading arrangements.

THE INTEGRATED TRADING MODEL

The integrated trading model derives from the operation of the old tight pools in the United States, and the traditional merit order dispatch used by utilities around the world. In advance of the actual time of delivery, traders tell the system operator their basic parameters: the plants from which they wish to generate; the amounts they wish to deliver to and take back from the transmission system in order to meet contract levels; and the prices and quantities at which they are prepared to bid to buy and sell less or more than these amounts. At the time of delivery, the system operator dispatches generators in merit order (i.e., in ascending order of the generator bid prices). This merit order is used in turn by the system operator to calculate spot prices. The spot prices are also the imbalance prices (see Figure 7.4).

This trading model should get to the same solution, that is, the same set of prices paid and quantities scheduled, as a perfectly efficient decentralized trading model. Next we describe why.

Optimization versus Bilateral Trading

Earlier we recommended congestion management through the ISO optimization process, and locational spot prices, with bottleneck fees for scheduled contracts as part of the integrated trading model. First we explain optimization and locational spot prices in more detail. This concept is familiar to electrical engineers and to many in the industry, so they could skip to the next section heading.

FIGURE 7.4 Merit order.

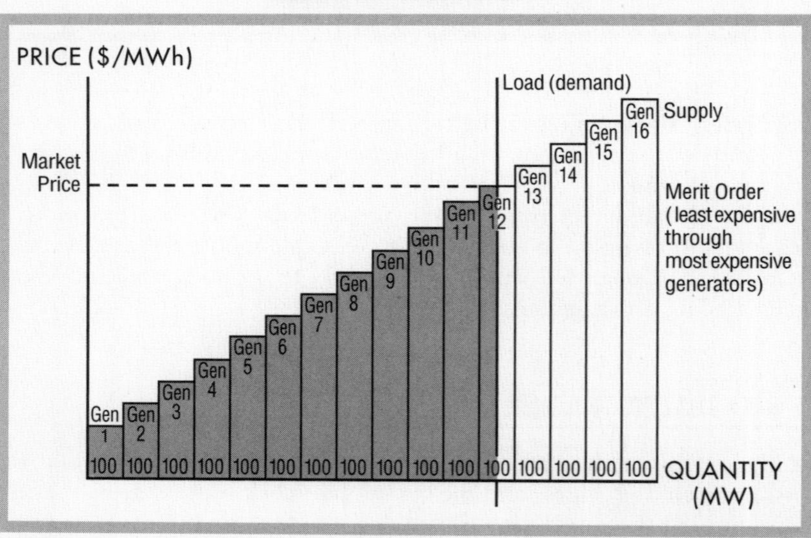

Optimization for Newcomers

Optimizing means *minimizing or maximizing something, subject to constraints.* In ordinary language we put things less formally:

- "He bought as big a house as he could afford" translated into formal terms, reads "He maximized the space he bought, subject to a budget constraint."
- "He was a fanatic about saving money except for the season ticket to the football games" translates as "He minimized expenditures subject to the football constraint."
- "He ran as fast as he could (*maximized his speed*)—although (*subject to the constraint that*) he was recovering from an operation."

There are two things we can note about these examples. In all these cases, we understand that he did not fully maximize or minimize whatever he was doing, because of the constraint—that he did not run as fast as he would have been able to had he not been recovering from an operation, or spend as much as he would have liked without the tight budget, or economized as much as he could have without the love of football. Actually, this is true of all binding constraints—*they prevent the thing that is being maximized or minimized from being as good as it could have been without the constraint.*

The second thing to observe is that it is possible to compute how much the constraint stands in the way of optimizing, but sometimes this requires us to know more about his universe. It may be obvious; if the runner is a champion we might say, "the operation added 25 seconds to his time." But in the other two cases we would need to know his alternatives—if there were no football season maybe he would have had another constraint—hockey perhaps. If he had more money, maybe he would not have spent it all on an even bigger house. We can surely say that the constraint affected the outcome, but it may be quite complicated to say by how much unless we know more. Even in ordinary language, the effect of a particular constraint depends on all the other potential constraints that did not come into play in this particular instance.

So let us see how this plays out in electricity. The system operator wants to *minimize total costs, subject to the constraint of not overloading the transmission system.* Suppose he just had three plants—he minimizes total cost by running the cheapest one first, then the second cheapest, and maybe part of the third. That is a "minimum cost optimization" but it does not need a computer to do it. Now suppose there is a transmission problem that effectively restricts the second plant, so he has to run less of the second and more of the third. He has increased total costs, because he has had to respect the transmission problem, but he has minimized cost insofar as he can (i.e., "optimized subject to the constraint").

Constraints on the Electric System When an electric system has many plants and many potential transmission constraints, the job of seeing what is the minimum cost solution becomes quite complex—one constraint may be important at one moment in time, but when things change slightly, another constraint may come into play.

This is the sort of mathematical problem that graduate students used to struggle with in miniature, before computing power and software became available to solve large real-world problems in seconds. System operators had to struggle with it, too. In the United Kingdom at the time of privatization and the development of the pool, the system operators scheduled the system using a 64k computer, and schematic drawings of the transmission system that they marked up with colors to show potential constraints—the result that was used for operations was called "the Picasso" because it looked like a Picasso drawing. But this is not needed now, because security-constrained dispatch software has now been available for years, as have high-powered computers, and these are used in electric system control rooms all around the globe.

If the software is presented with the problem of *minimizing cost,*[4] *subject to transmission constraints,* it produces a list of generators who should operate, and the level of their output. It also produces spot prices that correspond to the value of additional energy injected or taken—the balancing point of supply and demand bids. And the software is completely neutral about which plant it chooses and what price it puts out.

What relevance has this to competitive electric markets? *Competition produces the least-cost solution if competitive markets work properly. The software emulates the end result of thousands of efficient trades, and ends up at a point where no one would be better off by trading further.*

How is the software used, say in PJM and New York? The traders bid prices (not costs) into the spot market; these prices are *reservation prices*—the minimum price the producers are willing to accept, and the maximum price the buyers are willing to pay. The software is used to decide who will generate, and to produce spot prices. The system operator will buy and sell power at these prices. *At these prices, all generators who bid below the spot price will be generating, and all customers who bid above the spot price will be consuming. Everyone will be happy.*[5] *It is an incentive-compatible system for dispatch, congestion relief, and pricing, all rolled into one.*

---

[4] Including the cost of replacing transmission system losses.

[5] For a fuller explanation, refer to M. Morey, "Power Market Auction Design: Rules and Lessons in Market-Based Control for the New Electricity Industry," prepared for Edison Electric Institute, August 2001.

The system operator does not ask about *costs—he asks for bids.* How the traders bid will depend on the pricing rules and the competitive attributes of the market. The pricing rules in these markets should set the price at the intersection of supply and demand—*the highest supply bid or the lowest demand bid accepted by the system operator.* So there is no need for the traders to bid what they want to get; this is an auction and the market will set the price—they will all be price takers. However, their bids do something else as well—they determine which plants get to generate, *because the software will take all plants whose bid is below the market price.* When the traders in a competitive market strategize about how to bid—given these rules—they say to themselves, "I certainly do not want to generate if the price I am paid is below my marginal costs of operation. But I surely do want to generate if the price would more than cover my operating costs." So, in a competitive market, the incentives are for traders to bid close to their marginal cost; most of the time they will be paid more than this, making a contribution to the investment costs, but because the software implicitly sets the spot price at the highest bid selected, they do not need to add in the overhead when making their bids, and if they do they will not be selected to run as often.

Now it is true that thousands of bilateral trades can come to this same set of prices, and list of generators, given the same underlying cost structures, *if there is full information and time to do all the trades, and if the rules are not somehow restricting trading.* So, say some, why not just let the markets work—"my market is better than your computer program." But the time factor and the network interdependencies are critical here. Conditions change every second: congestion changes, demand changes, and prices change. The PJM software holds an auction every ten minutes. In effect, the system operator does the trading automatically. *An auction is a perfectly good way to run a market—a market does not have to be a series of bilateral trades to be a market. A computer can take the bids and decide the winner just as well as the more old-fashioned type of haggling, and with better results than market makers.*[6] A market does not have to support marketers and middlemen when the same result can be achieved directly. Indeed, bilateral haggling is no guarantee of an efficient, competitive outcome. NASDAQ market makers (brokerage houses) settled a class action suit for $1.03 billion for colluding to overcharge customers in their role as market maker—"doing deals" too expensively.

---

[6] For more on the subject of the trade off between centralized and decentralized, refer to Steven Stoft, *Power System Economics: Designing Markets for Electricity,* IEEE-Wiley Press, November 2001, Chapter 5-3, and R. Wilson, *Market Architecture,* Working Paper Stanford University, June 17, 1999.

There is little disagreement that these prices that come out of the software are the "right" prices, given the bids, which the traders still control—no one tells the traders what to bid. Nor is there much disagreement about the adequacy of the software. There will inevitably be some discretion required from the system operator in certain situations—this should be minimized—and some special procedures built into the pricing software. But these will be the exception, not the rule, and the exceptions should be auditable.

Locational Prices One of the outputs of the optimization process is a set of locational prices for electricity. We have said that if the electric markets had time to do all the necessary trading, they would come to the result of the optimization program. In natural gas, which moves much slower, the result is indeed achieved by trading. Figure 7.5 shows the results of decentralized trading of gas transmission rights, and the prices they have come to when hundreds of separate deals are done. The arrows show the direction of flows on interstate natural gas pipelines in April of 1996, and the natural gas spot price differences between selected points.

FIGURE 7.5 Natural gas spot price differences between select points, April 1996.

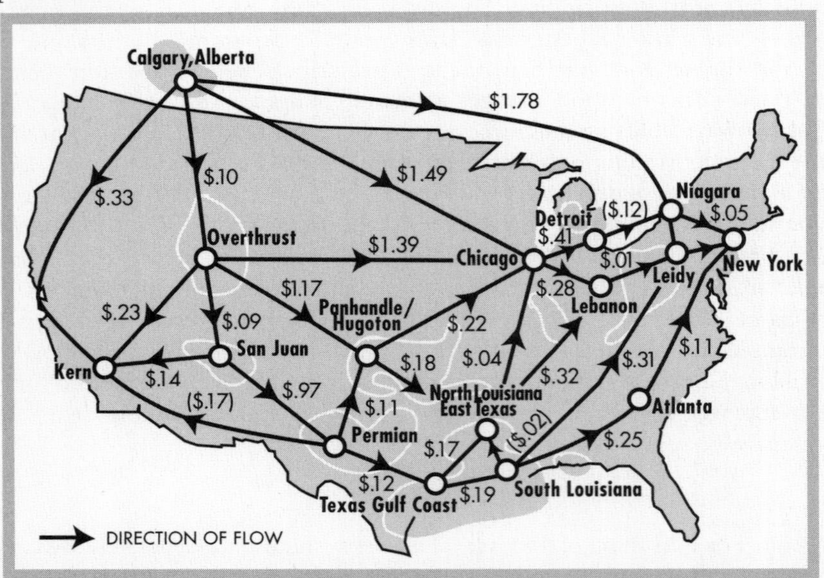

Source: State of the Markets, 2000, Measuring Performance in Energy Market Regulation, Federal Energy Regulatory Commission, March 2000, p. 22.

If we were to start at any particular point and assign a price to the gas (say at Henry Hub, in south Louisiana), we could then add the transport prices from hub to hub and come up with the gas price at any other location.[7] If the gas market has worked efficiently, it will not matter what route we have taken to get there—the gas price at each location will be consistent with that at every other location and related by the cost of transport between them. *Efficient spatial markets will produce a set of locational prices related by the cost of transport between them, or to look at it the other way, the cost of transport will settle at the difference in gas prices between various places. The two things are determined simultaneously.*

The constrained optimization process we have described at length above does this same thing in one pass every 10 minutes for electricity. There are many, many more *nodes* than there are in gas (perhaps one hundred thousand in the United States). If decentralized trading between buyers and sellers could conceivably come to a minimum cost solution every ten minutes that respected changing transmission constraints as they occurred, then we might recommend it, although as we have pointed out, haggling over the price is not the only way to run a market—many modern markets use computers to run auctions. But electricity moves 22 million times faster than gas. Because of the time constraints, and the absolute requirement for operator control, *we prefer without question that the system operator takes the traders' bids and, given those, arrives directly at the best solution.*

Two Ways to Look at the Same Thing It takes a while to see that this concept does the job. Optimization of the dispatch, subject to constraints does not sound much like scheduling contracts for delivery. Figure 7.6 is a picture of a daisy—or is it a Maltese cross? It depends which way you look at it—both are there but you cannot see both at once.

While the idea of delivering power as if it were a simple physical commodity like pork bellies (or grain) is fairly easy to understand (but wrong, in this context) the idea of a constrained optimization program to determine market prices, *given traders' bids and schedules,* does not immediately appeal to the average non-engineer. But this is where the right solution lies.

Apart from the non-intuitive nature of the solution, other objections come from those who hate to give a quasi-governmental, non-profit agency like a system operator so much authority to set the prices—computer program or no. Later, we will suggest that the system operator should be part of a regulated, profit-making entity that also owns transmission, which

[7] If the reader wants to perform this exercise, remember that direction matters—flow against the prevailing flow will have a negative transport price.

FIGURE 7.6 A daisy or a Maltese cross?

would provide better incentives for efficient operation. But there is really no way around the system operator having extensive control—it is the nature of electricity. He has to run the system and the only question is under what rules will he run it? The solution is not to hobble him and tie both hands behind his back, but to hold him accountable for enforcing clear and efficient rules and monitoring the transparency of the markets.

Larry Ruff puts it this way:

> *It is no coincidence that the opposition to system operator-administered real-time markets comes primarily from prospective market-makers and middlemen, who would naturally prefer a market in which market participants cannot function without large amounts of their services. The case is sometimes put just this bluntly. But the more subtle claim is that the system operator has such strong advantages in operating very-short-term markets that if it is allowed to do so its monopoly position will stifle innovation in contract terms, risk-management instruments, settlement processes, etc.*
>
> *There is no doubt that the system operator, as system operator, must have information and systems that give it strong natural advantages in operating very-short-term markets. The system operator must have good information about the system and every significant connected facility, must accept bids/offers to buy/sell energy for system balancing purposes, must issue operating instructions, and must assess*

charges and settle payments with and among market participants. Once the system operator has these capabilities, it is a relatively simple matter to add some machinery to determine market-clearing prices and to compute and manage the corresponding settlement, i.e., to operate a real-time market.

So independent marketers will indeed find it hard to offer very-short-term trading arrangements that can compete with a system operator-administered spot market. But that is just another way of saying that the system operator's integrated spot market/dispatch process is a valuable natural monopoly. This is a good reason to use careful, conscious, logical processes to design, govern and regulate the monopoly system operator. It is not a good reason to prohibit the system operator from operating a spot market just so that market-makers and middlemen can make money—at the expense of market participants and ultimately consumers—doing something that the system operator could do better if allowed to do so.[8]

Imbalances

How do contracts and imbalances work in the integrated model? In any wholesale power market, including the wheeling model and the decentralized model, generators and electricity buyers have reasons to enter into forward contracts, which may be of long-term duration, for the sale and purchase of power. Forward contracts provide generators with a means of hedging their exposure to fluctuations in the spot price of electricity—generators can negotiate a price for their output prior to the moment of producing it. This is particularly important for producers in electricity markets, as compared to markets in other products, because electricity cannot be stored, which leads to wide fluctuations in the spot price.

Of course, a similar situation applies to buyers. Properly structured forward contracts can benefit electricity buyers by providing them with the ability to lock in a fixed price for a fixed quantity of energy well in advance of delivery and consumption. This means that they need only face volatile real-time prices to the extent that their actual energy purchases differ from their forward purchases. Indeed, if a buyer's actual energy usage matches its forward market purchases, it can achieve a perfect hedge against high real-time prices and the benefit of complete price certainty in the face of real-time price volatility.

---

[8] Larry E. Ruff, "Competitive Electricity Markets: One Size Should Fit All," *The Electricity Journal,* November 1999.

Regardless of the market structure, it is normal that the terms of trade for 80 percent or more of the energy physically delivered will be established in forward contracts, prior to the moment of real-time delivery. The remainder is traded in real time, and as we have described previously, there will also be imbalances within the forward contracts.

In the integrated trading model, all differences between contract positions and actual production/consumption, regardless of cause, are traded at the market prices (spot prices) that come out of the system operator's optimization process. Whatever the traders' contract positions going into real time, they are not compelled to do any short-term contract trading to try to re-jig contracts to match updated expectations of actual operations. They are free to do so if they choose, but the alternative is to rely on the spot market to make the best trades. *The forward contracts in the integrated model are financial in nature only, providing only the thing that contracts need to provide: management of price risk.* We devote much of the next chapter to expanding on these concepts.

Congestion Management

What about congestion in the integrated model? We have said that the integrated model produces locational prices that differ by the cost of transport. What is the short-term cost of that transport when it comes to electricity? *It is the cost imposed by the transmission constraints and it is the cost imposed by transmission losses. The locational prices already include the impact of these two items.*

Ignoring losses for the moment, congestion management in the integrated model is, in essence, quite straightforward because the process is integrated with system and market operations. Congestion is solved as an integral part of the calculation of the least-cost dispatch, where cost is defined by generator offers. The system operator uses the information in the voluntary offers and his own knowledge of the physical system to determine the most economical way to operate the system within the physical constraints using the optimization software.

Pricing for congestion (i.e., the price charged for transporting electricity over scarce transmission) is also straightforward. *Traders who schedule contracts across valuable transmission lines are charged a transmission usage charge (a bottleneck fee) being equal to the energy price difference between the two ends of the transaction.* The value to traders of *moving* electricity from point A to point B is, after all, the price of electricity at B minus its price at A. And in the integrated model, the price at B minus the price at A reflects the congestion cost of transporting power from A to B.

Congestion pricing is thus integrated with energy pricing in the integrated model. Again, we devote much of the next chapter to expanding on this concept.

THE WHEELING TRADING MODEL

The wheeling model is interesting because many places are using it as a first step toward competition—most of the United States in fact. (In the United States, basic trading rules for wheeling were set out in Order No. 888, which is described in the second half of this book.) In the wheeling model, large loads such as municipalities arrange for independent generators to supply large blocks of their electricity needs instead of purchasing from the local utility, or alternatively, utilities arrange large blocks of "economy interchanges" between each other—and potentially across third-party transmission systems—to take advantage of regional differences in generation costs.

How the Wheeling Model Works

The trading rules of the wheeling model are all about *access* to the transmission of an integrated utility. The system operator—who is the local vertically integrated utility—figures out how much transmission capacity is needed to meet its own *native load,* and then tells the traders how much of its transmission capacity is spare and thus available for them to use on each transmission path. Native load gets priority, and what is left can be used for wheeling. Given that level of access, the (marginal) competitors trade with each other and, at some point prior to real time, the traders tell the system operator what they expect to do. They schedule flows over the system, naming the origin and destination of the electricity, after first obtaining *physical rights* to use the necessary *contract paths* upon payment of a tariff.

The system operator provides imbalance energy, congestion management, and ancillary services, which are charged at regulated prices. If the transmission system is unable to accommodate all the wheeling schedules, the system operator either reorganizes his own plants' output to allow trading to take place, or he may have to cut the transactions of the competing generators. (This should not happen often since the system operator can choose how much transmission to make available in the first place.) Since the system operator in the wheeling model is part of a vertically integrated utility, it can command sufficient plants to effectively and reliably manage the system.

But the wheeling model is heavily flawed. Because it relies on a system operator who is part of a vertically integrated utility, it does not allow full generation competition. In summary:

- Full competition requires that the system operator be independent of all market participants. But the wheeling model was designed with an integrated system operator in mind.
- The trading arrangements that support wheeling cannot be extended to support full competition. Wheeling just cannot scale up to so many transactions, and if it tries to do so, it uses the transmission network inefficiently.

We explain these problems in more detail next.

Independence of the System Operator

The trading arrangements necessary for full competition require that the system operator be fully independent of the generators (which is not true of the wheeling model). This is because once a generator's entire revenue depends on selling power into the market, the physical gatekeeper to the market has to be seen to be above possible conflicts, and above favoring the generation owned by his employer. It has been widely reasoned that when utilities control monopoly transmission facilities and also have competitive interests in the trading of electricity, they have poor incentives to provide equal quality transmission service to their competitors. This has been the major issue of independent generators in all marketplaces. Since the local utility is the system operator and still owns generating capacity, independent traders must be satisfied that the rules do not lead the system operator to favor his own generation to their detriment. For example, by holding too much transmission capacity back for native load, the local utility could prevent competitors from getting access to customers.

However, under wheeling, a utility system operator with his own plants is needed to provide the imbalances, congestion management, and ancillary services that are required to keep the system running. If the operator is independent, he will no longer control the plants that provide the necessary services. So wheeling has a built-in contradiction: independence of the system operator is required for competition; but if it is achieved, wheeling is not possible because wheeling presumes that the system operator owns generating plant, and if he is independent, he no longer does.

In Part Two we describe how FERC's Order No. 2000 rules were designed to improve the independence aspects of the original Order No. 888

rules in the United States. In particular, the responsibility for calculating how much transmission capacity to make available to traders is separated more fully from the utility system operator. But independence problems remain and there are still other problems with wheeling.

Wheeling Will Not Scale Up

The trading arrangements needed for full generating competition (where all the load is supplied competitively) are different in kind from the rules that are needed for marginal competition.[9] *None of the rules of the wheeling model translate well to full competition.* Full competition in generation requires a market-based framework to deal with scheduling, imbalances, congestion management, and ancillary services—the four pillars of the trading arrangements. A whole set of new rules and agreements are required to replace the old direct controls.

Under wheeling, the native load has first priority in *scheduling*. Native load is the load of the customers served by the vertically integrated utility. Actually, all load is served under all models of trading arrangements—it is the generating plant of the utility, other than that used for off-system sales, that gets the priority under wheeling. This scheduling priority cannot exist under competition.

Under wheeling, the issue of *imbalances* is relatively minor. Normally it is fairly easy for a wheeling customer to remain on schedule: Since wheeling trades are marginal trades, often made across more than one system operator's territory, they can be kept on schedule by the other system operators managing their generating plants in real time so as to keep the flows across control area boundaries at the prescheduled levels. System operators are very good at performing this function. In the instances when there are still imbalances, the imbalance is absorbed by the local system operator's generators at a regulated imbalance price. There are special penalties if imbalances get too high. But this cannot work when the market is truly competitive. The practical reality of electricity is that when almost all energy is bought and sold competitively—it is more than just wheeling of blocks of marginal economy energy—there are going to be quite significant levels of imbalances, and they need to be procured and sold competitively.

[9] The rules for open access enunciated by FERC in Order No. 888 apply best to the wheeling trading model in which the system operator has direct control (ownership or the equivalent) over most of the energy flowing on the system, and where there are few transactions.

The issue of *congestion* is usually relatively minor as well, with marginal trading under the wheeling model. In the wheeling model, congestion is defined as the situation where it is infeasible to use all of the firm physical rights that have been allocated. In the wheeling model, if there is congestion, the system operator has to reschedule his own plants to let scheduled firm transactions through, or follow predefined rules to curtail some of the traders' transactions. (The system operator does not want to reschedule his own plants too often since it adds costs, so he has incentives to calculate available firm physical transmission on a fairly conservative basis—therefore, there is little or no congestion, only a lack of available capacity.) Unfortunately again, the arrangements for congestion management under the wheeling model cannot be extended to full competition. The methods of allocating transmission and dealing with congestion do not scale up to full competition. Under wheeling, a market participant is told that some firm physical capacity along specific contract paths is available for marginal trades. This can work with a few trades in the context of finding *contract paths* across a traditional integrated electric company's service area. The utility just "dispatches around" the extra trades. But it cannot work with almost all energy being traded that way. The problem is that when almost all the energy is being traded, the difference between the transmission route scheduled (the contract path) and the reality of where the energy actually flows is too great for the wheeling rules to remain workable.

And finally, the provision of *ancillary services* in wheeling cannot work either, for full competition. The treatment of ancillary services, particularly operating reserves, in the wheeling model has usually been that the utility system operator wants to charge for the extra operating reserves necessary to support wheeling transactions; but since this generally leads to arguments about the price of these reserves, the users have been allowed to "self-provide." It has never been clear what exactly this means. There have to be operating reserves in particular locations, ready to run in the event of a contingency on the system. A wheeling transaction across a utility territory presupposes that the user does not have reserve plant in the territory, so how can it "provide operating reserves"? The truth is that it does not. If the competitor that is wheeling across a system leaves plant unused as "reserve," it will almost certainly be in the wrong place if needed. The utility effectively backstops the so-called self-provision. The convenient fiction of self-provision may work with a few transactions but cannot work with many; the system operator must have appropriate operating reserves in the right place for emergencies, and will need to be able to procure them without the fiction of self-provision.

The Fallacy of the Contract Path

The wheeling trading arrangements were based on the assumption that the power could be directed to follow a particular path in the network, in breach of the physical laws that dictate the flow of electricity. In practice, when there are many transactions, the difference between the contract paths and the actual flows is too large and unpredictable to be ignored or absorbed by the system operator. With full competition, there is no incumbent utility to adjust its own operations so that the trades will always go through. And there is no easy way for market participants to sort out among themselves who gets to use the transmission so that the people who value it the most use it.

To make matters worse, interactions between different schedules can be large and these interactions would change too quickly to be manageable, as system flows change in real time. The actual flow on any individual line absolutely must be controlled to be less than the capacity of the line, or the line will be destroyed. Yet, if firm physical capacity is allocated very conservatively to cope with the contract path fiction to prevent this happening, the transmission system will be used very inefficiently. Together with the lack of short-term control over generators, all these factors mean that the transmission rights would at best be allocated and used very conservatively—inefficiently—in order to maintain system reliability. This is in fact what is happening in the United States and much of Europe today.

The problems of the wheeling model are compounded when utility service areas are too small—the contract path fiction is exacerbated and the imbalances problem grows exponentially. For a would-be competitor whose transaction has to cross several congested territories, the wheeling model becomes a real barrier to trade. Again, the United States suffers from this problem. Part Two of this book contains a detailed description of the problems with the wheeling model in the United States, and how it has evolved with transmission loading relief (TLR) and other procedures to deal with increasing volumes of transactions and the fiction of the contract path methodology.

THE DECENTRALIZED TRADING MODEL

The decentralized model is half way between the wheeling model and the integrated model. *In this trading model, the system operator is independent of the generators (unlike the wheeling model) but its commercial responsibilities are deliberately minimized.* The aim is to get the system operator out of running integrated markets for spot energy, imbalance energy and congestion management, and to force trading into private markets. NETA (in England) is an example of such a system. So was the intended market design of the California system. (There are many differences between NETA and California, and we only refer here to the conceptual similarities.)

We do not recommend the decentralized model, for the reasons we explain in this section. However, a point to note immediately is that the integrated model can be set up before wholesale markets go live, because it is consistent with the way regulated utilities work, while the decentralized model needs completely new systems.

How the Decentralized Model Works

The decentralized and integrated models are most clearly distinguished by the differing roles of contracts in the procedures used to schedule and dispatch generation. While the integrated model treats the contracts essentially as financial agreements and dispatches generators to minimize overall costs, the decentralized model, like the wheeling model, requires the system operator to schedule the system explicitly using the contracts. The *transaction* is treated as the basic unit to be accommodated in real-time system operations.

In all trading models, market participants can make and trade contracts in diverse markets separate from the system operator. Traders may buy and sell contracts many times, in bilateral trades or on organized markets. They agree as to a quantity of energy to buy and sell, the origin and destination of the energy, the time the transaction will take place, and the price at which they will trade. At some predetermined moment in time prior to real-time operations, however, the system operator has to take over to deliver the contracts. The common feature of the decentralized trading model and the wheeling model is that regardless of how the transactions were arranged, the contract-defined physical plans of the remaining open transactions must be submitted to the system operator, and *he must take the origin and destination of contracts specifically into account in the scheduling and dispatch process*. Each seller must have a buyer, each buyer must have a seller—the amount bought must equal the amount sold. The system operator is not intended to facilitate a spot market—he simply schedules trades that have been arranged elsewhere. The aim of the decentralized model is to leave as much of the trading as possible to the traders. Whereas, in the integrated model, on the day and in real time the system operator makes the trades automatically, following the instructions incorporated in the traders' bids, in the decentralized model the system operator is prevented as far as possible from making efficient trades.

However, with so many trades, there will inevitably be imbalances between the amount actually sent and received under the contracts, and the system operator has to have some arrangements for dealing with these imbalances. And he will also have to deal with congestion.

Imbalances

Like in the integrated model, the system operator in the decentralized model does not own the resources necessary to provide imbalance service. The resources must therefore be acquired on some sort of commercial basis—either through some sort of a short-term "spot" basis, or through some form of longer term arrangement. As to the means of paying providers of imbalance service and charging users, there are two options: regulated prices or market-based prices. One possibility for charging users a regulated price, for example, is the method of the wheeling model; the system operator imposes predetermined (high) penalties on deviations between contract and actual quantities to encourage market participants to minimize such deviations through active short-term contract trading. Arbitrary and high penalties worked in the wheeling model because it assumed that suppliers could match their customers' loads quite precisely in real time. The wheeling model could afford to place stiff penalties on imbalances, knowing that imbalances are easier to manage for marginal trades through a vertically integrated system. But as we described earlier, the wheeling model cannot be extended to full competition where imbalances are prevalent and the system operator owns no assets. And the decentralized model cannot ignore imbalances or assume they are unimportant.

Furthermore, *arbitrary imbalance prices invite gaming*. If the imbalance price is too low, generators would produce less and rely on the imbalances to meet their customers' load. A cheap generator might be better off backing down, creating an imbalance, and relying on a more expensive generator to provide the imbalance energy. Equivalently, consumers would increase their reliance on imbalances, rather than contract at more expensive prices. (And at these low prices no one would want to supply imbalances.) If the price were too high, symmetric problems would arise. Either outcome would result in increased cost to the industry, as the system operator has to manage resources inefficiently to correct the imbalance. Anything other than a market-based imbalance price invites gaming.

The right price for imbalances is a market-based price. A market-based price for imbalance energy is incentive-compatible—a concept described earlier. It means in this case that if the price is low, it is a good thing that the generator reduces output from its contracted level because the imbalance

CINERGY AND GAMING OF IMBALANCES: Under the old system in the United States, which still obtains in some areas, imbalances were repaid under "gentlemen's agreements"—repayment in kind at some other time. But Cinergy, for example, gamed the system by buying imbalances at peak, when the value was high, and repaying off-peak when the value was low. For this it was reprimanded. Far better to have settled each imbalance at a market price, so no one can game and no "imbalance policemen" are needed. Regulated prices for imbalances have the same effect of encouraging gaming—it is only a market price that is incentive-compatible and prevents gaming.

market is a cheaper provider of energy. It means that if the price is high, it is a good thing that the generator increases output from its contracted level because it is a cheaper provider of energy than the alternative imbalance energy providers. And it means equivalent signals are sent to loads.

A market-based price for imbalances is also the right price because it sends the right signals to the contract markets. When market participants sign contracts, contract prices are compared to expected imbalance prices since imbalances are a direct substitute for contracted energy. So if imbalance prices were sending the wrong signals, contract prices would send wrong signals also. This would be to the detriment of investment in generation and of long-term efficiency.

Because the right price for imbalances is a market-based price, it follows that the right form of procurement of imbalances is a market-based one. Furthermore, since transmission system conditions change in real time, it also follows that imbalance markets should clear very frequently and procurement should be short-term (hourly) in nature. *If a decentralized system has market-based imbalance prices, then much of the inefficiency is removed. The imbalance price becomes the price at which the system operator will buy or sell energy, and pretty soon it becomes the de facto spot market.* The generators are able to buy in the imbalance market to meet their contracts if for some reason they are unavailable; the customers do not fear under-using or over-using against their contracts. A decentralized market with a market-based imbalance price comes closer to an integrated market.

However, in England and Wales, the old integrated system was abolished by the new Labour government, and an extreme version of a decentralized system has been introduced that intends to discourage the use of imbalances and force all trading into markets remote from the system operator.

Case Study: NETA and Deliberately Discouraging Imbalances

A feature of the new trading approach (begun in 2001) in England and Wales is that there is no single imbalance price, but both "spill" prices and "top-up" prices, known (somewhat confusingly) as the "System Sell Price" and "System Buy Price," respectively. Spill prices are paid to generators for generation in excess of contract nominations, and to buyers for consumption below contract nominations. Top-up prices are paid by generators for generation below contract nominations, and by buyers for consumption in excess of contract nominations. The trading arrangements are designed to ensure that the spill prices are lower than the top-up prices. The intention behind having two imbalance prices is that it will better encourage generation and load to minimize imbalances.

Example of Contract A: Suppose distribution company A's load is 100 MW more than contracted and generator A's output is 50 MW more than contracted. The system operator therefore needs to call on 50 MW of additional generation from B, with a cost of say \$40/MWh. With a dual imbalance price the system operator might pay (say) \$30/MWh to generator A and charge distribution company A \$50/MWh for its imbalance, even though the marginal value to the system and the cost to the system of each imbalance was actually \$40/MWh. Since generator A received \$10/MWh less than what would otherwise be the market price and distribution company A paid \$10/MWh more than this price, both of them are penalized. In contrast, in a system with a single price for imbalances, both generators would have been paid \$40/MWh and distribution company A would have been charged \$40/MWh for its imbalance.

The rationale for dual imbalance prices is flawed, and the wedge between the prices is arbitrary. The arbitrary wedge encourages generators and loads into short-term contract trading in an attempt to match contracts with output or consumption, thereby incurring unnecessary transaction costs. The transaction costs are unnecessary because these are trades the system operator could have arranged, given its knowledge of generator prices. Under NETA the transaction costs are real and must eventually be recovered through the price of electricity to consumers. NETA is a system designed to promote the interests of traders by increasing these transaction costs! NETA also increases the problems faced by the system operator in short-term management of frequency and network constraints.

Moreover, the prices emerging from NETA are asymmetric: The top-up price for deficits is many times greater (initially over \$100/MWh, since falling to $50/MWh) than the spill price for surpluses (initially often negative, but since stabilizing around $15/MWh). Many companies ensure that they are always spilling power, so that their net generation always exceeds their net contract sales, in order to avoid the punitive top-up price. As a result, the actual pattern of dispatch is affected by arbitrary penalties for imbalances, and does not reflect either a central optimization or efficient contract sales.

Perhaps more importantly, since portfolio generators and large retailers (or large retailing divisions of distribution companies) are able to diversify away much of their risks of imbalances; *a dual cash out price artificially encourages large market participants at the expense of small participants.* In the early days of NETA, small companies closed down their windmills, because the penalties made continued operation uneconomical. Investment in combined heat and power plant has stalled, because the value of spilled power is so low, and the British government is conducting a review of generation powered by renewable fuels, to see whether a special subsidy scheme is required. The owners of such plant have also submitted a proposed reform to NETA that would replace the current dual price system for imbalances with a single imbalance price—but only for renewable generators and other favored technologies.[10]

To design the trading arrangements so as to discourage imbalances is to purposely reduce the transparency of energy markets. Imbalance prices no longer signal efficient contract prices, transaction costs increase, and inefficiency is created. Large market participants are handed an advantage over smaller ones, back-up for small generators and renewables is removed, and consolidation of traders is necessary to internalize risk.

---

[10] In a curious footnote to the NETA reform, the former regulator, Stephen Littlechild, a prominent supporter of NETA, now states, "In most cases . . . it is not clear that a dual cash-out price is called for." Furthermore, ". . . a reduction in the spread of cash-out prices should be welcomed, together with increasing provision for default to a single cash-out price when there are relatively few balancing trades in the opposite direction." (Stephen Littlechild, *The Beesley Lectures on Regulation Series XI,* London England, October 9, 2001.) These suggested improvements in NETA's balancing mechanism would move NETA back toward the principles of the integrated marketplace, which was what NETA was set up (at a huge cost) to get away from.

Congestion Management

Congestion management in the decentralized model can occur in one of three ways:

1. There is something akin to the wheeling model where a finite number of transmission rights are issued, corresponding to the system capacity. (These types of rights are known as *physical transmission rights or PTRs.*) Traders then trade these with each other while making energy contracts, and use them to match with their energy contracts. The system operator then checks that a matching PTR is held before allowing a trader's contracted energy transaction to proceed.
2. There are allocation rules, such as first-come-first-served, or some other means of rationing transmission if the preferred schedules of all traders cannot feasibly fit on the transmission system at once.
3. There is an auction for available transmission capacity.

Without going into the details, which could fill a chapter by themselves, option 1 is unworkable in practice for the same reasons that wheeling cannot be extended to full competition. Network interactions of transmission systems are too great. It is not possible to come up with a set of PTRs so that (1) any PTR is always usable, no matter how all the others are being used, and (2) the PTRs allow the system to be used to its fullest potential. And in any event, option 1 relies on short-term trading of PTRs by traders as conditions change in real time. Yet traders are not system operators and don't see the big picture. Again, it is unworkable for full competition.

Allocation rules don't work either. For example, first-come-first served does not work—PJM tried it and everyone programmed their computers to submit bids at 12:00 precisely.

The third option, while still flawed, holds more promise. The decentralized model works best when the means of rationing scarce transmission is to run an auction. The auction determines which traders get to use the transmission bottleneck, and the price they will pay for that right. But again, in real time, there has to be a way for the system operator to manage the system.

Regardless of the means of congestion management, after the final schedule changes have been made to solve for congestion, the next step is the physical dispatch of generators in real time. In the concept of the decentralized model, the system operator will only deviate in the dispatch from the final contract schedules if he needs to do so in order to maintain system security, and he may not make efficient trades even if the traders ask him to, since there is no bidding mechanism for them to use to ask him. (In practice, some of the "decentralized" models do allow the system operator to make these trades, because it is so clear to everyone that it is desirable.)

The Decentralized Model Is Workable, but Has Problems

The decentralized model can work reasonably well if it is designed properly. It is capable of delivering competition if it includes *market-based congestion management solutions,* and *market-based imbalance solutions.* It certainly can be designed poorly, as the California effort is testimony (see Appendix C) but California should not be used to discredit the underlying philosophy. The decentralized model can achieve outcomes that the wheeling model cannot.

But, like the wheeling model, the decentralized model revolves around the notion that transactions should be physically scheduled, that buyers and sellers should be matched. The problem is that this matching is a fiction. Under any trading arrangement, the consumer just uses what he wants, and where those particular electrons come from is immaterial. So there is no particular reason to insist that contracts should be matched. The fact is that generators are delivering electricity to an enormously complicated marketplace (the transmission system) administered by a system operator, and customers are drawing electricity from the same complicated system. The reality of where the electrons are flowing within the marketplace is a mystery to everyone but the system operator. To insist that individual contracts be matched, and that individual contracts form the basis for scheduling and dispatch, is to unnecessarily constrain the process by which the market selects the lowest cost set of generators to meet load.

- It means that sometimes expensive generators are running because loads didn't know a cheaper generator was available; and
- It means that sometimes inexpensive generators are held back, in case they are needed for imbalances or congestion management, while more expensive generators belonging to others are running to meet contract requirements.

The decentralized model ends up requiring separate markets for congestion energy, imbalance energy, "regular" energy, and also for reserves. All of this is the same energy, at the same time, in the same place, and therefore, the same product. In an efficient market they should all be at the same price—the decentralized model creates complexity, bureaucracy, and inefficiency and does not ensure that the prices converge.

Marketers and brokers love the opportunities for arbitrage that such inefficiency creates—but the electricity industry is for the benefit of consumers, not traders.

ANCILLARY SERVICES

At the beginning of this chapter, we described ancillary services as one of the pillars of market design. Ancillary services are a "common good"; everybody using the transmission system shares them. The system operator must procure ancillary services on behalf of all users. Ancillary services arrangements are important and require careful handling, but here we will give it no more than a cursory visit.

In the United States, FERC has named six ancillary services:

1. Scheduling, System Control, and Dispatch Service;
2. Reactive Supply and Voltage Control from Generation Sources Service;
3. Regulation and Frequency Response Service;
4. Energy Imbalance Service;
5. Operating Reserve—Spinning Reserve Service; and
6. Operating Reserve—Supplemental Reserve Service.

These were the old system services that the utilities wanted to charge for in the fights over access—the extra costs that the vertically-integrated utilities incurred in wheeling. Note that imbalances are included in this list, although we earlier argued they should now be integrated into the spot market. Scheduling/control/dispatch is not really an ancillary service—or at least not a very interesting one—in that these functions can only be provided by the system operator. So in fact ancillary services boils down to frequency response, operating reserves, and reactive supply. In a book of this length we will ignore reactive supply, except to say that the needs for it are very localized. Some markets have added "black start" to the list of ancillary services—this is the capability required of some generators to restart the transmission system after a catastrophic failure—but we ignore this also because it is fairly uncontroversial.

Frequency response and operating reserves are therefore where most attention is focused.

Operating reserve is available capacity on generating plant that is able to run at short notice. Since the load goes up and down over the course of the day, and electricity cannot be stored, the number of plants actually generating is continually changing. Reserves are usually held on those plants that are about to start, or those that have just finished. They can be called into early (or late) operation at short notice if something unforeseen happens, such as a generator outage or transmission line outage. For system stability, the system operator needs operating reserves (depending on the size of the system) of about 7 percent to 10 percent of load.[11]

Frequency response, or regulation reserve is capacity that continually adjusts output at very short notice (every few seconds) based on instructions from the system operator, who uses it to ensure that supply always exactly equals demand from second to second. It is used to accommodate continual changes in load, and to cope at *very* short notice with anything that goes wrong with generators or with transmission, before operating reserves can kick in. Most of the time, regulation reserves are held on plants that are already running, and are a part of the operating reserve.

When a generator provides reserves, it incurs two types of cost:

1. *Operating costs:* Additional standby costs that would not otherwise be incurred if it was shut down; extra fuel costs from not running at optimal output; and extra wear and tear from having to modify operations suddenly.
2. If, by providing reserve, the generator is held back from profitably selling energy into spot energy markets it incurs an additional *opportunity cost,* equal to the profit foregone.

These reserves are not a separate service from energy—*they are options to buy energy if required.* They should be priced as options to call energy in the spot market. The way that options are priced in commodity markets is through the combination of an option fee (for standing ready) and a strike price (payment) if the option is called. Most of the time plants will not need to be paid terribly high option fees. The operating costs involved are quite a low proportion of total costs and the system operator, by minimizing total cost, should avoid holding back low cost plants for reserves, except in special circumstances. All up, ancillary services costs should be in the order of 1 percent to 3 percent of total costs.

In both the integrated and decentralized trading models, markets should exist for procurement of those ancillary services where competition is possible; others should be procured on a longer term cost-based/contract basis. Short-term markets are easiest for operating reserve and regulation reserve. Procurement of these reserves should be integrated with the least

[11] There are various types of reserve within the category of operating reserves. Here we simplify.

cost dispatch of the spot market (or the imbalance market, in the case of the decentralized model):

- Offers to sell these services should be simultaneous and of a consistent format with offers to the spot/imbalance market.
- The system operator should evaluate these offers and the energy offers simultaneously.

Market-based prices for reserves are not absolutely essential. PJM has done quite well with only frequency response being market-based, relying on some pay-as-bid rules for operating reserves when needed. Establishing competitive short-run markets in ancillary services—as opposed to more simplistic long-term arrangements—is laudable, but complicated, and adds less value than making sure the spot market is right. *It is essential, however, that procurement of reserves be integrated with the imbalance market, and that providers of reserve recover any opportunity costs they incur from following system operator instructions.*

Furthermore, and regardless of procurement method, the rules for allocating ancillary services cost to system users should be clear. The simple way is to divide the costs equally, but the more efficient way is to allocate some of them according to who created the need—reserve charges to those generators who fail in operation, reactive power charges to those who create the need for reactive power, and so on. Costs should also be allocated to exports and wheel-through transactions (i.e., loads at transmission system boundaries).

There is no sense in permitting self-provision of ancillary services because all market participants share ancillary services. Market participants who want to self provide should give operational control of their ancillary services over to the system operator, and the system operator should treat them like other providers. It should then allocate costs back to market

> **EXPERIENCE IN CALIFORNIA:** California established five separate markets for reserves, which worked incredibly badly. The reserves were not priced as options—they were priced as if reserves were a separate product in five independent markets. This does not work in theory and it turns out it did not work in practice either. The five markets were supposed to be run in order of the "value" of the reserves, but the prices were frequently reversed and capacity was frequently allocated inefficiently.

participants on a "net" basis, deducting the value of any services "self-provided" in this way.

SUMMARY OF TRADING MODELS

	Wheeling	Decentralized	Integrated
System operator	Utility operator	Independent operator	
Scheduling	Matched schedules		Contracts plus generator bids
Imbalances	Regulated price from system operator	Imbalance market	Integrated with spot market
Congestion	Rules exist for access to spare transmission capacity.	Congestion market (with bottleneck fees) or tradable transmission rights	Integrated with spot market
Market (spot) price	No	Short-term contract trading/Imbalance market	Yes
Custome response	No price response in the trading arrangements, only in the contracts		Demand bidding
Reserves	Regulated price from system operator	Reserve markets, preferably integrated with imbalance market	Reserve markets, integrated with spot market
Transmission rights *	Physical rights Regulated prices	Physical or financial rights	Financial rights

*Refer to Chapter 9 for details of transmission rights.

Wheeling Model

If the goal is full generation competition, then wheeling won't work. It is only useful for marginal trading:

- The system operator must own generation, so not all generators are subject to forces of competition. Consequently the market can not be fully competitive.

- The system operator is not fully independent, so independent generators are always suspicious.
- If all generators were independent and subject to competition, the system operator would not be able to provide imbalances.
- If all generators were independent and subject to competition, the system operator would not be able to efficiently allocate transmission capacity, or to efficiently manage congestion.

Decentralized Model

The decentralized model is an outgrowth of the wheeling model in which the system operator is independent:

- Consequently, new mechanisms for congestion management and imbalances are required. The model will only work properly if these are market based.
- The model is often defended by a flawed argument against integration of system operations and market operations.
- In order to work, separate markets are relied upon to come together to provide consistent outcomes—within short time frames and over complex electrical systems.
- The model is workable, but it is complex and can be inefficient.

Integrated Model

The integrated model solves the problems of the other models by integrating system operations and market operations, and by integrating markets for energy, imbalance, congestion management, and reserves.

- It is conceptually simple and it works in practice. It requires only minimal changes from the way the system was operated under vertical integration.
- It relies on traders giving instructions to an independent system operator prior to real time, and the system operator conducting system and market operations in real time consistent with everyone's instructions.
- It recognizes the unique nature of electricity and does not rely on contract path approximations, or an artificial requirement that contracts be matched.
- Contracts between traders are financial in nature, providing management of price risk, and do not interfere with system operations.

Case Study: New Zealand

In many ways, the New Zealand market design has been at the forefront of best practice. Furthermore, the electricity reform process in New Zealand involved extensive consideration of the essential ingredients of market design and the experience in other countries. The New Zealand electricity market provides fundamental design elements needed to support competition in generation and supply. A key feature of any such market is the use of a coordinated spot market to handle balancing, transmission usage, and security requirements. The New Zealand spot market includes a bid-based, security-constrained, economic dispatch with fully locational prices for real-time decisions. The bids summarize the preferences of the market participants and ensure that the final dispatch choices respect those preferences. The security constraints preserve the conditions needed to ensure reliable operations. The principles of economic dispatch define both the traditional engineering practice and the results of a competitive equilibrium. In this regard, the New Zealand model for real-time operations is aligned with the best international practice for a competitive electricity market.

Source: William Hogan, *Electricity Market Restructuring: Reforms of Reforms,* May 2001, 20th Annual Conference, Harvard University Center for Research in Regulated Industries, Rutgers University. (By "market design," Hogan is referring to trading arrangements here and not to requirements for competition in general.)

CHAPTER 8

Details of the Integrated Trading Model

The existence of a visible spot price is central to efficient operations; we have named some of the reasons earlier:

- It permits incentive-compatible handling of imbalances and congestion.
- It induces least-cost operation by being the de facto penalty for unavailable plants.
- It can be used in the pricing for final customers, permitting real-time price response and increasing reliability.
- It permits small plants to enter the market because they have automatic back up if the plant is unavailable. This reduces market concentration.
- The spot price feeds back into the contract market; the expected value of the (future) spot prices determines the contract price. Therefore, the spot price is an important determinant of the willingness of investors to construct new generating capacity.

If efforts are made to move spot trading out of the system operator and into private markets, not only does the spot price become much less transparent and therefore much less efficient at doing all these tasks, but also the inevitable rules necessary to suppress the system operator's imbalance market will drive traders to consolidate, increasing concentration. Together with the other factors we reasoned in the previous chapter, the preferred trading model is therefore the integrated model, in which short-run market and system operations are integrated.

This chapter describes in more detail how it works, and in particular, the role of spot market prices in the integrated trading model. We describe how prices must be set in the spot market so as to induce generator entry when it's needed, and the way forward contracts are handled. We expand on the description of how congestion management is dealt with and how locational prices come about. We describe the issues of prices that vary by location, different ways generators can offer their capacity to the system operator, and the potential benefits of system operator run day-ahead markets.

SETTING THE RIGHT SPOT PRICE

The spot market price must, in an efficient market, reflect the interaction of supply and demand. *The price in any competitive market, for any product, is set by the highest cost supplier actually selling product when there is plenty of supply, and by the marginal (lowest value) demand actually served when the supply is constrained.*

Sometimes, even when there is plenty of capacity available, the price can be high enough that some customers choose not to consume. This is just a normal interaction of supply and demand, familiar in other industries (see Figure 8.1).

Prices Must Be High Enough to Induce Entry

If the spot price in the market reflects the marginal cost of the last generator selected (which it will when supplies are available, that is, most of the time) how do generators ever get paid for their investment costs? There are two answers: Generators with lower running costs will make a profit from the market prices set at the highest bid—and this is a contribution to the

FIGURE 8.1 Normal supply and demand.

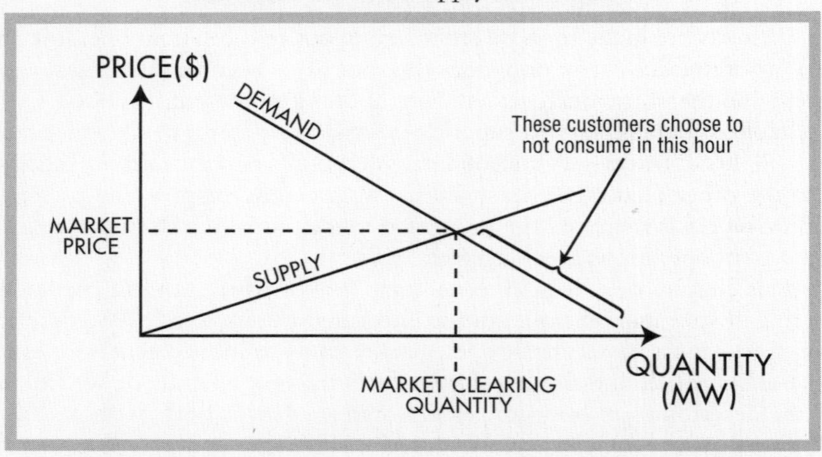

investment costs. But what of the last generator—how can he cover his investment? *The prices need to rise at the peak times to provide enough to cover the investment of the last generator on the system—and in fact it can be shown that all the generators need this amount to recover their investment.* It is the prospect of these returns that induces generators to invest.

What exactly happens in a market when prices are constrained by demand? One thing that happens is that when supplies get tight the price rises, eliciting a reduction in load. The price level that is required to achieve the necessary reduction sets the clearing price. In this way the price can rise above the marginal cost of the most expensive generator (see Figure 8.2).

When the price rises frequently enough or high enough that it is profitable to construct more capacity, the supply side of the market will respond. *The resultant prices and quantities of supply are those that are consistent with both consumer willingness to pay and producer willingness to sell.*

It is much easier to reflect generators' willingness to supply than it is to reflect customers' willingness to pay in designing the real-time markets for electricity. Generators bid different prices into the spot market to get dispatched. But most of the time customers simply take and are never asked about what they want. Yet even though it is difficult, it is a major error not to design into the market some direct or proxy form of price response. California did not do it. Retail customers saw—or were led to believe in—an infinite supply of electricity at a fixed price, and the wholesale

FIGURE 8.2 Price rises and consumers respond to supply shortage.

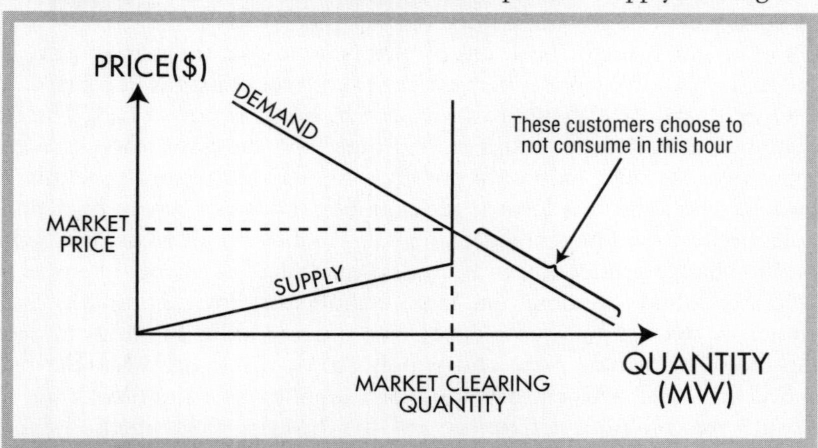

prices rose to amazing heights, far above what most customers would have been willing to pay, if only they had known and been able to respond.

Methods of Ensuring the Spot Price Is High Enough

There are three workable methods of ensuring that prices rise in times of tight supply to the level set by demand—demand bidding, a capacity payment, or a system of capacity obligations with capacity markets.

Demand Bidding Demand bidding refers to the normal intersection of a downward sloping demand curve with an upward sloping supply curve, such as in the diagrams just illustrated and repeated from Chapter 4. The

Demand Bidding in PJM

In PJM, demand bidding works like this: The system operator runs a day-ahead market where both the buyers and sellers make price-dependent bids, and the market price is set by the intersection of supply and demand. Accepted bids into this market are a binding financial commitment (i.e., a contract); if you do not do as you said, you cash out the difference at the real time price the next day.

In the day-ahead markets any customer can potentially make a price-dependent bid, and this bid could end up setting the market price, depending on the interaction of supply and demand. In real-time markets, in a pilot program in 2002, the only demand that can bid is that of customers who agree to be *dispatchable,* that is, they agree with the system operator to reduce load when the real-time price reaches their reservation level (or in the event of an emergency). Their cut-off prices do not set the market price, although they can influence it because the total level of load is decreased.

Overall, the PJM method is not perfect, but it is not so bad. The customers who agree to be cut off in real time (and the ones who cease consuming because their bids were not accepted day-ahead) are generally the ones whose valuation is lowest; for example, industries where high prices for electricity would be really detrimental—so they decide to use the opportunity to change production runs, or do something less energy-intensive.

In the United Kingdom, one large manufacturer, within months of the competitive market going into effect, had ordered all its factories to determine their reservation price and simply stop consuming when the price reached that level. This cut demand when supplies were tight *but it did not feed back into the price determination*—the PJM day-ahead method does.

interaction of supply and demand sets prices that ensure that customers are not overcharged and that generators are willing to build when new capacity is needed—that is what markets are about. With demand bidding in electricity markets, the customers or their representatives (the distribution companies or retailers, or large customers who participate in the process directly) bid for what they want to take and participate in setting the price.

Markets elicit supply and ration demand, but for reasons described in Chapter 4, the methods of rationing demand in existing U.S. competitive electricity markets are not yet working. Where programs are in place, for example, PJM, they are tiny. While the system operator has direct control over the generators, for the vast bulk of the load, he cannot control what they take, either directly or by calling them up to request reductions. Overall, demand curves are nearly vertical; demand bids don't exist, and can't set the price. The markets rely on generators bidding above marginal cost to get the price high enough, but since demand curves are vertical, they could bid far too high in times of scarcity. We have already described in Chapters 4 and 5 how this might make price caps necessary, until there is demand response.

It is a real priority for existing U.S. markets to get demand response and has largely been ignored. But what about other interim measures to make sure that prices are high enough to start with, to make sure that enough generators choose to stay in the market to reliably serve this unresponsive load? One option is to do nothing. California did nothing and generators certainly bid the prices up. Other U.S. markets have been forced to address the issue by imposing capacity obligations on load-serving entities. Outside of the United States, some markets have used *capacity payments.*

Capacity Payments The whole concept of *capacity* as being somehow separate from energy may be unique to electricity. It derives from the correct notion (explained more fully in Appendix E) that charging the marginal cost at all hours will, in a well-planned system, give generators just enough revenue if they also charge the "marginal cost of capacity" (the investment costs not recovered through marginal cost pricing) at peak times. This well-known theorem was the underpinning for marginal cost tariffs and for the rules of the tight pools. Utilities could buy and sell to each other at marginal cost, so long as either each utility held sufficient capacity of its own, which it charged to its captive customers; or so long as it paid another utility a "capacity payment" for using the other utility's capacity.

In the early competitive trading arrangements, like Argentina and the U.K. Pool, there was concern that the generators would not bid the price high enough to cover the cost of capacity. In the case of Argentina, the generators were only permitted to bid their marginal costs; in the United Kingdom, the worry was that with bids being made more than a day ahead, there would be no way for the generators to know that this was the day to bid higher. So capacity adders were included in the market prices in both places. The form adopted in the United Kingdom set the market price as the highest bid unless there was some probability of shortage, in which case the "value of lost load" (VOLL, an estimate of the value to consumers) came into play. The price was the weighted average of the highest bid and the VOLL, weighted by the probability that there would be a shortage: (highest bid) × (1–LOLP) + VOLL × LOLP. This formula also acted as a price cap of VOLL if the system was actually short of power.

However, there is no need for a capacity payment adder if the generators can bid up the price; and having such an adder can make the price too high. (In the long run, this will induce entry and push the price back to a proper market price by reducing the number of times the adder comes into effect, but in the short run the price can just be too high.) If there is an adder, it should be designed to reflect the value of the plant to the system, it should rise when supplies are tight and disappear when there is plenty of capacity; that is, it should simulate a market price.

Capacity Obligations Some of the rules of the new electricity markets, notably in the Northeast United States, have instead included installed reserve requirements, or *capacity obligations,* with associated *capacity markets.* These are an extension of the supply adequacy rules of the regulated regime.

The capacity obligation method works by requiring all load serving entities that serve final customers to acquire *capacity tickets.* The tickets can be acquired in capacity markets:

- The entities that serve final customers must buy enough tickets to cover the expected peak load of their customers, multiplied by (1 + X).
- X is calculated as a reserve margin, sufficient to meet some preplanned level of reliability to cope with random generator outages and so on that might otherwise cause customer outages if they occur at peak times.
- The people who sell the tickets must be generators. They must meet certain eligibility criteria, they must agree to make their generation available to the market under certain conditions defined by the system operator, and usually they must agree to some sort of system operator coordinated scheduling of maintenance.

In practice, capacity markets are workable but there are problems. The model relies on an administrative forecast of demand, which is problematic. They don't deal with retail competition very well because retailers' loads and reserve requirements change too quickly. There are policing

Theoretical Equivalence between Capacity Payment and Capacity Obligation Methods

In theory, there is an equivalence between expected prices in markets with capacity obligations and those using capacity payments based on VOLL × LOLP. In the capacity obligation method, capacity prices should settle at a level such that the marginal provider of capacity just recovers his costs. In the VOLL × LOLP model, VOLL × LOLP should settle at a level where VOLL × LOLP both provide just enough revenue so that the marginal provider of capacity recovers his costs, and the real level of likelihood of outages, LOLP, is acceptable to customers given those prices. Put another way, installed capacity obligations specify a required *quantity* of reserve capacity, which the capacity market converts into a *price* for capacity. It comes from the opposite direction to the LOLP × VOLL method, which specifies a *price* rule for reserve capacity from which the market decides the *quantity* of capacity to build.

---

and other problems with the sellers of capacity, because it is difficult to produce incentive-compatible capacity market rules. Generators who are being counted as reserve may sell the same capacity in another market, meaning it is not available in the first market when a generator outage or other problem arises.

In the long term, demand bidding is certainly the best solution, but in the *transition* to a fully competitive market, other mechanisms—in particular capacity payments that are related to the need for capacity in each hour—can do the job quite well.

Transition to Demand Response

Because of the steepness of the end of the supply curve (see Figure 5.5) a very small reduction in electric load from demand response can reduce the price a lot at peak periods. Consumers' refusal to consume sometimes caps the price by preventing suppliers from bidding it up. In other words, you get a big bang for a small buck on dynamic pricing response from demand. California experienced high prices and rolling blackouts in 2000 with only a few percentage points shortfall in supply, which would easily have been offset by virtually any system of customer response to the incredibly high wholesale prices—but there was none because the customers were all "benefiting" from regulated (frozen) retail prices, by order of the legislature.

Demand bidding does two things. It raises prices when supplies are tight, and this properly induces new investment. It also stops generators bidding up prices to excessive levels. Capacity payments and capacity obligations do not limit prices the same way. Arguably, by encouraging enough plants into the market, they reduce the number of times supply is tight. But they do nothing to limit prices in any particular hour in which supplies are tight, and hence the potential role of transitional price caps. Without them, when supply is tight, the generators could potentially bid as high as they like, and push the price up as they did in California, without limit. Then some regulator will cap the price at *cost* and not permit the peak prices that are necessary to induce investment.

TREATMENT OF CONTRACTS

Forward Contracts Provide Risk Management

We described in Chapter 6 that hourly variations in demand, a lack of storage, and a lack of customer response to changing conditions lead to extreme variations in hourly spot prices. In most markets in which supply and demand vary over time, inventories are relied upon to balance the market; often there will not be enough production capacity to serve all demand at all times, so inventories are drawn down during periods of high demand and replenished during low demand periods. As a result of inventory management in these markets, potential price differences over time are largely arbitraged away, and substantial price changes only occur as a result of some major unanticipated event with a major impact on demand or supply. But this doesn't usually happen in electricity markets and consequently *spot electricity prices are volatile.* (See, for example, Figure 8.3.) The lack of demand response exacerbates the problem.

The volatile short-term prices lead most (risk averse) people to want to enter into forward contracts. Both buyers and sellers need to contract, and they trade in the forward markets to do so. Customers do not need to be exposed to the short-term prices for all their purchases—in most electric markets 80 percent or more of the volume is under contract.

In the integrated model, traders can still make forward contracts in private and bilateral markets, just like they do in the wheeling and decentralized models. In the integrated model, the MW quantities, physical locations, and timing specified in each contract (the contract schedule) must be notified to the system operator only if one or both of the following conditions hold:

1. The traders in the contract prefer that the contract be inflexible; and/or
2. The trading arrangements require net settlement.

FIGURE 8.3 PJM west hourly prices ($/MWh), November 1999 to August 2000.

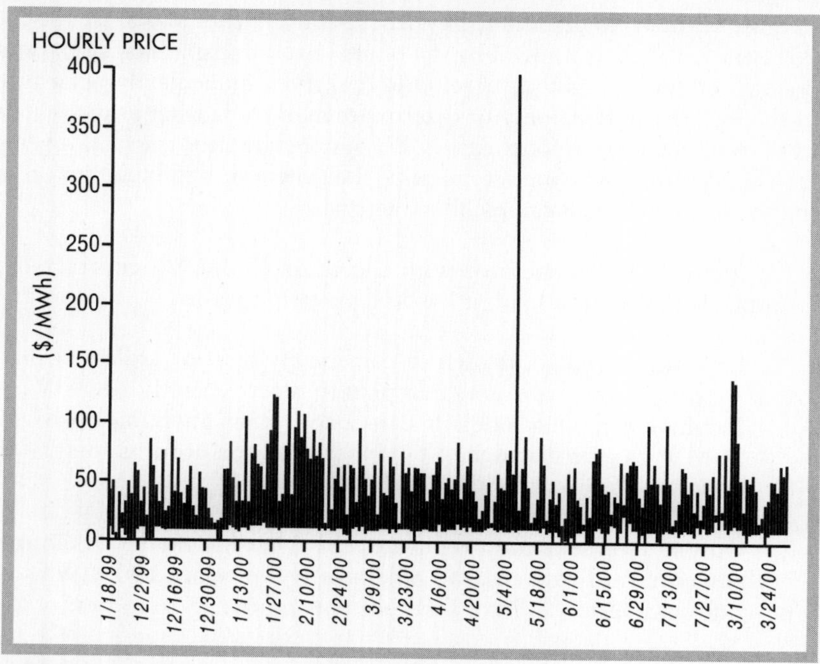

Source: PJM.

Otherwise, it is not necessary for the system operator to know anything about the forward contracts. We describe how this works and exactly what "inflexible" and "net settlement" mean next.

Offers Can Be Flexible or Inflexible

How do traders in the integrated model make contracts, but still take advantage of opportunities presented by the integrated model for the system operator to find mutually beneficial (cost-saving) deals in the spot market? In the integrated trading model, some time prior to real-time, traders can submit information to the system operator indicating their willingness (or unwillingness) to modify physical operations in response to real-time prices.

This information is represented by offer prices and offer quantities.[1] The system operator uses the offers of all traders (those with contracts, together with those without) to determine physical operations that maximize the economic benefit to all, as implied by the offers, given transmission constraints and actual conditions as they develop in real time. Immediately prior to or after the fact, the system operator determines market-clearing prices that are used to settle accounts among traders. If a system operator instructs a generator to deviate from its contract quantity, the generator will be better off for doing so. The following example illustrates why.

> If a 150 MW generator with a cost of $30/MWh contracted to supply 100 MW to a load, it has at least two options:
>
> 1. Make an *inflexible* offer. It can specify that, regardless of price, the system operator should plan to receive exactly 100 MW.
> 2. Make a *flexible* offer. It can specify that anything up to 150 MW can be dispatched by the system operator, as long as the spot price exceeds $30/MWh.
>
> Option 1 (inflexibility) replicates the wheeling model. As long as nothing untoward happens, the generator will produce 100 MW as per his contract. Option 2 (flexibility) presents more opportunities:
>
> - If the spot price falls to $20/MWh, the generator will not be dispatched by the system operator, and will meet its contract by purchasing electricity (i.e., imbalances) in the spot market. It will save $1,000 doing this because the market is $10/MWh less expensive than its own cost for the 100 MW.
> - Alternatively, if the spot price rises above $30/MWh to $40/MWh, the system operator will dispatch all 150 MW of the generator and the generator will have sold an extra 50 MW (i.e., of imbalances) into the spot market for an extra profit of $500.
>
> In all circumstances, the generator is better off being flexible than being inflexible. Indeed, in practice in the integrated markets that are operating, much of the generation is offered as flexibly as its production characteristics allow. The model is incentive-compatible because

[1] For simplicity, we use the terms *bid* and *offer* interchangeably to describe this process, although this usage is not strictly typical of the terminology used in the finance industry.

it rewards this flexibility. It aligns the incentives of generators with what is best for the industry (and society) as a whole.

Because the system operator has information on the prices at which market participants are willing to buy or sell energy, it is not even relevant for the system operator to know the contract schedules directly. The system operator will only know about a contract if the traders involved have chosen to be inflexible. Otherwise, market participants can submit offer prices and quantities and the system operator can identify the opportunities for profitable trades. In its simplest form, when all market participants are flexible—willing to modify operations from their contracted levels if profitable—the system operator's dispatch is fully separate from the forward contracts. *The forward contracts then become financial in nature only, providing only the things they were intended to provide in the first place: management of price risk.* The system operator dispatches generators in ascending order of offer price until all load is served. The offer price of the last flexible generator accepted becomes the imbalance price. The market-clearing quantities and prices from the spot market establish a set of real-time imbalance trades among market participants that the system operator automatically identifies, schedules through its dispatch process, and settles through its settlement process.

The mechanics and results of real-time operations are very different in the integrated model compared to the wheeling model, even if the contracts between traders are identical in all commercially relevant respects. Traders in the integrated model coming into real time know that they will be able easily to *cash out* at market-clearing prices any imbalances between their final contract positions and their actual physical operations. Thus, whatever the contract position going into the day—or even if the trader has no contracts at all—no one is compelled to do any short-term contract trading either prior to the day or during the day, although traders are free to do so if they choose. Instead of submitting his contract position or desired operating schedule to the system operator and then making adjustment transactions in external contract markets as real-time approaches, a trader can rely on the spot market to make the best trades. In other words, traders *can* make inflexible offers if they wish to stick to the contracted levels, or they can make them flexible if they want to take advantage of profitable trades, identified by the system operator, that might arise.

This also means that system operations are essentially unchanged in the integrated model from those in the vertically integrated old world. This can make the transition to full competition much less painful than if the wheeling or decentralized trading model is used, where new methods of operations must be built to accommodate contract trading up to the last minute.

Comparison: PJM, NETA, New York, and Inflexible Contracts

Traders are free to make inflexible schedules in PJM. However, PJM gives all generators an opportunity to participate in the imbalance market by submitting adjustment bids to an auction that is based on a least-cost security-constrained dispatch. In principle, this leads to a least-cost solution overall since PJM's locational spot prices give contracted traders an incentive to be flexible.

NETA (England and Wales), on the other hand, does not provide an opportunity for all generators to participate in such a real-time market because, as we described earlier, the balancing process is only used to adjust for imbalances between aggregate supply and demand and transmission constraints, and it violates the law of one price.

New York is very similar to PJM. In New York, whose market had its first full year of operation in 2000, inflexible schedules known as *physical bilaterals* accounted for as much as 60 percent of the market at the start of the year. By the end of the year, the proportion had fallen to closer to 40 percent (see Figure 8.4). *Note:* This fall does not indicate that forward contracting has declined since *financial* contracts executed through the day-ahead market may have increased, but it does indicate that generators have chosen to be more flexible.

Settlement Can Be Net or Gross

The original U.K. Pool used a system known as *gross settlement.* Under gross settlement, contracts are settled between participants after the real-time dispatch. This form of contract is known as a *contract for differences* because it "undoes" a trade at the market price, and replaces it with a transaction at the contract price.[2] The United Kingdom used this method because the system operators did not want to have to settle contracts.

Under *net settlement,* the system operator is made aware of the contract schedules between market participants. The contract schedules are used for financial settlement, not for physical dispatch: Imbalances are calculated

[2] A Contract for Differences (CfD) is an agreement to pay the difference between the market price and the contract price. A CfD acts as fixed price contract—either the seller pays the buyer (if the market price is above the contract price) or the buyer pays the seller (if the contract price is above the market price).

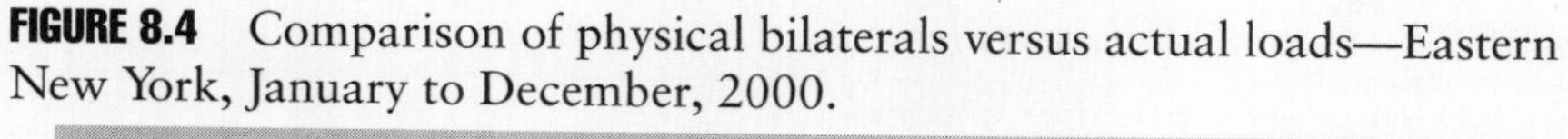

FIGURE 8.4 Comparison of physical bilaterals versus actual loads—Eastern New York, January to December, 2000.

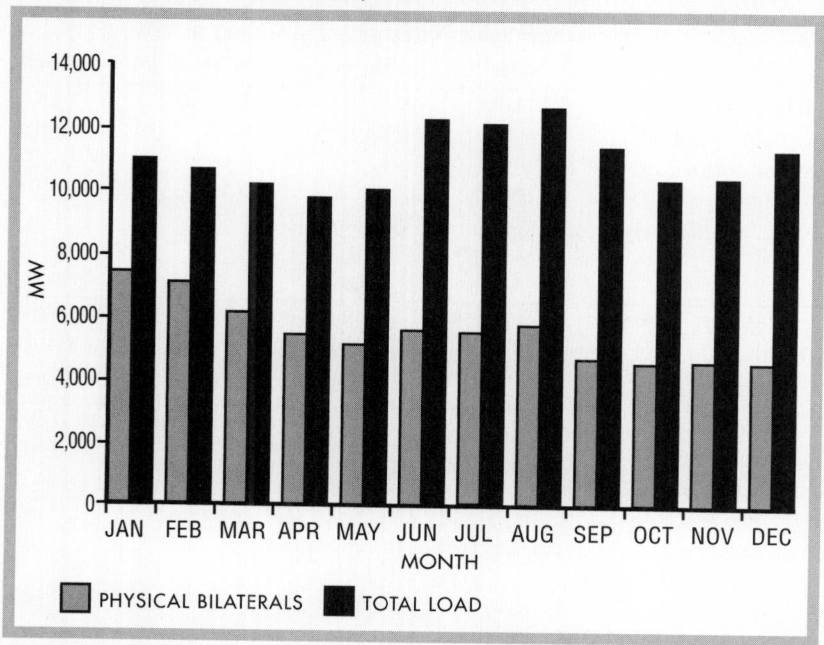

Source: Annual Assessment of the New York Electric Markets, 2000, p. 27. Presented to FERC Technical Conference, January 22, 2001. www.nyiso.com.

and settled by the system operator as actual metered deliveries *net* of contract sales volumes.[3]

These two methods of settlement come to the same result in accounting terms: Traders pay or receive the contract price for the contract quantity, and the real-time price (imbalance price) for any deviations between actual and contracted quantities. (See the example in Table 8.1.) Both methods are possible under the integrated trading model. We recommend net settlement because it is simple and efficient, reduces the level of funds at risk of default

[3]To qualify for net settlement, both sides of a bilateral transaction must nominate the same transaction. These nominations must correspond exactly (i.e., both sides must nominate the same quantity and location in terms of the pool settlement zone) for the transaction. If the nominations do not correspond, the system operator will not be able to assign responsibility for any imbalances from the contracted amount.

TABLE 8.1 Net and Gross Settlement

NET SETTLEMENT
With Contracts Settled by the System Operator (all quantities in MW)

	Seller	Buyer	Others	Total
Actual generation	110		10	120
Actual consumption		–120		–120
Contract notified to system operator	–100	100		
Imbalance settled with system operator at the spot price	10	–20	10	0

GROSS SETTLEMENT
With Contracts for Differences (CfDs) Settled Bilaterally (all quantities in MW)

	Seller	Buyer	Others	Total
Actual generation	110		10	120
Actual consumption		–120		–120
Contract notified to system operator	—	—	—	—
Imbalance settled with system operator at the spot price	110	–120	10	0
Contract amount settled bilaterally*	–100	100		
Difference effectively settled at the spot price	10	–20	10	0

*This quantity is settled at the contract price *minus* the spot price—the *difference* between contract and spot. Hence the contracts are called "contracts for differences" or CfDs.

in the spot market (i.e., reduces worries over credit) and doesn't preclude traders from using contracts for differences or other types of contracts if they want to.

"Scheduling" Contracts

PJM is an example of a market using the integrated trading model and net settlement, which allows both inflexible and flexible contracts. It is therefore possible to schedule contracts in PJM.

For example (and refer to the first part of Table 8.1):

- A generator tells the system operator that he will be supplying a 100 MW contract at 4 P.M.
- A customer says he will pay for 100 MW at 4 P.M. (The customer in this case is either a very large industrial customer who buys for himself in the wholesale market, or a retailer who buys for a large number of small customers.)
- These two notifications constitute the *contract delivery* no matter what actually happens on the system afterwards.
- The system operator decides which plants to run at 4 P.M. (How he does this is the subject of much of the previous chapter—load will be met at least cost from flexible and inflexible offers.) In Table 8.1, the generator with the contract produces 110 MW.
- The meters at each end tell what actually was sent and taken, and the settlement system goes to work. In Table 8.1, the customer consumes 120 MW.
- The contract amounts notified to PJM are subtracted from the metered amounts, and any differences (imbalances) are charged at the spot price. In Table 8.1, the generator with the contract is paid for 10 MW of imbalance energy at the spot price, and the customer is charged for 20 MW of imbalance energy at the spot price.

Contracts can be, and are constantly, scheduled for delivery, but we need to recognize that the link between the producer and the customer is in truth only a financial one—it could never conceivably be a physical one.

CONGESTION MANAGEMENT

In the previous chapter, we touched on the subject of congestion management in the integrated trading model. Here we expand on the subject of the role that spot prices play in congestion management.

To refresh on the economic definition of congestion: Transmission lines have finite capacity. When the capacity of one or more line is filled, the phenomenon is referred to as *transmission congestion.* When congestion occurs, transmission users are constrained from delivering more power. One way or the other, plants on the *import* side of the constraint have to increase production, and plants on the *export* side of the constraint have to decrease production, relative to the production schedules they would otherwise prefer, to serve load.

Vertically integrated utilities invariably say that grid congestion is not a serious problem on their system, and they are usually right in the sense that grid congestion is easy to manage for a monopolist who controls all the generation on the system. The monopoly dispatcher simply instructs some plants to produce a bit more and some to produce a bit less until the system is balanced within transmission constraints, and none of them have much reason to resist because they all work for the same boss and all costs are added together. Independents only get to use the transmission capacity that the utility doesn't need. The rules for allocating this spare capacity under wheeling normally make sure that the utility doesn't have to give too much capacity away, so it doesn't have to mess much with its own production schedule to manage extra demands on the transmission system.[4]

When there is *competition* in energy markets, congestion is a more important issue. The moment transmission is scarce it has a value. Those who get to use the scarce transmission to serve their customers in the import areas will capture that value. Those that don't get to use the transmission will not. They will have to get the energy for their customers in the import areas by purchasing it (or self-providing) from plants within that import area. And it stands to reason that spot prices of energy will be higher in this import area, relative to the export area, because of the restriction of supply in the import area.

So how exactly is the value of scarce transmission quantified in a competitive market? It is quite straightforward. *The value of congested transmission is equal to the price of energy in the import area, minus the price in the export area.* There are two ways of looking at this:

1. First, this is the value that someone gets when they don't have to purchase energy in the expensive import area. Instead, they can buy it where it is cheaper, in the export area, and use the scarce transmission to deliver it to the import area.
2. Second, and equivalently, this is the value of being able to deliver energy to the higher priced market, rather than having to sell it into the lower priced one.

How should this fact affect the design of trading arrangements? The value of scarce transmission just described is incredibly straightforward. *The value is entirely dependent on the differences in energy market prices from place to place.* After all, all transmission does is move energy from place to place. This suggests that the methods for allocating and pricing

[4] Because of *native load priority* in wheeling systems, it can appear that transmission is inadequate when in fact there is sufficient: There is great incentive for the utility system operator to reserve too much.

scarce transmission must be inextricably linked with the energy markets. (This is *not* the case in the wheeling model.) Wheeling model rules, in effect, specify who gets to go across the constraint. But these rules are totally separate from the energy markets.

The concept of who gets to go across the constraint is the heart of the problem of the wheeling model. Wheeling is based on the notion of *contract paths* and *physical rights* to those paths, and scheduled transactions between sellers and buyers, hoping imbalances will be small, and allowing the utility to charge a regulated rate for them. Since, as we have explained earlier, there is really no such thing as a *path,* trying to give *physical rights* to use them, *scheduling transactions* is the way to utter confusion. It can just about work, inefficiently, for five well-disciplined utility purchasers, who will not game the system. It cannot work for an army of unruly, profit-making, competitive generators, who will.

Transmission constraints must be respected or transmission lines will burn down. The right congestion model is the integrated model, which properly integrates the energy markets with the allocation and pricing of scarce transmission. In this model, scarce transmission is allocated as part of the optimization process. It is allocated so that the value of transmission is maximized. Traders who schedule a contract across valuable transmission lines are charged a transmission usage charge (a bottleneck fee) being equal to the energy price difference between the two ends of the transaction. That way, there is no difference for traders between (1) paying the bottleneck fee for scheduling a contract from the export zone to the import zone, and (2) selling their energy in the export zone and buying it back in the import zone. There is no reason to squabble over transmission allocation rules, which are a major problem in the wheeling model.

It is true that some features of the transmission rights from the wheeling model are extremely useful. They can define property rights to the transmission system, which encourage users to expand it, and they set in advance the cost of using the system. (There are no uncertain bottleneck fees to worry about.) *But each of these features can be obtained from an alternative instrument, known as financial transmission rights (FTRs), which we recommend should be adopted.* FTRs are described in the next chapter.

MORE ON HOW LOCATIONAL PRICES COME ABOUT

In a competitive electricity market, the spot price is the key piece of information that drives contract prices and gives incentives to produce, consume, and invest. Setting the right prices is therefore crucial for the system to be efficient. There can, for example, be one price for the whole system; there can be different prices in different zones or even different prices in every node of the system. In the next few sections, we describe issues of pricing and recommend solutions.

Transmission Congestion Causes Differences in Locational Prices

When there are no constraints on the transmission system, the schedule for dispatching generators will typically just consist of an ordered list of the least expensive generators (as indicated by their offer prices) necessary to meet demand on the system at that time, as shown in Figure 7.3.

When the transmission system is congested, the least-cost dispatch may involve some expensive generators running in some locations, while some cheaper generators are not running in other locations. In these cases it is not possible to transport additional energy from the "cheaper" locations to the "expensive" ones, because of the transmission constraints.

Figure 8.5 illustrates how generators (Gen 9 and Gen 10) might be *constrained-off* in such a situation and how it might be necessary to bring on other generators (Gen 13 and Gen 14) to replace them. When there is transmission congestion, and the overall electricity supply system is dispatched in a least cost manner, the marginal cost of energy will vary at each location.

FIGURE 8.5 Constrained generators.

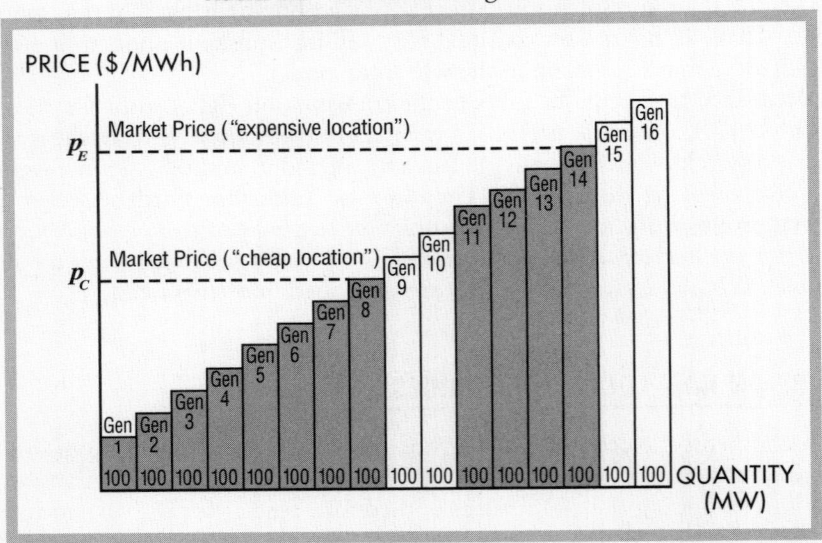

Under locational pricing of energy, the price in each location is set equal to the marginal cost at each location, as represented by the offers. Locational prices therefore incorporate any *congestion costs* arising from the need to dispatch the system to meet reliability and transmission constraints. (They can also incorporate the cost of transmission system losses, although losses are ignored for the moment, for simplicity.) Figure 8.5 shows how the market price rises in the expensive location and falls in the cheap one relative to the no congestion case in Figure 7.4, once the transmission constraint restricts the output of Gens 9 and 10 and forces Gens 13 and 14 to replace them. Under locational pricing, these are the prices at which real-time energy will be traded in the different locations. Generators will be paid their local price. Customers will be charged based on their local price.

Locational prices give efficient signals for the production and consumption of energy, and for the construction of new generation and transmission facilities. Generators in high-priced areas, where it is expensive to meet customer demand, will be paid higher prices than generators in low-priced areas. This encourages new generation facilities to be constructed in high-priced areas, where the new investments are needed, and discourages them from locating in the lower priced areas that may already have sufficient generation.

Locational prices provide the same incentives for consumers. High prices discourage customers from consuming in the high-cost areas, while low-cost areas will attract intensive users of electricity—like factories.

Finally, locational prices also provide signals for investment in new transmission facilities. A significant difference in prices between areas indicates that investments in new transmission facilities would be valuable. Additional transmission capacity would enable more power to flow from the low-priced to the high-priced regions. The marginal value of the new transmission investment is equal to the price difference between regions. This can be compared to the cost of new investment to determine whether new investment is efficient or not.

Another Example of Locational Prices

Figure 8.6 illustrates more visually how prices are calculated in a simple system when there are no transmission constraints, while the one that follows it demonstrates price calculations when the constraints are binding.

In Figure 8.6 area A has 400 MW of generation and only 200 MW of load. Area B has 400 MW of both generation and load. The system operator would choose the cheapest 600 MW of generation to meet the 600 MW of load, selecting four generators in Area A and two generators in Area B, as shown in the figure. The amount of power flowing from A to B is 200 MW, less than the capacity of the transmission link (300 MW). Since the

FIGURE 8.6 Dispatch with no transmission constraints.

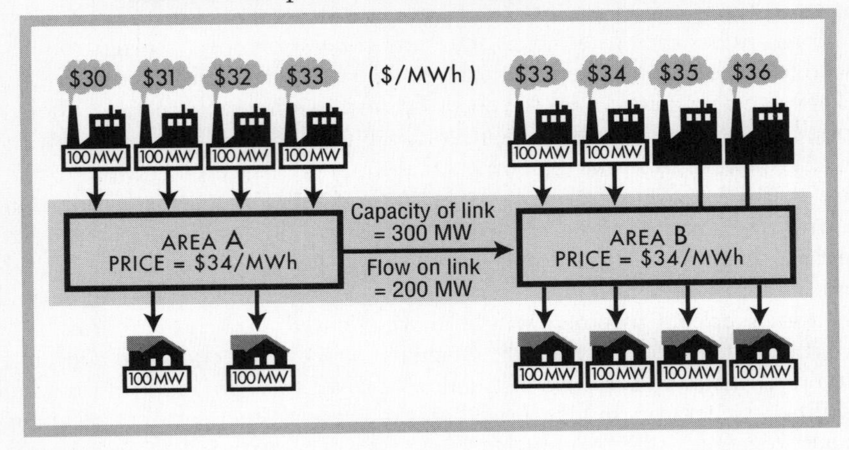

transmission constraint between the two areas is not reached, the price in both areas would be $34/MWh, the highest generator offer accepted.

Now assume that the link between Area A and Area B is limited to 100 MW, as shown in Figure 8.7. It is no longer possible to transport 200 MW from Area A to Area B. Hence, only 300 MW of generation can be dispatched at A, and an additional 100 MW must be dispatched at B, to meet the load. Since the constraint of the transmission link is reached, the prices in each area are set based on the last offer accepted in each area. The price in area A would be set at $32/MWh and the price in area B would equal $35/MWh.

FIGURE 8.7 Dispatch with transmission constraints.

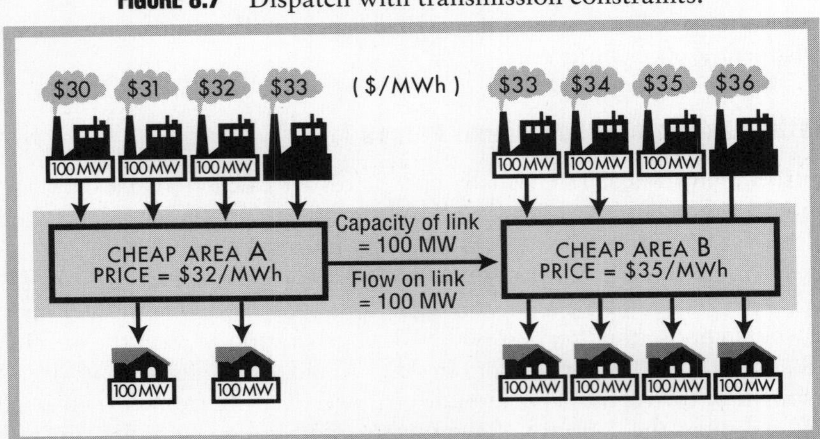

Transmission Losses Cause Differences in Locational Prices

Some energy is lost on the transmission system, due to the heating of the wires and the energizing of transformers. There are alternative ways to account for these losses in the integrated trading model. The best way is to include the marginal cost of losses in locational electricity prices.

Just like transmission congestion, transmission losses cause the marginal cost of serving load to vary from location to location. For example, if a distant city exists at the end of a long transmission line, and 5 percent of energy is lost as it travels down that line, then the cost of serving that distant city is 5 percent (actually 5.263 percent[5]) higher than the cost of serving a local city at the other end of the line. For every MWh consumed in the distant city, 1.05263 MW must be sent down the line. If the price is $30/MWh at the local end of the line, it should be ($30 × 1.05263 = $31.58/MWh) at the distant end. (See Figure 8.8.) The numbers work out and there is enough money to go around: If local generators produce 100 MW, they get paid $30 × 100 = $3,000. If the distant city consumes 95 MW, they pay $31.58 × 95 = $3,000.

If the price were not adjusted for losses, there would not be enough money to go around. Distant customers would pay $30 × 95 = $2,850, which would leave the system operator with a shortfall.

One alternative to including losses in the price is to make a quantity adjustment: Charge the distant customers the $30/MWh price, but multiply the

FIGURE 8.8 Prices with losses.

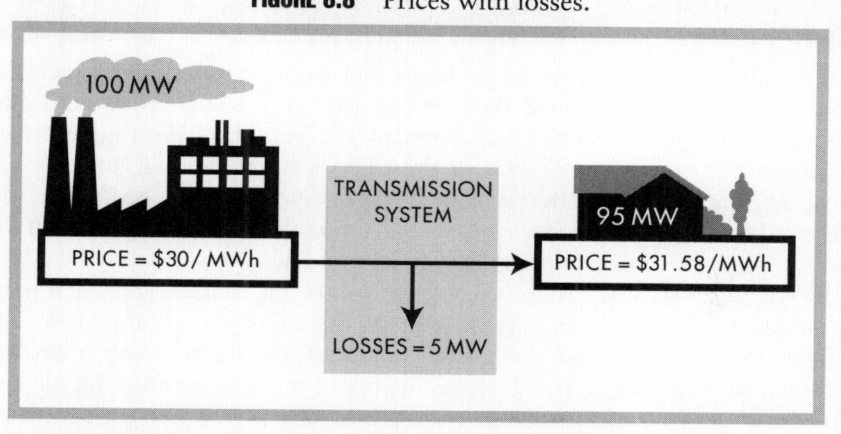

[5] The cost increase is given by the formula [100%/(100% – 5%)] – 100% = 5.263%.

95 MW quantity by 1.05263. This arrives back at $3,000. It has the same effect as including losses in the hourly price so long as the loss factor is updated every hour. It becomes a problem, however, when people are tempted to set the loss factors in advance based on expected conditions. Losses are never exactly as expected since transmission flows are never exactly as expected—especially on complicated networks. This method leads to inconsistencies that have to be mopped up by the system operator. A similar method of accounting for losses, used in the decentralized trading model where schedules must be balanced, is to insist that losses be replaced in kind (e.g., for every 95 MWh taken out, 100 must be put in). This method relies on setting loss factors in advance and runs into the same problems when loss factors are set in advance in the integrated model.

Including the cost of losses in the locational energy prices can prevent these problems. The marginal cost of serving load at a given location is a function of the marginal generator offer(s) accepted by the system operator, of transmission congestion, and of losses. These things are all intertwined and are all taken into account at the same time by the dispatch process. It makes no sense to separate these things and to treat them differently for pricing purposes.

For more detail on the hows and whys of locational prices, we refer readers to the many excellent papers written by Hogan on the subject, listed at the end of this chapter.

Marginal Losses

To be fully consistent with the principle that the locational price equals the marginal cost of serving load at a given location, locational prices should be based on *marginal* loss rates, not average loss rates. This is for the same reason that the energy component of the price is set at the marginal offered cost, not the average of offered costs. In the examples in this section we have referred to average losses for simplicity. Marginal losses are higher than average losses. (Meaning, for example, that more energy is lost from the 200th MWh sent down a line than is lost from the 100th.) The result when marginal prices are used is that the price in the distant city in Figure 8.6 will be higher than $31.58, and the system operator will be left with a surplus (known as *losses rent*). This losses rent should be used to offset aggregated fixed charges to traders, such as the transmission access charges described in Chapter 9.

ZONAL VERSUS NODAL VERSUS SINGLE PRICE

If prices should vary by location, then how many different locations (and thus prices) should there be?

At one extreme, it is possible to determine the unique price at every *node* of the transmission system. (A node is essentially any place where there is an intersection of transmission lines, or where a generator, large customer or the distribution system is connected.) At the other extreme, there could just be one price for the whole transmission system (and then prices are not locational at all). Somewhere in the middle is *zonal* pricing. Prices may feasibly be one of these things for buyers and another for sellers.

Precedents exist for each of the alternatives. PJM, New York, New Zealand, and others, for example, each have some form of nodal price. The pool that used to exist in England and Wales, and the New England system, used to have a single price. Some places have zonal pricing—particularly for buyers. The initial California system is an example here. Greece is an example of a market designed with prices that vary by location for reasons of losses, but not for reasons of congestion.[6]

Nodal pricing represents the true underlying prices that come out of the dispatch process. Zonal and single price systems are approximations. They are found by either averaging nodal prices, or by recalculating a simulation of the actual dispatch in which some or all of the losses and congestion are ignored.

Averages and approximations may save transaction costs. However, the approximations used in zonal and single price systems can run into problems. For example: If a generator with an offered price of $30/MWh is told by the system operator to run, and the market price is subsequently averaged down to $25/MWh, the market is no longer incentive-compatible. The generator is better off not following instructions because it will lose $5. Likewise, case 2: If the $30 generator is told *not* to run, and the market price is subsequently averaged up $40/MWh, the generator is better off running, even though it was told not to.

To solve these problems, zonal and single price systems need to provide *constrained-on payments* and *constrained-off payments* so that prices are fair, transparent, and incentive-compatible. The generator would get a $5

[6] Greece is using the quantity adjustment method of accounting for losses. Strictly speaking, all of Greece except the nonconnected islands have a single price each hour, however the practical effect of the losses adjustment is to create prices that vary by loss factor.

extra constrained-on payment in case 1, as long as it ran when instructed. It would get an extra $10 constrained-off payment in case 2, *for not running*. Customers would fund these payments through a surcharge rolled into their bills, often called an *uplift* charge. The calculation of the payments gets complicated in all but the simplest situations because it is necessary to know exactly *why* a generator was or wasn't running. It can become very messy. Since single-price systems make bigger approximations than zonal-price systems, the mess with single-price systems is bigger. The more zones, the smaller the mess.

Nodal prices are better for generators because they avoid this mess, and they give better (less approximate) market signals.

There is a valid argument that zonal prices are better for the demand side of the industry, however. Because the demand side is not very price-responsive yet, the problem of constrained-on and constrained-off payments doesn't really exist here. Because electrical locations can be quite different from physical locations (one side of a street might not be electrically connected to the other side) there can be cost differences to consumers that are hard to explain. It may be easier in the first instance at least to charge buyers on a zonal basis.[7]

COMPLEX VERSUS SIMPLE BIDS

When a generator tells the system operator its reservation price, it has specified the conditions under which it has *offered* to sell electricity. The trading arrangements can require the offers to be *simple,* or allow them to be *complex*. A simple offer says "pick me for up to X MW so long as the price is above $Y/MWh." However, the cost of running a generator is a complex function of many technical factors and constraints. A complex offer can say much more. It can allow the generators to give the system operator information about all sorts of costs and constraints: *start-up* costs; *no-load* costs; *nonconvex* operating costs; minimum run-time constraints; maximum run-time constraints; ramp-rate constraints; minimum output constraints; and many other complicated factors that we won't get into here.

The advantage of complex offers is that they allow the system operator to take account of the true characteristics of the generators and thus, potentially, do a more efficient job of minimizing cost. The disadvantage is that

[7] If sellers sell on a nodal basis and buyers buy on a zonal basis, there must be rules in place to ensure that buyers cannot resell, getting paid as if they were generators, or vice versa. This would be an instance of *gaming* the rules.

Zonal Prices in Australia

A few relatively low capacity transmission lines connect the states on the eastern coast of Australia. Each state is a pricing zone and this has caused problems because within a single state there may be transmission constraints that effectively create separate markets. One problem occurs between the states of Queensland and New South Wales (NSW):

- A line connects NSW to Tarong, a low-cost generation region in Queensland, and goes on to connect to the relatively large Queensland load center of Brisbane. Brisbane has access to other generation, but it is often more expensive than Tarong.

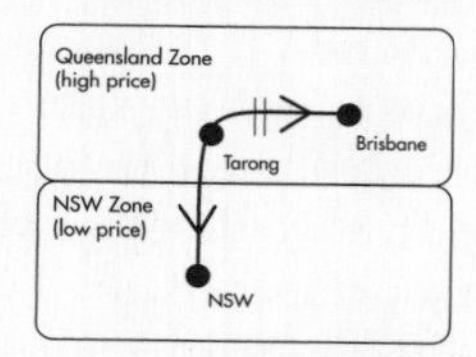

- The line between Tarong and Brisbane is often congested. Brisbane frequently imports as much as it can, but needs to use other high-cost generation to meet load.
- The zonal price in Queensland can often be high because of the relative size and cost of the other generation compared to Tarong.
- Meanwhile NSW, to the south, is also a large load center and imports from the cheap generation in Tarong. NSW's generation is not as expensive as that available to Brisbane and the NSW zonal price can often be lower than Queensland's.

The result? Energy travels from a high-priced zone (Queensland) to a low-priced zone (NSW). *Yet this violates the most basic principle of why anyone would transport any commodity.* We ship products to where we can sell them for more, not less! One practical result in Australia is that someone makes a loss on transporting the energy south, despite the fact that transporting it south was the sensible thing to do because it lowers total generating cost. (Under the Australian market rules, that "someone" is the holder of a contract which has similarities to the FTRs described in Chapter 9.)

These situations arise because under zonal pricing, the commercial aspects of the trading arrangements (which determine prices) can be inconsistent with the operational aspects (which schedule and dispatch generators). In Australia, the temporary fix has been to create extra operational rules to limit the output of generators in Tarong, and thus prevent the flow of power south when the situation arises. This fix has been made easier because the generators concerned are state-owned. But this is not a long-term solution.

setting prices is a nightmare. Price should still be set on the principle of marginal offered cost, but what if these prices no longer cover all the offered costs of the generator? For example, what if they don't cover a generator's start-up cost? If the system operator told the generator to run, it should be paid some constrained-on payment to make up the difference. This is incentive-compatible. But what if one of the generator's constraints prevented its output from being lowered by the system operator? Maybe it shouldn't get the payment in that case. What if some other constraint was the reason? The problem is that, again, *constrained-on and constrained-off payments get messy quickly.*

Trading arrangements with simple offers don't need to worry about this mess. If a generator's offer price is lower than the market price, it should run. If it is higher, it should *not* run. If for some reason there is an inconsistency, the constrained-off/constrained-on situation is straightforward. But because the offers are simple, generator owners must internalize many of the decisions the system operator would otherwise have made. They have to make sure that the system operator—with limited information, just an hourly offer price and quantity in the extreme—will not violate any of the technical constraints of the generator.

We believe that simple offers are preferable in systems where they are physically workable—hydro and modern gas-fired plants have less of a problem with them for example—and *precedent exists to show they can result in a minimal negative impact on efficiency. They provide a tremendous advantage in terms of trading simplicity and market price visibility.* We recognize, however, that in some circumstances there is no way to avoid complexity. Any offer complexity at all introduces the need to identify reasons—and the appropriate compensation—for constrained-on and constrained-off generators. *When complex offers are required, they should be designed with the objective of minimizing the constrained-on/constrained-off problem.*

PAY-AS-BID OR MARGINAL BID PRICING?

Almost without exception, prices in existing integrated electricity markets are determined the way we have described earlier; where supply meets demand, which is often a price equal to the offer of the highest priced generator selected.[8] This is widely known as "marginal bid" pricing since all generators are compensated equally, at the market price. However, some market commentators have suggested alternative "pay-as-bid" methodologies.

[8] There is good reason in auction theory to make this rule the lowest rejected offer price rather than the highest accepted offer, but that is not at issue here.

Their reasoning is that with marginal bid pricing generators get paid the offer of the marginal unit, but more efficient generators bid lower prices, so consumers would pay less if only we would pay generators their bid.

However, this reasoning is faulty because generators would not bid the same way if the auction rules were *pay-as-bid*. They would bid what they expect the clearing price to be. Ontario Hydro conducted an internal experiment with pay-as-bid pricing and found that generators quickly stopped bidding their marginal costs and began bidding at their best guess of the market-clearing price, thereby actually *increasing prices* and also distorting dispatch.

If traders all had good information, the market price would be the same under either method. But because the load, the dispatch and the price changes so frequently, it is virtually impossible for all the traders to have sufficient information to keep changing their bids to be at the market price. This lack of information has three implications:

1. Changing bids constantly in real time poses operational problems for the system operator. In real time the coordination with the dispatch is much simpler and more efficient if the system operator is given bids of a reserve price—"Don't dispatch me if the price is less than my bid." This gives the traders the incentive to bid close to their own marginal costs, which do not change much from hour to hour. The operator can optimize over a period of several hours ahead.
2. The dispatch will certainly be less efficient (further from least-cost) when everyone is guessing the clearing price.
3. Lack of information increases the risk to generators and more so to the efficient baseload; they make a big operating profit from running, and if their bid were marginally above the market price, they would not run, forfeiting their profits.

The response of generators to this increased risk is either to bid low to ensure dispatch; or to contract everything in advance, so as not to have to sell anything in a spot market:

- By reducing revenues to baseload plants, pay-as-bid makes them less profitable and less likely to be built; generators will lean towards building less efficient plants thereby reducing the overall efficiency of the system.
- Selling everything at contract prices removes flexibility from the system, and encourages consolidation to internalize the risks—small generators need to be able to buy and sell at spot prices to offload uncontracted power and to buy back up if plants are not available.

The problems for the system operator of constantly changing bids creates an inefficient dispatch and increases costs, which we consider more than sufficient reason for marginal bid pricing.

In particular, this pay-as-bid suggestion has been put forward in the case of markets in which market power is suspected, in order to force advance contracting. But if there is market power in a market, it will simply be moved to the contract markets where it is more difficult to police. And the risks introduced by pay-as-bid force consolidation to internalize the risks, exacerbating market power. If there is market power, it may be easier to detect it when the price is set by marginal bid methods—since that method encourages traders to bid close to marginal cost, there is more information to work with about who is trying to manipulate the market.

Moreover, the bidders in a pay-as bid auction will still attempt to guess the market price, *even if that market price has been set by the use of market power,* and the same points outlined above—problems for the system operator, and inefficient dispatch—still apply.

Pay-as-bid is a bad idea.

DAY-AHEAD MARKETS

In most circumstances, when generators take more than an hour to start up, it is beneficial to have the system operator run *two* energy markets: a *day-ahead market* in addition to a spot market. This is indeed how New York and PJM operate. (They refer to themselves as having a "two-settlement system.") We have made references to day-ahead markets already. Here we look at how they can be beneficial.

A day-ahead market, as its name implies, operates a day in advance of the spot market. At 2 P.M. on a Wednesday, for example, a day-ahead auction might be held for energy delivery for each hour of Thursday. It is essentially a forward contract market. Where it exists, other forward contracts arranged privately and independently between traders more than a day in advance can be cleared against the day-ahead price, rather than the spot price. The same can be true for FTRs (described in Chapter 9). Transactions in the day-ahead market then become contracts that are settled against spot prices.

A day-ahead market can be beneficial in three ways.

First, it can be beneficial if generators have high start-up costs and "cycle" daily—i.e., start and stop each day. For example, old gas units can fall into this category. When this is the case, generators can benefit from the system operator integrating their start/stop decision into a longer-term dispatch process (called the "scheduling" process). Effectively this means that the time horizon for optimizing dispatch decisions is a day, not an hour or

Case Study: New York Day-Ahead Market

Figure 8.9 shows a monthly comparison of the average day ahead and spot energy prices in New York in 2000. Like all forward markets, the average prices in the day-ahead markets converged to the spot prices, although they are never exactly the same.* The day-ahead and spot energy price differences in New York are comparable to the differences experienced in PJM since the implementation of PJM's day-ahead market.

FIGURE 8.9 Monthly average energy prices in New York.

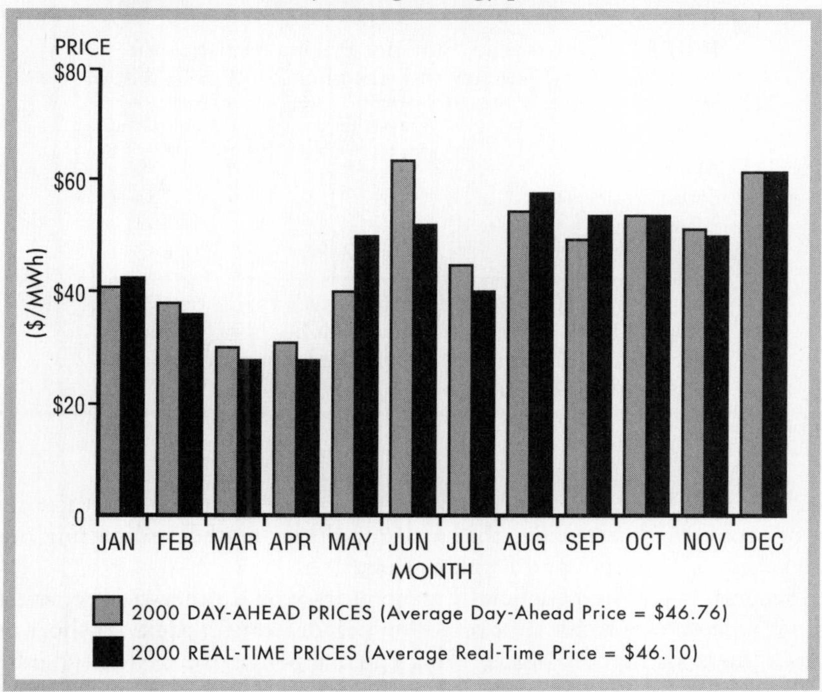

Source: Annual Assessment of the New York Electric Markets, 2000, p. 29. Presented to the Joint Board of Directors/Management Committee Meeting, New York ISO Market Advisor, April 17, 2000. www.nyiso.com.

*A price "spike" on June 26 heavily influenced average June 2000 day-ahead prices in New York. The spike was caused by a number of factors, including a very hot day, expected transmission congestion and a large number of inflexible schedules across an important transmission interface, and the outage of a major nuclear plant.

(continued)

Case Study: New York Day-Ahead Market (Continued)

Day-ahead electricity prices tend to be less volatile than spot prices. Higher volatility of spot prices vs. day-ahead prices is caused, in part, by the smaller number of options the real-time dispatch software (called SCD in New York) has available to resolve system constraints and meet load in real-time relative to the day-ahead software (called SCUC in New York). Table 8.2 compares day-ahead and spot price volatility in New York City. The standard deviation of prices in the spot market is considerably higher than in the day-ahead—more than twice as high.

TABLE 8.2 Day-Ahead and Spot Pricing Statistics for New York City, January to December 2000 ($/MWh)

	Day-Ahead	Real-Time
Mean	49	50
Standard deviation	37	83
Minimum	0	(903)
Maximum	1,012	1,862

Source: Annual Assessment of the New York Electric Markets, 2000, p. 27. Presented to the Joint Board of Directors/ Management Committee Meeting, New York ISO Market Advisor, April 17, 2000. www.nyiso.com.

less. The alternative to a day-ahead market in this context is to let the generators concerned internalize the start/stop decision when submitting their own schedule of output and flexible offers.

Second, it can be beneficial if generators would otherwise be able to "game" the market to lift spot prices by withdrawing capacity at short notice—a form of market power. This can happen if the system operator needs to plan operations a few hours ahead of time, relies on generator promises of availability, and must call on expensive quick-start alternatives if those promises are reneged on at the last moment (thus lifting spot prices to high levels). In this case, day-ahead contracts can remove the gaming incentive from generators because they no longer benefit from high spot prices; their prices are locked in day-ahead, and they can't play the same "game" in the day-ahead market because more alternatives are available day-ahead than in real-time.

Third, as we mention elsewhere, a day-ahead market can promote demand response. The day-ahead price is a day-out forecast of the spot price, and a price that consumers can lock in, in advance, to meet their requirements. If the price is high, they can choose not to buy, and they have a day to plan for alternative arrangements. They don't have to wait until real-time, in the volatile spot market, to find out what the cost of their purchases is going to be.

REFERENCES

Hogan, William, *Contract Networks for Electricity Power Transmission:* Technical reference, Harvard Electricity Policy Group, September 1990–revised February 1992.

Hogan, William, *Transmission Congestion: The Nodal-Zonal Debate Revisited,* Harvard Electricity Policy Group, February 1999.

Hogan, William, *Getting the Prices Right in PJM: A Summary April 1998 through September 1999,* Harvard Electricity Policy Group, October 1999.

Hogan, William, Harvey, Scott M., and Pope, Susan L., *Nodal and Zonal Congestion Management and the Exercise of Market Power,* Harvard Electricity Policy Group, February 2000.

Hogan, William, *Flowgate Rights and Wrongs,* Harvard Electricity Policy Group, August 2000.

CHAPTER 9

Transmission Business Model

One of the things that has not been clearly established by the industry is the best business model for transmission in a competitive world. Transmission is still a regulated business. Who should own it? What functions should it perform? How should it be regulated? How should it price its product? How should it invest? What type of contracts should it offer? In this area more than any other there is not a complete international model ready to be adopted.

TRANSMISSION FUNCTIONS

The business of transmission consists of several activities, including:

- *Maintenance* is the process of keeping the transmission system in good working order, checking for wear and tear, replacing defective or worn parts, trimming trees that might interfere with the wires, and so on. Normally maintenance is carried out by the transmission owner under the instruction—or at least with coordination—of the system operator. In some instances the system operator and the transmission owner are the same company so there is no distinction.
- *Operations* is the process of physically changing the physical configuration of the transmission system by throwing switches to take parts of the network into or out of service, to activate transmission equipment such as capacitors, and so on. Operations are a fairly insignificant part of the transmission business. Not very many changes take place in a day. The transmission owner normally carries out operations, although many operations are so straightforward that the system operator carries them out directly and automatically. Again, in some instances the system operator and the transmission owner are the same company so there is no distinction.

- *Control* is the process of deciding what switches should be thrown and giving operating instructions to throw them. The system operator carries out transmission control. There is a subtle difference between transmission control and other control responsibilities of the system operator. Transmission control refers only to control of the transmission assets, but the control room of a system operator also gives operating instructions to generators and other users of the transmission system.
- *Expansion and upgrade* are components of a multipart process. It is the process of evaluating the need for new transmission assets, deciding where and when to build new lines or upgrade existing lines, dealing with the necessary economic and environmental approvals, and physically building and commissioning the facilities. Transmission expansion and upgrade involves all the stakeholders in the industry and is a complicated process, as we describe later.

The business of transmission is price-regulated because the transmission system is the only highway over which electricity can be delivered. The transmission business is a natural monopoly so it must be regulated to ensure that transmission users (market participants) pay a fair price, to ensure it is run as efficiently, reliably and fairly as possible, and to ensure the right amount of investment is made. These rules should be incentive-compatible as far as possible. In addition, where transmission owners are also market participants, rules are needed to ensure that some market participants are not favored at the expense of others.

The regulation of transmission can be considered as part of the trading arrangements because of the tight link between the generation and transmission of electricity, and because the rules for transmission are so commercially important for the market participants. Lack of availability of transmission, transmission congestion, and transmission prices all affect the ability of market participants to trade and affect the price that generators are able to offer customers.

The rules for transmission fall into five main categories: conditions for *access* (in both the short and long run and including the rules for maintenance); the rules for *pricing* of transmission; the rules for long-term *expansion and upgrade* of the system; the method of transmission *contracting*; and the arrangements for *ownership and control* of transmission.

LONG-TERM ACCESS

The story of access to the transmission system in the *short term* was described in the previous two chapters. However, whatever the specific form of the short-run rules, market participants also need to feel comfortable that their access is assured in the *long term*. They need agreements linking themselves, the transmission owner(s) and the system operator, specifying the conditions under which they will be connected and maintain access to the transmission system. These include:

- Transmission connection agreements, which ensure that connections are properly provided, maintained and modified at terms that are efficient and fair to the connected parties; and
- Transmission use-of-service agreements, which regulate the terms and charges for use of the system.

The first thing that generators, in particular, are concerned about is that they have access to use the transmission system on *stable* terms. Having built a plant that will exist for 30 years, they do not welcome being told two years after construction that the access rules or charges will fundamentally change. The second thing they are concerned about is that they continue to have access to the transmission system on *fair* terms, especially so that the old vertically-integrated utility doesn't attain some sort of preferred access it can use to undercut their prices in the marketplace.[1]

In return for stable and fair access rules, generators expect to meet certain conditions required by the system operator. They expect to follow short-term instructions from the system operator, which must be issued to keep the system secure. They expect these rules to be incentive-compatible; that they be paid a fair price when they are instructed by the system operator to do something that wouldn't otherwise be in their interest. Buyers also seek stable and fair rules from a marketplace. Resellers require this before they in turn are willing to make commitments to final consumers.

Stability over time and fairness apply to all the rules—the operating rules of the system operator, the rules for buying and selling electricity, the connection agreements, and the use-of-system agreements. To the extent these rules are not perceived as stable and fair over the long term, participants will be reluctant to come to the party. It is all too tempting to get a market up and running as soon as possible and fix things that go wrong on

---

[1] Long-run access rules tend to be a much bigger issue for generators than for consumers, because generators are large and must make capital-intensive investment decisions. They tend to have more to lose if the rules are changed, whereas consumers are accustomed to a history of protection from the regulator (and electricity is a small part of the costs of a typical consumer, but most or all of the revenue of a typical generator).

the fly. But this is exactly what we must not do if we want efficient entry and want to avoid endless litigation.

TRANSMISSION PRICING

Since most of the costs of the transmission company are fixed investments, a simple way to price the transmission system would be to take all the investment costs, divide them by some number representing total usage, and charge this amount per unit of use. But once the investment is in the ground, the marginal costs of usage are much lower than this simple calculation would indicate, and charging this way drives a cost wedge between buyer and seller and limits usage of the facility.

In 1938, Harold Hotelling pointed out this very problem with charging investment costs to usage, and suggested that the solution was to charge only the marginal cost for the actual use, and charge the investment costs in some other way. Hotelling's insight has had a big impact on many policy issues. There are other ways to charge, with some form of fixed fee and lower usage payment, which make transactions more efficient. The Federal Highway Administration did this when it developed the interstate highway system with 90 to 10 federal-state sharing of tax funds, and a *requirement for toll-free roads* if the federal funds were used.[2]

But in the United States, at least, many companies' prices for electric transmission are still set in the "simple" way. The problem is worsened when prices are *pancaked*. Whenever a transaction is deemed to cross two or more areas, each transmission owner crossed charges its own fee. This stacking up of fees, referred to as pancaking, further inhibits trade because it makes the wedge bigger.

A Model for Pricing Transmission

Exactly what sort of transmission pricing should we shoot for? Ideally, to be efficient and to meet Hotelling's standard, but without the taxpayer picking up the overhead costs, a transmission pricing scheme would meet the following criteria:

- Costs would be directly attributed to those for whom the costs were incurred, where those market participants can be identified. This includes:

[2] The *gasoline tax* is a form of usage charge, however, which corresponds in a general way with usage costs. Gasoline usage varies with distance traveled, with the weight of the vehicle, and with congestion.

- —Short-run costs where the short-term marginal costs of transmission usage can be identified.
- —Directly attributable long-term costs such as the cost of connecting a generator to the transmission system.
- Other long-run costs would be socialized and recovered from market participants in a manner that is fair, and minimizes distortion to the efficiency of the day-to-day running of the electricity markets.

An ideal transmission pricing scheme will therefore be comprised of three parts: a transmission usage charge, a transmission connection charge, and a transmission access charge.

Transmission Usage Charges An efficient pricing system will charge the short-term marginal cost of transmission for short-term use of transmission. As we described earlier, this consists of two parts: the electrical losses on the system and the cost of congestion.

To refresh: Electrical *losses* occur in transmission because the transmission wires heat up. More electricity is generated than is consumed by customers, and the system operator has to make up for the losses by calling for extra generation. Loss varies with distance, with the size of the wires (large ones lose less than small ones) and with the amount being carried—when the lines are near capacity, losses can get very high. Overall losses come to over 7 percent in the United States,[3] but over long distances when the wires are full, losses can get up to 12 percent or more. You can think of losses as equivalent to fuel in other transport systems. They are part of the marginal cost of transporting power, just as gasoline is part of the marginal cost of trucking. The difference is that the electrical "fuel" is provided by the same product as is being transported—it's as if a gasoline delivery truck uses some of the same gasoline in its main tank for fuel.[4]

We described in the previous chapters that *congestion* occurs in transmission when the flow on one or more line reaches the line limit. When there is congestion, in order to accommodate market participants who want to produce an extra MW on the export side and consume an extra (marginal) MW on the import side, it is not possible to send the MW over the transmission line. Instead, a separate plant on the import side (generator A) must produce an *extra* MW to serve the load there, and another separate

[3] This figure includes distribution losses. (Department of Energy, Energy Information Administration, Mitigating Greenhouse Gas Emissions: Voluntary Reporting, October 1997.)

[4] For more on losses and pricing for losses, refer to S. Stoft, *Power System Economics: Designing Markets for Electricity*, IEEE-Wiley Press, November 2001, Chapters 5-7 and 5-8.

plant on the export side (generator B) must produce a MW *less* to accommodate the extra generation there. That is the only way to accommodate the transaction. The marginal cost of the transaction, therefore, is the marginal cost of production of A, minus the marginal cost of production of B. This is also the cost that would be saved if one less MW of someone else's transaction were using the transmission line.

Good pricing of marginal transmission costs is dependent on efficient congestion management and a decent method of accounting for losses. The integrated model, and, to a lesser extent, the decentralized model, are capable of properly accounting for marginal transmission costs. The wheeling model is not.

To summarize what we have already said about transmission usage pricing under the integrated model: Charging for transmission usage is straightforward when energy is priced on a locational basis. With locational prices (nodal or zonal), the price of energy at a location is equal to the marginal cost of supplying energy to that location. First, this includes the effects of congestion. In the case just described for example, the price in the import area is set by the marginal cost of generator A, and the price in the export area is set by the marginal cost of generator B. Second, the locational price should also include the cost of losses in reaching a location; a distant part of the import area might have higher losses and thus a higher price than a central one, for example. The charge for transmission usage is the difference in energy prices between locations (i.e., the bottleneck fee described earlier).

How are these charges settled? Under *net settlement* (refer to previous chapter) the system operator charges traders with *scheduled contracts* this price difference between the origin and destination of the contract. *Spot* transactions are implicitly charged the same thing—the generators sell at their local spot price, and the buyers buy at their local spot price. Since the electricity flows from generators to buyers, the generators' prices overall will be lower than the buyers' prices; the difference is *implicit* transmission usage charges. Under *gross settlement,* the transmission usage charges are exactly the same, except all of them are implicit because the system operator does not deal with scheduled contracts.

Transmission Connection Charges For a variety of reasons, transmission usage charges based on marginal congestion and losses costs will probably always fall well short of recovering the total costs of transmission investment. Therefore, regulated transmission connection charges and transmission access charges are needed to recover the rest.

Transmission connection charges recover directly attributable long-run costs such as the cost of connecting a generator to the transmission system. These charges can either be calculated on a "deep" basis, where we really try to allocate as much cost individually to market participants as possible, or on a "shallow" basis, where we only allocate the costs we are really sure about. Deep is best, but shallow is easier.

Deep charges have the benefit of apportioning as much of the "blame" for cost as possible. This means that less cost has to be spread around (socialized) and recovered through access charges. The problem with deep charges is that the deeper they go the more contentious they get. For instance, it is clear that the line that connects a generator to the nearest junction of the transmission system is unlikely to be benefiting anyone but the generator concerned. However, it may also be true that even further into the network there are other lines that are built with that generator in mind. Perhaps they are needed as an alternative outlet for the energy if one line should fail, perhaps to take account of additional risks the generator's presence on the system creates, perhaps to share the load with another generator located a few miles away. The problem with proving *why* a line is built or who benefits from it lies with the fact that the generator concerned doesn't want to pay for it. It is very difficult to create a simple and transparent rule-based means of determining deep connection charges.

Shallow connection charges on the other hand have the advantage that they are less contentious. The disadvantage is that they cause more costs to be socialized in access charges. Why should I share in the cost of a transmission reinforcement made hundreds of miles away to accommodate a new generator, especially if that generator is my competitor?

There is no easy solution to the question of deep versus shallow charges. An acceptable compromise must be found, with criteria based on clearly defined engineering and economic conditions. The criteria and other rules must be stable over time. There are some economic principles to help. Where behavior is not affected much by the allocation of costs we can allocate more of the *overhead* or *joint costs* without causing distortions. Various economists[5] have proposed that such charges should be priced so as to minimize distortions in market decisions. Transmission cost allocation is more likely to affect generator location decisions than customer connection decisions and efforts should be expended to calculate the total impact of new generator connections.

Transmission Access Charges Finally, transmission access charges must recover the approved costs that are not recovered by usage and connection charges.

[5] See, for example, Frank P. Ramsey, "A Contribution to the Theory of Taxation," *Economic Journal* (1927), XXXVII: 47–61.

Like connection charges, the basis by which they are charged is controversial and there is no perfect answer, but the rules should be simple and stable over the long term. Transmission access charges should be applied with a compromise in mind, tying them to factors that *reflect usage*—for fairness and long-term efficiency, but *minimize distortion to usage*—for short-term efficiency. The issues are:

1. There is no perfect way to determine who should be *allocated* these charges. Final consumers are ultimately the only source of revenue in the industry, charging final customers is less likely to distort market decisions, and it is simple to charge them. This is a typical arrangement in the regions of the old U.S. tight pools.
2. There is no perfect *billing determinant*. Charges may be by a per-unit-of-use charge on all transactions if that is not too distortionary, or by an annual or monthly charge based on peak use, or some combination.
3. There is no perfect way to determine what *locational element,* if any, to incorporate. A common and simple solution is to have a single system wide rate (known as a *postage stamp* rate).

Conceptual issues still remain in the area of transmission access charges. The jury is still somewhat out on the third point for example; do connection charges and locational energy prices alone provide the best locational signals for investment in new factories and generation? (Or should there be a locational element in the access charge also?) Prices that vary by region, and transmission usage prices derived from these, signal to generators that they should build in regions where power is most valuable. They signal to industries to build factories in areas where power is less valuable. The issue is whether the addition of a regional component in transmission access charges would capture the effect of some long-term location-specific transmission costs that connection charges and locational prices might be missing.[6]

One thing that mustn't be done is to charge on the basis of the contract path implied by the source and destination locations specified in energy

[6]It can be argued that locational price signals fail to capture some regional differences in long-run transmission costs. Some of these differences might arise, for example, if central transmission planners are required to build enough transmission so that reliability of supply is more or less equated around the network. Achieving the same reliability costs considerably more on a per kW basis in low load regions and/or distant regions. Furthermore, if power prices are capped below consumer valuations (VOLL) in a market, or if prices are otherwise not allowed to ever rise to VOLL, then transmission usage prices (locational price differences) might never rise to truly reflect the costs saved by transmission used to prevent load outages in a region.

contracts. Some people have suggested this, with "highway" and "local road" tolls accumulated along the path. Like the contract path rule from wheeling, this requires that all trades be matched. But the contract path and matching fictions are eliminated in the integrated model. The road toll method can also easily be gamed. A trade from A to B can get together with a trade from B to A, for example, creating new trades from A to A and from B to B, and thus avoid access charges. Big traders with many transactions are favored over small, who have no such opportunities.

A better alternative to postage stamp pricing, if one is needed, is the United Kingdom method. Access charges could be different by zone and levied on some measure of peak usage. This method uses a *load flow analysis* to roughly determine how long-run transmission costs vary depending on the zone of new generation or load. However, it should be noted that in practice this method of allocating regional differences relies on so many assumptions and approximations that is at best arbitrary. And any similar method will contain arbitrary elements. The decision of a postage stamp rate vs. a rate that differs by region again boils down to a trade-off between the benefits of apportioning blame for cost causation, vs. the cost of making arbitrary and therefore contentious allocations.[7]

TRANSMISSION EXPANSION

Next to pricing and long-term stability of the rules, the thing that market participants are most concerned about regarding transmission is the set of arrangements for expansion. They are concerned about this because changes to the transmission system can dramatically change their ability to access the market, and/or the price at which electricity can be either bought or sold.

Regardless of the trading model, market participants understand that the competitive dynamic of entry and exit by others will affect their profitability. This is true under all trading models because this is how *deregulated* markets work. Entry and exit are driven by market price signals and the profit motive. What traders are concerned about is how the *regulated* business of transmission goes about deciding where and when to expand

[7] Earlier we mentioned pancaking. Pancaking is a form of locational signal because it discourages traders from importing or exporting *between* neighboring transmission regions. Pancaking can not exist *within* a region using the integrated trading model because pancaked fees can only be applied if trades are matched, with a source and a destination. We describe the problems of pancaking in the United States in Part Two, and that when fragmented transmission systems are consolidated over large regions and integrated, pancaking is less of a problem. When solving the pancaking problem, the first question is therefore how big to make the transmission region.

transmission capacity, if the regulated business does not have incentives in line with their own. These decisions have just as much impact on their profits, and can either increase or decrease the energy market profitability of generators or consumers, depending on where the line is built. Furthermore, market participants will eventually be required to pay for all new lines, so they have an additional direct interest in the process of how the decision to build new lines is made.[8]

Market participants need to know that someone is in charge of expanding the transmission system, the rules under which they will expand it, and that they will not be discriminated against. The basic questions are: Who proposes new lines? Who pays for them? Who decides?

Recall that earlier we said that good models exist for reform. Transmission expansion is one of the few areas where there is still conceptual work to be done. Stripped of complicating factors the central idea is quite simple: It is economic to build a line if the value of additional power transported is greater than the cost of the line. The value of transporting the power is the cost difference between generating at A and generating at B. This is always the fundamental cost-benefit analysis that should be done for a new line. How do we translate this concept into a workable plan for transmission expansion? The alternatives are market-based mechanisms and centralized decisions.

Market-Based Mechanisms

Market-based mechanisms for transmission expansion would be nice, and sound fine in theory, but are difficult or perhaps impossible in practice. A huge amount of academic horsepower has been devoted to the subject.[9] The theory goes like this:

- If we define a thing called a transmission right, and give it to people who expand the transmission system, then people will have incentives to expand the system if these rights are valuable.
- The rights *can* be valuable because they will give the owner the right to move power from one end of the line they paid for to the other. They get to use what they paid for and built.

---

[8] Transmission expansion can widen the geographic boundaries that define electricity marketplaces, reducing price differences between regions caused by congestion and losses. It can increase the intensity of competition and help solve market power problems.

[9] Refer to, for example, William Hogan, *Market-Based Transmission Investments and Competitive Electricity Markets,* Harvard Electricity Policy Group, August 1999.

- The rights *will* be valuable when transmission is scarce (i.e., when there is congestion) and so people will have incentives to build when and where transmission is needed. The incentives will match the need because the alternative to building will be to pay the cost of congestion.

Many factors complicate transmission rights, and most can be solved in theory. The main problem is that in a fully competitive market there are too many simultaneous transactions for the system operator to be able to check that everybody is only using the transmission they paid for. Since power flows where it will and can't be told where to go, it is known for sure that everybody is in fact sharing everybody else's transmission. So, to make sure that the network actually gets used efficiently and that people receive the value of their investments, the system operator must drop the fiction that people actually use the transmission capacity they paid for. He must do two things:

1. He must ignore who built what transmission and who owns what rights and instead instruct generators to operate in such a way that the transmission network *as a whole* is used most efficiently (i.e., *using the integrated trading model*).
2. He must reward the individual owners of transmission rights, consistent with the way the network was used. *It can do this by paying them the price of energy at one end of the line corresponding to the right, minus the price at the other (and minus the cost of energy lost).* This is, after all, the value of the line to whoever used it—power was moved from a place with cheap energy to a place where it is more expensive. This money is available to be paid to the transmission rights owner because the system operator collects it through transmission usage charges—collected directly from those who schedule contracts, and as implicit transmission usage charges, from the difference between the locational prices in the spot transactions.

So the main complicating factor with market-based mechanisms for transmission expansion can be solved. (The type of transmission right that allows these things is the *financial transmission right*—described later in this chapter.) But there are still many unresolved practical problems with the theory. There is a free-riding problem:

- Transmission investments are lumpy. They have massive economies of scale. Once the land has been purchased and the towers built, there isn't much difference in cost between a low capacity line and a high capacity one. You can't build transmission lines in increments of 1 MW in most cases. You might as well build a high capacity line if you are going to build one at all.

- Because they tend to be large and infrequently built, once they are built they tend to eliminate congestion.
- If they eliminate congestion, then the transmission rights will have no value. This is not a problem per se—even if congestion is fully eliminated, the investment might still be cost-effective because it allows more cheap power to substitute for expensive alternatives. Cheap but previously isolated generators get to sell their power into the same market at the same prices as everyone else.[10]
- But all this means there are some strong incentives for "free riding." If I, as cheap generator, benefit from congestion being eliminated, then I may be better off waiting and hoping that someone else will come along and build transmission first. That will save me the cost of building. But if everybody thinks that way then there will be a stalemate and nothing will be built.
- Many potential transmission investments are huge and may be bigger in scale than individual market participants, and so coalitions of interested parties may be necessary. But the free riding problem doesn't go away and in fact could get worse when coalitions are needed.

Other problems exist:

- Other potential investments are not huge but they are highly interdependent with existing network facilities. Building any transmission line can actually increase network capacity by *more* than the capacity of the line because of network effects. It can also *decrease* capacity in some parts of the system. The *net* amount of capacity increase to associate with a transmission right is a contentious issue that inevitably involves some system operator judgment, and therefore some opaqueness. It is particularly contentious if a right is granted for capacity increases on lines built by other people, and if the rights are good for the life of the investment (they should be), which may be a matter of decades.
- Some quite small and cheap gizmos can be added to the network, which increase capacity, and more appear to be on the way. Who gets to add these and claim the new capacity?
- Finally, the biggest problem of all. There is a real concern that the theory of market-driven transmission investment is untested in the real

[10] When the new lines investors have funded are uncongested, they will receive access to the grid, where the new lines connect, to buy or sell power. When the lines are congested, the owners of FTRs will receive the financial equivalent of access, in the form of payments equal to the difference in energy price between their locations and the location at the other end of the lines they have funded. (See Appendix F.)

world. Given all the uncertainties, including how long it takes to get the necessary approvals to build transmission lines, to form coalitions, to wait for long-term market prices to signal the value of new transmission there is a fear that investment will come too late, that the reward of transmission rights will not induce enough capacity.

It is also possible that market participants can have too much incentive to expand. Unfortunately, adding transmission is a bit like free trade—the importing customers and the exporting generators win, while the customers in the exporting zone and the generators in the importing zone lose. So the net benefit is always smaller than the individual benefits to one set of generators and customers. If a large amount of generation in an export region is selling uncontracted energy to local loads, for example, it can collectively have incentives to build unnecessary transmission, so as to lift local prices to the level in the export zone. Defining the net benefit is quite hard, and even if it *is* clear, there will still be winners and losers.

Moreover, with transmission investment there may be more than private benefits at stake. Increased transmission can reduce market power, increase network reliability, and enhance national security, so even if we could solve all the problems of market-based expansion, we might still want additional transmission.

Centralized Decisions

The alternative to a market-based mechanism for transmission expansion is a centralized one. This is the method still used more or less everywhere. The system operator/transmission owner and perhaps the regulator come up with a transparent and stable set of rules for identifying, evaluating, building, and charging for required new facilities that are necessary, feasible, and in the public good. But centralized planning is difficult too. The problems are of identifying and proving which investments are cost-effective, and allocating costs to market participants. Virtually any expansion will create winners and losers and the nature of the business is such that the rules will always involve some interpretation and hence some arbitrariness. The losers will fight any decisions. The goal is stable rules, efficient decisions, and to avoid endless litigation.

Combined Market-Based/Centralized Decisions

The alternative to choosing between the market-based and centralized methods is to have a combination of the two. In the long term, the best method of transmission expansion is to have such a compromise. It must inevitably rely heavily on a central planning backstop: To bring coalitions together; to verify and approve the cost effectiveness of projects; and to ensure that transmission gets built in time. It must mesh with the energy trading arrangements and be based around the structure of transmission contracts: Whether centrally planned or not, transmission rights should be created and allocated when new transmission is built.

Inevitably a compromise is necessary, but the extent to which decisions can be market-based should be maximized. Like the model for pricing of the transmission system, market-based expansion aligns the responsibility for cost with the beneficiaries of expansion. The transmission rights created from the market process should be transferred to the entity concerned, in return for the system operator being granted control of the assets and appropriate arrangements being put in place for their long term maintenance. The greater the percentage of cost of the required transmission that can be aligned this way, the less that remains to be socialized and recovered from market participants under some allocation rule.

The transmission rights created under the central planning process (i.e., when there is no specific entity or group of entities funding the line) should be auctioned off to the highest bidder. The proceeds should be used to reduce the remaining revenue requirement of the transmission owner to be recovered in transmission access charges.

The compromise process should define rules for how potential projects, whether identified in the central planning process or not, can be secured by private parties for funding.

Perhaps it is lucky, because it is delaying the pain, but for the moment it is very difficult in the United States at least to expand transmission by any mechanism in any event. The United States has gone BANANAS—Building Absolutely Nothing Anywhere Near Anybody. Nobody wants ugly transmission towers in his backyard any more, and the construction of new transmission lines has almost ground to a halt. There are eminent domain problems.[11] The exact details of how to mesh the centralized and market-based models still need to be fully shaken out.

[11] Eminent domain problems mean that it is more difficult to get siting approval for new transmission paths. But meanwhile, new technologies are offering some promising alternatives for increasing capacity without new towers, and they may offer increased relief in the near future. See, for example, *New York Times,* p. C1, August 11, 2001.

TRANSMISSION RIGHTS

How exactly do transmission rights work, and what is so special about Financial Transmission Rights?

The Precedent in the U.S. Gas Industry

The arrangements for pricing and expanding pipelines are exemplary in the U.S. gas industry, and rudimentary in electric. Most of the work in gas has been to price the pipeline service and introduce tradable contacts, which electricity has—for the most part—yet to get to.

Gas pipeline contract prices are regulated by the FERC, but the contracts are renewable virtually in perpetuity, and the capacity can be sublet on competitive terms, so the pipeline market is very competitive. The holders of the contracts essentially have a "property right" to the pipeline capacity. They pay the (minimal) usage charges for pipeline operating costs. To restrain any potential monopolization of the pipeline by holders of contracts, there is a "use it or lose it" feature. *The contracts are tradable and must be traded.* This is the aspect of the gas model that should be copied.

The users, who benefit directly and unambiguously, and get long-term contracts in return, pay for gas pipeline expansions. The prices are based on the incremental cost of the expansion, and are not rolled into an existing rate base. The pipeline contracts are not complicated—they are for physical point-to-point transport on a given system—a *contract path*. This is the part that is hard to copy in electricity.

In electricity, except in unusual circumstances, the beneficiaries of a transmission expansion are difficult to identify, since expansion benefits all the users to some extent by increasing the capacity of the network. In electricity, the transmission is a grid; the laws of physics mean that electricity does not flow over the designated and physical contract path. What this means is that the *laws governing flows of electricity on the grid make it extremely difficult to create a system of tradable property rights in transmission capacity that can facilitate trading*. Physical transmission contracts that would be analogous to gas are too difficult to define, enforce, and trade. In other words, as we have already said, the wheeling model cannot be extended to full competition.

However, there are some aspects of the gas contracting system that can be replicated. The Financial Transmission Rights (FTRs) we recommend are the economic equivalent of physical rights that are tradable and traded—gas contracts at the speed of light. Electricity travels 22 million times faster than gas. So if we take the principle adopted in gas—point-to-point rights that are tradable and must be traded—and just have the system operator do the trades instead of waiting for them to happen, we have Financial Transmission Rights.

The U.S. gas experience is described in more detail in Appendix D.

Financial Transmission Rights

The transmission right we have proposed is known as a *Financial Transmission Right*,[12] because using one doesn't affect the way the system operator dispatches the system. This is a different kind of right than *Physical Transmission Rights* (PTRs) in the gas market or in the electricity wheeling model. The difference is that the use of PTRs does affect the dispatch of the system.

A Financial Transmission Right is the right to collect, net of the cost of losses, the transmission usage charges (bottleneck fees) and implicit transmission usage charges between one defined location on the system and another. Normally traders would want the rights between locations where they typically buy and sell energy, and in that way they receive back exactly what they pay for congestion in transmission usage charges.

In practice, it makes the rights more flexible if they are defined to and from central hubs. This makes it easy for a buyer and a seller each to have one FTR from the same hub. When they make a contract, the two FTRs together hedge the transmission usage charge; but the buyer is not tied forever to the same seller. (*Hub and spoking* of FTRs also make secondary markets for FTRs more liquid.)

Financial Transmission Rights should be used to:

- Provide a means for traders to lock in the price of transmission usage (net of losses) in advance of scheduling a transaction—the locked-in price is the price of acquiring the FTR contract. A contract may be acquired either by building the transmission lines, or purchasing it on a secondary market. This encourages market participants to enter into long-term generation or purchase arrangements because it hedges the uncertainty of transmission usage charges.
- Give good incentives to regulated transmission owners to maintain their transmission properly.
- Help address market power problems.

[12] William Hogan has written extensively on the subject of FTRs. See www.ksg.harvard.edu/whogan. Refer also to an "Introduction to FTRs," Parmesano, Fraser, & Lyons, *Electricity Journal,* November 2000. The equivalent to an FTR exists in New York and is known as a Transmission Congestion Contract (TCC). In PJM it is known as a Fixed Transmission Right (FTR).

- Encourage market participants to make transmission expansion investments as we have described earlier.

In theory either physical or financial transmission rights should be able to provide these benefits. But, again, in practice, because of the 22 million factor, the lack of storability and the contract path fiction, only FTRs can.

Before describing how FTRs provide these benefits, how do FTRs work? FTRs are contracts that exist between a trader—in fact any individual or organization—and the system operator. FTRs are defined from a source location to a destination location. They are also denominated in a MW amount corresponding to a transfer capability between these two locations. FTRs can exist in the integrated trading model with locational spot prices, and unlike in the wheeling model, they do not confer an exclusive right to use the transmission. Instead, the system operator dispatches the system in a least-cost manner without regard to who holds FTRs, and calculates the locational prices that result. FTRs confer their holders the right to payments equal to the price difference—net of losses—between the source and destination locations specified for the denominated MW. As such, *FTRs rely on the fact that energy prices are set on a locational basis as they are in the integrated trading model.*[13]

FTR payments represent exactly the financial benefit that would accrue to a market participant that owned its own line, or to the owner of a physical right that sold its right to the highest bidder. In effect, FTRs are tradable PTRs that are automatically assigned to other users who place higher value on them. For example if the holder of an FTR is a generator that does not have a low enough offer price to be dispatched, it nonetheless will receive the financial equivalent of having sold the right to the generator who does get dispatched.

As we said earlier, funding of FTR payments is guaranteed from: (1) the transmission usage charges (bottleneck fees) that the system operator collects from traders who schedule contracts over congested transmission; plus (2) the equivalent funds (implicit transmission usage charges) that the system operator collects when traders make spot transactions in the energy market, rather than scheduling contracts.[14] It can be shown that as long as

---

[13] FTRs can also be used in the decentralized trading model, when congestion management is by auction.

[14] For example, in a market where all trades are made at spot—and none are contracted—and 100 MW flows across congested transmission from A to B, the system operator is a net buyer of 100 MW at A and a net seller of 100 MW at B. The funds it retains (price at B minus price at A, multiplied by 100 MW) are the same as the bottleneck fee it would have charged a scheduled contract to use the transmission.

the aggregate combination of FTRs awarded represents a feasible pattern of electricity flow on the transmission system, the system operator will always collect enough funds in any alternative, actual, flow on the same system, in order to be able to meet all its FTR payment obligations.[15]

Hedging Transmission Usage Charges Market participants in bilateral transactions who purchase or otherwise acquire FTRs can use FTR payments to offset transmission usage charges. They can thus convert uncertain future transmission usage charges into certain up-front FTR acquisition costs. Reducing this uncertainty is important to facilitate an efficient electricity market.

With *physical* transmission rights, ownership of a right *guarantees delivery of electricity between specified locations.* Rights can be acquired at a fixed price, and as long as the right is in effect, there are no additional charges for transmission usage, other than the costs of losses in transmission. Financial Transmission Rights provide the financial equivalent in the integrated trading model. The price of transmission usage is a function of transmission system congestion. This price will change from hour to hour. If an FTR is configured to match a transaction in size and location, the non-losses component of the transmission usage charge is exactly offset—the same result as having a physical transmission right.

Financial Transmission Rights can be subdivided and traded to market participants in a secondary market. FTRs can be reconfigured in terms of size (e.g., a 100 MW FTR could be sold as two 50 MW FTRs). FTRs can be reconfigured in terms of time (e.g., an FTR could be split so that one portion covers next week only, or only the hours from 6 P.M. to 8 P.M). FTRs can be reconfigured in terms of location (e.g., an FTR from A to C could be reconfigured as an FTR from A to B and an FTR from B to C). (Reconfiguring of this type might typically involve an industry standard hub location at B, to ensure the maximum liquidity and possible combinations of reconfigurations.)

Incentives to Transmission Owners If the system operator is not able to meet all its FTR payment obligations due to unplanned transmission outages that

---

[15] More than once in this discussion, we have said that FTR payments are net of transmission *losses*. Losses contribute to spot prices and thus to transmission usage charges (except in trading models that require losses to be repaid in kind). However, due to the way the revenue adequacy condition just cited works, FTR payments as they have been implemented in PJM and New York only apply to the differences between locational spot prices that are caused by *congestion*. The difference between location spot prices that are caused by losses are used to recover the cost of losses, and the losses rents (see Chapter 8) are set against transmission access charges, rather than paid in FTRs.

reduce system transfer capability, *the regulator can make the transmission owner liable for its FTR payments shortfall.* This gives transmission owners the right incentives to maintain the transmission, which we explain in more detail on page 213.

Market Power FTRs avoid the market power problems of PTRs. A major problem with PTRs is that they give the ability to exclude users from the use of transmission capacity. This could allow market participants to raise prices to uncompetitive levels in some locations and/or to depress them in others by withholding access. For example, a holder of PTRs from A to B who has generation at B might prevent generators at A from using the transmission. This would maintain a high price at B and also enables energy prices to be distorted or manipulated. To prevent manipulation of gas market prices, the gas regulator requires gas contracts to be used on any day or they will be reassigned. FTRs solve this problem for electricity because, as we described earlier, the economic effect of FTRs is to act as if they were tradable physical rights that are automatically traded—the system operator assigns them to the users who place the highest value on them.[16]

Other Considerations We described in the last section how transmission rights can encourage market participants to make transmission expansion investments. In Appendix F we expand on the decision criteria for transmission investments in general, and the specific role of FTRs.

Financial Transmission Rights can be awarded for the existing transmission system, not just expansions. This has been the case in PJM and New York already. Some historical transmission rights have been grandfathered—swapped for FTRs—and FTRs corresponding to the residual transmission capacity have been auctioned. The revenue from these auctions is beneficial in reducing access charges, although the value of FTRs that sold is not nearly sufficient to fully offset the total embedded cost of existing transmission investments.

In summary, a system of FTRs is not absolutely necessary to make a market work, but a system of PTRs will result in a market that doesn't work. Strictly speaking, successfully restructured markets do exist that don't use FTRs. But FTRs are very useful. They define property rights for market participants to use the transmission system. This means that market participants can buy something and in return get a guarantee that they will always be able to move power from A to B. This gives them valuable price certainty when negotiating energy supply contracts, and it means for people who are willing to build transmission that they get a valuable asset in return. It means new generators thinking about entering the market have a

[16] Refer to footnote 8 p. 99.

method to guarantee their product can get to their customers.[17] FTRs can provide a valuable service in giving transmission owners good incentives, and they can solve market power problems.

OWNERSHIP AND CONTROL: TRANSCOs VERSUS ISOs

Finally, who will run the transmission business? The most difficult restructuring issue regarding transmission concerns the relationship between the system operator and the transmission owner(s). One option is to set up a separate company, completely independent of all traders, which combines ownership of the transmission with system operations. The general name for this sort of company is a *Transco,* and the model is the National Grid Company (NGC) in the United Kingdom. (See Appendix B for a description of NGC.) This is also the model in Spain and Scandinavia. The Transco is a regulated, profit-making company.

The second option is to separate the system operator into a separate organization—an *Independent System Operator* or ISO, and to separate the transmission ownership into a second independent entity—the Gridco. This is the model in a few countries (Argentina and most of Australia, for example). The Gridco in this set-up is regulated and profit making—it does nothing but own, expand, and maintain the transmission network, and earn a return on the assets through charges levied on users. The ISO advises on transmission expansion and maintenance but does not have responsibility to physically carry out these functions. The ISO is generally a "not-for-profit" organization (owned by the government in some countries). It has to be regulated, since it's a natural monopoly, but since it has no assets except a control room, it cannot possibly be "for-profit" in the sense of being allowed to make returns on its assets. So the issue here is how to give it incentives to operate efficiently (see Figure 9.1).

In the United States, there are ISOs in California, New England, New York, PJM, and Texas, but transmission ownership in each of these regions remains with the old utilities, so transmission ownership is fragmented.

Transcos or Gridco + ISO?

As to the arguments between independent regulated ISO + Gridcos and independent regulated Transcos: Both models operate somewhere in the

[17] In New England, when the market was first restructured, generators were not able to obtain such a guarantee.

FIGURE 9.1 Transco.

Gridco + ISO = Transco

world, so far quite adequately. The disagreements on this issue are not fundamental, but they are informative.

The arguments in favor of the ISO/independent Gridco come down to distaste for a large and powerful monopoly Transco, which is potentially hard to control and regulate. The tension between the ISO and the Gridco, it is asserted, will lead to constructive solutions—two heads are better than one. Most people however agree that NGC seems to work rather well in the United Kingdom, which Gridco proponents put down to the British tolerance of monopolies of all sorts.

The arguments in favor of Transcos start with the fact that a stand-alone ISO is a not-for-profit, asset-free organization. An ISO is given control over expensive transmission assets owned by others, but it is not ultimately responsible for maintaining or expanding them, or even to ensure that they are properly used and not overloaded. The transmission control agreement between the owner of the assets and the ISO is difficult to write and enforce. A Transco by contrast is a profit-making regulated entity with assets. It can be sued. Liability is aligned with decision-making and ownership, so potentially a Transco can better be held accountable for its actions than an ISO. A Transco requires a serious Board of Directors to see that it meets its financial responsibilities to shareholders.

Significantly, a Transco can more easily be given incentives by the regulator in the rate-making process to do its job properly. A Transco can more readily be regulated under performance-based rate-making (PBR).[18] For example, as we alluded to earlier, the regulator can make a Transco liable for any shortfall between the transmission usage fees it collects and the FTR payments it is obliged to pay out. Such a shortfall might arise if the Transco does a bad job of maintaining full transmission capacity. The incentives to the Transco to do proper maintenance can therefore be aligned with the

[18] PBR is a form of regulation that can give better incentives to the company being regulated. It is designed to align responsibility for additional costs with benefits from additional revenues. Traditionally, regulated companies have been responsible for little or no risk. But placing all risks on a company might be too much. PBR implies a level of risk sharing.

benefits to transmission users of the maintenance being done, and there is no ambiguity of whether it was the transmission owner or the ISO responsible if there is a problem.

A Transco can better choose between maintenance and investment decisions; because it more fully encompasses both functions, it can better choose the right trade-off. Transcos need to be carefully regulated however. For example, we said earlier that transmission rights created under the central planning expansion process should be auctioned and the proceeds used to reduce transmission access charges. If the rights were not auctioned, and the Transco kept the transmission usage charges, the Transco would have a conflict of interest in its role as system operator because it could be better off dispatching the system in a way that causes congestion. And the Transco's investment decisions must be independently approved, because otherwise it could have incentives to over-invest.

But whether in an ISO/Gridco form or in a Transco form, the structural reality is that *both operations and transmission really need to be separated from generation* to avoid conflicts of interest. *We prefer the Transco format, because of the advantages just listed.*

ISO and the Utility Transmission Owner

Mostly though, in practice, the ISO structure where it exists in the United States and in Europe is a compromise, *leaving the transmission ownership with the existing utilities as a quid pro quo for agreeing to give up system operations.* In other words, while the system operator may be independent, the transmission is not separate from the generation at all. In our view this is not a viable solution for the long term, since it creates conflicts that are impossible to police. (In the United States there are tax problems associated with divestiture of transmission, which are on the list of simple things that need to be fixed. We return to this much later, when we discuss the current U.S. situation.)

Once vertically integrated companies have given up the system operations and planning functions to the ISO, the main reason for vertical integration is gone. Under the wheeling model, the integrated company can still benefit from over-reserving transmission, and keeping competitors out, but this advantage also disappears if the integrated trading model is introduced. Once system operations are separated and an integrated trading model introduced, utilities that own generation would be better off to avoid conflicts, to ensure that they get adequate compensation for their assets, and to divest them into a Transco.

There is an interesting question if a utility has divested its generation and system operations but retains transmission. The generation has gone so there is no generation/transmission conflict. Does it need to divest its transmission? Here the issue is not the conflicts, which are already solved. The problem is then whether transmission should be divested to promote regional consolidation, which we turn to in the next section. However, in some cases, what has always been called "transmission," because it is high voltage, is not really part of an integrated regional network, but is more closely integrated with a networked distribution system. (This is particularly true in big cities.) The balance has to be struck between integration of transmission and distribution at the local level, and the need for consolidation of transmission at the regional level.

Regional Consolidation

Finally, whether a Transco or a Gridco, the transmission business must be of sufficient geographic scope. In the U.S. (and Europe) they are currently too fragmented. We have already mentioned how consolidation helps solve the pancaking problem, but there are other problems of fragmentation.

Between each pair of contiguous areas there has to be an interconnection agreement—specifying how the system operators will arrange power flows and payments between the areas. Evidently, the more areas there are, the more interconnection agreements have to be made, and the required number of agreements grows exponentially. It becomes more complicated to run the system efficiently. This is especially true if the areas are not natural market areas, separated by just a few transmission constraints. Consolidation should be achieved so that seams between transmission systems reflect natural market boundaries caused by electrical characteristics such as congestion and losses, rather than political boundaries that make no sense from either an electrical or market point of view.

Fragmentation can cause problems in either the wheeling trading model or the integrated model, although perhaps less so in the integrated model. In the wheeling trading model, traders have to be specific about the assumed path over which a contract will follow. The smaller the individual transmission systems, the more specific the transmission user needs to be, and the bigger the contract path fiction. Traders might even be able to shop from alternative transmission paths, and this exacerbates the problem. For example, two paths might connect location A to location F: A to B to C to F, and A to D to E to F. A trader will pick ABCF if it is cheaper, but operationally this could be nonsense. Electricity flows where it will—perhaps half on ABCF and half on ADEF due to loop flow. To allow for the possibility of such an ABCF trade, system operators in D and E have to be conservative about how much of their transmission capacity they make available to others. They can't sell everything they have. Meanwhile, system operators in B and C can't assume that they will have spare capacity if they sell access for an ABCF trade—it depends what else is happening on the transmission system, so they also need to be conservative. Furthermore, if the ABCF trade does occur, the recovery of transmission cost is not fair. Traders are using D and E's transmission assets, but not contributing to D and E's fixed costs.

Consolidation helps reduce some of these problems. It does this by reducing the impact of the contract path fiction. In its simplest form, if A, B, C, D, E, and F are all consolidated within a single system operator, the trade simply needs to be nominated as going from location A to F. The system operator is able to internalize the consequence of where the electricity does actually flow, and it doesn't have to hold back as much capacity to deal with other people's trades interfering with its system. Consolidation widens the marketplace and provides one stop shopping for transmission users.

Consolidation improves efficiency under the integrated trading model as well. Under the integrated model, a system operator controls generators and optimizes the use of transmission *within* its region—this is the scope of its control—and generally it schedules power flows *between* regions on interconnectors at the request of traders. The interregional scheduling is required in advance of real time because (usually) the system operators do not have real-time control of any units outside of their regions. Since the system operator control is limited to its own region, it can't maximize value between regions. (At least, not unless there is a system of economic coordination between system operators, as Hogan and others have suggested.[19]) Consequently, in this process of managing the use of interconnectors it is normal to use something similar to Physical Transmission Rights. Consolidation reduces reliance on these interconnector PTRs, and by doing so, allows more efficient trading over large regions.

Furthermore, consolidation can deliver considerable cost savings to the transmission owners; the business of transmission has large economies of scale. And it can fix a real problem of uncoordinated regional expansion planning.

In recent times, FERC has devoted considerable attention to the issue of regional consolidation of transmission in the U.S. Regional Transmission Organizations (RTOs) go some of the way. We return to this subject in Part Two of the book.

---

[19]Refer to Michael Cadwalader, Scott Harvey, William Hogan, and Susan Pope, *Coordination of Congestion Relief Across Multiple Regions,* Center for Business and Government, Harvard University, October 7, 1999.

CHAPTER 10

Issues in the Retail and Distribution Business

This chapter addresses the problems of retail access. Retail access is customer choice—the Model 4 organization of the industry. There is a relatively simple core of needs for retail access—wholesale competition, and a settlement system for retailing—and a complicated set of practical difficulties. Some of these are problems of scaling up access for millions rather than hundreds or thousands of customers. But some of them arise, in the United States at least, because the process was done back to front—the state regulators had to make up the rules as they went along to offset the problems of not having implemented wholesale competition first.

Before retail access, every utility had *distribution divisions* that were responsible *for delivering the power that another division in the company produced or sometimes purchased.*[1] Customers purchased standard electricity service from the local utility. The customers purchased distribution service as part of the bundled package, although they did not realize it. The main functions of the distribution divisions were:

1. Planning for, installing and maintaining the poles and wires, and restoring them after storms or accidents—the "wires" functions. This is a natural monopoly because it requires a heavy fixed investment in the distribution grid that is inefficient to duplicate. To date, few have seriously considered allowing multiple firms to string their wires overhead or to dig up streets to place them underground. (There are one or two cities where this is allowed but no other jurisdictions have followed their lead.)

[1] Alternatively, some Model 1 and Model 2 systems had separate distribution and generating companies umbilically attached (see Chapter 2).

2. Metering, billing, and customer service.
3. Plans for interrupting customers in the event of generation shortfalls.

In the world of retail access, customers have the choice of who provides the electricity, and distribution companies will *deliver power produced by someone else*—there may be hundreds of competing retailers. Under retail access the role of the distribution divisions—now the distribution companies or Distcos—becomes more complex. But exactly what functions they should have under retail access has been a matter of some controversy.

THE EVENTUAL RETAIL ACCESS FRAMEWORK

In this chapter, we lay out the basic model of an eventual retail access framework, namely:

- A regulated Distco who provides, maintains, and charges for the delivery system (the poles and wires) and the distribution losses;
- Functioning wholesale markets, including hourly metering of final consumers, and a transparent spot price;
- Competing retailers, serving all customers, with a small residual retail function for those whose retailers go out of business, or who are credit risks (the provider of last resort or POLR); and
- A settlement system to decide who sold what to whom. Infrastructure for metering, billing, and information transfer.

These are the core requirements. There are also a series of metering and billing issues—who should provide the meters, who should send the bills, and what to do about customers who do not yet have hourly meters (so-called *load profiling*).

The Distco may also be required to sell at regulated rates as a default provider. We distinguish *default provider* (for couch potatoes who cannot be bothered to choose) from *provider of last resort* or POLR (for customers whose retailers have gone out of business, or whom retailers will not serve). This nomenclature is not universally used—there is no standard terminology—and we apologize in advance for appropriating words that may have been used differently elsewhere.

Additionally, much of the confusion and dispute in the United States over retail access arises from not having followed a logical order in reforming the system, and consequent ad-hoc measures to offset various problems. The most important of these are the problems arising from "top-down rate design" used to solve stranded cost problems, leading to lack of competition in the retail markets and hokey methods of setting "shopping credits." This is mainly a U.S. problem, because the industry is privately owned, and we leave detailed discussion of it to Part Two. Our strong preference for stranded cost recovery (as discussed in Chapter 3) is early valuation by agreement or by divestiture, which gets the problem settled and out of the way.

This chapter first reviews the core requirements for retail access. Then it considers the additional issues of competition in metering and billing, and load profiling when metering is inadequate; and finally we discuss whether the Distco should be required to retail as default provider, and its role as POLR.

A COMPETITIVE WHOLESALE MARKET

The functioning of the wholesale markets is the subject of the whole of the preceding part of this book. *We assert that effective wholesale markets with a transparent spot price are essential for retail competition,* which may need some explanation since it has not been universally implemented. The competitive wholesale market is the mechanism for controlling the price of electricity; this is what protects final customers, in place of regulation. Competition is what protects them in most other parts of the economy and, if it is working well, it will protect them in electricity also.

For several reasons, having a transparent spot price is a critical element of an effective retail market. It is important for the wholesale markets for reasons discussed earlier:

- A significant number of customers should pay a spot price (for marginal consumption, not for all) so that there is sufficient demand response to clear the market and balance the market power of generators.
- Generators (especially small, new entrants) need a spot market and a spot price because it provides them automatically with the back up they need if their plants are out of service. This increases reliability and inhibits market power.

But a transparent wholesale spot price is also important for retail access:

- The inevitable discrepancies (imbalances) between customers' consumption and sellers' deliveries must be settled. A spot price is the right price for this purpose.

- The spot price indicates the value of generation and is important to many stranded cost computation approaches, and for penalties for failure to supply.
- Consumers need a spot price to evaluate the reasonableness of competitive generation offers.
- Suppliers of default service (and other marketers) need a spot market to evaluate proposed contracts with generators.
- Consumers need a history of spot price volatility to decide whether they want to purchase a "price protection product" to reduce bill uncertainty.

In the United States, some states have tried to introduce retail access without functioning wholesale markets, and without a transparent spot price, which has created serious problems. (For more details on this, see Part Two.)

COMPETING RETAILERS

The competitiveness of the retail market depends on the establishment of clear and enforceable rules and procedures governing retailer eligibility and retailer codes of conduct. The rules also need to set out the responsibility of the competing retailers, and any penalties for failure to supply.

The problem is that when prices in the spot market get high, competing retailers may find it more advantageous to sell power (their own, or the contracts they own) back into the spot market, rather than make good on their contracts with customers. But someone has to serve the customers of the defaulting retailer; the question is who, and at what price.

One solution is for the customers simply to pay the spot price if their retailer defaults; but they expected to be protected by making contracts. The utility is open to considerable risk if customers can simply be dumped back into regulated default service, at tariff prices, because the cost of the extra power will exceed the tariff charges. Although the customers could sue to enforce the contract, this is expensive and time consuming, for relatively little individual benefit.

The retailers themselves should probably be discouraged from walking away from their contracts by bonding provisions and penalties for defaulting. If penalties are written into bonding provisions, the "right" penalty is based on the value of the electricity not provided (the spot price).

Likewise, competitive retailing depends on fair practices by the utility, which must provide the same quality of delivery service regardless of a consumer's choice of supplier, not use its monopoly business to subsidize its competitive activities, and not provide competitively useful information about customers to its retailing subsidiary that it does not provide to competing retailers. (See the discussion of codes of conduct in Chapter 3.)

Eligibility

At one extreme, a retailer can be just a middleman—arranging energy supplies to match the consumption of its customers. At the other extreme, a retailer can be a large corporation that also owns generation. Because the behavior of any retailer affects the entire system, it is important to have a set of rules laying out the responsibilities and qualifications for being a retailer. Often these rules include letters of credit or other financial arrangements to ensure that retailers do not run off without paying for the energy and delivery services their customers have used. Other rules are designed to protect consumers from retailers who have no resources (in markets where purchasing all requirements from the spot market is not allowed), from misleading marketing campaigns, and from slamming (switching a customer from one marketer to another without the customer's permission).

In spite of efforts to ensure that only qualified and responsible retailers are permitted to operate, there is no way to force a retailer that wants to exit the market to continue operating. For example, AES Power Direct (the largest alternative supplier in New Jersey) dropped over 15,000 residential and small commercial customers in early 2001[2] and there was some confusion about who was responsible for paying for the energy these customers used. Enron did the same in California in 2000.

Market Conditions That Make Competitive Retailing Difficult

The probability of retailing is, as we have discussed earlier, quite limited. Therefore it is all the more important that in those areas where the retailers do add value, competition should not be foreclosed by assigning potential value-added tasks exclusively to the utility. For example:

- Fixed prices for default service make it hard for competitors to offer hedges;

[2] U.S. Department of Energy, *Electric Utility Restructuring Weekly Update,* January 26, 2001.

- Low fixed prices for standard offers or default service, based on historic costs of the utility, undercut entrants;
- Not permitting retailers to bill customers directly can undercut the benefits of simple bills, or complex bills that give real information, that retailers might offer and customers might appreciate; and
- While we believe that competition in metering itself is problematic for reasons of timing and potential cheating (and is a distraction from the main issues), we believe that Distco should leave the market to provide the value-added services such as automatic cut-off of appliances when the price gets high.

Some of these may be unavoidable in the transition, but if competitive retailing is the goal, the rules should be made with caution.

SETTLEMENT FOR RETAIL ACCESS

Deciding who sold what to whom requires an enormous accounting (settlement) system. This is complicated and boring, so it is often left to the last minute, but it has created massive confusion and expense when done badly. Some entity must provide meters at customer premises, read them, transmit the information to a billing system, prepare bills, send them out, and follow up for payment. Meter reading does not happen on a single day at the end of the month—meter reading cycles are continuous, there are missed readings, estimated readings and all the messiness of the real world to deal with, which becomes much more complicated when customers can change suppliers.

The move from wholesale to retail competition involves a host of new responsibilities, decisions, rules, and protocols. The more customers involved, the more complex and costly the systems necessary. The entire flow of funds, from customer to eventual supplier, is now broken into multiple parts, and the billing and accounting systems now have to ensure that the customers get the right bill, that they pay them, and that the Distco, the retailer, the transmission company, and the ultimate generators all get paid. This is a very much more complex system of information and control than under the old integrated utility.

In the United States, agreeing on the details for metering, billing, and information transfer has been very time consuming, involving endless stakeholder committee meetings. Done on a state-by-state basis, the result has been a different set of rules in each state. There is a national effort to produce uniform rules and uniform business practices, but this effort is proceeding slowly.

Information Requirements for Settlement under Retail Access

Information for settlement must be collected from four sources:

1. Generator meters—this information is collected by the system operator;
2. Transmission/distribution interface meters—this information is collected by Distcos; and
3. Customer meters—this information is collected by Distcos as well.
4. The generator must tell the settlement agent that he has contracts with the following people, and the customers agree. So this contract is the fourth piece of information, linking the generator with the customer. (It becomes more complicated when there are retailers involved, but the principle is the same—for clarity let us just suppose that generators sell directly to customers.)

There is no way for the ultimate supplier of power to track his output to the final customer. What he produced will inevitably be different from what the aggregate of his customers take, and the difference is made up in *imbalances* in the wholesale markets. The only way to tell which customer was served by whom is to have an accounting system that records contracts between generators and customers. The question is where should all this information be lodged? Who should be the settlement agent?

System Operator or Local Settlement

The question is whether the system operator or SO (or a *central settlement agent* who serves all the Distcos served by the SO), should keep a big central accounting system that records all the millions of customers' meter readings and matches them both with the contracts and the generators' output; or whether the Distco should be a local settlement agent, and in some sense be interposed between the SO and the customer for settlement purposes.

We recommend that the Disco take on the retail settlement role, and that sufficient time be allowed to get this right. The reason the local settlement would make sense is that Distcos have been managing large scale accounting for their customers for years, and anyway, all these people are still their customers, for the wires business if not for the energy itself. The Distco has to measure their usage and bill them anyway. For the SO it is a major new job, and distinctly different from its main task of operating the system.

If the Distco acts as settlement agent, it (not the SO) receives notice of the contracted suppliers for customers within the distribution area. It aggregates the meter readings for all those customers who have the same generator supplying them, and sends the aggregated amounts to the SO (perhaps 10 pieces of information per hour, not millions, for the SO). The SO then aggregates across all Distcos for that generator, and computes the "imbalances" to be purchased by or sold to that generator at the spot price in the wholesale market. The SO does not need to know the prices in the contracts or the details of the meter readings, just the aggregate quantities.

Meanwhile the Distco uses the contracts to settle with the generators. In the simplest system, the Distco also acts as the generator's billing agent—it bills the customer for the price shown in the contract and passes the revenues on to the generators. Or the Distco can pass the meter reading to the generators and they can bill the customers themselves.

Retailers interposed between generators and consumers add another layer of complexity. Then the Distco sends the aggregate amount for each retailer to the SO and the SO has to settle the wholesale contracts between retailers and generators. The wholesale contract is sent to the SO—the retail contract to the Distco. In Argentina, the Distcos are the settlement agent for all but the largest customers, and things have worked well. This is also the model in PJM.

Competing retailers sometimes fear that having the Distco settle contracts will increase conflicts of interest, and this is certainly possible. Our preference for local settlement is a judgment about costs and benefits, not an absolute preference.

Two horror stories follow.

Horror Stories Many retail access pilots and full programs have floundered because the necessary metering, billing and information transfer infrastructure was not in place. California and England and Wales are examples.

Each of the three California utilities had different billing and communication systems that were relatively old and inflexible. Adapting them to work for retail access was costly and time-consuming because:

- System changes necessary to facilitate the exchange of meter data between the utilities and retailers took longer than anticipated and the regulator made changes to the standards in midstream.
- Operation of the meter read database was problematic as some marketers provide meter read data on paper, not electronically as was originally envisioned.
- There were also problems with consolidated billing by utilities, which were supposed to be able to accept bill-ready information from the retailers and print that information on customers' bills without further

computations. PG&E's billing system was unable to handle bill-ready information; instead retailers had to submit their rate schedules and PG&E computed the retailers' charges before printing them on the customer's bill.

In England and Wales, lack of adequate billing, metering, and settlement systems proved to be a serious and costly problem in the introduction of retail access. Beginning in 1990, the large customers settled centrally through the system operator (the Pool). There were only 4,000 of them to start with, and things went smoothly. But as the numbers of customers with retail access increased, England and Wales just went on with central billing (and complicated online data collection), and fell into all sorts of major problems, including:

- In 1994, retail choice was extended to customers with demand over 100 kW (about 50,000 customers), before the necessary half-hourly meters were in place. (Previously only consumers of over 1 MW were able to choose their supplier.) Only about 30 percent of the sites registering for retail competition had the necessary meters and communication links installed in time. Therefore, in the short term, suppliers and distributors had to rely on load profiling to bill customers. Substantial billing errors resulted and bills were delayed for months. *The total cost of introducing retail access for this group of customers was estimated as £24 million, rather than the expected £10 million (£1 = about $1.5).*
- Problems arose again in 1999, when the extension of retail access to all small commercial and residential customers (24 million of them) had to be postponed almost a year because the marketers did not have the necessary software and settlement systems in place. There were significant discrepancies between the meter readings made by customers when they switched supplier and the meter data fed into the system by data collectors. These discrepancies resulted in incorrect bills being issued and problems with data passed to the Pool for settlement.

Texas also had problems with centralized settlement:

> *Computer and communication problems continue to plague the Texas agency working to implement a retail electric choice pilot program.*
>
> *Officials with the Electric Reliability Council of Texas, or Ercot, told market participants late Friday that they are unable to increase the number of requests the staff can handle from the roughly 330 a day, despite ongoing computer upgrades.*

> *A backlog of more than 95,000 requests submitted by retail electric providers, or REPs, to switch customers to new suppliers still is waiting to be handled. About 2,000 requests have been successfully processed so far.*[3]

METERING ISSUES

Accurate metering is critical, not only for normal commercial purposes, but also for the financial stability of the Distco. This is a special quirk in electricity. For reasons that are unique to electricity, *it is not the retailer but the Distco that stands to lose plenty of money if meter readings for final customers are inaccurate*. This is a major reason for leaving the Distcos in control of reading (and owning) the meters for final customers.

In most businesses, it is the retailer who loses if the scales read light—he has to pay the wholesaler for the correct weight, and if he sells 2 pounds of apples and only charges for 1.5, then he loses money. If he tries to charge for 2.5 pounds, the customer is there as a counterweight, with opposing incentives. But in electricity, the same meters that say how much electricity the customer used are the very same meters used to say how much the retailer has to pay the producer for, or how much he owes in the imbalance market. *So the retailer has no incentive to get it right. If the meter reads low, he pays less, too.*

The difference between measured consumption at the customer meter, and energy measured when it flows into the Distco's service territory, is treated as a "loss" on the distribution system. (About 4 percent to 6 percent of power is normally lost in transit, due to heating of the wires and physical characteristics of transformers and other equipment.) If customers' meters or meter readings are inaccurate, the difference will grow, and will be treated as a distribution loss. Depending on the rules for dealing with the shortfall, this difference may be considered as:

- Higher-than-expected distribution losses, to be borne by the distribution company until the next time distribution tariffs are set. This can amount to a very high charge on the Distcos. In New Jersey, for instance, a 5 percent reduction in total customer revenues from low meter readings would result in an under-recovery of approximately $200 million, which is over 25 percent of distribution revenues of PSE&G, and far in excess of the Distco's profits.

---

[3] Dow Jones & Company, Inc., August 27, 2001.

- Or the excess "losses" may be spread to all consumers (or retailers) through an uplift charge.

Either way, the customer with the slow meter (or underreported consumption) gains at the expense of someone else, and the retailer has no incentives to avoid under-recording. The cost never falls directly to the retailer who sold the power or the customer who bought it. Because of the poor incentives for retailers to perform these functions accurately and the need for the Distco to control shut-offs for nonpayment, we believe it is essential for the Distcos to keep control of the metering and settlement.

Competitive Metering?

We would exclude meter provision and meter reading from the list of tasks that should be competitive for several reasons:

- Metering and meter reading has a particular quirk in electricity as explained above—the retailer and the customer have the same incentives for the meter to read low. This could in principle be offset by having yet another set of traffic cops to check meters, but it is easiest to leave it with the Distco.
- The regulatory arguments over standards, requirements, accuracy, and so on that we have observed in places where attempts have been made to introduce competitive metering, suggest that it is a distraction from the main goal and should be left aside while the main goals are accomplished. The places in the United States that are actually implementing extensive hourly metering seem to be the places where competition in metering is not allowed, and even where retail access is not contemplated—Washington and Wisconsin.
- The timing in the restructuring cycle—hourly metering should be in place before competitive retailing, so that the wholesale markets work well.
- There may also be a question of scale economies in metering—if it costs much less for a single provider to handle metering than for many competitors, then this is a case for monopoly provision; however, it is an empirical matter as to whether there are such scale economies—it depends on the technology, which is developing fast.

Against these arguments is the possibility that the Distco will choose the wrong technology—too expensive or too limited. There is no good answer to this, other than regulatory oversight and plenty of bids.

Use of Load Profiles for Small Customers

Customers who do not yet have hourly meters will need to have their monthly total kWh usage apportioned to the hours of the month, mainly so that their retailers can be charged properly in the wholesale markets. The way this is done is to create a standard *load profile* of how much the average person in a particular group of customers (a load) uses in each hour—a load profile is simply a set of standard weights to apply to compute an *average price* for the month. Customers who have hourly meters do not need load profiles.

The customer's own monthly kWh usage is used to multiply this average price to get the bill—the profile simply decides how much of their usage is deemed to be in the appropriate period (would have been counted in that period if the metering were in place and they used the same as others in their group). This is simple enough in theory, but in practice, with meter reading cycles differing and with estimated bills, there is a massive amount of data to compute: the cost in England and Wales for implementing retail access for small customers was $1.2 billion largely because of the costs associated with load profiling. And after all that expense, these customers are still not able to respond to prices signals, and are still cross-subsidizing each other, since the expenditure was made on load profiling and not on hourly meters.

There is often controversy over how many load profiles are necessary; who should compute them (the utility, the regulator, etc.); whether they should be computed on a fixed schedule (such as once a year) or dynamically to follow the actual consumption of a sample of customers with hourly meters over the specific days in each consumer's billing period.

For people whose use is less peaky than average, the load profile overcharges. Norway came up with a way to use this fact to encourage voluntary conversion to hourly metering. It computed the profile for the residual load, after the hourly-metered consumption is removed. In this way, those who believe they can do better than the profile by having an hourly meter get themselves a meter, leaving nonmetered customers with an increasingly less attractive load profile and providing more incentives to get an hourly meter.

There is some opportunity for gaming if a customer can influence the load profile to which he is assigned. However, load profiles are not subject to gaming by retailers because the pattern of consumption dictated by a consumer's load profile should be the pattern that the retailer is held responsible for supplying. Even if a consumer uses less electricity in the high cost hours than the load profile assumes, his retailer does not benefit because the retailer has to supply the higher load-profiled amount.

California's rules got this wrong, too—consumers' shopping credits are based on the load profiles, even if they have hourly metering, but their retailers are responsible for providing the energy registered by the hourly meter. So by cherry-picking consumers who use less in high cost hours than the load profile implies, retailers can make additional profits—the resulting losses are spread to all other customers.

Degree of Unbundling on Bills

Consumers need to know what they are paying for the elements of service over which they have choice. Anything more simply causes confusion. The default bills should be unbundled to show the delivery charges, and the energy charges by the hour, so that customers have a clear choice, and know the cost of the alternative. The California PUC required bills supplied by both retailers or utilities to show in excruciating detail, even on residential bills, competition transition charge, generation cost, transmission cost, distribution cost, securitization charges, system benefits charges, 10 percent discount required by restructuring legislation, and so on. There was no way for even sophisticated consumers to determine *how their bill would change if they used more or less electricity, or if they changed suppliers.* California went too far in bill unbundling and regulatory control of the bill's appearance.

The retailers should be allowed to send their own bills. In the United Kingdom, one of the main selling points for retailers is their offer of simple bills—flat per kWh charges or various combinations of fixed and variable charges. If regulators insist on unbundling charges that consumers have no control over (you cannot buy a different amount of transmission and distribution), hiding the marginal price, and forbidding retailers from structuring their own bills, many of the promised innovation benefits of retail access and responses to efficient price signals will be lost.

SHOULD THE DISTCO RETAIL AT REGULATED RATES?

We distinguish the *default service* for couch potatoes who do not wish to choose, from the *POLR service* to customers that no retailer wants because they are credit risks, or those whose retailers have gone out of business. Both services might require the Distco to retail at regulated prices, but there are different issues involved. (As noted before, these terms are not standardized, and are often used differently.)

In Model 3 where the Distco is the only provider to the medium-sized and small customers, the Distco has to retail at regulated rates, and there are problems with contracting for the purchase of power, which we reviewed in Chapter 3. In Model 4, retail competition, the end point should be to get out of this problem, *and not provide default service at regulated prices for anyone.* New Zealand went straight to this solution many years ago, and has had few problems with it. England and Wales are moving to this solution after 10 years of transition.

POLR

In the old world, the franchise utility had to supply whatever load came along in its service territory. It could require a deposit from a customer with a bad payment history, but could not refuse service.[4] Retail access changes that. Retailers can pick and choose the customers they wish to serve. But what of those that no one chooses? The POLR function should be a very small function, serving very few customers, rather like the "assigned risk pool" in auto insurance—if it is priced according to the risks, it will be more expensive than the competition, and customers will try to get off it as soon as possible. The price will need to be regulated; the price should account for the risks; and customers should be clearly informed that they are in the assigned risk pool, paying more than they could probably find elsewhere.

This function could be contracted out so that the distribution company is not the POLR although this has not been universally successful: Maine went to the extreme of requiring divestiture of generation and forbidding the utility from providing standard offer service, but this approach backfired when the Maine PUC was unable to find suitable bidders to perform this function. Overall it probably makes sense for the Distco to provide POLR service by simply passing through the spot price, with an adder for the administrative costs and credit risks. *We do not recommend this for default service for reasons discussed next.*

Required Default Service

Required default service is in a way just continuing what the utility has always done—provide the whole bundled service at regulated prices, but unbundling the prices on the bill so that the customers can choose to go elsewhere if they wish, and not pay the commodity portion to the Distco. (This is different from the situation where the Distco has a retail affiliate who provides competitively. There, competition is supposed to keep the price down. Here we are talking about required regulated provision.)

---

[4] A utility could disconnect for nonpayment, but only after following detailed and lengthy procedures prescribed by the PUC, and often not even then during periods of extremely hot or cold weather.

There are four sets of problems when the Distco *is required to retail at regulated prices* in competition with retailers. We reviewed these in Chapter 2.

1. Is the Distco charging customers a fair price for the power it is selling? The problem arises if the Distco has to contract for power—policing the contracts is difficult.
2. When the Distco is selling from its own plants someone also has to police what it is charging itself, and passing on to its customers.
3. Does the default offering prevent competing generators from entering the market, or create conflicts of interest for the Distco?
4. Does requiring the Distco to retail put an unfair risk on the Distco? This is a regulatory problem as to what costs the Distco will be allowed to recover.

One school of thought is that if wholesale markets are working well, when retail competition (Model 4) is introduced *the Distco should never have any regulated retail default responsibility* so that the there can be no conflicts or cross-subsidies; all retail sales are made by competitive retailers and there is no risk on the Distco. At the other extreme, some jurisdictions *required* Distcos to offer retail tariffs as a condition of their licenses.

The main reason for not going all the way to abolishing regulated default service is the concern of regulators for the couch potatoes—those customers who cannot be bothered with making a choice, and would just like all this extra administrative work to go away and leave their evenings free (of whom I must confess your author is one). For these people, the Distco as *regulated default provider* is seen as an *enhancement* of customer choice—I choose to let the Distco and the regulator deal with it for me. There is some evidence from marketing research that I am not alone—customers want a choice of pricing plans, but not necessarily a choice of supplier; they would be satisfied to have several utility-offered options from which to choose.

Most places have required regulated default service at least as a transition, in deference to the couch potatoes, although when the Distco has retail responsibilities it requires more regulatory oversight. This may be considered a socialization of my private costs—no one watches over my other competitive purchases for me unless I pay them to do so, so why should an army of electric regulators protect me at the public expense, unless the competitive wholesale markets are not working? It has been the fear that the wholesale markets would not be competitive that has led to some of the belt-and-suspenders-too protections of default service.

But regulators often consider more than just the inertia of the lazy and the busy—they believe that small users, poor people, less educated people, are more likely to be confused and make bad choices; or even that no one has the real information to decide between alternatives that have not established a track record, and need some trusted fall-back. These are not unreasonable positions, at least in a transition period.

In most cases, only the regulators and the couch potatoes like the regulated default service option—the Distcos themselves and the competing retailers do not. The competing retailers call it unfair competition—taking advantage of inertia—while the Distcos complain that it is a no-win situation; if they make contracts that turn out to be higher than the spot price, they will be penalized two ways—the regulator will disallow the contracts, and the couch potatoes will wake up and go elsewhere, leaving the Distco with stranded contracts. Or if the reverse happens, and market prices rise, customers will flock to the regulated offering, and the Distco will have to purchase at higher costs than the tariff to meet its obligation. There are ways out of this problem with properly designed tariffs. On the whole, in spite of my personal inertia, the solution of no regulated offering at all does seem to be the best end point.

Design Issues in Default Service for Small Customers

The regulators will determine how generation is *acquired* by the Distco to supply default service for small customers. Alternatives include spot purchases, full-requirements contracts, contracts with the new owners of the utility's former generation units, and some combination. There is an additional question of what generation service it should *provide*—spot market pass through (virtual direct access), fixed prices, or some combination of contract and market prices. These choices are related—the Distco will want to back its retail offering with a purchase having much the same risk characteristics.

Virtual Direct Access One very simple option is to make default service a form of virtual direct access. Under this approach, *consumers purchase energy from the utility at the spot market price* (averaged over the month if the customer does not have an hourly meter). If the customer does not like the volatility of the spot price, he can choose a retailer.

We recommend this for default service for large customers, and for POLR for small customers, but not for *default service* for small customers. In fact, virtual direct access is not only simple, but it gives ample room for competing retailers.

However, as a transition mechanism, *we would not recommend pass-through of the spot price as the default service for small customers* for two reasons: first, if there are indeed many couch potatoes and much inertia, this solution makes too much electricity pass through the spot markets—the wholesale markets need contracts to reduce market power. Second, it does not afford the couch potatoes or the vulnerable customers the relative price certainty of the default service that they are used to, and what they are used to is the primary reason for offering default service at all.

Difficulties of Distcos Contracting Forward Since many small and unsophisticated customers will end up on default service, at least in the early years of retail access, providing some degree of price certainty in default service is probably appropriate. To avoid unacceptable risks, the Distco offering default service with fixed prices must have its own generation or contract with generators for a fixed-price supply.

Forward contracting by Distcos solves the two problems above: Small consumers would have less price volatility than if they paid a spot market pass-through exclusively. Market power by generators would be balanced by market power of Distcos. The existence of a large contracting market would reduce risks for developers (including small ones) of new generation, thereby increasing capacity and competition.

However, contracting creates its own problems and many of these problems are equally applicable to marketers entering into contracts to supply their loads. Some of these problems are:

- How much power should the Distcos purchase under contract? If consumers can switch at any time, the Distco never knows how much load it will have. The Distco could try to require its customers to sign long-term contracts, but this is a departure from the goal of not disturbing things too much, and regulators have wanted to give consumers maximum flexibility and protection.[5]
- If default service based on long-term contracts turns out to be more expensive than shorter-term options, customers will switch, leaving the default provider with unrecovered costs.
- Since the Distcos are not final consumers, they will have no incentive to minimize contract prices; this function will have to be regulated.
- How will the contracts markets be regulated? It will be difficult to determine whether the default provider acted prudently in contracting.

[5] Some state regulators have even set rules to allow consumers to switch suppliers within their monthly billing cycle, requiring a special meter read and billing.

Regulators will tend to second-guess—if the spot price is lower than the contract, you should have bought spot; if the spot price is high, you should have contracted.

- The Distcos may need prior approval for the contracts, which will make the contracting process cumbersome and costly.
- A Distco that owns generation and has to contract for power may favor its own generation.

Possible Solutions There are a number of possible solutions to the problems arising from the Distco being the default provider and needing to make contracts, including:

- The Distco with generation could be required to bid out a portfolio of medium-term contracts at auction (and be allowed to bid itself). The form of the contracts would have to be specified to facilitate bid comparison. (This is what New Jersey did.)
- The default function itself could be bid out, as was attempted in Maine (and Pennsylvania for 20 percent of residential load). This also requires specifying the details so that the bids can be compared, which led to problems in Maine, but could perhaps be accomplished better.
- The Distco could negotiate contracts to provide fixed-price generation service only to the smallest residential customers. Customers whose consumption falls outside the limit would be required to choose another supplier or pay hourly spot market prices or spot prices computed monthly, depending on their metering.
- Default customers could be required to sign a one-year contract and *nominate a specific amount of energy* (perhaps varying by season) that would be supplied at a fixed price from contracted supplies. Any deviations from this amount would be charged (or credited) at the spot price. Again, the fixed price loads would be relatively predictable, simplifying the contracting and bid evaluation processes.

The latter option gives bill stability to consumers. It protects the Distco from excessive risk. It sends price signals at the margin to a large number of consumers. Let us look at it further.

Efficient Tariff Design for Default Service under Competition *The most efficient design for default service rates involves a fixed price for a block of energy, and a spot price (credit) for energy used (conserved) above (below) the contracted block size.* This design was described in Chapter 4 and illustrated in Figure 4.3. The first block can be based on historic consumption, or 80 percent of historic consumption, or an amount chosen by the customer. The customer might choose to fix the price for 250 kWh a month, and pay (or get credited) the spot price for any additional (or reduced) use.

By varying the size of the fixed price block, consumers would control the amount of price volatility they face. This program would ideally use hourly prices for the deviations from the designated block. (However, it would also work with prices averaged over a month for customers without hourly meters.)

Even this is complicated for couch potatoes and the vulnerables. None of the default solutions is perfect, and on the whole *we suggest that full price certainty in the default option should probably be offered only to small residential customers.* Larger customers do not need this degree of protection. Certainly anyone who is running a business should certainly be able to choose an appropriate provider for electricity, using the same skills and techniques they use to acquire all the other goods and services they purchase. Nor is there much reason to protect large residential consumers.

This means that contracting for fixed-price default service may be quite limited, but assumes that alternative offers are available to consumers. Customers should be removed from default service by gradually closing the option to them, with sufficient information and advance notice. Customers who fail to choose should then be assigned to the POLR option. (Our preference for POLR pricing, noted earlier, is a pass-through of the spot price [virtual direct access], increased for the excess risks of the POLR group, who should jointly pay the excess costs of credit risks.)

The Relation between Prices for Shopping Customers and Default Service

If shopping and default customers, or POLR customers, are treated consistently:

- A shopping customer should pay the Distco's unbundled distribution and transmission charges (plus stranded costs and system benefits); and
- A default customer should pay this amount plus the Distco's cost of default or POLR generation service.

In other words, there should be an explicit correspondence between rates for bundled service and rates for delivery only. In Spain, there is no such relationship. In Illinois, shopping customers get a special discount, called a *mitigation factor* that is supposed to spur the utility to reduce its stranded costs.

Should Customers Who Do Not Choose Be Assigned to a Retailer?

At least initially, most small consumers will not choose an alternative supplier. Some retailers argue that consumers who do not make an explicit choice should be assigned randomly to other retailers rather than remaining with the utility. Other parties contend that this is slamming. When Georgia assigned gas customers to retailers, the retailers were overwhelmed by the volume of customers and had serious problems with metering and billing. *We believe that there is no need to force customers to move to new suppliers and that failure to switch is a legitimate exercise of choice, while there is a default option.*

PBR FOR DISTRIBUTION

Performance-based ratemaking (PBR) for Distcos in general is a good idea because it provides incentives for those who expand, operate, and maintain the distribution system to increase efficiency (and their profits). The two key elements of a PBR system are:

1. Rules about how often and by how much tariffs change between major tariff reviews; and
2. Quality standards (with penalties and possibly rewards) to ensure that the Distco does not expand its profits at the expense of service quality or safety.

There are many types of PBR programs and the details are beyond the scope of this book. However, there are several aspects of PBR that are important to retail access and do warrant mention in a book on that subject. First, experience shows that there is room for efficiency improvements in distribution, metering, billing, and customer service. Take restoration of distribution outages and scheduling of connections and disconnections requested by customers. It is appropriate to set standards for these activities and to penalize the utility for failing to meet the standards. *Particularly in a world of retail access, the penalty should be paid to the customers who received inadequate service, rather than being flowed through distribution charges to all customers.* In this way the Distco will not only have an incentive to keep quality up, but will also have no incentive to give less service quality to customers who have chosen another supplier. Utilities in a number of jurisdictions have moved to this form of penalty for missed appointments, excessive delays in restoring power, and so on.

Second, customers with poor payment history impose costs on the utility and on customers who pay on time. This is clearly an area where efficiency improvements are possible. *There is growing evidence that the non-payment problem can be significantly reduced by installing pay-as-you-go meters for customers who have difficulty paying their bills.* These meters, which allow energy to flow only if there is money remaining on a *refillable* card inserted in the device, are very popular with low-income customers who may be able to pay $5 a week for electricity, but not $20 at the end of the monthly billing cycle. These customers become very knowledgeable about which appliances are the big energy users and quickly learn to control their electricity costs. Pay-as-you-go meters are compatible with time-of-use pricing, but (in the absence of communication equipment) cannot be used with dynamic hourly prices. However, they are ideal for POLR customers—who tend to be poor credit risks. Whether or not PBR is applied to Distcos, they should be allowed to recover any cost of pay-as-you-go meters beyond what the customers using them can afford.

SUMMARY AND CONCLUSIONS ON RETAIL ACCESS

Retail access is complicated. Without a proper market design and careful preparation, it can be a disaster.

A Functioning Competitive Wholesale Market

If the utility keeps its generation or has life-of-plant contracts with the new owners of plants it has sold, there will be little chance for new entrants. If the trading arrangements are not changed, there will be little opportunity for retailers. A spot price is essential for balancing and settlement, for tracking stranded cost recovery, as a benchmark for evaluating contracts, and as a price signal for consumers. Hourly metering is essential for functioning wholesale markets.

Codes of Conduct for the Distcos

If a Distco is affiliated with a competitive retailer, a code of conduct must be established to obviate conflicts of interest and cross subsidies.

Rules for Retailer Eligibility, Behavior, and Shopping Credits

Because the behavior of any retailer affects the entire system, there must be rules about the responsibilities of retailers qualifications and financial guarantees. Shopping credits are the retailers' price-to-beat and must reflect market prices if retail access is to succeed. (If there is a default service there is always a price to beat.)

A Settlement Mechanism

With many market participants, settlement becomes much more complicated. The right price for settlement is the spot price. The Distco is best situated to handle settlement at the customer's end—determining what was consumed and which retailer was responsible for that energy.

Infrastructure and Protocols for Metering, Billing, and Information Transfer

Numerous details such as load profiling, estimation of meter reads, and true up with actual reads, rules about partial payments by consumers, and treatment of losses must be worked out.

Stranded Cost Recovery

A stranded cost recovery mechanism that minimizes the ability of consumers to bypass their share of stranded costs is an essential element of the retail access plan. We have left the details to Part Two on the United States, and include a summary here for completeness. The bottom-up approach requires a specific valuation of stranded costs. The top-down approach is easier to implement. However, setting the "shopping credits" often becomes a political exercise. The fixed prices nullify demand response, and also keep out competing retailers. In addition the whole top-down approach as implemented has posed considerable risk for utilities, especially if they are required to divest their generation.

Other Matters

Some entity must have responsibility for supplying generation services to customers who have no other retailer—the power will flow to customers no matter what their retailers do. Default service should be provided only to small customers, on a fixed-plus-variable pricing scheme, and should be phased out. POLR service should be priced at spot market prices plus a risk premium.

CHAPTER 11

Summary and Conclusions to Part One

In the preceding chapters we have looked at four models of industry organization, the requirements for competition and the conflicts that can arise. In Part One we looked at the underlying issues that need to be addressed in electricity, and explained *why* things work. We offered a standard prescription, but since we are never starting from a clean slate, we also tried to consider which elements are critical, which are optional, how to think about transitions, and what to do if things are not perfect.

Here is a summary of Part One—the standard prescription in the form of a checklist of what needs to be done in an ideal world. Note that full retail access is the last step of the process, not the first.

THE STANDARD PRESCRIPTION

General Requirements

1. Analyze natural market areas (within transmission constraints) to determine the existing configuration of market areas, and where they could be fairly easily expanded though release of transmission constraints. (This is not necessarily the same as the areas for trading arrangements—ideally trading arrangements would cover the whole country—but if they do not, they should at least be as large as natural market areas.)
2. Expand the transmission system to remove constraints and increase market areas, where necessary. Natural market areas can be enlarged by judicious construction of transmission to relieve constraints; this helps remove market power. (But more efficient trading arrangements will make better use of the existing capacity, at least in the United States.)
3. Unbundle the accounts and the functions of existing companies into generation, operations, transmission, and distribution.

Demand Side

4. Arrange for hourly metering of a large proportion of load as a prerequisite for getting enough demand response. Currently, wholesale prices vary by the hour but retail prices cannot. This is a crucial element that has so far been largely ignored. Normal markets clear because both supply and demand are price-responsive; in electricity, the final customers in most places are unable and have no reason to respond to wholesale price changes. Electricity markets will not work properly until they do. Demand response is critical to control of market power.
5. Change traditional pricing forms. Prices of high-cost peak hours and low-cost off-peak hours have always been averaged. This cannot survive competition, and it requires hourly metering to unbundle them. There are ways to make utility tariffs, other than the traditional fixed price, that can expose customers to spot prices for increases or decreases in their consumption.
6. Establish how many wholesale buyers there will be in the competitive markets, and set up the infrastructure to meter and bill them. We recommend against immediate introduction of full retail access, because we believe the wholesale markets need time to get established and the infrastructure for retail access takes time to arrange. But wholesale markets need enough buyers—distribution companies and large customers (who normally account for a large proportion of the consumption and are a very small proportion of the customers) should be sufficient.

Trading Arrangements

7. Impose requirements for open access to transmission (this step has already been taken in the United States for most of the transmission). But this step is only a prerequisite: Making open access happen requires real work to establish workable trading arrangements. *This is because of the special complexities of electricity,* which requires unique real time coordination between production and the transmission system.
8. Establish trading areas in which the trading arrangements for access would be the same. Different sets of trading rules inhibit trade. At the very least, the trading areas should be as big as the natural market areas. In fact, the whole country could usefully have the same rules.
9. Separate generation from transmission and system operations. This is a necessity, because the system operator has enormous ability to influence who gets to sell power and who doesn't, and hence the profitability of the generators. The transmission owner has similar influence in the longer term. Everyone knows this separation has to happen, but it

requires restructuring of existing companies, which may require legislation, and will certainly take time.

10. Establish regional system operator(s). In each of the market areas, a single system operator should be set up independent of any of the traders. Ideally, all transmission and all generators should be subject to the system operators requirements.
11. Forward energy contracts should be determined by bilateral trading between market participants or on organized forward or futures markets that do not need to be set up by electricity regulators. This is a necessary step, but one that will set itself up once demanded by traders.
12. Develop detailed trading arrangements for delivery of forward contracts. This is the most intellectually challenging of the things that have to be done, and the most contentious. The old wheeling arrangements will not work for full competition. There are dozens of different models, but we believe a clear winner has emerged, broadly similar to PJM, New York, and New Zealand (although each of these is deficient in some respects). The four paragraphs that follow are elements of the "integrated" trading arrangements.
13. Arrange for the system operator to buy and sell enough energy to offset "imbalances" between forward contracts and actual deliveries, which will inevitably be different because of the nature of the transmission network. The best price for imbalances is a market price, not a regulated price.
14. Encourage liquid forward markets through transparent spot prices. Electricity forward markets are intrinsically less liquid than most commodity markets, and transparent spot prices make these markets more liquid. In the trading model we propose, the system operator runs the spot market, integrated with the imbalance market. The demand side should participate in setting the spot price. The spot prices should vary by location.
15. Develop arrangements for efficient congestion management, to maximize the value of the transmission network. Managing congestion efficiently in real time requires spot purchases and sales of power. The trading model we propose integrates congestion management with procurement of power for imbalances and for the spot market. (Same power, same time, same place—should all be at the same price. The integrated model ensures that they are.)
16. Develop arrangements for efficient procurement of operating reserves and other ancillary services, again integrated with the energy market. Reserves are not a separate product—they are an option to buy energy. Physical self-provision does not make sense—the system operator should procure them.

17. Develop governance and regulatory mechanisms to ensure that the system operator performs these functions fairly and efficiently.

Transmission Business Model

18. Consolidate transmission into regional companies for cohesive planning and implementation of maintenance and expansion. Preferably, combine system operator and transmission ownership in a Transco. The two functions need to coordinate in so many ways that it makes sense to combine them.
19. Develop business models and regulation for transmission companies. These companies must be regulated as to the prices they can charge and the contractual assurances they can offer, and they must have incentives to expand the transmission efficiently.
20. Develop better transmission pricing than that currently in operation in the United States, which inhibits trade. We propose pricing at short-run marginal costs (the cost of congestion and losses) with the overhead costs assigned to the generators and customers in the area, and to exiting trades. This integrates well with the recommended trading arrangements.
21. Create property rights in the form of *financial transmission rights* for the use of the transmission system. Physical transmission rights limit the use of the system and increase market power. Financial transmission rights do not. Financial transmission rights can also be used in the regulation of the transmission company to increase incentives for good management of the transmission, and for expansion. They require locational spot prices, another reason for preferring the proposed integrated trading model.
22. Transform existing explicit physical rights into financial rights. Existing generating plant and load have implicit physical rights and these should also be reflected in the initial allocation of FTRs.

Supply Side

23. Establish a market value of generating plant to enable a fair transition from regulation to competition. Stranded costs (or the reverse, plants whose value is above book value) have hampered U.S. restructuring decisions for years. The value of plants should be established, by agreement or by divestiture if necessary, so that things can move forward. Arrange for buy-out of the old regime.
24. Analyze concentration in the market areas and break up the generation where necessary to establish enough sellers in each market area. Buy out the contracted IPPs if feasible. The most critical of the bulwarks against market power in production markets is having enough different

generators in the first place. This may require divestiture, which may require legislation if the companies are private.

25. Remove barriers to entry of independent generators (including legal barriers). In the regulated world, the regulators needed to ensure that the generators did not overbuild, and set up rules and processes for approvals. Now it is the other way around—these processes and agencies need to be dismantled.
26. Develop regulatory mechanisms for detection and control of market power.
27. Distribution companies purchasing on behalf of their smaller customers need to make contracts with generators, and regulators need to see that the contracts are arm's-length and to agree to pass those contract prices through to consumers. The distribution companies should not "pass through the spot price" because the wholesale markets need contracts to reduce market power. If distribution companies own generation, the contracts should be purchased in an auction.
28. As a transition mechanism, vesting contracts are recommended. These expose the generators to competition for the make-or-buy decisions, but not for the final price.
29. Remove price regulation of generators and regulation of retail sales to large buyers. Note that deregulated production markets do not require fully deregulated retail markets. It can be argued that the step of full retail access costs more than it is really worth. (The incremental costs many depend on how much is built into the metering upgrading recommended in step 4.) However, we believe that retail access should be the eventual aim since it removes various conflicts, and customers seem to want it.
30. Establish environmental regulations, if necessary. The best form of emission regulation for major environmental programs is the cap-and-trade method.
31. Establish subsidy programs, for green power or low-income consumers if necessary. Subsidy programs should be designed in a way that preserves the maximum efficiency and competition in the markets.

Retail Access

32. Arrange for settlement and billing for retail access for millions of smaller customers; this is quite complex with various quirks that are again specific to electricity. It has been badly done in many places and is a major reason for delaying and phasing in retail access.
33. Develop codes of conduct for Distcos with affiliated competitive retailers and requirements for competing retailers.

34. Arrange for default provision by the distribution company, for those who prefer not to choose; this is for their benefit. After a transition period, which may need to extend for a decade while customers get accustomed to the new arrangements, the default provision can be terminated. (We do not think it necessary for the Distco to have any default obligation to the large customers who can look after themselves.)
35. However, the distribution company will probably always need to stand as Provider of Last Resort, a role akin to the mandated automobile insurance pool. The pricing for this function should reflect the increased risk of the residual customer pool and be an incentive to get off it.
36. Remove regulation of retail sales to smaller customers, preferably in phases.

THE FIVE MAJOR ISSUES

Summarizing, the five major changes required are:

1. *Demand side:* Hourly metering for most of the consumption, and price designs that expose customers to the spot price for some of their consumption.
2. *Trading arrangements:* System operations separate from traders and regionally consolidated. Trading arrangements based on an integrated model, with central dispatch and locational energy prices.
3. *Transmission business model:* Control of transmission separate from traders; pricing and expansion arrangements; our preference is for regional profit-making regulated Transcos incorporating the system operator.
4. *Supply side:* Remove barriers to entry. Buy out of the old regime by valuing assets and dealing with stranded costs. Expand market areas by improving transmission. If necessary for market power control, divest utility generation into smaller parcels.
5. *Retail access:* When production markets are working, choice for all customers. This needs an extensive settlement mechanism and customer education, and decisions about default provision.

TRANSITION ISSUES

No one does everything perfectly—everyone lives with second-best to some extent, makes mid-course corrections, applies Band-Aids. We have set out a list of 36 things to do. They are our preferred prescription, but what if they cannot all be done? What can be left till later, what is optional? What substitutes are available? How can you tell which elements are structural and which are cladding? And what should be done in situations that have already gotten into advanced muddles?

If we are to talk coherently about second best, we have to decide at what level it is appropriate. The recommendations are at different levels—like a decision tree. For example:

Overall goals: *Efficiency.*

Instrumental goals for efficiency: *Competition, regulation.*

Specific requirements: for example, *many suppliers in any market.*

Design to achieve these specifics: for example, *build more transmission.*

To keep the book of manageable length, we have taken it as given that efficiency is the appropriate *overall* goal for the electric industry and that competition is an appropriate *instrumental* goal for efficient electricity production, at least in the United States, which is stuck in the middle of a reform process and needs to get out of it. Then we have set out the economist's prescription for a competitive industry: *Specific requirements* of many buyers and sellers; price-responsive demand and supply; liquid and efficient marketplaces with prices set by supply and demand; resolution of conflicts of interests; good regulation of the parts that remain monopolies. These are the necessities for competition: the structure, not the cladding. There is no second-best. They may be done well or badly, but these things are needed for competitive markets to work. The question is how to achieve them in the real world—the design issues.

It is at the level of the design issues that there can be workable alternatives. If the design elements we have suggested are unobtainable, then the alternative should be judged by whether it can meet the specific requirements for competition. On some issues there may well be better ways than we have proposed. This list can be done—it is not a theoretician's dream world—but we have given examples of second-best alternatives throughout Part One. For example:

- If demand response is not in place, price caps may have to be used.
- If price caps are used, they should approximate the hourly supply/demand intersection in the market (intelligent price caps).
- If structural remedies for market power are not available, behavioral or outcome remedies may have to be imposed.
- There is no right way to charge the nonmarginal transmission costs, but there is a well-developed theory of second best for pricing.

- Integrated trading arrangements are clearly preferable, but some forms of decentralized model are not too bad.
- Neither decentralized nor centralized transmission expansion is clearly preferable, and we propose a mixture.
- We prefer Transcos, but there are respectable arguments for other arrangements.
- We think transmission should be divested to create separation, but there are ways to separate transmission short of divestiture.
- Codes of conduct are a way to steer between conflict of interest and loss of scope economies.
- Retail access for small consumers is expensive: It can wait and be phased in.

So the tests for alternative designs would be these: How does the proposal meet the specific objectives? Is it incentive-compatible? How will it be gamed, and does it require rules and policemen to make it work? Will avoiding the need to legislate a fundamental change lead to half-baked solutions that do not do the job? Or can we wait and see whether the solutions are actually so half-baked after all? Is it cost-effective, or is trying to avoid the expense of metering, say, going to require enormous expenditures for load profiling (as it did in the United Kingdom)?

In any real case, if the standard prescription cannot be applied for some reason, go back to the fundamentals and see if the fixes that are proposed will cure and not kill the patient.

PART two

The United States

CHAPTER 12

The Structure of the Industry

In Part One of this book, we laid out a feasible end-state for a restructured electric industry, and reduced the recommendations to a short list of five big issues. In Part Two, we explore how to go about achieving that end-state in the United States, where we stand on the five big issues, and what remains to be done to get to a stable, workable solution.

What has been done in the United States can be likened to a meal without the main course; the appetizers and dessert have been served without the meat and potatoes. Retail access should be the last step, not the first. Requiring access to the transmission system for wholesale power sales (a necessary precondition for competition) was carried out between 1992 and 1996; retail access followed from 1994 onward. But the main course, competitive generating markets and appropriate trading arrangements, is still in the kitchen in most of the country, or causing indigestion in much of the rest.

The primary reason the United States did it like this is that no agency has the authority to take an overall view of what should be done. The United States has a strong national policy favoring competition in general, but it has not been well implemented in the electric industry; no general consensus has been reached on how to proceed, no framework has been established. Restructuring has been done piecemeal. The aim of Part Two is to describe and analyze the current situation, and to make recommendations for a workable policy framework.

In this chapter, we describe the complicated structure of the "old industry" in existence until 1992; how it worked and how it was regulated. In Chapters 13 and 14, we describe the structural and legislative changes since 1992, the federal law EPAct that permitted the federal regulator to order open access to the transmission, and removed constraints on entry of generators, the Orders setting out trading arrangements and encouraging regional consolidation, the state initiatives on retail access, the new players and the current situation.

In Chapters 15 to 18, we look in more detail at the current issues in the United States in trading arrangements, transmission business models, control of market power and retail access. (Note that there are no U.S.-specific issues in metering and demand response, other than the fact that almost nothing is happening.) We explain the changes that have already shifted jurisdiction towards FERC and away from the states.

Finally we gather together the various stands and ask what next? Chapters 19 and 20 review what needs to be done, what efficiencies can be gained if some things are done and not others, what changes need to be legislated for, and where a change of jurisdiction would help matters. The conclusion is that the federal regulator needs the power to resolve the issues of trading arrangements and transmission organization, where its authority is currently too limited to impose a solution. On the question of whether there should also be federal preemption of generation, to promote competition at the national level, the issues are not so clear. Retail access for small customers can clearly be left to the states.

KEY FACTS AND DATES

The U.S. electric utility industry has annual revenues of over $200 billion per year. The United States has more than 800,000 MW of generating capacity, which is about a quarter of the generating capacity of the world. Of that 800,000 MW, over a half is coal-fired. The fastest growing fuel type is gas, which currently accounts for 16 percent of U.S. capacity. (See Table 12.1 and Figures 12.1 and 12.2.)

One of the big problems novelists and filmmakers face in structuring a story is how to introduce the "back-story"—where were all these characters before they arrived at where we now meet them? In our case, the back-story is much longer for some than for others. The changes that began in 1992 with the federal Energy Policy Act have affected some states in radical ways,

TABLE 12.1 U.S. Electric Key Statistics, 2000

Retail sales	3,413,000,000 MWh
Average retail price	6.68 cents/kWh
Retail revenue	$228 billion
Installed capacity	811,625 MW

Source: Department of Energy, Energy Information Administration, *Electric Power Annual 2000: Volume 1.*

FIGURE 12.1 World generating capacity.

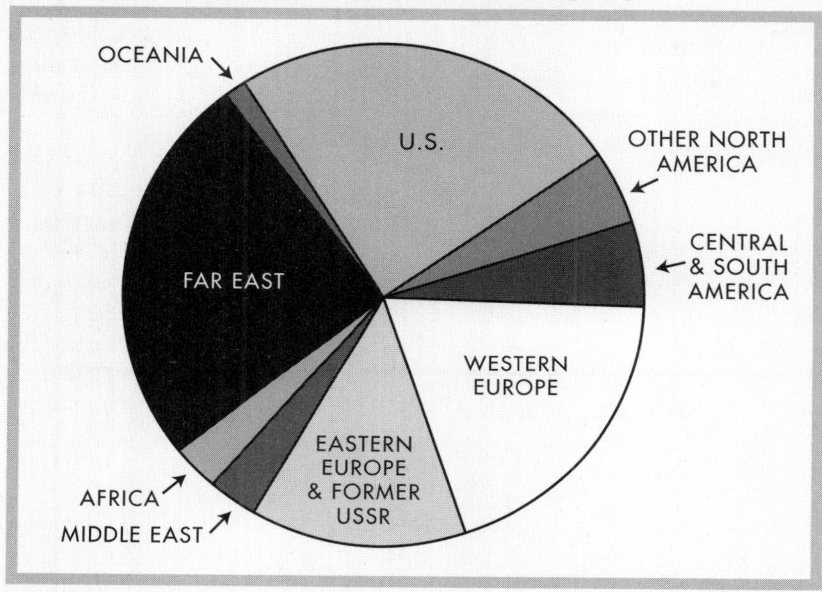

FIGURE 12.2 U.S. electric industry net generation by fuel type, 2000.

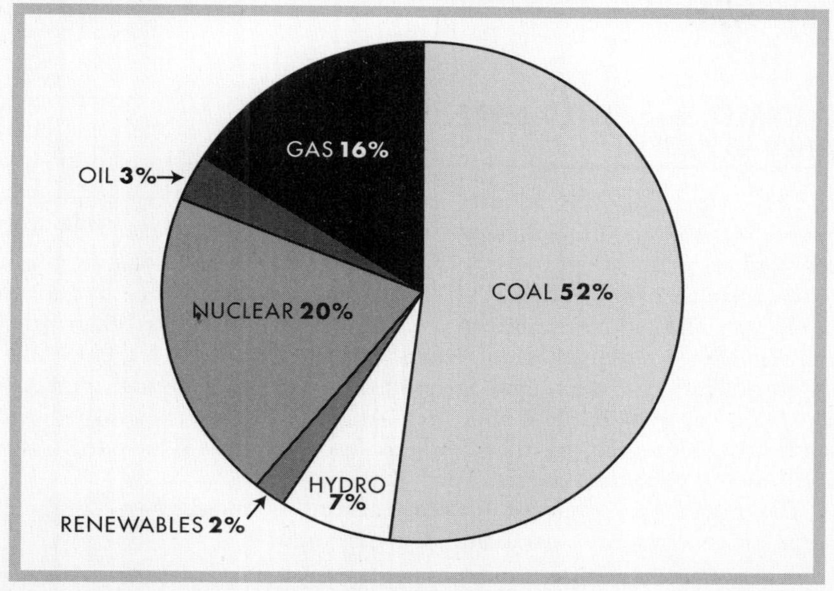

FIGURE 12.3 Timeline of events in the United States.

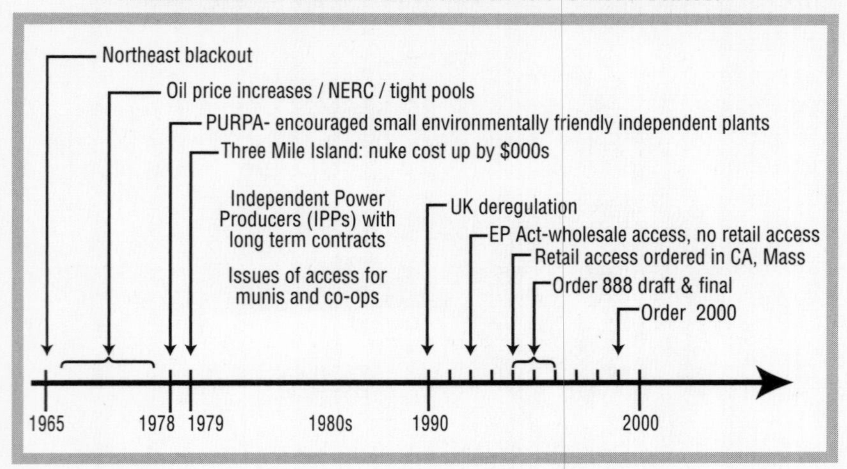

whereas others have hardly changed at all. So in describing the industry pre-1992, we are in many cases describing the current situation in many states. Figure 12.3 shows a time line of major events and issues that will be referred to in the text.

VERTICALLY INTEGRATED INVESTOR OWNED UTILITIES

In 1992, 75 percent of the industry consisted of about 200 investor-owned utilities (IOUs)—private companies listed on the stock markets. They were almost all vertically integrated—they comprised all the functions, from generation (production) through reading customers' meters. They had a monopoly over all final consumers in their service territories, and their prices were regulated by the states. In return for their monopoly franchise, they had an obligation to serve and to build or contract for enough power to provide for everyone in the service area—the native load. They owned their own transmission, and, for the most part (except for the tight pools), controlled their own system operations.

The prices they charged to customers were *bundled*—a combined charge for generation, transmission, and distribution.

NOTE ON TERMINOLOGY: In the United States, regulated prices are called *rates* and the word *tariff* technically refers to the rates plus all the terms and conditions. We prefer to use the term *prices*. If we use tariff, it refers to the schedules of regulated prices—as in bundled tariffs.

Retail consumers used to be called ratepayers—we call them customers: final customers are end users who are served at retail; wholesale customers are those who buy to resell. The whole group of final customers is sometimes referred to as *the load*.

Regulation of IOUs

The IOUs are regulated by state public utility commissions (PUCs).[1] Some IOUs are active in several states and are regulated by several PUCs. The states had started to regulate utilities early in the century, and by 1935 most states had passed legislation giving state PUCs the duty to set prices, requiring "just and reasonable rates" for privately owned utilities serving customers within each state.

State PUCs reach well beyond simply setting prices—they need to control quality and cost as well, and therefore they approve new plants, set required reserve margins, and in the years before 1992 were very busy enforcing state legislation mandating programs for energy conservation.

The 1935 Federal Power Act was a compromise that kept most of the regulatory authority in the hands of the states—only "wholesale sales" (sales for resale) are federally regulated. Wholesale sales were (and are) very narrowly defined. Most sales are regulated by the states. The state agencies are not arms of the federal regulator. They have independent jurisdiction over different aspects of the industry.

The Federal Energy Regulatory Commission (FERC),[2] which administered the Federal Power Act, had relatively little to do with the electricity industry until the 1980s, when issues of transmission access began to arise. After 1992, its responsibilities expanded enormously, but as we shall see, its authority (and its budget) did not expand along with the task.

This fragmented structure of local integrated companies, and of bifurcated regulation, persists to this day.

---

[1] The state commissions are called various names such as Public Service Commission, Department of Public Utilities, and so on.

[2] Known as the Federal Power Commission until 1978.

FIGURE 12.4 Interconnects and the U.S. boundaries of the 10 North American Electric Reliability Council regions.

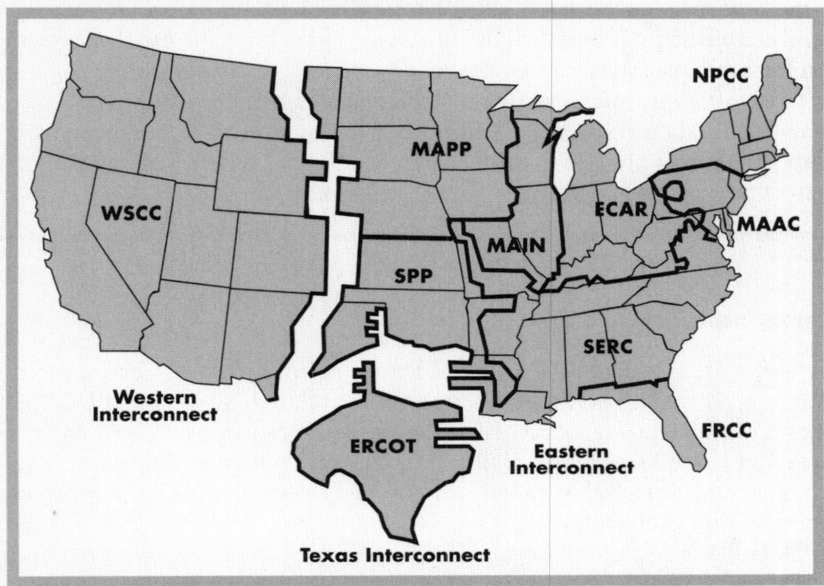

NERC and Reliability

After the 1965 blackouts in the Northeast, the industry made strenuous efforts to interconnect neighboring utilities so as to increase reliability by allowing neighbors to call on each other for power in the event of problems. It set up the North American Electric Reliability Council (NERC) to facilitate these interchanges by establishing technical operating standards followed (voluntarily) by everyone in the industry. NERC is really a series of ten regional reliability councils that set out and monitored guidelines for the industry to follow (see Figure 12.4). NERC has no formal authority other than the consent of the governed.

CO-OPERATIVES

About 1,000 co-operatives are owned by their customers. Most are rural co-ops and are eligible for low-cost federal loans. Some of them own generation, but most do not. Their focus is on buying electricity in bulk and providing local distribution services. Many have joint membership and receive their power from generation and transmission co-operatives, but most of their power comes from IOUs or government-owned generators. They are not considered public power, although in the text we sometimes refer to municipal utilities and co-operatives—munis and co-ops—together.

PUBLIC POWER

There are three major components to public power: generating-only companies, principally the federally owned power marketing agencies (PMAs); a few vertically integrated entities; and thousands of small distribution-only entities, mainly small municipal utilities. All of these entities are tax-exempt to one degree or another.

The economic regulation—the authority to set the price—of the public power entities is in the hands of the government that owns them, federal, state, or local, and even when they are state-owned, they are generally not regulated by the state public utility commissions.

Federal Entities

The federal entities, which produce 8 percent of the total output, make the federal government the largest producer of power in the United States. The four main PMAs are the Bonneville, Southeastern, Southwestern, and Western Area Power Administrations (the Alaska PMA has been privatized). The Tennessee Valley Authority (TVA) is also owned by the federal government but was set up under different legislation. The PMAs and TVA were originally set up to harness hydroelectric power on major rivers, but in some cases expanded into nuclear power and other types of generation.[3] They sell to local

[3] New York State has the NY Power Authority, set up for the same reason, which also built or acquired nuclear and oil plants. New York also created the Long Island Power Authority (LIPA) to rescue the customers and shareholders of LILCO (an IOU on Long Island, NY) from the consequences of the very expensive Shoreham nuclear plant, by using the state's tax-exempt bond financing to replace the shareholder equity of the company and reduce prices, *at the same time that it was deregulating the rest of New York's utilities*. LIPA is a corporate municipal instrument of the state of New York and was created by state legislation enacted in 1986. On May 28, 1998, LIPA acquired LILCO's transmission and distribution system, its interest in the Nine Mile Point 2 plant and its Shoreham regulatory asset along with the responsibility for serving electric customers in the LIPA service area.

municipalities or co-ops, and since their hydro output is limited and generally cheaper than other sources, preference is given in complicated ways to certain groups of customers. The federal entities also own transmission lines, which fall under limited federal (FERC) jurisdiction, although they comprise about 25 percent of all transmission.

Municipal Utilities and Other Public Power

There are a few vertically integrated municipal utilities—the largest being the Los Angeles Department of Water and Power. Some municipal utilities are partially integrated—they own some of their own generation, but purchase the rest from PMAs and IOUs. There are about 2,000 small towns and rural areas served by a local distribution-only utility that purchases power from PMAs or neighboring IOUs. Prices for final consumers are set by local boards or by local governments. The prices charged by the IOUs are regulated by FERC under their "sales for resale" authority. There are also public power districts, irrigation districts, and other organizations. The whole of Nebraska is served by public power in one form or another.

Issues in Public Power

A major issue prior to 1992 was the desire of the munis and co-ops for access to the transmission lines of the IOUs. They had always purchased power and in principle they were able to choose their suppliers, but in practice they could not, because they could not get access to transmission wires owned by the IOUs. This resulted in many years of litigation before FERC, and was a major factor in the 1992 legislation. California and Florida particularly had severe issues with access for municipal utilities. This issue was solved in principle by the 1992 legislation (see the next section), and there were also several antitrust suits, the most important of which was *Otter Tail Power,* a case decided by the Supreme Court.

Public power has always been subsidized through its financing—either through low-cost government-backed bonds, or in the case of TVA, by direct government ownership and absorption of losses. TVA and Bonneville both went into nuclear power in a big way in the 1980s and both failed spectacularly. But these two entities, and the other PMAs, are very large players in their respective regions. The issue that remains is whether they can be players in the new markets, or whether they distort the markets, either because of the subsidies or because of their sheer size.

Subsidies to public power also take the form of low-cost (tax-exempt) financing for investment in distribution wires. This is less a problem for competition than it is a problem for getting municipals to join a regional market. To get this financing there are two requirements—a showing of public purpose, and a showing that the expenditures are truly local (the "two county" rule). Municipalities have been afraid that by joining a regional market they would lose the financing.

These last two issues are still with us, and are important for the development of competition.

INDEPENDENT POWER PRODUCERS

The Public Utility Regulatory Policies Act of 1978 (PURPA), designed to promote environmentally benign and small sources of power was, perhaps unintentionally, the first chink in the armor of vertical integration. It required utilities to purchase power from certain types of independents power producers[4] at the utility's *avoided cost*. Avoided cost was the cost the utility "avoided" by not having to build its own plants, a perfectly good concept, but very hard to measure in practice without competitive markets. The history of the QF contracts would fill a book, but suffice it to say that some state regulators' notion of future avoided costs was so exaggerated that the QF contracts became a very lucrative business for the owners, a big expense to the utilities and their customers, and a major portion of the "stranded costs" that have proved such a problem. Later, when costs in the real world turned out to be lower, the utilities and their customers were stuck with inflexible contracts at unrealistically high prices.

Following this, various states permitted or encouraged utilities to hold auctions for life-of-plant contracts with independent power producers (IPPs) for the power they needed at lowest cost. The contracts counted as part of the required capacity the utility needed to hold to serve its native load. In addition to unregulated independents with no utility ownership connection, some utilities set up unregulated subsidiaries to build IPP plants, in their own service territories (where this was permitted), in those of others, and abroad.

The IPPs became quite a force in the industry, and a major source of technical change. By 1992, they were building 60 percent of new capacity in the United States (although 1992 was a really low year for construction and not much has been built anywhere in the United States since 1992 until recently).

[4] Principally small plants and co-generators: These were called Qualifying Facilities (QFs)—qualifying for avoided cost treatment.

SHORT-TERM TRADING MARKETS

Prior to 1992, the principal forms of trading were long-term contracts: private utilities and the power marketing agencies of the federal government selling to munis and co-ops; IPPs selling to utilities and some long-term inter-utility contracts. Short-term trading, such as it was, was done in the "bulk power markets," of which there were two types—the tight pools, and the markets for bilateral trades between utilities. The United States had two models for short-term trading, and when it was later faced with the need to accommodate more transactions, it chose the wrong one.

Economy and Reliability Trades

Economy trading goes back to at least the 1930s, but grew a lot in the 1970s, as costs diverged between utilities; the arrangements for reliability grew into arrangements for trading at the margin. Although the utilities were obliged to hold enough for their own use, many times the next plant on one system would be cheaper than the next plant on another system, and the cheaper system would sell to the more expensive. These "economy interchanges" were still wholesale sales, regulated by FERC. They were, however, a very small part of a utility's costs.

Bilateral Trading

This bilateral trading between utilities is the basis for the wheeling model of trading. In fact, these are the only trades it is suitable for. *The only transactions where the supply and the demand ever matched exactly were the inter-utility transactions between two system operators, for some number of megawatts at a given hour.* The two system operators raised the output of the utility seller, and reduced the output of the utility buyer by exactly the same amount, so that the electricity flowed between them. There was no need for arrangements for imbalances or congestion management, because there were no imbalances, and if there was congestion, transactions simply were not scheduled. In many cases the trading rules were informal—to pay back energy borrowed at another time, for example. In other cases, the trades were priced by bilateral bargaining.

The Tight Pools

In the Northeast, three regional tight pools were set up to improve reliability, by allowing automatic interchanges between neighboring utilities without the system operators having to negotiate terms each time. These were:

PJM (the Pennsylvania—New Jersey—Maryland interconnection), the New York Power Pool, and the New England Power Pool. PJM was actually set up in 1927, the others after the blackout of 1965. These pools had central scheduling and control of all the plants in the region, and central control of the system operations. The pricing of short-term inter-utility transactions was based upon a formula designed to "share the savings" between higher and lower cost generation. These agreements for the short term were always bound to longer term agreements requiring the members to build enough generating and transmission capacity.

In later years, these pools formed the basis of the integrated model for competitive trading arrangements, and each of them became the basis on which deregulating states in the region were able to create the new trading arrangements.[5]

Market-Based Prices

Although it had the power to set prices in these *bulk power markets*, FERC decided in the 1980s that it did not need to review each sale individually if the markets were reasonably competitive. So it began to issue *market-based pricing authority* to exempt arm's-length transactions between utilities from regulatory scrutiny. It did this after a finding that the potential seller had no market power because it had less than 20 percent of the relevant market; authority for market-based prices was granted for three-year periods (subject to renewal) with little oversight until recently.

PRICE DIFFERENCES EMERGE

The regulated IOUs were generally required by their state regulators to build or contract for sufficient capacity to serve their native load (their captive customers). Municipal distribution utilities, and rural electric co-ops that did not own their own power plants also contracted, usually with a neighboring utility, to buy power and have it transported to the muni's or co-op's distribution system. The munis and co-ops were therefore wholesale customers of the IOUs.

During the 1980s, demand growth slowed, and some IOUs found themselves with excess capacity. The nuclear plant boom had turned into a bust,

[5]At the time they were set up they were not competitive—they were generators' clubs. It required extensive changes in the rules to make them into the new arrangements, but the basic ideas were there.

as the costs escalated wildly after the incident at Three Mile Island in 1979. In fact, the last nuclear plant that ever came into service was ordered in 1976—all subsequent orders were cancelled.[6] But the plants that had been ordered earlier were coming into service by the end of the 1980s. The Shoreham nuclear plant in Long Island, perhaps the most egregious example, was originally proposed for less than $100 million in the 1960s, finally ended up costing about $6 billion, and never produced a single kWh of commercial power.[7] In some areas, like California, Texas, Maine, Connecticut, and New York, the QF contracts were a large proportion of total cost, and well above market prices. The high QF payments attracted too much supply.[8] New York went so far as to enact a statute that required its utilities to pay 6 cents/kWh to all comers; California had four *standard offers,* one of which was based on the assumption that the price of a barrel of oil would reach $100/barrel (it has never yet gone above $40/barrel).

The electric industry has also been used as a vehicle for the implementation of various social programs such as low prices for low-income consumers, and for socialized development of such desirables as energy-saving measures and electric cars. The programs for demand-side management were a case in point. In normal markets, prices limit consumption. But in electric markets, the traditional forms of rate-making prevented customers knowing the current costs of production; prices were (and still are) rolled-in averages of high-cost hours and low-cost hours, of historic investments and new investments. So it was understood that demand could not respond appropriately. Rather than fix the underlying problem of the averaged prices, many regulatory commissions instituted costly and inefficient methods of

---

[6] This was also a failure of regulation—many of the utilities with partly built nuclear plants would have been glad to cancel them if some arrangement could have been made with the regulators to pass the costs of the unfinished construction to the customers. The regulators declined; if the utilities had been private companies they would have taken a (large) loss and gone on with their business. But instead they continued to build in the expectation that a completed plant, being "used and useful" would be able to be charged to the customers.

[7] In 1965, LILCO first announced its intention to build a nuclear plant somewhere in Suffolk County. Within a year, LILCO was declaring its new plant would be on line by 1973, at a cost of $65 million to $75 million. In 1968, LILCO decided to increase the size of Shoreham from 540 to 820 megawatts. By the late 1970s the price was approaching $2 billion. Shoreham was fully decommissioned on October 12, 1999 with a $6 billion price tag—about 85 times higher than the original estimate (Dan Fagin, "Lights Out at Shoreham, Long Island Our History," www.lihistory.com).

[8] Paul Joskow, "Regulatory Failure, Regulatory Reform and Structural Change in the Electric Power Industry," Brookings Paper on Economic Activity: *Microeconomics,* 1989, p. 174.

persuading customers to conserve energy, and charged the costs to all users. In this they undermined the development of a competitive conservation sector and added to utility costs.

These factors increased the prices charged by the utilities that had invested in nuclear plants and that had QF contracts or demand-side management programs. Worse, new plants were being developed that could come on line at below the regulated (historic cost) prices that the utilities were charging.[9] Customers in some places were paying well above the cost of the new generation (as part of their bundled tariffs). Large industrial customers, and also the munis and co-ops, wanted to choose their suppliers, either another IOU with lower prices, or an independent generator who could build new. For this, they needed access to the transmission wires of the IOUs.

Munis and Co-Ops Seek Access

Most of the contested requests to FERC for transmission access in the 1970s and 1980s were from munis and co-ops that wished to change suppliers. Utilities owned most of the transmission, and those whose transmission was required for another utility to take delivery were often unwilling to make space available, which made trading difficult or impossible. The utilities would argue (with some justice) that the transmission was paid for by its own customers—the native load—and was built to carry a particular pattern of generation. Additional use would cause congestion, increase costs, and require additional reserves to be available in case of sudden changes in flows (the standard problems of congestion, imbalances, and ancillary services that we meet throughout the discussion of trading arrangements—they used to be called system services).

But behind all this, the transmitting utility would prefer to sell to the receiving customer itself. The IOUs held that they had built plants to serve the munis and co-ops that were planning to leave, and that the native load customers would be saddled with these *stranded costs*.

The open access cases, which were almost entirely about access for munis and co-ops, numbered in the hundreds in the 1970s and 1980s. By 1992 there was very little *open access*. It was very galling to high-cost IOUs to think that they might have to open their transmission to allow competitors to steal their wholesale customers, especially when the price differences arose from historic costs, not from the sort of going-forward efficiency or lower costs that a "free trade" argument would assume (see Chapter 2).

[9] The Combined Cycle Gas Turbines—see Chapter 2. The Fuel Use Act of 1978 prohibited the use of gas as a fuel for new electric generation. It was later repealed.

Industrial Customers Want Choice

The large industrial customers also wanted to leave and find cheaper power elsewhere. (Industrials are one-third of load in the United States, but under a half of 1 percent of customers.) They could not get access to the transmission wires, but in addition, they were subject to state regulation that required them to purchase only from the local utility. In fact the industrials had been quite successful in getting themselves, as a class, regulated prices that were lower than those paid by other classes (commercial and residential), but they still felt they could do better. They agitated a lot, with some success; this was a major reason that restructuring in the United States started with retail access rather than generating competition, which would have been the right place to start. What the industrials, and also the munis and co-ops wanted was access to low-cost power supplies without bearing any responsibility for the existing high-cost generators that had been built to serve them.

Independent Power Producers

The independent generators also lobbied for access to customers. Some of them had international business and were constructing or purchasing plants in newly deregulated markets abroad. But in the United States they were constrained, and not only by lack of transmission access to potential municipal customers; they could not legally sell to industrial customers, and they were hamstrung by the rules of the Public Utility Holding Company Act (PUHCA) of 1935, which imposed stringent requirements on any company that engages in anything other than utility business in a single state. For instance, General Electric had thought of purchasing the assets of Public Service Company of New Hampshire, which went bankrupt in 1988, but had dropped the idea because of the PUHCA requirements. So the independents needed not only access, but also some relief from PUHCA.

Stranded Costs

The IOUs could just about imagine the munis and co-ops and a few pushy industrials leaving—in many cases they paid barely profitable rates anyway—but the thought that *all retail customers* or even all industrials might also be able to choose, caused a mild panic. Retail access might mean a deregulated market in generation, which is what had been happening abroad.

For the high-cost utilities, a deregulated production market would almost certainly mean a fall in revenues—market prices would tend, in the long run, to approximate the costs of new entrants, and in the short run, if there was excess capacity (which there often was in the early 1990s), market prices would be even lower. If market prices were to prevail in generation markets, some high-priced utilities could stand to lose, in stranded costs, more than their entire equity in the company. Congress was in favor of competition, but that way could lie disaster for the high-cost IOUs.

The low-cost IOUs were not necessarily in favor of competition either. Although some of them felt that they might be able to gain from market prices that were above their historic costs, many of them realized that their customers would not want to pay the (higher) market prices, and that therefore their regulators would want to arrange for any "negative stranded costs" to be assigned in some way to the customers. It seemed like a lot of bother to restructure an entire industry for competition, when the customers in low-cost states were doing better than the market anyway. This also is an issue that is still with us.

The industry opposed *retail wheeling,* as it was then called, because of the unresolved stranded cost issue. But some of the high-cost utilities privately hoped that the introduction of market forces might act on unruly regulators to stop forcing ever-higher costs on them.

EXAMPLES IN OTHER INDUSTRIES

Apart from the internal pressures, there were examples from elsewhere. The gas industry in the United States had been unbundled and gas production deregulated by FERC in a series of Orders in the 1970s and 1980s; this appeared to have been successful. (See Appendix D on the U.S. gas experience.) Many gas marketers had made a lot of money trading in the deregulated gas markets, and gas companies were building electric generating plants in the deregulated markets abroad. Enron, the biggest of these companies, was a major player in all phases of U.S. electric market deregulation.

FERC however does not have the same jurisdiction over the electric industry as it does in gas, although in both industries FERC has jurisdiction over wholesale sales. The essential difference between gas and electricity with respect to FERC's jurisdiction is that in electricity, *production is regulated by the states when the production is in an integrated operating company,* because there is no wholesale sale. Originally gas was also produced by integrated companies; this was "town gas" made from coal at the smelly gas works. But when gas production moved from "town gas" to the distant natural gas fields, and local distribution companies purchased gas from the pipelines, the purchase became a wholesale transaction and hence FERC jurisdictional. (The retail sales were, and still are, regulated by the states.) FERC was therefore able to deregulate gas production when it believed the markets were competitive, and also set up a very good regulatory regime for the pipelines. But in electricity, FERC had very limited (practically useless) authority under the Federal Power Act to order access to the electric transmission, until the EPAct of 1992.

Other examples came from countries that had been restructuring their electric industries—the most influential reform being that of the United Kingdom, which in 1990 restructured from a government-owned monopoly into a competitive generating market with regulated transmission and distribution, and retail access in phases for all customers. We examine the United Kingdom in more detail in Appendices A and B. The primary difference between these countries and the United States is that in most places abroad, the government originally owned the industry, and also had the authority to make the necessary changes—most of these changes were done in the run-up to privatization. Prior government ownership does make things much simpler. There are many fewer stakeholders, fewer conflicting interests, and, therefore, few compromises. A unitary design that can withstand stresses is a far more likely outcome. Furthermore, the government can generally absorb any losses in the book value of assets consequent on the transition to competition, whereas this is a major problem for investor-owned companies.

CHAPTER 13

Changes in the 1990s

We have mentioned that the munis and co-ops and also the industrial customers wanted access to the transmission to purchase from independents, or from more distant utilities. FERC did not feel that it had a mandate to order any sort of access—it only had jurisdiction to set prices for wholesale sales and associated transmission. In the 1990s, there was only one piece of federal legislation related to the electric industry—the Energy Policy Act of 1992 (EPAct). No one was saying competitive generation might be a good thing—what do we need to do to establish generating competition? The issue was open access.

EPACT (1992)—OPEN ACCESS FOR WHOLESALE ONLY

In EPAct Congress decided that FERC could order open access for wholesale transactions (inter-utility sales, and contracts with the munis and co-ops) but it was specifically prohibited from ordering access for final customers. The states could order retail access if they wished. It is this limited mandate, to order access for wholesale transactions, that set FERC on the wrong path for the design of trading arrangements. The wheeling design FERC chose, and has not yet abandoned, is really only suitable for this type of very limited trading.

EPAct also made provision to exempt independent generators from the onerous provisions of the Public Utility Holding Company Act, which had stymied the growth of independent generators. Note that at this stage, the buyers from independents had to be munis and co-ops or utilities. No retail customer, large or small, in the United States could choose its supplier and changing this was in the jurisdiction of the states. The industrials, and their potential independent suppliers, were mortified by this restriction and threatened to "municipalize the hell out of the country" (i.e., get friendly towns where they were located to condemn the distribution system and take it over). They started working on the states to give them retail access.

The stranded cost issue then took center stage for several years. Was there a regulatory compact that entitled the regulated utilities to recoup their stranded costs in the event of deregulation? Or was that just part of the risk of running a business? And did permitting customers to switch to suppliers who had lower historic costs but just the same marginal costs of supply actually increase competition, or was it just moving money around?[1]

In 1995, FERC put out the first draft of Order No. 888, a generic rule ordering all IOUs subject to its authority to provide open access to their transmission systems. This was finalized in 1996. It tried to answer these questions.[2]

ORDER NO. 888 (1996)—STRANDED COSTS AND TRADING RULES

It ruled that stranded costs due to lost wholesale sales could be recouped from the departing wholesale customer, provided that efforts had been made to mitigate the effects. This was an enormous relief to the IOUs, for although it referred only to wholesale sales, it set the tone for the later discussions at the state level, and effectively put the stranded cost issue to bed, at least in principle. In practice, the recovery of stranded costs has posed some knotty problems of rate design (see Chapter 18) and is one of the things that have dogged the subsequent restructuring, especially in California.

Order No. 888 also set out rules for open access, the trading arrangements, which we review in Chapter 15, and it required separation of trading and system operations.

ORDER NO. 888: The order put out by FERC in 1996 that dictates much of the way energy is traded in the United States today.

[1] An influential article by W. Baumol, P. Joskow, and A. Kahn gives a good review of these issues: "The Challenge for Federal and State Regulators: Transition from Regulation to Efficient Competition in Electric Power," December 1994, submitted by the Edison Electric Institute to FERC in the rulemaking proceeding that led to Order No. 888.

[2] From 1992 to 1996 FERC adjudicated access requests on a case-by-case basis. This was slow and cumbersome, so in 1996, in Order No. 888 and a companion Order No. 889, FERC codified its previous individual decisions on access into general rules.

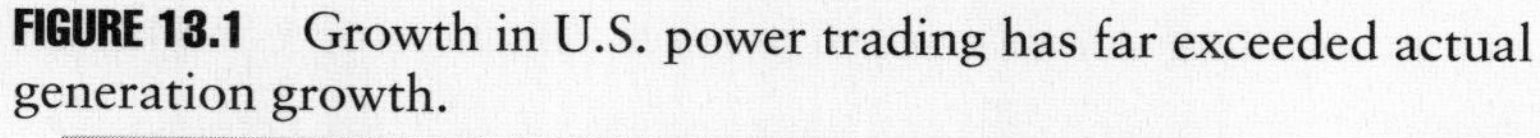

FIGURE 13.1 Growth in U.S. power trading has far exceeded actual generation growth.

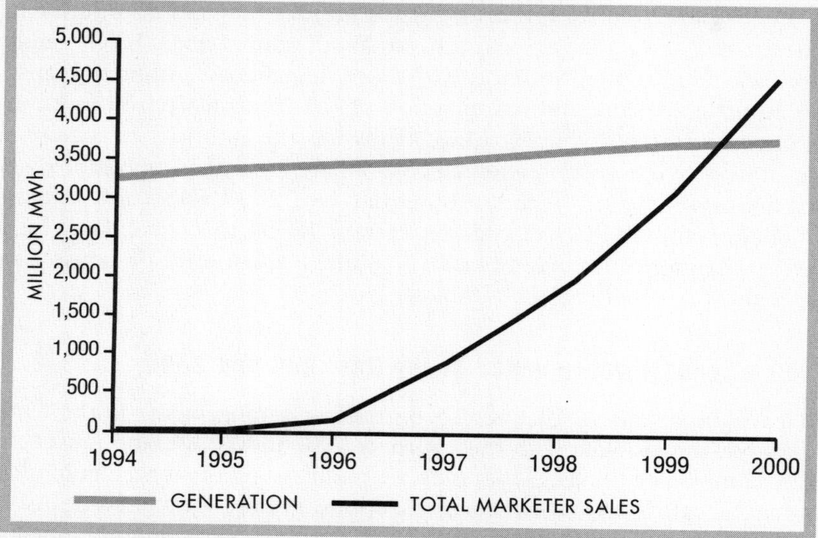

Source: Generation—Department of Energy, Energy Information Administration, Annual Energy Review, 1994–2000. Total Marketer Sales—McGraw Hill Quarterly Power Marketer Database, 1994–2000. (These numbers include bilateral sales that do not go through organized markets, and include multiple sales of the same energy.)

Trading grew fast after 1996 when Order No. 888 was finalized (see Figure 13.1), guaranteeing equal access to the wires for delivery. Nonetheless, much of this trading is still *marginal competition,* when most of the power is coming from utilities and going to buyers who still have a monopoly over final consumers.

ORDER NO. 2000 (1999)—CONSOLIDATION

By 1999 it was obvious that *vertical integration* of trading and system operations was not the only, or perhaps even the major, barrier to trade. We have mentioned before that the ownership of transmission and control of system operations is extremely fragmented. There are approximately 140 different control areas in the U.S. grid and more owners of transmission facilities. The *geographic fragmentation* of transmission was inhibiting trade. Electricity market boundaries transcend franchise territories and state boundaries, and trading across control areas is much more complicated than trading within a single area.

Order No. 2000 told investor-owned utilities they had to find dancing partners and join up in regional transmission organizations (RTOs) and report back. They did report back, with more than a dozen different plans for trading arrangements and organization of the transmission business. It is not clear, to this day, whether FERC really has the authority to require private (state-regulated) companies to consolidate even their operations when they are unwilling to. Technically, Order No. 2000 asked for voluntary compliance and FERC has ordered certain RTOs to consolidate. FERC, however, cannot order private utilities to divest themselves of transmission into a new regulated regional Transco.

Trading Arrangements under Order Nos. 888 and 2000

We leave the details to Chapter 15 on trading arrangements in the United States, but the problem with these Orders (888 and 2000), and most of the utility compliance filings, is that they are premised on the wheeling model of trading: on rather few wholesale transactions, in the context of a utility system operator running the transmission system, and providing the ancillary services. FERC has not actually imposed specific trading arrangements, but it has issued general requirements that presuppose a utility system operator who owns generation. Since Order No. 2000, FERC has had a number of technical conferences and further orders that move towards more consolidations and more sensible trading arrangements and has also taken encouraging steps in the direction of standardized market design. They say they are going to impose new trading arrangements. *It is a major thesis of this book that the trading arrangements required by Order Nos. 888 and 2000 are not sufficient to support competition and retail access. What are needed are new trading arrangements entirely.*

Separation of the System Operator in Order Nos.888 and 2000

When competition is introduced, the traders will not trust the system operator if he is also a competitor. The system operator has to be separated in some way from the generators owned by the same company, or he will naturally favor them in offering access. The physical gatekeeper to the transmission has to be seen to be above possible conflicts.

In 1996, in Order No. 888, FERC chose a minimum separation—the system operators had to be separated physically from the utility's wholesale traders, treat them the same as everyone else, and charge them the same prices. In Order No. 888, FERC "encouraged" the formation of independent system operators (ISOs)—organizations completely separate from the utility, controlling system operations, and consolidated on a regional basis, which by then were forming anyway in the new marketplaces.

By 1999, FERC was not satisfied that this solved the access problem. It was still getting many complaints about subtle forms of discrimination in favor of the utility's own trades, and it reasoned that for every filed complaint there were probably other instances that did not result in formal complaints. So it needed to go further. Order No. 2000 required many system operator activities to be separated from the utility.

It said it would like to see, but would not mandate, *corporate separation* of the transmission, such as, divestiture.

Regional Consolidation in Order No. 2000

Many of the difficult issues in trading arrangements are in setting up rules for using someone else's transmission to make a trade across multiple control areas. The areas the trade is passing through have to accommodate it if space is available, and the system operators have to make adjustments all the time to accommodate the trade. For internal trading, the system operator has to control the generating plants internal to the area, but if the trading arrangements are those we recommend, he has a big computer model to help him do this. The requests for trades across control areas add a layer of complexity that require additional rules, pricing, reorganization of in-area generation, provision of reserves, and so on. And importantly, since electricity flows where it will, the transaction may be designated, and paid for, as if it were flowing on one *contract path,* and actually be flowing on another, over another control area. This is called *loop flow.* Consolidating into many fewer areas would greatly reduce the number of cross-area trades and loop flow problems by making them internal.

FERC's solution was the formation of Regional Transmission Organizations or RTOs. Order No. 2000 directed that all transmission-owning entities in the United States, *including nonpublic utility entities,* place their transmission facilities under the *control* of RTOs. This meant they had to consolidate operations and produce new trading arrangements, but left open the question of the transmission organization and ownership. However, the RTOs must have a governance structure and staff that are independent of other market participants; and they must have the authority to file with FERC the terms and conditions for access to the transmission. Some of the options are:[3]

[3] The full list of independence conditions is contained in FERC's Order No. 2000.

- The RTOs can be organized as ISOs (as in PJM), where the utilities continue to own transmission;
- They could be Transcos of the type we propose in Part One, where a regulated company owns the transmission assets and runs the system operations;
- FERC also left the door open for other structures (like the Gridco plus ISO form) as long as the independence criteria are achieved; and
- The Alliance proposal in the Midwest, for example, is called a Transco, but the transmission assets were essentially leased to the Transco, who would have acted as ISO.

FERC ordered the creation of RTOs for operations, without mandating the corporate divestiture of transmission that it said it preferred, but there is some doubt as to FERC's authority even to order this much consolidation.

We return to the organization of transmission, and transmission pricing, in Chapter 17.

DEREGULATING STATE BY STATE

EPAct left retail access, and the deregulation of generation, in the hands of the states. The first state to announce retail access was California in 1994, followed later that year by Massachusetts, although Rhode Island was the first state actually to implement retail access, in 1997. High prices for generation, compared to prevailing and predicted wholesale prices were a major reason these states moved for reform, under pressure from the industrial customers. Figure 13.2 shows the dates of retail access and the average *industrial* price in 1997. On the whole, the high priced states went first, at the urging of their industrial customers (see also Table 13.1 and Figure 13.3 on page 274).

The big states and the states in the tight pools of the Northeast historically had some of the highest prices, which gave them incentives to reform, and they were also the easiest to reform either because of their size or history of pooling.

We do not propose to go into the details of each state's changes. Of the states that have introduced retail access, there are three groups—the group that grew out of the tight pools; the big states that have gone it alone, but have put in new trading arrangements; and the states that have begun retail reforms without competitive generation markets in place.

FIGURE 13.2 Average industrial price and retail access date.

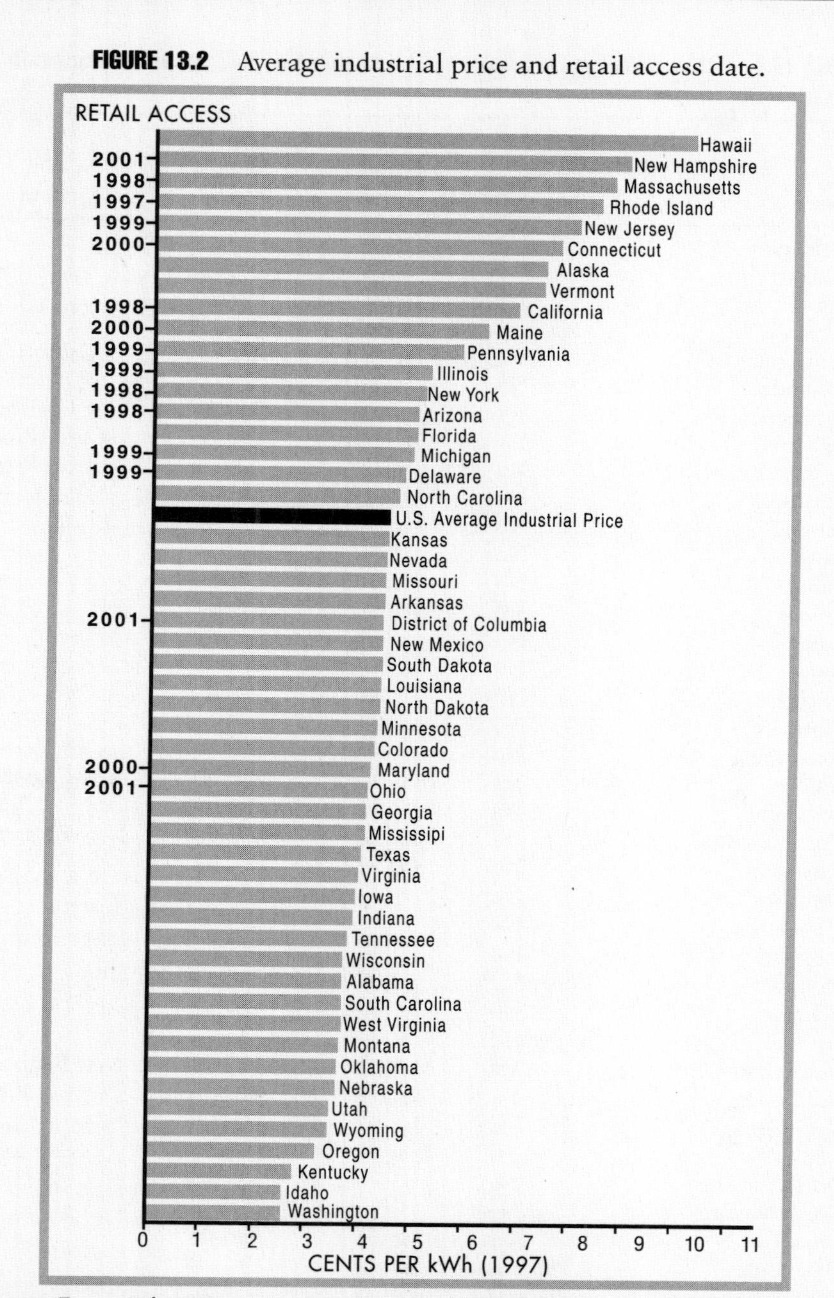

Source: Energy Information Administration, Monthly Average Revenue per Kilowatt-Hour for Industrial Sales by State, 1990–2201 and Status of Electricity Restructuring Activity as of September 2001. www.eia.doe.gov.

TABLE 13.1 Retail Access by State and Implementation Date and Regional System Operator

State	Retail Access	Retail Access (Start Date)	Full Retail Access	System Operator
Alabama	No	—	—	—
Alaska	No	—	—	—
Arizona	Yes	Dec-98	Jan-01	*
Arkansas	Planned	Oct-03	Oct-03	—
California	Yes	Mar-98	Mar-98	California
Colorado	No	—	—	—
Connecticut	Yes	Jan-00	Jul-00	New England
Delaware	Yes	Oct-99	Apr-01	PJM
District of Columbia	Yes	Jan-01	—	PJM
Florida	No	—	—	—
Georgia	No	—	—	—
Hawaii	No	—	—	—
Idaho	No	—	—	—
Illinois	Yes	Oct-99	May-02	*
Indiana	No	—	—	—
Iowa	No	—	—	—
Kansas	No	—	—	—
Kentucky	No	—	—	—
Louisiana	No	—	—	—
Maine	Yes	Mar-00	Mar-00	New England
Maryland	Yes	Jul-00	Jul-02	PJM
Massachusetts	Yes	Mar-98	Mar-98	New England
Michigan	Yes	Sep-99	Dec-02	*
Minnesota	No	—	—	—
Mississippi	No	—	—	—
Missouri	No	—	—	—
Montana	Suspended	Jul-98	Jul-04	—
Nebraska	No	—	—	—
Nevada	Suspended	—	—	—
New Hampshire	Yes	May-01	—	New England
New Jersey	Yes	Aug-99	Aug-99	PJM
New Mexico	Planned	Jan-07	Jul-08	—
New York	Yes	May-98	Dec-01	New York
North Carolina	No	—	—	—
North Dakota	No	—	—	—
Ohio	Yes	Jan-01	Jan-01	*
Oklahoma	Planned	Jan-04	—	—
Oregon	Planned	Mar-02	—	—
Pennsylvania	Yes	Jan-99	Jan-00	PJM

TABLE 13.1 *(Continued)*

State	Retail Access	Retail Access (Start Date)	Full Retail Access	System Operator
Rhode Island	Yes	Jul-97	Jan-98	New England
South Carolina	No	—	—	—
South Dakota	No	—	—	—
Tennessee	No	—	—	—
Texas	Planned	Jan-02	—	ERCOT
Utah	No	—	—	—
Vermont	No	—	—	New England
Virginia	Planned	Jan-02	Jan-04	PJM
Washington	No	—	—	—
West Virginia	Planned	—	—	—
Wisconsin	No	—	—	—
Wyoming	No	—	—	—

Source: Department of Energy, Energy Information Administration Status of State Electric Industry Restructuring Activity as of September 2001 (www.eia.doe.gov). Connecticut Department of Public Utility Control, Nevada Assembly Bill AB369 and New Hampshire Public Utility Commission.
*These states introduced retail access without changes in the trading arrangements.

States in the Tight Pools

The tight pools, now ISOs, of PJM, New York, and New England, operated in the high-population Northeast states (see Figure 13.4). They operated in Connecticut, Delaware, Maine, Maryland, Massachusetts, New Hampshire, New Jersey, New York, Pennsylvania, Rhode Island, Vermont, and the District of Columbia. The boundaries do not exactly correspond state lines; for example, some of Virginia is in PJM, and not all of Pennsylvania is.

The main reason the new markets came to the Northeast is the history of pooling there. In New York for example, the utilities created the New York Power Pool (NYPP) many years ago in response to reliability problems. (New York was sufficiently large that they felt it was not necessary to pool with other States.) After Order No. 888 many years later, New York complied by opening the NYPP club to allow municipalities and others comparable access terms to the utilities, and allowed merchant generators access to sell power to the pool under the same terms as the utilities. The pricing rules were changed, but everything was fairly straightforward to arrange given the history of pooling.

FIGURE 13.3 Estimated average revenue per kWh for all sectors at electric utilities by state, 1999.

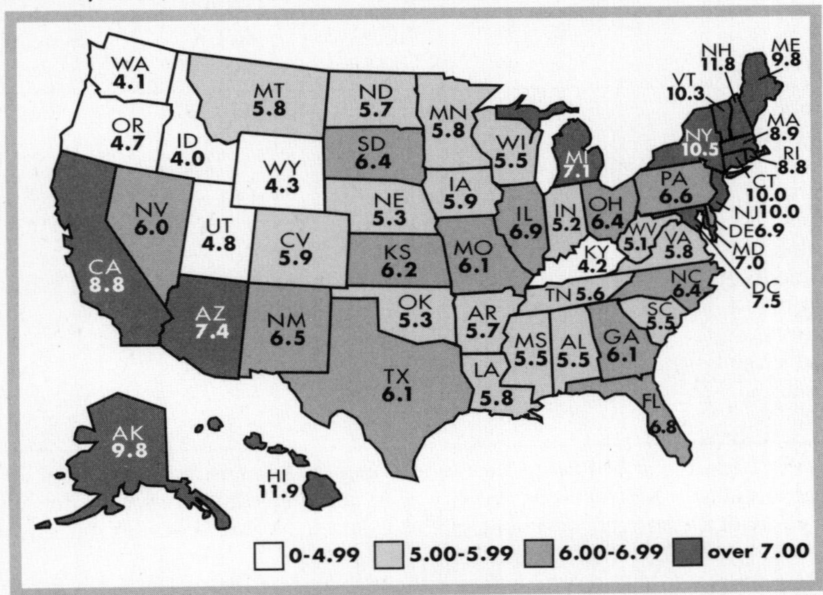

Source: Energy Information Administration, Form EIA-826 monthly electric utility sales and revenue report with state distributions.

FIGURE 13.4 States comprising the "tight pools" in the Northeast.

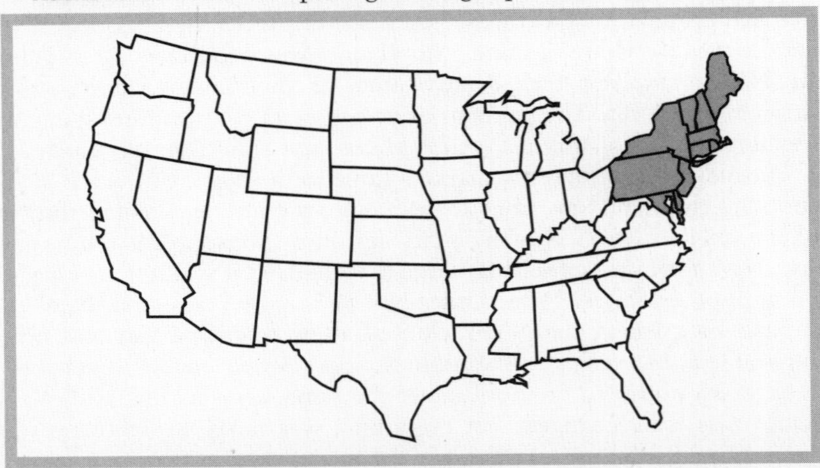

The situation in PJM and New England is essentially the same as that in New York except that PJM and New England have a history of multistate pooling.

The history of retail access and reform of state regulation varies by state within the tight pools. But they all made changes around the same time (between 1997 and 2001) and in this area only Vermont has not gone to retail access.

Big States That Have Gone It Alone

California and Texas are different stories (see Figure 13.5). In each, the state itself was large enough to take the initiative to deregulate within its boundaries—although California is really part of the larger Western market, which creates some problems of its own. Texas is not interconnected with the rest of the United States. *Both of these states had to invent a new trading system.* As everyone knows there were serious problems in California. (We devote Appendix C to describing the California crisis of 2000–2001.) Texas operates its own regional grid and has no oversight from FERC. It established its own rules and trading arrangements.

States That Have Begun Reforms without Market Institutions in Place

Other states, such as Arizona, Ohio, Montana, Illinois, Virginia, and Michigan have begun reforms without wholesale market institutions in place. The

FIGURE 13.5 The big states that have gone it alone—Texas and California.

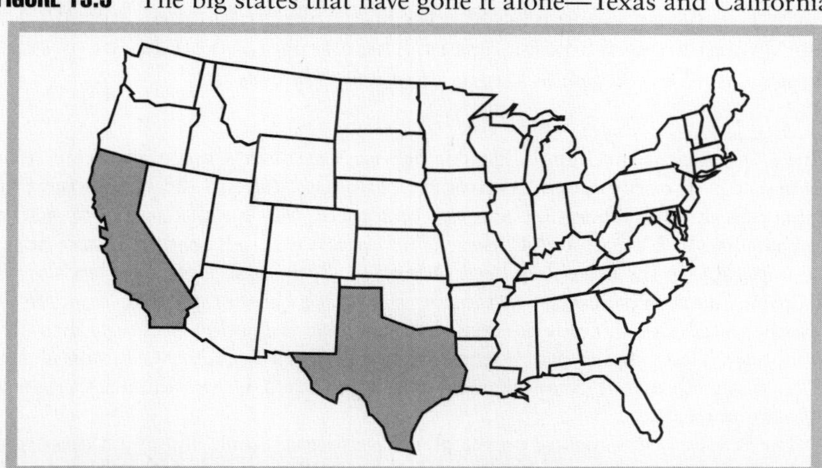

FIGURE 13.6 Arizona, Ohio, Montana, Illinois, Michigan, and Virginia.

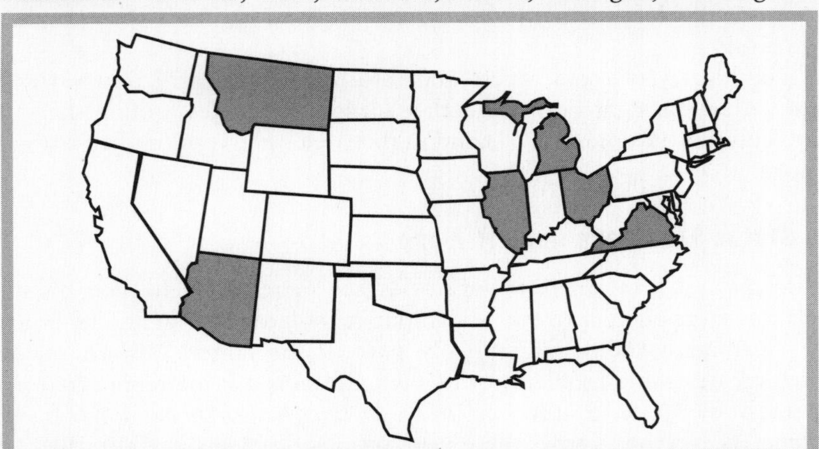

trading arrangements have not been changed; tests for market power have not been made. These states do not have competitive generation markets, yet have forged ahead with retail access (see Figure 13.6).

Trying to do retail access without a wholesale market and a spot price causes all sorts of problems. For example, in Illinois, efforts to create an Independent System Operator and a centralized market for the real-time bidding of electricity supply lagged behind state initiatives to introduce retail choice. Because there are no new trading arrangements, and no spot price on which to base a shopping credit, the state uses an administrative process to set annual proxy wholesale prices. These generation credits or *prices to beat* are called *market values,* instead of *shopping credits.*[4]

[4]Illinois introduced the Illinois Electric Service Customer Choice and Rate Relief Law in 1997. Its purpose was to introduce customer choice. It did not envisage full competition in the generating market, and there was no discussion of trading arrangements. In 2001 in Illinois, there is no operational independent system operator comparable to the ISOs elsewhere. During 1998, the first year of the law's implementation, many residential customers received a base rate reduction. As of December 31, 2000, all nonresidential customers had the option to choose their electric supplier. That supplier may be the current electric utility, another Illinois electric utility, or an alternative retail electric supplier certified by the Illinois Commerce Commission (ICC).

The law does not require power plant divestiture. Some Illinois utilities transferred ownership of their generating facilities to affiliated companies. For example,

Initially, Illinois used a *Neutral Fact Finder* (NFF) to calculate these market values. However, the NFF's method did not produce accurate estimates. They did not properly reflect the seasonality of actual market values and were updated only once a year. NFF market values were significantly lower than actual prices observed in the market during the summer period, and too high at other times. As a result there was gaming by marketers to serve retail customers in the winter and dump them back to the utility in the summer. The NFF process was then changed to an index based on real transactions that more closely resemble market activity. However, the wholesale market arrangement still needs a great deal of work.

In Montana, it has been a real muddle. Montana Power sold all its generating assets to PPL Resources in December 1999 (without breaking them up, and with no trading arrangements in place), planning to introduce full retail access in July 2002. In June 2001, spooked by California, Montana decided to delay complete retail access for all consumers from July 2002 to July 2004 because the state did not have a competitive power supply market in place. (A wise move.) The state regulatory commission then ruled that Montana Power's rates (including power supply) would be regulated through 2007. PPL filed a suit against the commission ruling.

Central Illinois Public Service transferred its generation facilities to an affiliate, Ameren Energy, and Illinois Power Company transferred its generation facilities to a generation subsidiary of Illinois Power's Houston, Texas based parent, Dynegy, Inc. These affiliates are free to sell electricity to their affiliated utilities and to unrelated companies. This transfer puts generating assets under FERC jurisdiction.

CHAPTER 14

The New Players

Since 1992, there are many new players on the U.S. scene—independent system operators (ISOs), Transcos, marketers and brokers, retailers and the new/old independent generators, whose role has changed; FERC itself is a new/old player—it has acquired by accident rather than by design a much wider set of responsibilities, without additional staff and without additional mandate.

INDEPENDENT SYSTEM OPERATORS

Restructuring involves unbundling functions that have always been integrated. One function that needs to be unbundled is that of system operations, because the system operator stands at the gateway to the market. If you cannot get your power delivered, you cannot compete. If the system operator is part of a company whose generation is in competition with yours, you are suspicious of his motives. Even with transparent rules and audits of the system operator to check it is following the rules, it is incredibly hard to police all these second by second decisions. So the system operator has to be independent of all the generators.

Most of the world has gone further and unbundled transmission along with system operations. They have independent Transcos, which combine independent[1] ownership of a consolidated transmission with system operations. In a few places (parts of Australia, for example) the ISO and market operations are combined and there is a separate Gridco, owning all the transmission. In Argentina there is decentralized expansion of transmission, and an ISO, which is owned by the government.

But the fragmented nature of the U.S. ownership of transmission made the task of separating and consolidating transmission too difficult to take

[1] Independent, that is, of the generators and other market participants.

on, politically. So the notion was promoted of separating the system operator from the utility and combining the *operations* of several utilities into ISOs, while leaving the transmission under fragmented utility ownership. Throughout the United States, the notion of the ISO has taken hold—the term was unknown before 1994. By 2001, five ISOs existed in the United States—California ISO, ERCOT (Texas), New York ISO, ISO New England, and PJM. They are not-for-profit organizations run by boards of directors.

TRANSCOS

A Transco is a profit-making company that owns transmission and also runs the system operations. The model is National Grid Company in the United Kingdom. (See Appendix B.) A Transco should be independent of generators. There were several proposals to FERC for Transcos owned by generators, and several for Transcos that would be more independent. As yet there is no agreed policy as to whether a Transco is a good thing (we recommended it in Part One); it would require divestiture by the utilities of their transmission, and there is no authority to require this in the United States, although the Wisconsin legislature working cooperatively with the utilities, required the Wisconsin utilities do this.

MARKETERS AND BROKERS

Marketers and brokers buy and sell power without necessarily owning power plants; marketers take positions and therefore risk; brokers simply match buyers and sellers and take a cut. Trading in power increased enormously after 1996 with the final Order No. 888; many liquid trading hubs have sprung up. Forward markets (marketplaces) in electricity have developed a lot since 1996. Figure 14.1 shows location and trading volumes in 2000. Enron was the biggest trader by far as of this date, although the Enron bankruptcy in January 2002 clearly changed that.

These private markets are having a major impact on thinking in the industry, and should play an important role as more states deregulate. Buyers and sellers have the choice to enter into bilateral transactions, or participate in organized markets. In the organized markets, traders are increasingly willing to take "positions" where they either buy forward contracts and later sell them back (having no intention or ability even to produce power) or sell forward contracts and later buy them back (having no intention to ever consume the power). Power is often bought and sold many times before

FIGURE 14.1 U.S. electricity trading hubs, 2000.

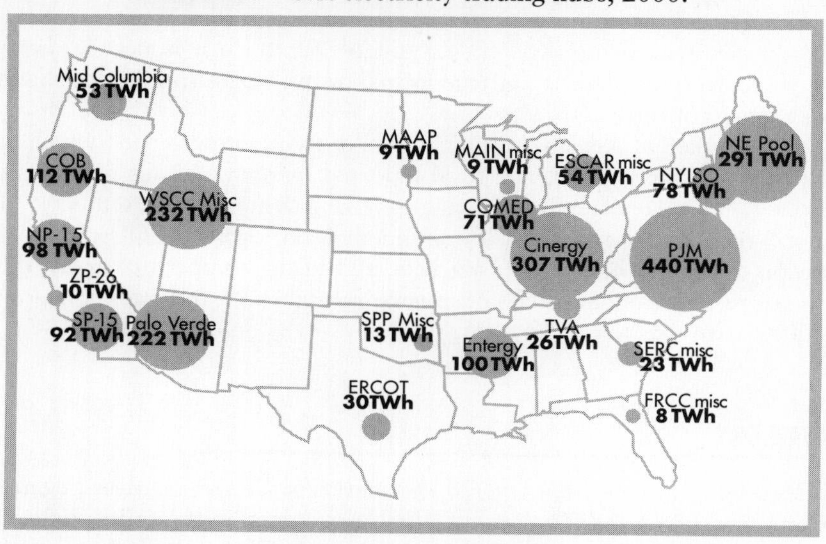

delivery. In this respect, the new electricity markets are much like other forward commodity markets, and regulated not by energy regulators but by securities regulators.

There is also unregulated trading in forward contracts when they are traded bilaterally between parties, often facilitated by a broker. In addition to "voice" brokers, electronic platforms that match buyers and sellers (e.g., InterContinental Exchange, Bloomberg, or Altra) have become popular and are replacing traditional phone and fax trading for the simpler type of contract. Enron Online was an electronic platform in which Enron acted as market-maker, escaping regulation because Enron was counterparty to all the traders.

A futures market trades standardized forward (futures) contracts through an exchange. NYMEX offers standardized futures contracts for principal hubs throughout the United States.[2] The Minnesota Grain Exchange offers futures for Minnesota delivery. The Chicago Board of Trade listed electricity futures for a period of less than two years from September 1998 to June 2000[3] but exited the market due to lack of trading volume.

[2] NYMEX ceased trading in these contracts days before this book went to press.
[3] Market Information Department, Chicago Board of Trade.

One of the big problems of organized futures markets in electricity is standardizing the contracts when spot prices move hourly. There are 8,760 hours in a year; it is hard to define a suitable set of those hours that everyone wants to trade. This is not true in gas, or oil, where spot prices change much less frequently.

The marketers' sales figures include sales to other marketers, which are 90 percent of the volume, and total reported marketers' sales now exceed total actual U.S. production. (See Figure 13.1.) Who are they selling to? In the still-regulated areas they sell to municipals, co-ops, and IOUs, in an expansion of the old bulk power markets; and in the competitive areas, they also sell to retailers and final consumers. But when all the trading is done, the power still has to be delivered.

RETAILERS

Independent retailers have entered the market since retail access began in various states in 1998. They sell to final consumers, in the states that have permitted retail access, and they generally need to be registered with some oversight agency in the state to do so. Virtually all utilities created unregulated retail subsidiaries, and many other private companies also entered the market. But as of 2000, in the United States non-utility retailers were serving only 3 percent of final customers.

INDEPENDENT GENERATORS

Independent generators existed and had a growing role in the pre-1992 world. However, their role changes in the new world; the business model is no longer life-of-plant contracts with insulation from changes in market prices or technology. What is important, in theory and also borne out in practice, is that generators will not enter a market unless they have one of two things:

1. Long term, life-of-plant contracts with a single buyer;
2. Or a liquid market into which to sell the output.

The theory is that if there is only one potential buyer (the local utility) then the independent can be expropriated after he has built the plant, and his price pushed down to his marginal cost. He needs the protection of a long-term contract. So before the 1990s, there were independents, and in fact by 1992, 60 percent of new plants were being built by independents, *but the old independents all had long-term contracts with utilities.* Not until 1998–1999, when utilities began selling their generating plants, and competition in generation became a reality, did the independents' competitive capacity really take off. They bought plants that were offered for sale, and they also constructed new plants.

In some areas, New England and New York, divestiture was more or less complete. In other areas like Ohio and Michigan, there has been no divestiture at all. In other states, the generation has been partially divested, and in still others it has just been moved to deregulated subsidiaries. "Independent" generation was reported in 2000 to be 30 percent of the total generating market, and in the competitive areas, 70 percent. However, this is a little misleading—the data include the old independents, with life-of-plant contracts, and some newly "deregulated" utility generation with long-term contracts back to their parent companies.

THE NEW JURISDICTIONAL SPLIT

FERC now finds itself with much more on its plate than it ever imagined a decade ago. In 1992, it was given the power to mandate access to utility transmission for wholesale sales only. This implied pricing the use of transmission, as well as issuing orders; but it has grown into mandating ever more complex trading arrangements and efforts at regional consolidation of transmission. Furthermore, trading has increased as the states have deregulated. With no legislative changes since 1992 at the federal level, regulatory responsibility has shifted toward FERC and away from the deregulating states, because as the states have deregulated, the volume of output that is classified as wholesale sales has expanded.

About 30 percent of plants (the independent plants and those in utility subsidiaries) are FERC-regulated. The rest are with the states, except for that portion of the output that is sold in the bulk power markets.

FERC now has control over the important issues of trading arrangements, transmission consolidation, transmission pricing, market power detection, market monitoring, and price controls, on a much greater scale than was envisaged in 1992, and without the resources to handle all the new responsibilities. FERC has only limited expertise in actual market operation. It has recently established a market oversight office, but it may have trouble attracting talent and expertise into the federal salary structure—entry level electricity traders are paid more than top-level FERC officials.

Moreover, FERC has traditionally been unwilling to hire consultants with the necessary expertise.[4]

Rather than establishing a model for trading arrangements and regional organizations, FERC's policy (in the words of one of the commissioners) has been to "let a thousand flowers bloom." This has resulted in dozens of different proposals, which not only slows up progress, but also puts enormous burdens on the staff to review and critique them.

THE NEW NERC

NERC has inherited enormous responsibilities of ensuring the reliability of day-to-day system operations. It has proposed legislation to give it more authority to enforce its rules—but we will argue that what is really needed is new rules that would largely enforce themselves (be incentive-compatible).

[4]This may sound self-serving from an ex-consultant, but the U.S. government daily rates, and in the case of FERC the almost complete absence for many crucial years of a consulting budget, mean that the national expertise is contracted to utilities and other stakeholders in the process of reform. This small fact by itself may explain a large part of the impasse in the United States. Governments abroad have generally been more prepared to pay market rates for sound advice.

CHAPTER 15

Trading Arrangements in the United States

In this chapter, we look at the current trading arrangements in the U.S. electric industry. We describe the existing markets and the problems of access and operations, and why and how trading arrangements based on Order No. 888 must be totally revised.

Recall from Part One that replicating the system operator's control in a disaggregated industry involves a host of new agreements, protocols, and contractual arrangements—the trading arrangements. These new trading arrangements need to accomplish everything the system operator in an integrated utility used to do by command and control, but now using rules and prices. The trading arrangements are the rules governing the relation of the system operator to the traders. We have argued that detailed trading arrangements designed specifically for the electricity industry are a prerequisite to generation competition.

Before the reforms of the 1990s, there were no organized forward markets, no independent system operators, no spot markets with visible spot prices, no uncontracted independent generators, and no final users who were free to choose. There were only a few wholesale sales (to utilities or munis or co-ops); a few long-term contracts; some short term bilateral trading for economy and reliability in the bulk power markets and the tight pools. Since 1996, there has been an enormous increase in forward trading, *but these forward contracts need to be deliverable.*

When all the trading in forward markets is finished, the practical reality is that the transmission system is limited in what it can deliver. Electricity contracted in the forward markets can only be delivered over a single network of transmission wires. The trading arrangements for delivery have to be designed to respect the short-term operational concerns of the system operators, and with incentive-compatible rules so that the traders obey the system operator without a police force to ensure compliance.

In the United States, these issues in delivery are far from settled. They have been debated for years and they are not solved yet. They are all in FERC's jurisdiction, and FERC has addressed them in Order No. 888 (1996) and in Order No. 2000 (1999) and has started a standard market design process (2001). But FERC's current rules are based on the wheeling model—a model that simply does not work for competition, and does not work particularly well anywhere. We describe some of the specific problems the United States has run into with this model, in the section called *Acronym Soup*.

THE BIG STATES AND THE TIGHT POOLS

However, before the reader gets bewildered by the complexity of the current arrangements, we should note that these problems have in fact been (more or less) solved in the United States, with the approval of FERC. Delivery arrangements that deal with all these complexities have been established in the new competitive areas—namely, PJM, New York, New England, California, and Texas. We will refer to these as "the new trading arrangements" or the "new marketplaces" or the "new markets." In these areas, new trading arrangements have been developed using the decentralized and the integrated market models (refer to Part One) to underpin competitive production markets.

The rules in each new marketplace are different: The three in the Northeast (New York, PJM, New England) developed from the old tight pools, and have a family resemblance, using the integrated trading model that we recommend in Part One. The tight pool model worked efficiently in the old system, and the adaptations of it are working well in the new competitive world. In fact, the tight pools were the original blueprint for the development of competitive trading arrangements around the world. *It is no accident that competition found its easiest home in the tight pool states.* The access and pricing rules were changed to accommodate competition, and it was fairly straightforward to arrange given the history of pooling.

California had to invent a new trading system. The California trading arrangements were truly badly designed—deficient in virtually every respect (see Appendix C)—and many of the other aspects of the design of the market itself were also bad. Texas deregulated early in 2002, although its ISO had been in place for several years, an approach worth emulating. The Texas design is partly decentralized.

Look again at the map in Figure 14.1 showing the major private forward trading hubs: *the majority of the trading is being done in connection with the new market places.* The vast bulk of the trading on this map is within, or on the borders of, California, PJM, New York, and New

England. (The Texas market was not operational at the time of this map.) Elsewhere, except for Cinergy,[1] the trading is tiny. The new markets do actually encourage competition.

These new trading arrangements were developed by the utilities that use them, in conjunction with the states that they serve. *They are not the trading arrangements that FERC has been ordering in 888 and 2000.* They certainly comply with FERC's requirements, but have been made to fit—something akin to shaving the corners off a square peg so it will fit in a round hole. And although FERC said in 1997 "we have seen the future and the future is PJM," FERC has not actually ordered that the rest of the country adopt the PJM model. It believes it does not have the authority to do so.

So the United States is at an impasse. We believe that transformation of the trading arrangements is essential for competition, but appropriate trading arrangements have so far only been introduced where there was low-hanging fruit—where an existing tight pool could be transformed, or where a state was big enough to go it alone. Meanwhile, FERC only has limited jurisdiction; it does not sit over the states—it has jurisdiction over only a part of what goes on. It is dealing only with wholesale sales, unless asked by the states to go further. And its Orders have reflected the partial nature of its authority.

PROBLEMS ELSEWHERE

Despite the existence of these new markets and some others gingerly making some steps towards competition, most of the country has not instituted trading arrangements that could underpin competition. Most of the United States is not competitive at all. Overall, the industry consists of about 800,000 MW of generating capacity. Only about 250,000 MW of this participates in the big states and the tight pool states listed earlier. By far the bulk still exists outside of competitive markets.

To turn from the new markets, that can accommodate everything required for competition, and then to read the orders of FERC, one would imagine that we were in two different worlds, which in a way we are. The competitive markets have trading arrangements that are almost unrecognizable in the context of FERC's jargon. But in all parts of the country outside the new competitive markets, the FERC Order Nos. 888 and 2000 governing the

[1] Cinergy is an interesting case, where a utility system operator (not an ISO) dispatches bilateral contracts arrived at in an OTC forward market that appears to be quite liquid. The secret may be the relative lack of transmission constraints in the Midwest of the United States due to the very robust transmission system of American Electric Power (AEP).

activities of the industry with respect to access, pricing, and operations are adhered to more literally.

What exactly is wrong with the trading arrangements used in most of the United States? The wheeling model asks the wrong question, and therefore comes to the wrong answer. The wheeling question is this: "What is the right charge for a delivery of a scheduled flow of power over a utility's transmission lines?" It starts from a delivery schedule, which is a fiction in electricity anyway and piles on a dozen more unanswerable questions, creating serious inefficiencies but also major operational headaches, including:

- First it makes a preliminary cut—the right charge is a proportion of the annual cost of the investment being used.
- Then it has to define a contract path to decide on whose investment is being used. The contract path is a fiction, but once we have decided to work with this fiction, it has to be made operational, and traders have to request a reservation of a path.
- Since the utility gets first priority for its own native load, the utility has to decide on which paths are actually available for wheeling.
- Then there have to be rules for priority among those who want to use the available paths, and physical rights for the winners to use the system.
- But since the contract paths bear little relation to reality, someone has to decide what the utility is permitted do in real time when the real system does not correspond to the imaginary system of contract paths. Can the utility just curtail transactions; or, if it has to reorganize (redispatch) its own plants, what it can charge for that?
- Then almost as an afterthought, it has to worry about appropriate charges for losses, imbalances and ancillary services, at regulated prices.

Each of these steps is a problem. The delivery schedule is a fiction. Electricity is not carpets—you don't order one and complain if they deliver you a different one. Electricity is exactly the same everywhere. It is generated and flows over the transmission network where it will. Customers do not get the same electricity their supplier sends, and no one believes they do. They get whatever electricity happens to be flowing their way at the time, since electricity does not go where we tell it. We just talk as if there is a delivery schedule that gets one producer's electricity to his own customers, and this is what leads to errors. Metaphors can be useful but when taken literally, as the metaphorical "delivery schedule" was in California, whole edifices can be constructed on an erroneous concept.

Instead of thinking of a path or a bridge or a pipeline we have to think of a network, because that is what we have. Dozens of generators and

DISINGENUOUS: It is not entirely clear that the designers of the awful California trading arrangements, among whom Enron was prominent, were incompetent; they may just have been disingenuous. One could be forgiven for thinking the rules in California were designed to give arbitrageurs the ability to make money off an inefficient market. Steven Stoft initially pointed this out in a prescient article "What Should a Power Marketer Want?" (Electricity Journal, June 1997). And indeed Enron has publicly admitted that its goal was to create initial confusion in markets so that the company could profit from arbitrage trading. The *New York Times* ("Regulators Struggle with a Marketplace Created by Enron," Business Day, p. C1, November 10, 2001) reported as follows:

> *For years, the Enron Corporation used its political muscle to build the markets in which it thrived, pushing relentlessly on Capitol Hill and in bureaucratic backwaters to deregulate the nation's natural gas and electricity businesses. Its achievement, as one Enron executive said today, in creating a "regulatory black hole" fit nicely with what he called the company's "core management philosophy," which was to be the first mover into a market and to make money in the initial chaos and lack of transparency.*

millions of customers are scattered around the network (at the *nodes*—a node is a physical place on the transmission system where either a generator or a load is connected). There is no such thing as a supplier getting his power to a specific customer—it is all intermingled. In real time we only have to worry about the generators, and having sufficient power produced to serve all the load—we do not have to worry about who is supposed to be serving whom—that is taken care of in the settlement process.

Against the background of the utility providing almost all the power for almost all the customers, we can imagine a single transaction as a *delivery* with an origin and destination. But once the delivery schedule is the centerpiece of the design, it leads to paths and reservations and physical rights. These cause inefficiencies and operational problems.

- The utility will obviously try to over-reserve transmission capacity for itself rather than be caught short.

- The priorities for transmission usage established on a first-come first served basis will not ensure the highest and best use of the transmission, and also, the physical rights enhance market power.
- Redispatch (see next section) requires a utility system operator to have his own plants to adjust in the event of congestion.
- And imbalances, losses, and ancillary services have to be continually provided or absorbed by the system operator at pre-set, regulated prices. Soon the traders want to provide their own losses, imbalances, and ancillary services.

This system can barely work for a few transactions. It simply cannot be scaled up for the situation where *everything that is going on the network is a delivery.*

The right approach is to presolve the problem, and ask the question: "When competition has done the job of making the best use of the existing generating plants and the best use of the transmission, what will the system look like—who will be generating and how loaded will the transmission lines be?" Actually, we know the answer to this—it is just what the utilities have been doing for years by command and control—making the best use at lowest cost of the existing system. Now that we have in mind what the end point will be, the question is: "How do we get there from here? Can we set up incentive-compatible rules to ensure that it gets there by the traders' own actions, without command and control?" This is exactly what the integrated trading model does.

To summarize, what is wrong with the conceptual model in Order Nos. 888 and 2000 is the limited view of what it has to accomplish. The trading arrangements assume a utility system operator; they assume delivery schedules; they assume a utility system operator over whose territory "foreign" transactions are flowing, and they try to impose charges on each transaction. Furthermore, wheeling presupposes a system operator who owns most of the generating plant on the system and provides congestion management, imbalances, and ancillary services at regulated prices. In competition the system operator has to be independent—he does not own any generating plant. He has to get the competitive generators to provide the energy for congestion management, imbalances, and ancillary services. And they will not do it at pre-set regulated prices—it requires market mechanisms, which are intrinsic to the integrated model.

The United States has a special problem with the wheeling model because of the large number of utility control areas. Transactions *between* control areas are indeed "scheduled" and thus suffer from the contract path fiction. Congestion management, imbalances, ancillary services, scheduling, and dispatch are all made more difficult and the contract path fiction more troublesome when system operator control areas are small. Making the RTOs bigger can help solve this problem, but the foremost solution is to avoid wheeling entirely.

ACRONYM SOUP—THE CURRENT NERC METHODS

Recall that in 1992, EPAct gave FERC the power to order access *for wholesale sales only*. This partial mandate is part of the current problem—FERC could only deal with wholesale access, and wholesale sales in 1992 were a very small part of total output—most of the generation went to regulated sales to the native load. As the states have deregulated, FERC has tried to accommodate the need for additional transactions, but without changing the basic concepts. This has led to a really confused operational situation.

When FERC wrote Order No. 888 based on the old world paradigms of wheeling and contract paths, so many special terms were created to tie the old way of doing things to the new, that it was a case of acronym soup. And it immediately created serious problems.

For example, shortly after the adoption of Order No. 888, the North American Electric Reliability Council (NERC), the organization responsible for system reliability, recognized that contract-path scheduling created incentives to overload the electric network system. NERC immediately adopted transmission loading relief (TLR) protocols to undo the damage whenever the system became constrained. *In essence, NERC created an administrative unscheduling system to counteract the effects of the FERC-mandated scheduling system.*[2] The NERC system did not work well. However, something was necessary in order to keep the lights on.

NLP (Native Load Priority) and CBM (Capacity Benefit Margins)

How do the FERC and NERC methods work?

- Order No. 888 automatically granted (grandfathered) rights, called *native load priority* (NLP), to the local utility's transmission system for all native load customers.
- It also provided utilities with a transmission reserve margin, called a *capacity benefit margin* (CBM) to ensure sufficient transmission capacity

[2] William Hogan, "Electricity Market Restructuring: Reforms of Reforms," Center for Business and Government, Harvard University, Massachusetts 02138, May 25, 2001, p. 8.

on interconnections between utility systems was available to serve the native load in case an emergency, such as loss of a critical generating unit, necessitated importing power from adjacent areas.

- After allocating transmission line capacity sufficient to cover NLP and CBM to the vertically integrated utilities, the remaining *available transmission capacity* (ATC) (obtained by subtracting NLP and CBM from *total transmission capacity* [TTC]) could be allocated on a first-come first-served basis to other wholesale transmission users under terms defined by Order No. 888.
- The available capacity must be posted on the OASIS[3] web page, and the utility's own traders must get their information from OASIS, not by internal communications.
- Under this scheme, transmission customers can purchase "network" service, "point-to-point firm," or "point-to-point nonfirm" transmission service.

ATC (Available Transmission Capacity)

There are several problems with this scheme. The fundamental problem with allocating of ATC among the three types of transmission service rights *is its use of embedded cost pricing that bears little or no relationship to the economic value customers place on those rights*. Therefore, transmission capacity does not get allocated (except coincidentally) to those who value it most highly.

Equal access under EPAct meant equal treatment of competitors for wholesale sales only, with priority for native load. Native load is allocated first priority, which seems right, until you realize that all load is served anyway. What is really allocated first priority is the generating plant that is used to serve native load. This can have two inefficient effects—it can give priority to a generator who is not the least cost; and it can reserve too much of the transmission, leaving capacity unused.

Another problem exists when the ATC calculated and allocated in advance doesn't turn out to match the real-time available transmission capacity. When this happens—and it does because of the contract path fiction—some transactions must be curtailed, interrupted, or the system redispatched to relieve the constrained element. Since transmission capacity rights are not rationed economically under Order No. 888, the curtailment

[3] OASIS is the Open Access Same-time Information System, required by FERC in Order No. 889 so as to give comparable information to all users of a transmission system, and to allow reservation and purchase of transmission capacity.

rules must follow the "natural" order of priority established by service type and level of firmness: network service has highest priority, followed by firm service, and finally nonfirm service.[4] The problem in a nutshell is that property rights are not well defined, since even an energy transaction that is covered by a long-term firm transmission right can be (partially) curtailed if the congestion problem is severe enough.

TLR (Transmission Loading Relief)

Order No. 888's curtailment priority schedule for managing transmission congestion is further complicated by the obligation of system operators to obey curtailment rules established by NERC and its regional reliability councils, referred to as *transmission loading relief* (TLR) procedures. These procedures enable system operators to address transmission congestion in terms of the physical reality of power flows on the network, curtailing transactions in proportion to their contribution to the congestion problem on a particular transmission system element, which also meant they addressed congestion caused by loop flows. Under the open access regime created by Order No. 888, the substantial increase in wholesale power transactions between and across regions, and the increased use of the transmission grid in general, have made the problem a more frequent occurrence on many individual transmission systems. Using the TLR procedures, a transmission provider whose system becomes congested as a result of loop flows can require the curtailment of the transactions creating the loop flows. NERC has long sought additional authority to make its rules apply to all transactions and to give FERC oversight authority over reliability rules. FERC, the Department of Energy (DOE), and several administrations have supported the change. But no significant electricity legislation has been enacted since 1992 because of an impasse on how much authority should be given to the FERC. Clearly, FERC needs more authority to do the job right, and this should include more authority over government-owned transmission.

Tagging in TLR Procedures

An energy transaction that, according to its contract path, sends power on a line from a point A to a point B, can actually send the power on several other

[4] Priorities are further subdivided on the basis of contract length: long-term firm service (a contract for service covering a period of a year or longer) has higher priority that short-term firm service.

lines as well, using up capacity on someone else's line not party to the transaction. And when such a transmission right is sold by one user to another who may use it differently, its side effects change. This means that an enormous effort must be undertaken to *tag* and track every transaction to find out how much ATC is really available in near real time. Often too many ATC-based rights are sold by competing adjacent transmission providers and the result is congestion that requires invoking TLR procedures. The problems with ATC style rights and the TLR procedures to mitigate congestion stem principally from the difficulty of maintaining inter-regional ATC rights coordination. There is a simultaneous, uncoordinated commitment of ATC reservations (i.e., issuance of transmission rights) that will naturally flow on parallel systems. Individual coordinators do not have sufficient information about adjacent regions to know what might be an optimal allocation of rights on their own systems. NERC's Congestion Management Subcommittee believes that ATC coordination remains a major issue in the over-commitment of transmission capacity and is looking for a market-based solution.

System Redispatch

But there are other problems with the TLR process as well. It has been used to interrupt many interchange transactions to maintain transmission security in recent years, but it does not always succeed in mitigating the congestion or, when it is used, can easily restrict transactions that were not part of the problem. With these problems growing over time, NERC directed the Regional Reliability Councils to develop methods of congestion management that would mitigate the negative effects of the TLR transaction curtailment process. *System redispatch* has emerged as one such alternative. System redispatch is sort-of like the *congestion auction* in the decentralized model described in Chapter 7. With system redispatch, the system operator for the region adjusts the dispatch of the generators subject to its control to relieve the constrained transmission element. System redispatch can be used in lieu of TLR curtailments. Also, system redispatch may often be an attractive alternative, because the amount of redispatch required to relieve a given constraint will often be much less than the amount of transactions that must be interrupted to eliminate the loop flows that are contributing to the congestion.

At best, system redispatch helps the old Order No. 888 method start to look a bit more like the decentralized trading model. But for the moment, basic problems with it still exist. The lack of uniformity among transmission providers offering a redispatch option means that a single transaction flowing across or through several systems may be treated quite differently. The result: confusion, uncertainty about the cost of the redispatch option, and inefficient choices made to protect (or hedge) against the risks of either TLR or redispatch.

Flowgates

One proposal that has received more than its fair share of airtime in policy debates is that of flowgates. What is a flowgate? A flowgate is a name given to the boundary between two parts of a transmission system, across which there can be congestion. A flowgate can encompass multiple transmission lines. The main criteria for grouping multiple lines together and defining them as a flowgate is that the amount of power that can flow across the grouping should have a well-defined limit.

The idea of flowgates was initially that they might solve some of the problems of the wheeling model and the contract path fiction. The idea was that *flowgate rights* could be a type of physical transmission right (PTR), used by traders to schedule power over scarce transmission. Because of the grouping, there would be fewer commercially significant flowgate rights to worry about than there would be PTRs under the normal wheeling model. Flowgates would be easy to identify, and have well-defined capacities.

The problem is none of these ideas hold up sufficiently well in practice to be compelling. It turns out a normal system still has many commercially significant flowgates. They are not always easy to identify. And their capacities are not well defined. The flowgate idea does not get around the basic failings of the wheeling model.

Hybrid versions of the flowgate proposal have been put forward under the integrated model. But how are flowgate rights settled in the integrated model? What good are flowgate rights if traders can have financial transmission rights (FTRs)? (Refer to Chapter 9 for a description of FTRs.) Again, the rationale is not compelling.

THE TRADING ARRANGEMENTS MUST BE TOTALLY REVISED

The FERC Orders Are Not Doing the Job

FERC clearly has jurisdiction over trading arrangements:

- EPAct (1992) gave it authority to order wheeling for wholesale sales (mainly to munis and co-ops) on a case by case basis.
- Order No. 888 (1996) codified this into general rules.
- FERC approved the new trading arrangements of California, PJM, New England, and New York ISOs (1997–1999 and continuing).

- Order No. 2000 (1999) required utilities to join into RTOs and produce their own trading arrangements. It still relied on the basic concepts of Order No. 888.

Full competition requires establishing a completely different relationship of generators to the system operator. The conceptual model underlying Order No. 888 simply will not be able to underpin full competition.

FERC Understands This Problem

The problems of the wheeling model were not lost on FERC when it wrote Order No. 888. As Hogan points out, as is its custom, FERC included in Order No. 888 a review of the public comments and problem diagnoses. A close reading finds an extensive discussion of the obstacles to electricity markets created by the need for instantaneous balancing and managing the complexities of transmission usage. In particular, FERC recognized that the traditional wheeling model was built on the fiction of the contract path. A simple reading of Order No. 888 shows plainly that FERC knew this, but in the end FERC embraced the wheeling model for the expedient reason that it did not have clear legal authority or support from stakeholders or Congress to go further.[5] The result is that FERC has approved new rules, agreements, and protocols in several systems in the West, Midwest, and Northeast, but the rules are still in the context of the old wheeling methodology.

In Order No. 2000, FERC made great advances in responding to the need for market design that is suitable for full competition and recognizes the complexity of electricity markets. It defined the regional transmission organization (RTO) concept, and told utilities to get together and form them. It required that an RTO have *operational authority* for all transmission facilities under its control and that it also must be the security coordinator for its region. FERC stated that its objective is for all transmission-owning entities in the United States, *including nonpublic utility entities*, to place their transmission facilities under the control of appropriate RTOs in a timely manner. It concluded, among many other things, that:

[5] As this book was going to press, the U.S. Supreme Court decided an appeal against Order No. 888 (*New York et al. vs FERC*) and confirmed FERC jurisdiction over transmission used for wholesale and retail sales, which opens the door for the next generation of competitive reforms. But FERC still lacks jurisdiction over municipal-owned companies and cooperatives.

- All RTOs must be *independent of market participants*;
- The RTO would itself *determine the available transmission capacity* based on data developed partially or totally by the RTO—as opposed to relying only on values or data from the transmission owners;
- An RTO must ensure that its transmission customers have access to *a real-time balancing market*; and
- An RTO must ensure the development and operation of *market mechanisms to manage congestion,* with efficient price signals.

In other words, *Order No. 2000 allows all the things that would make for full competition, but it does not require them. It does not eliminate the vestiges of the wheeling model, and indeed it requires some of them.* Order No. 2000 has the feeling that it was written by two people—one who defines the necessary criteria for full competition, and the other who ties the requirements back to accommodate the constraints of the wheeling model, of OASIS, and all the paraphernalia of defining paths through someone else's system. Consequently, it is still unclear how the new arrangements will be built, or indeed whether FERC thinks that further tinkering to the old arrangements will do for the meantime.

Order No. 2000 is clearly a step in the right direction, but it is still a high-level policy document. Because it has been written in sympathy with the wheeling model (albeit less so than Order No. 888 before it) it has still not led to substantial change in the industry. It has not, for example, led to RTOs of sufficient scope or to competitive generating markets.

The need for standard cohesive trading arrangements that are conceived "in the public interest" (i.e., with efficiency, liquidity, and transparency as a major objective) is at the heart of the current institutional problems. It has held center stage for nigh on a decade and has not been resolved, deflecting corporate and regulatory energy from arguably more fundamental issues. During the period in which this book was being completed, there were encouraging signs that FERC is ready to make major changes in the direction of a standard market design which would be very gratifying, so long, of course, as they are the right changes.

Short-Term Stability Is at Risk

One thing the pre-1992 system did really well was to maintain short-term system stability. The frequency and the voltage were kept in check second by second, because the generators always obeyed the system operator. The new markets also maintain system stability; the Order No. 888 rules we reviewed in the last section do not, without the additional NERC interventions. The current situation is not good, and the problems it creates are a major reason for cutting through the impasse we are in as fast as possible.

NERC, struggling to implement the Order No. 888 rules, has asked for legislation to enable it to enforce these rules in the face of increasing competition. But the problem is less that NERC cannot enforce the rules than that the rules are not incentive-compatible. People can gain by cheating, and they cheat much more than the old utilities would dream of doing because the old utilities did not have real money at stake. When people do not obey the rules, and cheat, it impairs the reliability of the system. The solution is not to have more policemen; it is to have incentive-compatible rules. The integrated model we propose has these; it works. It does not need legislation to provide more authority for enforcing bad rules—it needs FERC to impose a set of trading arrangements that is better suited to inducing system reliability. FERC should just hire Bill Hogan to set out the coherent set of trading arrangements that he has been advocating indefatigably for a decade, and drop all the paraphernalia of wheeling.

The question is whether, in the parts of the country where deregulation is not happening, any harm would be done by mandating a consistent set of trading arrangements based on the integrated model, and doing away with OASIS and ATC and TLR and all that stuff. The answer has to be that no harm would be done; it is feasible, there are working models—it would be a great step forward. The tight pools worked this way long before competition was on the horizon.

But FERC would also have to prescribe the RTO areas for those who cannot make up their minds. It would have to prescribe a model set of trading arrangements, and it would have to enforce the reorganization that would be required. This is asking a lot of an agency with so limited a current legislative mandate. The conclusion has to be:

- To ensure full competition, FERC needs to abandon the wheeling paradigm completely, bring about trading arrangements that conclusively support full competition. FERC should choose the integrated model and abandon contract paths, ATC, CBMs, TLRs, flowgates, and all the paraphernalia of wheeling.
- It should take steps to ensure that RTOs of sufficient size and configuration are actually created.
- It should assert or obtain jurisdiction over all access to all transmission, including that owned by the government entities.

CHAPTER 16

Transmission Business Model

How is the transmission business to be organized? In this chapter, we look at the current situation, and the reasons it has to change, irrespective of what happens in deregulation. The organizational model we proposed in Part One is similar to the National Grid Company (NGC) in the United Kingdom, although organized regionally in the United States. (Appendix B describes NGC.)

CURRENT SITUATION

The transmission business model needs to cover the question of who owns the transmission, how do they permit access to it, how do they price it, what types of contracts are used, and how do they expand it? We have covered the general questions of ownership, access pricing, contracting, and expansion in Part One, and the U.S. rules for access (the trading arrangements) in the previous chapter.

In the pre-1992 world, the utility built transmission for its own needs. After the blackouts of 1965, utilities built extra transmission to be able to make economy trades with each other. The regulators approved the expansions and allowed the costs to be charged to the native load customers. The utilities did not have to charge themselves for using their own transmission—it was not an issue, as it is in the competitive world. (See Chapter 9 in Part One.)

In the United States at present, the system is basically, with few exceptions, as follows:

- Utilities own the transmission, just as they always have. FERC is trying to order consolidation of system control and transmission into independent regional organizations, but probably does not have the authority to require it. In the five new markets, system control is consolidated into ISOs, but transmission ownership remains with the utilities.

- Utilities are required by EPAct to provide equal access. It is now a decade since EPAct and the issues are not resolved. In addition to the trading arrangements described in the previous chapter, the implications for the organization of the transmission business have not been resolved.
- The pricing is set out by FERC in Order No. 888. It is a full-cost usage charge, of the type we characterized as inhibiting to trade in Part One. Moreover, the charges are levied as a toll at the boundary of each jurisdiction (pancaked). FERC wants to remove the pancaking. We discuss this more next.
- The contracts are physical transmission rights, with the exception of some financial transmission rights in the new markets of PJM, New York, and California. These physical rights inhibit trading and can increase market power.
- System expansion has more or less come to a halt except in Texas. Currently under Order No. 888 the utility gets first priority on limited transmission facilities, and no one really wants to build transmission to give more access to their competitors to steal their customers.

UNBUNDLING OF ISO AND TRANSMISSION FUNCTIONS

The issues of ownership and control in the United States are first the independence question—how far should the unbundling of operations from generation go, and second, should the transmission go with it? Figure 16.1 shows the myriad of possibilities.

Everyone agrees in principle that the system operator has to be completely corporately separated and independent, even for trading in areas that have not deregulated; *but this has not happened yet, outside the five new markets.* It is waiting on resolution of the question of transmission organization: Should the transmission also be completely separated, divested, and consolidated, or can it continue to be owned by the utilities under some less rigorous form of separation? Should the roles of the system operator and the transmission owner be combined into a Transco structure, or should the system operator be a separate organization, an ISO, with the transmission in a Gridco?

Separation under Order Nos. 888 and 2000

In Order No. 888 in 1996, FERC required *functional* separation—a functionally separate division of the company would determine the available transmission capacity on its system, and allocate it to transmission users—

FIGURE 16.1 Ownership and control possibilities.

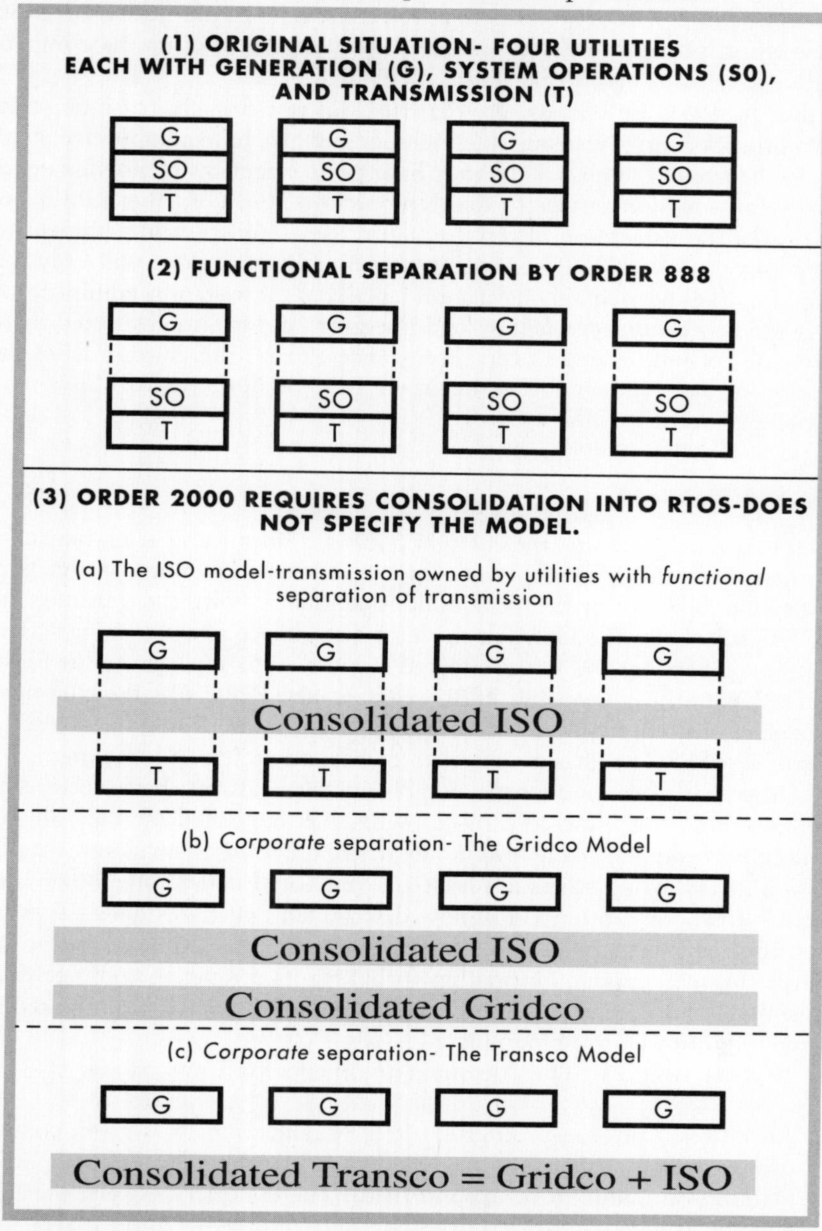

(1) ORIGINAL SITUATION- FOUR UTILITIES EACH WITH GENERATION (G), SYSTEM OPERATIONS (SO), AND TRANSMISSION (T)

G SO T | G SO T | G SO T | G SO T

(2) FUNCTIONAL SEPARATION BY ORDER 888

G | G | G | G

SO T | SO T | SO T | SO T

(3) ORDER 2000 REQUIRES CONSOLIDATION INTO RTOS-DOES NOT SPECIFY THE MODEL.

(a) The ISO model-transmission owned by utilities with *functional* separation of transmission

G | G | G | G

Consolidated ISO

T | T | T | T

(b) *Corporate* separation- The Gridco Model

G | G | G | G

Consolidated ISO

Consolidated Gridco

(c) *Corporate* separation- The Transco Model

G | G | G | G

Consolidated Transco = Gridco + ISO

including its own parent company's traders—using a rule-based system approved by FERC. Order No. 888 required companies to put traders on a different floor, post transmission availability on OASIS, and not discriminate in allocating transmission capacity.

But by 1999, FERC was sure that this was not enough, reasoning that when utilities control transmission facilities and also have competitive interests in the trading of electricity, they have poor incentives to provide equal quality transmission service to their competitors. FERC further said it believes even the *perception* of discrimination is a significant impediment to competitive markets, that efficient and competitive markets will only develop if market participants have confidence that the system is administered fairly (and by an *independent* system operator) and it also suspected there were cases of self-serving in certain instances. FERC therefore ordered the creation of independent RTOs, but there is some doubt as to FERC's authority even to order this.

ISOs and Transcos

So far in the United States, the old tight pools, California and Texas have chosen to separate the system operator into an independent entity: an independent system operator or ISO. The utilities continue to own the transmission. The ISO solution was adopted as the least disturbance of the existing system of utility ownership, and it was adopted in most of these places before FERC required it, but it is not what FERC really wants. FERC sees the continued ownership of transmission by companies that also own generation as leading to trouble—FERC just has no power to go beyond urging and cajoling.

Other parts of the country, notably in the Midwest, have decided to combine these roles into a Transco. What has happened (at the Alliance Transco for example) is a hybrid model where the Transco owns some transmission assets, while others are leased, or managed under some other contractual arrangement. FERC has now determined that the Alliance Transco does not qualify as an RTO, a decision with negative implications for the Transco business model. Florida has forbidden its utilities to combine their transmission into a profit-making Transco, while Wisconsin has required it. Again 1,000 flowers are blooming.

To recap from Part One, the main arguments for Transcos are:

- An ISO is a not-for–profit, asset-free organization. It is given control over expensive transmission assets owned by others, but it is not in its mandate to maintain or expand them. The contract between the ISO and the owners is hard to negotiate and enforce—a good reason for combining them.

- A Transco is a profit-making regulated entity with assets. A for-profit Transco that causes damage to a market participant is in a position to assume the consequence of its failure—and thus it has an incentive to avoid failing—but a not-for-profit ISO can only pass the cost of damages back through to the market participants.
- Transmission investment and transmission maintenance can be optimally coordinated. Transcos can potentially do this much better than ISOs. Rather than having two separate entities making separate decisions, one entity can decide whether maintenance or new construction is the best choice in a given situation, or a combination of the two.
- Transcos also can have good commercial incentives to operate the system efficiently—taking on the responsibility for congestion costs if they fail to deliver in accordance with the transmission rights they have issued, for example.
- Transcos have been adopted in most other countries in the world where generation has been deregulated.
- But there is concern that a Transco might be too independent, and become a fiefdom of its own, with too much power; and also concern that there could be conflicts between the roles of ISO and owner of transmission.

The pure Transco model would have all the transmission owned by the Transco. One way to ensure this is to insist that utilities *sell* their transmission assets to an independent Transco. Many companies are reluctant to be forced into such a divestiture, and therefore forcing it could be a long and tortuous legal road. On the other hand, why would utilities want to keep the transmission if they received just compensation for their assets? Once the generation is separated, isn't ownership of the transmission asset just a lawsuit waiting to happen? In many cases, the reluctance of the utilities stems from a series of tax issues, and the lack of compensation. In most cases, the tax issue could be solved by narrow legislation assuring that divestiture into a Transco would not be a taxable event.

Government-Owned Transmission

There is a further issue about the jurisdiction of FERC over government-owned transmission. We cannot have a national or even a regional system if 25 percent of the transmission is not included; the paradoxical thing is that this is mainly owned by other arms of the federal government. The transmission owed by the municipalities has an additional problem—some of it was funded by tax-exempt bonds. They were permitted the tax exemption under two doctrines—the public purpose doctrine and the *two-county rule* (the facilities could not serve more than two counties) and the tax exemption might be jeopardized if it were to be consolidated with other transmission. These matters could clearly be solved with appropriate narrow legislation.

Issues in Ownership and Control

The ownership and control issues in the United States are these:

- Is full ownership separation of transmission really needed? Order No. 2000 didn't go that far (it ordered separation *of control* into independent RTOs) but should it have?
- Is it enough to have realistic caps on ownership, and governance controls that don't allow undue influence to any stakeholder in the energy markets?
- Is it necessary to bite the bullet and legislate divestiture of the transmission assets, with just compensation, to a regional company?

Our answer would be that getting ahead with the inevitable regional reorganization of the transmission business is a high priority in the United States, if only because larger areas are necessary to develop efficient trading arrangements. We believe that Transcos are the way to go, and that the legislation necessary to make this happen, which would involve divestiture of utility company assets, ought to take care of the tax and compensation problems. The U.S. House of Representatives has passed legislation that would make tax-free transfers of utilities transmission systems to Transcos possible. It does not mandate divestiture.

PRICING

Order No. 888 required utilities to submit pro forma tariffs for the use of their systems. The tariffs take the annual charges on the transmission system and divide it by some measure of total usage: This is the charge for each transaction. It is not charged by distance, it has no relation to congestion. It is a full-cost usage charge of the type we warned against in Part One as inhibiting trade. The rational for the tolls is that the native load of the utility has paid for the transmission, and if someone else wants to use it they should pay their fair share.

Simplified Example Utility A has a revenue requirement for transmission of $4 million/year. It has a load (total kilowatt-hours passing out of the system, to final users or to the next control area) of 400 million kWh. The price is determined simply by dividing 4 million by 400 million = 1 cent per kWh.

This price is only charged to *wholesale trades*—the regular retail load of the utility is charged its share of the transmission costs in the bundled rates determined by the states. The people who actually pay the transmission charge under the FERC pricing are those who trade over the wires, including the utility's own traders when they sell off-system. (In other words, tourists pay tolls for usage—residents pay in their base charges.)

Eliminating Pancaking

Under Order No. 888, tolls are charged by each jurisdiction over whose territory a transaction passes—stacking them up like a pile of hotcakes—this is called *pancaking charges*. So if, in the previous example, two adjoining areas each had a 1-cent charge, then a transaction over both areas would cost 2 cents. Over three areas it would cost 3 cents, and so on. Order No. 2000 says reforms are needed. It tells utilities to band together into RTOs, average out their charges, and eliminate pancaking.[1] But some utilities are understandably reluctant to follow—look at the arithmetic in the examples that follow.

It should be fairly obvious that if three 3-cent charges have to be unpancaked and reduced to one, there will be a loss of revenue somewhere. Instead of three charges there is now just one. Someone has to take the loss. But this is only a loss on the trades that cross the boundaries—trades within the boundaries were only ever charged once. For a small control area that had many trades across the area, it could be real loss, but for larger areas, where more trading stays within the boundary, it may be quite small. But the loss is immediate and tangible, and creates resistance to consolidation.

This loss of pancaking revenue is the immediate issue that utilities face when told to form an RTO. But the bigger problem is cost shifting between regions, which can occur in the longer term. Suppose the utility A charges 1 cent for transmission access. And utility B, instead of charging 1 cent, had made really big investments in transmission and its charges were not 1 cent but 2 cents. Then when the utilities place their assets into an RTO, the charges are averaged, and the average price becomes 1.5 cents. (Assume for simplicity that the utilities are the same size.) This 1.5 cents is the uniform price charged per transaction over the entire area of the RTO, as required by FERC.

Initially, nothing changes for the utility if it retains ownership of the transmission or for the utility customers on bundled state-regulated tariffs. Utility A incurs transmission costs in region A, most of which are recovered

[1] Pancaking is the practice of charging each transaction a price for transmission usage in each jurisdiction it passes through. Since there are so many jurisdictions, this greatly inhibits trade, although just the practice of including overheads in the usage price is inefficient in itself.

from the bundled tariffs. Access charges applied to independent users of the system are collected by the RTO, who then allocates them back to the transmission-owning utilities in proportion to an agreed ratio: for example, 1:2. The cash flow to the utilities remains the same. The problems start to arise when either customer rates are unbundled (for retail access) and/or when the utility divests the transmission assets to the RTO/Transco.

- When customer rates are unbundled, the independent supplying the customer will be charged 1.5 cents for transmission access. However, customers in region A have been accustomed to paying a bundled rate that included only 1 cent for transmission. These customers, or the state regulators that represent them, may be reluctant to accept this unless other benefits exceed the half-cent difference. (Of course, people in region B will have no such qualms.)
- If utility A divests the transmission assets, the RTO will be required to charge it 1.5 cents for transmission access to serve all its customers. If the state regulators do not allow this cost increase to be passed through to local customers, the utility will incur a cost.

In summary, unless a low-cost utility is allowed to pass through increased transmission costs, or delay the averaging of costs until it is able to do so, it will be reluctant to join the RTO. Final customers in low cost areas with retail access may have a similar reluctance. The problems of averaging, cost shifting and the revenue reduction make forming RTOs difficult. The process, even when beneficial in aggregate, can produce individual winners and losers among the utilities. The losers resist change, but here the problem of overlapping jurisdictions applies. FERC makes the changes in the rules, but the lost revenues can only be retrieved from the native load through a state rate case. Otherwise, the company simply absorbs the loss.

The only practical solution here is to phase into RTO pricing slowly so that cost shifting and revenue reduction can be ironed out over time, as different regulated prices come up for review. The decisions of exactly how to price should be made now, and that pricing scheme should be phased in over a transition period.

A Better Solution

The development of RTOs allows a more fundamental change in pricing to solve the problems of pancaking. Recall that the idea of this sort of *full-cost* pricing was to make travelers who had not contributed to the overhead charges pay their fair share by charging a toll for passing through. This is inefficient but perhaps unavoidable when that is the only way to avoid free riding. But in the larger areas of the RTOs, there will automatically be more residents and fewer tourists—more of the trading will be internal to the RTO. This permits a redesign of the pricing scheme.

We have described an alternative workable pricing scheme in Part One, based on congestion and losses, with the overhead costs being paid by all the generators and customers in the area. Charges should not be levied on trades as such—trades should be charged at the marginal cost, which means charging for the congestion and losses, as we explained in Part One. But this presupposes a fairly large area, with few cross-area transactions that need to be charged tolls. Once RTOs are established, many more of the transactions are internal to the area, very little is going across or over the boundaries—charges can be levied on customers' usage, not on trades.

Here again, FERC is constrained by not having the authority to work as if its job was to provide the underpinnings for competitive markets. Its only legislated mandate is to provide access for wholesale sales. The form of pricing that it uses is perhaps the only way to charge if the underlying picture is of 140 control areas, with trading across them, and if the main problem is seen as getting traders to pay their fair share.

SYSTEM EXPANSION

Under regulation, each company planned its own transmission for its own use. Each company planned transmission jointly with the plan for generation expansion, because:

- The location of generation affects the need for transmission in way that are not always obvious—on a network a new generator in one location can affect the carrying capacity in other locations not directly affected, and a badly sited generator can actually destroy transfer capacity.
- Plants can be located close to fuel sources or close to loads. The choice is often a question of the cost of transporting the fuel versus the cost of transmitting the electricity. The locational trade-off was always made internally in the utility planning department.
- Transmission is sometimes a substitute for generation—if a distant producer (Hydro-Quebec, for example) can produce more than it needs quite cheaply, but the long distance transmission required is very expensive, then again the decision as to whether to build generation locally or buy and build transmission was made internally.

The regulated utilities generally arrived at what they hoped was a minimum cost solution, then charged the customers more or less equally, rolling in the costs of transmission with the costs of generation, and the costs of distant plants with those near the load.

System Expansion in the Restructured World

Prices for transmission in the restructured world have to do much of the job that the system planners used to do—the job of helping generators decide where to locate. (See Appendices E and F.) If generators are not held responsible for the costs they impose on the system, they will locate near the fuel sources and wait for their competitors to share the cost; or they will locate in places that destroy capacity elsewhere on the system.

For example, it is generally the case that it is cheaper to transport gas in pipelines than to transport the electricity that results from gas-fired generating plants. But if transmission pricing is done wrong, expensive new transmission can end up being built when lower cost new pipelines would have been a better choice. With coal it depends on railroad pricing—the Mount Storm mine-mouth generating plant in Virginia was built at a long distance from the load because of the prices the railroads proposed to charge for transporting coal, and started a trend for "coal by wire."

The proposed integrated trading arrangements have locational signals in the locational prices for energy—although they may not be strong enough (refer to Chapter 9). But the current system has usage charges with no locational signals at all except for the effect of pancaking; the further a generator is from its contracted load, the higher the stack of pancaked charges. Therefore, pancaking, while inhibiting trade, inhibits distant trades more than local ones. Some have argued that this goes some way toward getting the right locational signals. There might be some truth to this, but the bottom line is that the size and the number of the charges being pancaked is a function of political boundaries (not electrical ones), the contract path fiction, and averaging of historic (sunk) costs. The result is a price for transmission that is just too arbitrary.

Furthermore, the current situation in the United States is that utilities even in the competitive states still own transmission; the ISOs are supposed to tell the utilities when to expand the system, even if the expansion benefits the utility's competitors. But if the utilities do not build, there are no sanctions; states can still delay or refuse permission for transmission that benefits primarily other states. (Connecticut refused for some months to permit a line that would benefit mainly New York and although that situation was resolved, it is not an isolated example.) FERC is still getting complaints about subtle forms of discrimination by transmission owners in making their lines available.

We have destroyed the old system and have put nothing in its place. The question of who is responsible for transmission expansion and who pays, are unsolved questions. In other countries, a regulated Transco has incentives, through rate of return, and special performance incentives analogous to the financial transmission rights we propose. In the United States, no one has jurisdiction over transmission expansion on a national or regional basis. Siting authority is with the states.

President Bush has proposed giving FERC siting authority, but State regulators have opposed the proposal because they would lose some of their authority. Federal siting is clearly appropriate to support a multistate transmission grid. FERC has siting authority for gas pipelines.

A National Grid?

The National Power Grid System Study in 1976[2] concluded that the federal government had no need to promote a national grid—things were moving that way by themselves. In fact the net additions to transmission from 1978 through 1998 normalized for summer peak demand were negative. No one has explored what it would take to relieve congestion for the U.S. as a whole. It might even be worth considering a program analogous to the Federal Highway Program with matching funds for relief of major congested ties. The FHWA matching program had different levels of matching depending on the capacity of the road. At the highest level, the FHWA match was 90 percent of the total capital expenditure. This percent federal share was reserved for interstate highways. Such highways were 4 lanes or more and were capable of handling interstate trucks of all sizes. A two-lane highway would receive a lesser match—70 percent. One of the reasons for the higher match for the higher capacity routes is that they were arguably part of national defense. Operating expenses were the responsibility of the local areas.

The interstate highway program had (perhaps unintended) locational effects: For example, in urban areas, radial highways extended residential development outward whereas circumferential highways caused a clustering of economic activity in rings around the central urban areas. (It is also credited with expanding greatly the share of freight handled by motor carriers at the expense of the railroads.)

But the main problem may not be with financing—it may be with siting. The utilities in many states had *powers of eminent domain,* and still

[2]National Power Grid System Study, prepared by the Congressional Research Service, U.S. Government Printing Office, 1976.

had trouble siting transmission. In the deregulated world, the need is greater, and the opposition will also be greater.

NERC's Reliability Assessment for 2000 puts it like this:

> *The changing electric market may be breaking down the social compact behind the principle of eminent domain . . . the segments of the population impacted by new transmission construction will not be the same segments that are benefiting from the profits the new lines create. This disparity will increase the legitimacy of the political opposition to new transmission line construction. The fragmentation of the industry into segments not easily identifiable with the familiar local utility may make matters worse. The step of limiting the power of eminent domain . . . may be an easy one for legislators.*

A Solution Using Incentives (Instead of Fighting Them)

A very simple solution, long proposed by Paul Joskow, would be to establish the regional Transcos and regulate their charges on the traditional rate of return basis. There is no avoiding an independent regulator to adjudicate the need for expansion, and to approve expenditures, rates of return, and prices. The theoretical literature says that rate of return regulation gives incentives to utilities to overbuild. If this is true in the case of transmission, which is a relatively small part of total costs, and where the need to build is (probably) quite extensive, we should take advantage of the supposed inefficiencies of traditional regulation—the incentives to overbuild if the rate of return is high enough. With a generous rate of return on investment, the Transcos would no doubt do as utilities always have done—find ways to compensate communities that are unwilling for lines to be sited in their back yards, rather than fighting over eminent domain.

CHAPTER 17

Control of Market Power

On the supply side of the market, the most important thing is to control market power. We looked at market power in general in Part One. Here we look at the situation in the United States.

The diagnosis of market power is difficult under the best circumstances. Especially at times at which load is close to system capacity and demand response is weak, such small amounts of withholding can so radically affect price that it is almost impossible to tell the difference between withholding and genuine lack of capacity. Consequently, we should focus on remedies. The major remedies are having enough competitors to start with, demand responsiveness, and expansion of, or better use of, transmission capacity to expand the market size.

DIVESTITURE TO ACHIEVE ENOUGH COMPETITORS

In some areas of the country where transmission is robust, there may be enough competition in a market area. But in others, divestiture (sale of the generating assets) may be the only way to get enough competitors in the markets. *As a regulatory matter, no one has the authority to order divestiture of an IOU's assets.* Divestiture has in every jurisdiction been the subject of negotiation between the utility and the regulator, be it a PUC or state legislature. In those jurisdictions that have required divestiture, utility acquiescence stemmed from other terms of the total package, for example:

- In some cases (e.g., Massachusetts), the utilities have volunteered to divest mainly to establish the size of stranded costs.
- In California, they were "encouraged" to divest at least 50 percent of their fossil plant by the suggestion that they would earn less on the assets they chose to retain.

- In Illinois, the legislature gave substantial incentives for divestiture.
- At least one utility, GPU, has divested its generation assets entirely voluntarily.
- In Maine, they were ordered to divest.
- By contrast, the Texas legislation explicitly prohibits any company from owning *and controlling* more than 20 percent of the capacity in ERCOT.

Forced divestiture without the utility's consent presents legal problems—it could arguably be a "taking" under the U.S. Constitution with compensation required. Since FERC has no power to solve the underlying problem, it has to use secondary and inferior methods such as price caps to address market power issues.

DEMAND RESPONSE

Demand response, as we demonstrated in Part One, is the first bulwark against market power where it still exists. If customers have the ability to say no, then even if some market power exists, the prices could not possibly rise to the levels we saw in California. Demand response is to some extent a substitute for an increased number of suppliers. With no demand response, even a large number of suppliers may prove uncompetitive at certain times.

Very few states have ordered installation of hourly meters. Even those that have hourly metering on large customers do not charge the form of tariff that would permit response to the spot prices.

TRANSMISSION TO EXPAND MARKET AREAS

Transmission constraints reduce the size of markets. Texas ordered additional transmission lines to be built as part of the implementation of the competitive market there, and charged the cost to all users. But this has not been the general practice.

Furthermore, the existence of transmission constraints can augment the possibilities for the exercise of market power. The current U.S. trading regime is, for the most part, based on physical rights to use particular constrained paths. Participants can sometimes exercise market power by *withholding transmission capacity from the market.* Transmission owners can do it by over-reserving transmission capacity for their own use; other participants can do it by taking but not using a physical right. *This exercise of market power can only happen if the rights are physical rights—financial transmission rights (FTRs) obviate the problem, because they cannot be withheld.* (See Chapter 9.)

FERC'S ROLE IN PRIOR APPROVALS

FERC reviews market power in several contexts, deriving from the requirement of the Federal Power Act that it ensure that wholesale rates are just and reasonable. It has authority to grant *market-based rates* (rather than regulated rates) to sellers of wholesale electricity; it approves the trading arrangements of the new markets and it has to approve mergers. It is looking for market power, but the methods that it uses do not catch all the market power problems that have arisen with restructuring. There are two types of markets in the United States:

1. There are those where the generation has not been deregulated, and where the "markets" are for the power *in excess of native load requirements*—these are also known as the bulk power markets, or (confusingly) the wholesale markets. Here the relevant market is the excess over the requirements for native load customers.
2. There are the five new marketplaces, where all the generation has been deregulated. Here the relevant market is all the generating resources.

Regulated utilities are required to own or contract for sufficient power to meet their own loads plus some quite substantial reserve. So in the bulk power markets there should be plenty of available supply evenly spread between utilities and relatively little demand. When utilities purchase for economy reasons, their own more expensive plant is idle; the price they will pay is always naturally capped by the costs of the plant they chose to leave idle—the demand has responsiveness built in. These markets stand a good chance of being highly competitive, and even if they were not, a very tiny proportion of total production passes through them, so the impact on final customers is tiny.

But in the second case, *where the entire load is being purchased competitively, the problems with market power are much more intense and require more sophisticated methods of detection.* The prices here matter, because the customers pay them directly or indirectly through their contracts; the demand and supply are more evenly matched and there is at present little or no demand response.

The methods used to detect market power in the new markets need to be more sophisticated than the ones used for the old bulk power markets.

Market-Based Rates

These days virtually all wholesale sellers have market-based rates. To get them, sellers need to show lack of market power. The applicant can demonstrate the lack of market power if it can show that it, together with its affiliates: (1) does not dominate the generation of power in the relevant market (*horizontal market power*), (2) lacks the ability to block buyers from reaching other sellers using transmission facilities which it owns or controls *(vertical market power),* and (3) cannot erect or control any other barrier to market entry.

The test for horizontal market power (except for the new markets) was, and technically still is, a concentration analysis using the old hub-and-spoke method, which defines a market for each utility as the capacity in place one wheel away from the seller. The seller's share of total capacity and uncommitted capacity is calculated for each market—the entire market, comprising all generating plant, and the residual, or bulk power market, comprising only plant that is not used to serve native load. FERC, like the Department of Justice (DOJ), uses a benchmark of a 20 percent market share to evaluate market dominance, but has no hard and fast rule. New plants, no matter what the ownership, do not need to do step 1 of the above analysis—it is assumed that they have no dominance in the market automatically. Small owners can get market-based rates even in a concentrated market.

The New Markets

For the new competitive markets (California, PJM, New York, New England), FERC approves the trading arrangements, as it did for the old pools. Now the market has to be "workably competitive" to ensure that rates are just and reasonable. Sellers that wish to supply into a FERC-approved pool must still apply for market-based rates. (If the pool is deemed competitive, all the sellers get market-based rates.) The market power analysis submitted by 1995 for FERC approval of the California pool, caused FERC to rule that there would be market power in the proposed new energy markets. FERC sent the finding back telling California to devise a set of market power mitigation measures; under pressure from the CPUC, the utilities eventually decided to divest themselves of most of their fossil plant. FERC has no power of its own to require divestiture—although the power to refuse market-based rates when requested is a fairly serious stick.

FERC's Appendix A

In its Merger Policy Statement, FERC adopted the DOJ/FTC Merger Guidelines as the appropriate framework for analyzing the effects of electric utility mergers on market power. One of the important precursors to determining whether a merger could lead to the exercise market power is the *definition of the geographic market.* Market shares and measures of market concentration are computed based on the definition of the geographic market. In Appendix A of the Merger Policy Statement and in other statements, FERC has set out a methodology for identifying geographic markets in electric power from which market shares are calculated. *However, the methodology set out in Appendix A is not entirely consistent with the Merger Guidelines.*

The critical difference between FERC's Appendix A and the Merger Guidelines is that Appendix A (like the hub-and-spoke method) focuses on *destination markets*—specifically, utilities interconnected with the merging utilities or other large wholesale customers that are likely to be harmed as a result of the merger. In defining geographic markets, the Merger Guidelines focuses on finding *the set of generators, which if acting as a single monopolist could profitably raise its prices.* As a result, the Appendix A methodology can easily lead to false positives and false negatives, in which benign mergers are deemed anticompetitive, and anticompetitive mergers are deemed benign.

Analysts have been submitting the Appendix A study to analyze market power in the new markets. The Appendix A analysis differs from the hub and spoke in two important ways—whereas hub and spoke looks at all capacity, however expensive to run and however much the cost in losses and transmission charges, Appendix A made total capacity into economic capacity by including a "delivered price test"—could the power be generated and delivered into the area at a competitive price? Appendix A has two effects as compared with the hub-and-spoke analysis. The exclusion of uneconomic capacity raises the share of a would-be monopolist; on the other hand, generation more than one wheel away is now added to the market.

Nonetheless, Appendix A is not sufficient to detect market power in complex strategic interactions of players in competitive electricity markets—it is a static analysis of market shares. It can act as a screen, but it cannot predict strategic behavior. FERC has in fact proposed changes to the current methods. The Standard Market Assessment (SMA) test (floated in December 2001) proposes to look at whether the utility's generating capacity is necessary to serve the load in its region. Those who flunked the test could not sell any power at market-based rates. This caused a firestorm of opposition, since virtually any utility would flunk the test.

Market Monitoring

California proposed, and FERC agreed, that two market monitoring groups be set up to report to FERC on the actual operations of the California markets. This has been repeated in the other new markets. The market monitors could potentially be a useful arm of FERC in the markets, to review how markets actually work, rather than how they might work.

But however good the detection of market power becomes, the best solution is to have sufficient generators to start with, to ensure demand response, to eliminate transmission constraints, have efficient trading arrangements and a transparent spot price, and encourage contract cover. These structural solutions are much better than after the fact penalties, but FERC does not have the authority to impose them.

PRICE CAPS

One problem in the competitive markets, and particularly California, has been how and when FERC should institute price caps. In California, it capped various prices that seemed to be "too high" in a way that only exacerbated the problems, but then was slow to cap the prices when it was clear that the market was dysfunctional.

Functional, competitive markets for any commodity—including electricity—should not require price caps. High prices some of the time are what create the incentive for new generators to enter; if the prices are capped when they get high it will choke off entry. But some markets, for example the Californian electricity market in 2000/2001, are *dysfunctional*. In the presence of extreme inelasticities of both demand and supply and in the presence of extreme shortages, such as have characterized California at times of peak demand, unregulated markets don't work very well. They are dysfunctional. The problem with a dysfunctional market of this nature is that there is no limit on prices because of the lack of demand response.

The following should guide us regarding price controls in the United States:

- Price controls must only be applied if the market is dysfunctional and the alternative is market failure.
- The level at which prices are controlled must be carefully established so that the value of entry is signaled when entry is needed, and the consequences of the controls on reliability of supply are understood and acceptable. The price controls should not interfere with the incentives of investors to construct new generating plants.

Price controls, when necessary, must be a transitional measure. Price elasticity of electric energy, particularly from the demand side, is the best long-term solution. In the meantime, by dampening price signals, price controls are impeding the growth of an active demand side. (For a fuller discussion, refer to "The Adequacy of Prospective Returns on General Investments Under Price Control Mechanisms," Alfred Kahn, *Electricity Journal,* March 2002.)

Dysfunctional Markets: The Letter of Ten Economists

In May 2001, ten noted economists wrote to President Bush regarding their concerns in California. The following is an extract:

> We write to express our deep concern about the failure of the Federal Energy Regulatory Commission (FERC) to act effectively to enforce the provisions of the Federal Power Act that require it to set just and reasonable wholesale prices for electricity in California. Under the terms of the Act, FERC is required to ensure that wholesale electricity prices are just and reasonable. FERC historically met this responsibility by approving wholesale prices that were no higher than the total costs suppliers incur to produce electricity. More recently, FERC has given suppliers "market-based pricing authority" in situations where it was able to conclude that market-based pricing would lead to better outcomes than continued cost-based regulation.
>
> FERC retains the responsibility to ensure that wholesale prices are just and reasonable when a state decides to rely on a competitive wholesale electricity market to provide for its citizens' electricity needs. In particular, once FERC has granted suppliers market-based pricing authority it has an ongoing responsibility to ensure that these prices reflect the outcomes of well-functioning competitive markets. If well-functioning competitive markets do not exist and, as a consequence, the resulting prices are not just and reasonable, then FERC should act either to remedy the market failures or to return to cost-based regulation. . . .
>
> Well-designed competitive wholesale electricity markets can provide long-term benefits to consumers. For sixty years FERC implemented its obligations to set just and reasonable rates under the Federal Power Act by regulating wholesale market prices. During the 1990s, based on the belief that if appropriate criteria were met "market-based rates" could produce lower prices and a more efficient electric power system, FERC changed its policy. It began to allow suppliers to sell wholesale electricity at market-based rates but, consistent with FERC's continuing responsibilities under the Federal Power Act, only if the suppliers could demonstrate that the resulting prices would be just and reasonable. Generally, FERC allowed suppliers to sell at market-based rates if they met a set of specific criteria,

(continued)

Letter of Ten Economists (Continued)

including a demonstration that the relevant markets would be characterized by effective competition.

All generators and marketers selling power into California were granted the ability to receive market-based rates rather than cost-of-service rates because they were able to demonstrate to FERC that their participation in the California market would result in market prices reflecting the interplay of supply and demand in well-functioning competitive markets. These showings were based on a variety of market-structure screens adopted by FERC before California's wholesale electricity markets went into operation. Numerous subsequent studies based on actual market behavior and performance have identified a number of serious problems of market design, supplier behavior, and market performance that were not anticipated or considered in FERC's initial market-structure screens.

There are numerous flaws in California's wholesale electricity markets, and their consequences have been significantly exacerbated by the tight supply situation in the Western U.S. We cannot expect a market to operate to benefit consumers or for the resulting wholesale prices to satisfy the requirements of the Federal Power Act if effective competition does not exist.

Source: Office of California Governor Gray Davis, May 29, 2001, Economists Express "Deep Concern" over Wholesale Electricity Prices, Letter to President George W. Bush, Speaker of the House of Representatives J. Dennis Hastert, and Senate Majority Leader Trent Lott by Roger Bohn, Peter Cramton, Severin Borenstein, Alfred Kahn, Paul Joskow, James Bushnell, Alvin K. Klevorick, Robert Porter, Frank Wolak, and Carl Shapiro. The letter is publicly available.

CHAPTER 18
Retail Regimes

In Part One we reviewed various issues in retail access, including default service, metering, and settlement. Here we see how it is working in the United States; and we also explain the top-down/bottom-up pricing issue.

PROPOSED MODEL

The regime we propose for retail access in Part One has five main elements:

1. A gradual phase-in with large customers first;
2. Local settlement;
3. Hourly metering for a substantial proportion of the load to start with (the rest being load-profiled), and eventually for all;
4. Tariffs for default service that has some element set at the spot price, with perhaps full price-certainty only being offered to small residential customers; and
5. Eventually all customers removed from default service, with a minimal POLR responsibility remaining, perhaps with the Distco.

Additionally, we prefer *bottom-up pricing* as a means of stranded cost collection. (We describe the meaning of bottom-up in this chapter.)

Use of these elements permits a retail access program that promotes real retail competition. Retailers have a role in hedging risk for consumers and in providing pricing structures (including alternative bundles of high-priced and low-priced hours) that consumers want to buy. The all-important spot price signals are loud and clear—to retailers if not to every consumer. Game playing with load profiling is minimized. Retailers can count on stable market rules—a sudden change in the administratively determined shopping credit will not put them out of business.

The details of the proposed regime are discussed next.

Gradual Phase-In with Large Customers Free to Shop First

Because retail access is complicated, phasing in by size of customer makes sense. Programs that start with the largest customers and gradually work down to inclusion of the smallest customers have a number of advantages:

- A large share of total demand can be moved to the competitive market with only a small number of customers involved.
- The large customers are those most attractive to retailers because marketing costs are small relative to sales; therefore, many retailers are likely to be interested in the market.
- Hourly metering costs are lower on a per kWh basis for large customers, and they often have pre-existing meters capable of recording hourly usage.
- Information transfer and settlement systems can be tested on a small number of transactions and any bugs worked out.

Local Settlement

Settlement—the process of deciding who used how much, who delivered how much, and what the cost of imbalances was—can be accomplished by the system operator for all market participants or can be handled locally by distribution companies or other local companies on behalf of consumers and producers. With a large number of buyers and sellers in the market, it is most efficient for this function to be performed *locally*. However, this is not a structural requirement—it is simply our view of the most effective solution.

Hourly Metering

The key to an effective demand side to the market is hourly metering. Hourly metering is a prerequisite for charging time-sensitive prices, whether contract, tariff, or spot prices. It is a prerequisite for production competition, not just for retail access. *Hourly metering should precede retail access, not follow it.* Before there is a spot price, a simplified form of time-of-use pricing is better than nothing; this at least gets customers familiar with the idea that prices change more often than annually.

Load profiles used for customers who do not yet have hourly metering should be updated frequently. As the customers with less-expensive profiles adopt hourly meters to get better deals, the load profiles of the remaining group will become increasingly expensive.

While every customer should eventually have an hourly meter, the expensive communication equipment necessary for real-time price signaling and meter reading is not essential, although here also prices have come down. Consumers can check hourly prices on the internet or other public media and the meters can be read monthly. The cost of hourly metering for small consumers can be subsidized through the system benefits charge, if necessary, because the benefits of a more robust competitive market accrue to all consumers.

Tariff Reform

Unregulated retailers are free to offer customers any pricing plan the retail market demands.[1] For default service, however, the most efficient plan (proposed in Part One) involves a fixed price for a fixed block of energy, and the spot price charged (or credited) for energy used above (or below) the contracted block size. This block can be based on some percentage of historic consumption, or an amount chosen by the customer. An example of this proposed pricing design was illustrated in Figure 4.3. Full price certainty in the default option, if offered, should probably be offered only to small residential customers.

To provide fixed price blocks or otherwise hedge against market price volatility, the utility must either be allowed to keep generation or sign (regulated) contracts with generators. The former situation opens the door to self-dealing. The latter puts the regulator in the middle of contract negotiations, in the position of administering auctions (which led to very unsatisfactory results in Maine), or in the role of after-the-fact prudence reviews of the utility's contracting efforts. During the transition period, self-dealing between generators and Distcos can be a problem and default service should eventually be phased out.

Eventual Phase-Out of Default Service

Customers should be removed from default service by gradually closing the option to them, with sufficient information and advance notice. The exception could be a POLR offering for very small (and very undesirable)

[1] The equivalent of retail access could be achieved by the utility's passing the wholesale spot price through to consumers, which has been done in some places. However, if customers want stable prices, they must be allowed to contract for power from competing retailers. In fact, they should be encouraged to contract, because contracts limit market power in the generation market.

consumers. At the end of the transition period, a minimal POLR responsibility should remain, serving very few customers. These will be customers in the process of choosing a new supplier, or customers who cannot be bothered to choose one. Overall, it probably makes sense for the Distco to provide this POLR service by simply passing through the spot price, with an adder for the administrative costs and credit risks.

Since most of the POLR customers will be credit risks, we advise the adoption of prepayment meters, which virtually eliminates the problem.

Bottom-Up Pricing with Market Price for Generation

Bottom-up pricing—explicit charges for stranded costs and delivery, plus a market-based charge for generation that tracks hourly spot prices—is the preferable means of stranded cost recovery in a competitive market. The alternative, top-down pricing, involves freezing retail prices at or near historical (high) levels until stranded costs are fully recovered. Top-down eliminates the benefits of hourly metering, and effectively postpones retail and demand-side reform until stranded costs are recovered.

WHAT THE UNITED STATES HAS

Unfortunately, retail access in the United States bears little resemblance to the program outlined. The situation in the United States can be summarized as:

- California, Maine, Massachusetts, New Jersey, and Ohio allowed all customers to choose their provider from the start date of retail access. However, most United States jurisdictions with retail access have used some form of phase-in, although not always with the largest customers freed to shop first. Rhode Island, Montana, Illinois, Delaware, New Hampshire, D.C., and Niagara Mohawk in New York followed the largest first rule, for example. Connecticut, Pennsylvania, Rochester, and Consolidated Edison in New York used a phase-in, but opened competition to a percentage of each major customer group.
- Utilities in Washington and Wisconsin are installing hourly meters on many customers even though these states do not yet have retail access. The states with retail access tend to require hourly metering only on the largest customers, if any.
- The question of hourly metering has gotten tangled up in endless arguments over competitive metering in many states. In our view the benefits of hourly metering of all market participants greatly exceeds any

possible benefits to consumers of having a choice of meter supplier (refer to Chapter 10 for our reasons why).

- Bottom-up pricing is common in other countries, but rare in the United States where stranded cost recovery has been such a big problem. Maine uses bottom-up pricing because its distribution companies are not permitted to sell energy. There essentially the PUC acquires generation for standard offer service and customers pay the utility's delivery rates (including a stranded cost component) plus the standard offer generation cost. New York is working on bottom-up pricing as the bundled rate freeze period ends for the various utilities.
- Most utilities' standard offers are top-down versions of the old bundled rates, with a fixed, administratively determined shopping credit that bears no resemblance to actual market prices. Retailers have little to offer, since the prices charged by the incumbent are fixed. There is nothing to hedge. Standard offers not tied to market prices do not work.
- The situation is even worse in states such as Pennsylvania and Ohio where the legislatures are so set on making retail access "a success" that they set artificially high shopping credits. For a while these standard offers can entice consumers to leave the incumbent, but if the wholesale market price rises above the shopping credit, there is a flood of consumers back to the incumbent and the retailers pack up and leave the state.
- Despite the huge amount of effort that has gone into reforming the retail regime in the United States, by 2000 unregulated sales accounted for only 3 percent of total retail sales.[2] In the states with retail access, most customers remain on default service.

Retail regimes in the United States are far from standard. Although most have not experienced the problems faced in California, this is largely the result of luck rather than good program design.

[2] Under retail access, small customers have switched in significant numbers only when they received a subsidy to do so. A higher proportion of large customers have switched; evidently these customers have greater reason to exercise choice, and have the full-time employees who can do so wisely. However, switching is not a good test of the success of retail access. What counts is whether prices are lower than they otherwise would have been; and whether new pricing and service options that customers value are available. But the U.S. retail markets have not succeeded yet by those measures either. The point is that with retail access, customers have a choice; competitive markets tend toward a single price if customers can switch, and if some of them do switch, it keeps the markets honest.

RATE DESIGN FOR STRANDED COST COLLECTION

How should stranded costs be recovered in a competitive market? In the remainder of this chapter we look at the complications in the United States over tariff design for stranded cost collection, shopping credits, and the "price to beat."

As a reminder, *stranded costs* are the difference between the market value and the book value of a utility's generation assets.[3] Before retail access, these costs were included in the revenue requirement and recovered in rates, but no one knew about them because, without retail access, these costs were not strandable.

To quantify stranded costs to be recovered, it is necessary to determine the market value of generating plants. The clearest way to do this is divestiture, as we described in Part One. The price that the highest bidder is willing to pay is unambiguously the value of an asset. Alternatively, and with more difficulty, a utility might be able to agree on a valuation with its regulator if the utility wishes to retain its generation. If it can reach such as agreement, and does not have a market power or conflict of interest requirement to divest, a utility might be able to retain ownership. A variation on this possibility is a partial divestiture by IPO, which establishes a market value for the assets on the stock exchange. But regardless of the way the valuation is established, in most countries it is obvious that the way to go for pricing and stranded cost recovery is the bottom-up design:

- Unbundle the various costs;
- Charge a regulated price for distribution,[4] transmission, and an explicit *stranded cost* component (this requires amortizing the total amount of the stranded costs over some period); and
- Add the generation component, whether this is provided by a competing supplier, or by the utility's default service.

In this case it is easy to see that the *price to beat* for the competitors is the generation component of the utility default service. Figure 18.1 illustrates bottom-up pricing. However, in the United States the unbundling has

[3] These assets are physical generating plant and *regulatory assets* that are past promises by the regulator that the utility will be allowed to recover certain costs in the future, and also contracts for the purchase of power.

[4] *System benefits costs* (such as low-income subsidies and costs of DSM and renewables programs) imposed by regulators also typically end up in distribution charges.

FIGURE 18.1 Bottom-up pricing.

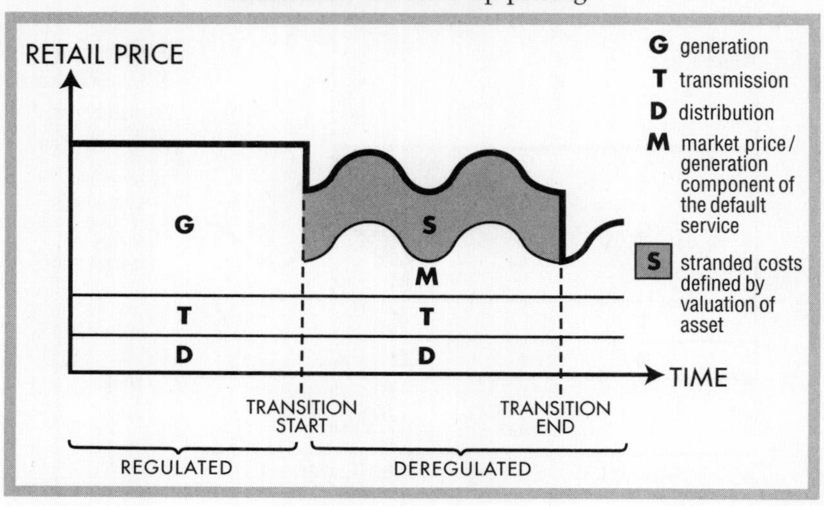

gotten mixed up with the issue of stranded cost collection. Although some states have gone for full divestiture, in other places agreement could not be reached as to valuations. Legislatures have been keen to ensure some guaranteed reduction in the bill when retail access is introduced; and the result has been what we call *top-down prices,* plus endless arguments about shopping credits.

The top-down method is based on the concept that the current regulated prices are recovering the stranded costs. If the market price of electricity is deducted from bundled kWh prices, the residual is the sum of distribution, transmission, and stranded costs, although these cost elements are not separately identified. Charging delivery rates equal to this residual amount recovers from every customer the same amount of stranded costs after retail access as before. Figure 18.2 shows recovery of stranded cost under the top-down method.

Figure 18.3 shows a variation of the top-down method in which customers receive a guaranteed rate reduction (as was the plan in California). The retail price is reduced, but stranded cost is collected over an increased amount of time so the total amount of stranded cost recovered is the same.

All in all we recommend buying out of the old regime and starting again with a clean slate, using the bottom-up approach. This is because of the multiple problems with the top-down approach that we review next.

FIGURE 18.2 Top-down pricing.

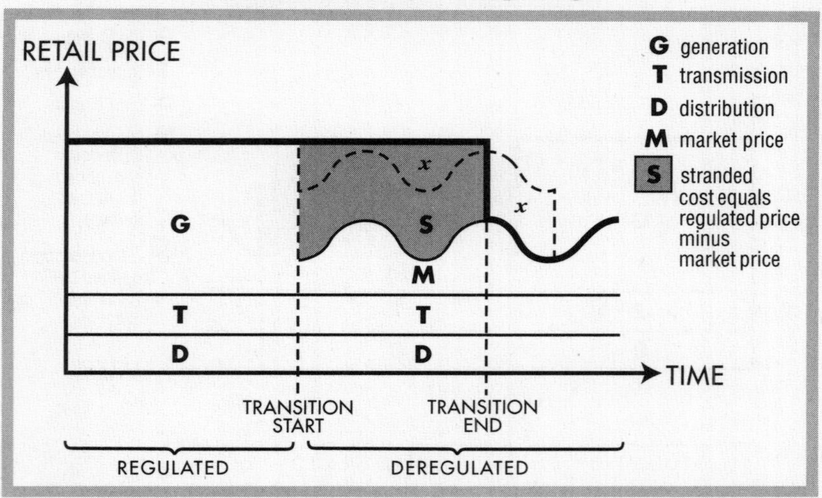

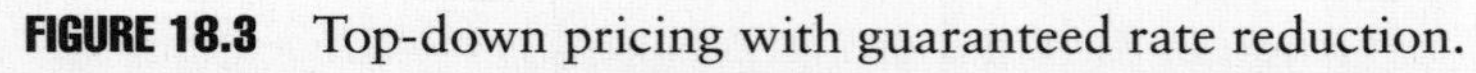

FIGURE 18.3 Top-down pricing with guaranteed rate reduction.

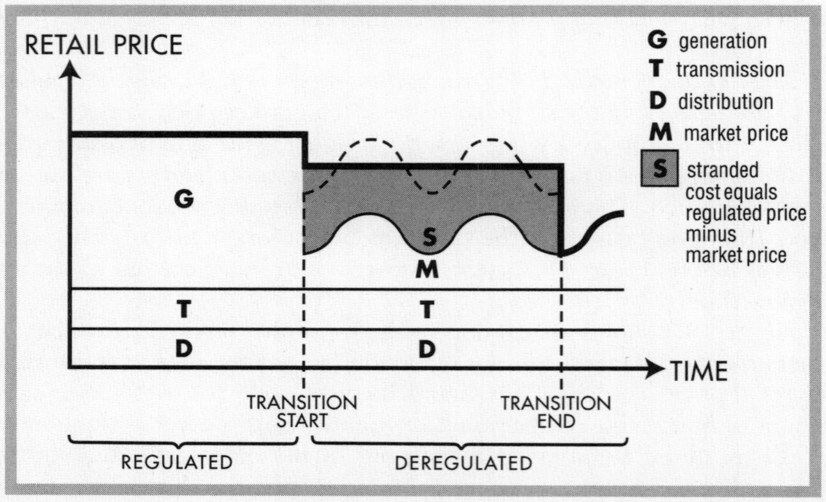

Bottom-Up Approach

Before listing disadvantages of the top-down approach, we should say that the bottom-up approach is not as simple as it sounds. It requires an explicit computation of stranded cost, generally by divestiture, and what are often arbitrary allocations of the total stranded cost to classes and rate elements. This approach can also lead to significant cost shifting. It requires new unbundled cost studies and a careful analysis of the costs of miscellaneous functions the Distco must perform.[5]

Top-Down Approach

The advantage of the top-down approach is that it leaves things as they are for a transition period. It postpones the hard decisions and does not require divestiture, or estimating stranded costs, assigning them to classes, and structuring a separate stranded cost charge. It also avoids cost shifting. It leaves the prices just where they were before. Or if the legislature wants a 5 percent reduction, then it is clear what that means. However, the top-down approach has major disadvantages, including:

1. It prevents the demand side from being responsive.
2. It inhibits (virtually prevents) competing retailers from entering, since there is no price variability to insure against.
3. If the utility has divested generation, the logic of top-down becomes strained.
4. It does not eliminate the eventual need for an explicit estimate of stranded cost.
5. It prolongs cross-subsidies.
6. It encourages uneconomic values for shopping credits.

First, the top-down method, by fixing rates, prevents the demand side from responding to price changes—even those who have hourly meters. (See Appendix C on California—this was one of the problems in the 2000–2001 crisis.) This would be a problem even if the other aspects were not.

[5]The unbundled cost studies (whether marginal or embedded) necessary for the bottom-up approach are much more complex that standard cost studies because they require explicit consideration of functions not typically tracked in the accounts and budgets of the utility. For example, what is the cost of scheduling hourly loads? What is the cost of standing by to provide generation and billing services to a customer who wants to return to default service?

Second, the major offering of competing retailers is hedging the spot price by offering fixed price contracts. But under top-down pricing, there is no variability to hedge against. *When the market price goes up, the stranded cost component of the rate goes down to match and the total cost is unchanged.* The retailers have no value added to sell, unless the shopping credit is overstated.

Third, the top-down approach does not provide the right amount of stranded cost recovery if the utility does not continue to own the generation. As the market price varies, the stranded cost component implicit in the residual changes in the opposite direction. This makes sense if the Distco's parent company still owns the above-market generating units, because a higher market price really does translate into lower stranded costs—the generating units are earning the market price, and therefore the stranded costs really are lower.

However, if some of the generating units have been divested, *higher* market prices go to the new owners—the divestiture fixed the amount of stranded costs once and for all, for those plants. So the utility would be under-recovering under top-down pricing. The opposite could also be true—*lower* market prices go to the new owners and the utility would be over-recovering. This makes any eventual recovery much more complicated or, if the recovery is time-limited, as it was in California, exposes the utility to tremendous risk (see Figure 18.4).

Fourth, the top-down approach still eventually requires an explicit and agreed determination of the market value of the generating units. At some point the transition to retail access will end and no further stranded cost recovery will be allowed; there will be a switch to the bottom-up approach. At this time, it is necessary to estimate the remaining difference between book value and market value of the generating units. There may even be stranded benefits that should be refunded to consumers. To use the top-down approach is to delay the inevitable bottom-up approach, not avoid it forever.

Fifth, keeping the current revenue allocation to classes and rate structures may be counter-productive if there are cross-subsidies and tariff structures that do not reflect the structure of market prices.

Sixth, *the top-down approach requires setting a specific "shopping credit"* to be deducted from the original bundled rates if customers choose another retailer than the Distco. In the theory of top-down pricing (which is used in various industries where a bundled product has to be partially unbundled), this credit should be the avoided cost of the company losing the customer. In the case of electricity, this is the market price of power. *But because the whole top-down scenario effectively bars competing retailers from entering, there has been a tendency for regulators to increase the credit so as*

FIGURE 18.4 Top-down pricing with unexpected market price increase.

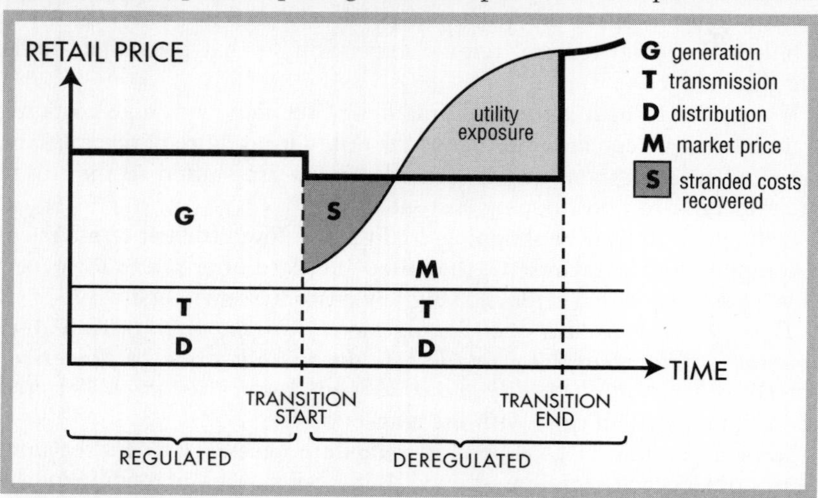

to induce retailers to enter (see the section on Pennsylvania that follows). This is inefficient, and can also backfire, because fixed shopping credits may seem to be high when set, but later price increases in the market can send customers scurrying back to the Distco, when the shopping credit looks too low compared to the market price.

These are the reasons we prefer bottom-up pricing—establishing once and for all the difference between market and book values, and then recovering this stranded cost under the bottom-up approach.

SHOPPING CREDITS AND THE PRICE OF DEFAULT SERVICE

Critical to the success of retail access in the presence of default service by the utility, is the establishment of a transparent, market-based shopping credit. Under top-down pricing, the shopping credit is the reduction off the bundled rates for customers who choose an alternative supplier. Under bottom-up pricing, where rates are unbundled, the shopping credit is simply the price for default generation service.

The shopping credit is the price to beat that consumers use to compare suppliers. Customers cannot make prudent choices about shifting to or from utility-supplied default service if they do not know what the utility is charging. The shopping credit should be clearly and separately shown on the bill. It is crucial for real retail competition so that consumers understand their choices.

If the price to beat is too high, inefficient retailers with high costs relative to the utility's can compete. Since the utility loses more in revenues than it saves when a customer leaves, stranded costs are shifted to the utility's shareholders or to nonshopping customers.

If the price to beat or shopping credit is too low, efficient retailers cannot compete. In Massachusetts, the initial standard offer prices for generation were set below market level. Very few customers switched.

The right price to beat or shopping credit from the point of view of encouraging efficient entry by retailers is the market price of power plus whatever other costs the utility avoids when it loses a customer. The credit should change dynamically with the market price.

Some argue that large shopping credits are necessary to get the infant industry of electricity retailing started. But retailers are often companies already providing conservation or other utility services, for example, and utilities entering new territories. Such retailers are well-established companies and do not need an infant-industry assist.

Retailers believe the shopping credit should also include an allowance for *retailing* because they must spend money to attract customers, manage accounts, arrange for suppliers, and so on. However, since a utility offering default or standard offer service will not be spending money to attract customers to these services, they will still have to track customer usage and payments (for delivery services) and will still be arranging generation and scheduling loads for default customers, there is little opportunity for the utility to avoid such retailing costs.

Since the market price is not a fixed number, the shopping credits should not be fixed either. Shopping credits that were not sufficiently seasonally-differentiated have created problems in virtually every retail access market—*the retailers sign up customers when market prices are lower than the fixed shopping credits, but then dump the customers back on default service once the market price rises above the shopping credit.* Shopping credits that are fixed, with no true up for actual market prices, are bound to be either too low or too high.

Not every customer will have an hourly meter and small customers probably need some price stability. However, since shopping credits are the marketer's price to beat, it is essential that they reflect market prices. The question of how to arrange for supply to default customers and how to structure default charges was discussed in Part One.

Massachusetts—Low Standard Offer

Under the Massachusetts plan, consumers were given the opportunity to select a competitive electricity supplier or accept standard offer service if they did not. If a customer selected a competitive electric supplier—that is, someone other than its regular utility—then that supplier could buy the required energy for its customer from the New England market. The standard offer service was designed to give a 10 percent rate reduction from prevailing rates in 1998, increasing to 15 percent in 1999. Massachusetts started with a seven-year market price forecast as the basis for default service, but the forecast was well below market prices by the time retail access began. But very few customers switched because the shopping credit was too low. This approach created problems because the utilities were unable to acquire supplies at the price set by the standard offer and began to incur losses. Standard offer prices had to be increased as energy and fuel prices in the New England market increased.

Pennsylvania—High Shopping Credit

Pennsylvania is the poster child for high shopping credits. In Pennsylvania, retail access started in 1999 and competing suppliers can buy their energy from the PJM market. The shopping credit was set at a high level to encourage

TABLE 18.1 Customer Load (MW) Served by Alternative Suppliers in Pennsylvania from January 1999 through July 2001

Date	MW	Percentage of PA MW
April 1999	6.959	29
July 1999	7,006	30
January 1999	7,166	30
January 2000	7,488	32
April 2000	8,320	35
July 2000	5,509	23
October 2000	6,088	26
January 2001	6,147	26
April 2001	5,371	23
July 2001	**2,040**	9

Source: Electricity Competition in the Keystone State, *Public Utilities Fortnightly,* October 15, 2001.

rapid shifts to new suppliers. As Table 18.1 shows, shifting was initially impressive, but once market prices caught up with the shopping credits, customers shifted back to the utilities. The utilities' prices are frozen at what is now below-market prices, so new competitors cannot compete.

Ohio—Targets for Switching

The Ohio legislature had an over-riding concern that significant switching take place—20 percent of each major customer group (residential, commercial, industrial, public authority) within three years of the beginning of retail access. Utilities were ordered to predict switching and set their shopping credits to achieve these goals. If the goals are not achieved, shopping credits will be further increased. But, as explained earlier, shopping credits set above the utility's avoided cost provide a subsidy to alternative suppliers and increase the costs of electricity service as a whole by allowing inefficient suppliers to operate. The Ohio approach defines success of retail access in terms of switching rates and makes arbitrary targets the primary goal at the expense of development of an efficient competitive market.

Switching by retail customers is not a good test of whether there is a competitive market. If nobody switched, that might indicate a problem—but the point is to give people the choice.

CHAPTER 19

Current Jurisdictional Situation

Initially, the federal government was not involved at all in regulating the electric industry—the states set up the early regulatory mechanisms. In 1935, the Federal Power Act (FPA) intruded the federal nose into the industry, but did not occupy the space—it asserted federal jurisdiction only over the price of *wholesale* sales—that is, inter-utility sales, called *sales for resale*—and over the prices charged for transmission of electricity in interstate commerce. Prices of *retail* sales were regulated by the states. For all practical purposes, since there were few wholesale sales, the states regulated the industry. Now FERC regulates much of the industry. The 1935 definition of a wholesale sale has not changed—but the industry has.

There may not have been much interstate transmission in 1935, but by 1992 the country was covered with three interconnections—most of Texas (known as ERCOT, or Electric Reliability Council of Texas), the Eastern interconnection, and the Western interconnection. Texas stands alone, and has never been regulated by the FERC; but my computer outlet in New York is joined by an unbroken series of wires with Florida, Newfoundland, Chicago, and Alabama. In the West, the interconnection extends into Mexico (Baja California) and Canada. *Everything outside Texas is in interstate commerce, whichever way you look at it.* (Excluding, of course, Alaska and Hawaii. Even Texas is interconnected by small DC lines and some power plants located on the border of ERCOT can sell into that market.)

But while there is no doubt that electricity is in interstate commerce, that is only the threshold question in determining jurisdiction. It is the legislation that rules.

WHAT IS A WHOLESALE SALE?

The definition of wholesale sales in the 1935 Act was quite limited.[1] Almost every private utility was vertically integrated, generated for its own customers and was *set up with the generation in the operating company.* Under the 1935 division of jurisdiction, this form of organization meant that there was no wholesale sale within the utility, and therefore the regulation of generation, as part of the bundled utility price, fell to the states. The states also regulated the price of transmission other than that used for wholesale sales.

One company (New England Electric System) was set up as a *holding* company, with a generating subsidiary (New England Power), and 3 distribution subsidiaries. Because the generation and distribution were not in the same *operating* company, the transfers from the generating company to the distribution companies were "sales for resale"—wholesale sales—and the price was therefore regulated by FERC. NEES was in practice no different from any other utility—but the formal difference between a holding company and an operating company changed the regulatory jurisdiction. It was as if NEP had a regulated contract (with prices set by FERC) with its distribution companies. Although this model was not widely copied, it may be a useful model to note as part of a solution to the current restructuring problems—*when generation owned by an IOU is put into a separate subsidiary its sales to its affiliated companies (sales for resale) are regulated by FERC.*

[1] The Federal Power Act gives FERC jurisdiction over all wholesale power transactions. A wholesale power transaction is a "sale of power for resale." It covers any sale of power except to an end-user (a retail customer). Generation of electricity by a vertically integrated utility is not covered as long as there is no "sale" of power from one affiliate to another. So, when SCE (Southern California Edison) owned its generating plants, generation from its generating plants for its own distribution company load was not subject to FERC jurisdiction because there was no sale of power. It was all internal to the same OPERATING COMPANY. Power that SCE supplied to, say, the City of Riverside, was subject to FERC jurisdiction because it was a sale of power from one company to another. Vertical integration here is defined in a very narrow way. The generating assets must be owned by the same operating company as the distribution/retailing business relying on them to serve retail customers. NEES (New England Electric System) was a holding company whose generating plants were owned by New England Power Company (NEP). NEP supplied power to affiliated distribution companies—Mass Electric, Granite State, and Narragansett Electric. These were all separate operating companies within a holding company structure. While an economist would consider these entities to be vertically integrated, in fact under the Federal Power Act the production of electricity in NEP was a "sale for resale" to Mass Electric, and was regulated by FERC.

The state commissions who regulated the NEES distribution companies were obliged to pass through the FERC-approved generating cost to retail customers under the "filed rate doctrine."[2] This should protect utilities from buying at one FERC-regulated price and having to sell at another price determined by the state PUC.

EXPANSION OF FERC JURISDICTION

The prices in the prederegulation bulk power markets for inter-utility sales, and the rules of the tight pools, were regulated by FERC, although FERC allowed market based rates to virtually all applicants. The prices of transmission for inter-utility sales and for wheeling to munis and co-ops were set on a case-by-case basis—the main issue was whether there should be access, not what the prices should be.

The responsibilities FERC acquired under EPAct in 1992 were simply to provide access for wholesale sales. But this has become a massive job. FERC has tried to specify trading arrangements for wholesale access, under EPAct, but meanwhile states are deregulating and ordering retail access. FERC's main focus has been on:

- Geographic consolidation of operations into RTOs;
- Separation of transmission from generation; and
- More market-oriented trading arrangements.

But as the states deregulate generation, FERC also acquires additional jurisdiction:

- The price of sales from those deregulated plants become wholesale sales under FERC jurisdiction.
- And in addition, if a utility company puts its generation into a subsidiary, the transfer from the generating subsidiary to the distribution subsidiary becomes a wholesale sale, subject to FERC regulation. Illinois Power, Exelon, Pacific Gas and Electric, and others have done this, or have plans to do so.

[2] There have however been some instances (not in Massachusetts) of exceptions to the filed rate doctrine. And the price of electricity bought from a spot market is not a "filed rate"—which is why the California utilities could not appeal to the filed rate doctrine when their state commission ordered them to buy in the spot market and sell at fixed prices.

- The pricing of all transmission in deregulating states falls into FERC jurisdiction.
- The design of trading arrangements in the new markets falls under FERC's jurisdiction, because the markets are where the wholesale prices are determined, and FERC, under the Federal Power Act has to say they will be "just and reasonable" prices.
- The determination of market power (needed before market-based rates are approved) has become much more difficult.
- The detection of market power when the markets are operating falls under FERC's jurisdiction.
- The imposition of price caps in the new markets also falls to FERC—the extraordinary sight of the governor of California (a state that passed its own legislation to deregulate and dared the FERC to interfere), pleading to have prices capped by FERC, and rebates ordered, emphasizes this point graphically.

As a result of all these changes, FERC's area of authority has expanded greatly. In the current situation, FERC has responsibility for many, but not all, of the important issues in competitive markets. However, FERC has severely limited authority to impose an overall solution if it involves restructuring companies, or changes in the retail arrangements that are in the power of the states. And even where it clearly has authority, it is not yet set up as an agency with a budget and staff to take on all the new roles that have been thrust upon it.[3]

THE JURISDICTIONAL IMPASSE

Although FERC has acquired much more authority, it does not have the authority necessary to do what would need to be done to establish competition in the electric industry of the United States. First, it has jurisdiction only over the private industry; the government owned industry is part of the sector too, and a large part in many places. It is simply bizarre that privatization of the electric industry, which has been a major priority in many countries as they struggle to make the industry more competitive and efficient, should

[3] Legislation to give FERC additional authority has been pending in Congress since 1996. Congress has hesitated to act because of unresolved disputes over the treatment to be given to munis and co-ops under the new regime and because of opposition by some states and utilities to giving FERC more power.

not be part of the restructuring in the United States. The Clinton Administration proposed to privatize the Federal PMAs, but ran into major opposition and failed. However, this book is already long enough, and a review of the inefficiencies of government ownership is not included here.

The restructuring of existing companies, both to separate transmission and to divest and break up generation if required, almost certainly requires legislation and just compensation, and probably also changes in the tax code, unless it is to be done by cajoling.

Transmission access and trading arrangements are clearly in federal jurisdiction. The FERC has complete authority over the trading arrangements. We believe that what it has done so far is not sufficient, for reasons we have explained at length earlier.

The business model for transmission, that would enable the necessary coordination of generation investment with transmission investment, is unresolved. The traditional pricing paradigm is uneconomic and inhibits trade; the organization of transmission is fragmented into 140 control areas, and while FERC has ordered consolidation into regional transmission organizations in Order No. 2000, it may not have the authority even to do this. It almost certainly (no one knows for sure) does not have the authority to order companies to divest their transmission into Transcos, on the model of NGC, which would be the one we would suggest. This would almost certainly require legislation and changes in the tax code.

The other elements needed for competition are largely in the hands of the individual states.

The regulation (and hence the deregulation) of generation is where the big regulatory problem lies. Jurisdiction is divided in a complicated way: Only the states can deregulate the generation, but once they do, it passes into federal jurisdiction and obviously state regulators are not happy about losing their powers. *But natural markets are larger than a single state, and hence no state can ensure competition throughout the market, although it can deregulate within the state. The states cannot set up trading arrangements; they cannot expand transmission capacity throughout the market; they probably cannot even require the companies they regulate to divest capacity to ensure competition; they certainly cannot require generators in other states to do so; and FERC cannot either. So no one has the authority to bring about production competition in the remaining states.*

At the retail level, there is no harmonized set of principles for the retail regime, and all the states are working under different rules. There is no authority to order hourly metering at the federal level, and no requirement for final customers to be exposed to market prices even if they have hourly meters. At least setting out the principles for rate design, metering, stranded cost collection, and POLR responsibility would be a step forward, but again, no one has the responsibility to do this.

POSSIBLE SOLUTIONS

In our view, federal jurisdiction over the transmission and trading arrangements is inescapable. We set out the reasons in more detail in the following chapter. FERC cannot do its job with one hand tied behind its back. It needs legislation to give it authority to require separation of generation from transmission, regional consolidation, and appropriate trading arrangements. It needs clear authority over the government owned entities in the matter. This legislation should address and solve the various tax and tax-exemption problems and allow for compensation for the utilities.

There is also a good case for federal requirements for hourly metering, and for appropriate tariff structures for final customers. (See Chapter 20 for details.)

So far, this much seems self-evident; what is not clear is what to do about generation, which is regulated by state or federal entities according to who is the buyer. Were it not hallowed by history, this would appear to be a peculiar way to regulate.

One obvious solution would be to make all output from generating plants (other than self-generation) subject to the same jurisdiction. This would mean a revamping of the state-federal boundary established in 1935, so that the federal government regulated all generation. That is essentially what happened in gas, for different reasons—FERC regulated the sales from the gas fields and was able to deregulate when the production markets were potentially competitive. (See Appendix D on the gas experience.) At the simplest level, federal jurisdiction could be accomplished by requiring utilities to put their generation into a subsidiary, which would immediately make all sales from generating plants wholesale sales. Independent plants are already in FERC's jurisdiction; several utilities have put their plants into subsidiaries and are therefore now FERC jurisdictional. It makes no sense to have jurisdiction over this critical function so scattered.

FERC would then have clear authority to require generating subsidiaries to join regional transmission organizations, and to sign up for their trading rules. The regulated generators would simply dispatch into the regional organization (this is analogous to the operations of the old tight pools). Then, when the trading arrangements were working well, the regional generation market could be deregulated. If the states wished to designate the distribution company as the sole retail provider in its service area, and avoid the additional infrastructure needed for retail access, they could do so. Or they could phase in retail access, as we suggest.

However, short of this, there is something that could be done immediately, without legislation. FERC long ago stopped regulating the price of arms-length wholesale transactions, permitting market-based prices on a showing that the relevant market was competitive. When states deregulate, there are many more wholesale sales than before, and the generators have to apply to FERC for "market based prices" for the new markets. Small generators and new plants get such approval automatically, but requests by large companies, or companies with a big share in the particular market, get more scrutiny. This has so far been interpreted as approval of the trading arrangements and an examination of the expected concentration of generators in the market.

Although FERC has not so far done so, we believe it clearly has the authority to examine all the arrangements in the market, including those that fall within the state regulators jurisdiction, and to condition approval of market based prices on showing that all necessary conditions are met. This would include the retail regime, the metering, the entry conditions, the transmission constraints, and so on, even if they were state jurisdictional. It would be a big step forward if FERC were to issue a list of the requirements for competition, and to insist on their being met before approving market-based prices. FERC does not have enough staff, or the right kind of staff, to do this right now, but it would not require any legislation.

However, this would only solve part of the problem. FERC can only condition approval in this way *when it is asked for approval.* And it is the sellers who ask for the approvals—they have no authority to make the markets competitive, install hourly meters, order divestiture, establish the retail regime, or anything else. More important perhaps is that no one today is asking for market-based rates for new markets, because the situation is at an impasse—the big states and the tight pools have deregulated; and in the rest of the country the markets are bigger than the remaining states.

Even if FERC were to follow our suggestion and spread a wider net in conditioning approvals for market-based rates, that would not solve all the problems—and it might not solve any of the real problems facing the industry today. Consider:

- What of the areas of the country that have not taken steps, and might never do so, to introduce competition? All the low-hanging fruit—the big states, and the ones with the pre-existing multi-state arrangements—have instituted reforms. What is left are market areas that comprise more than one state. What happens if some of the states wish to change and others in the same market do not?

- Is it necessary to insist on all the states in a region becoming competitive? Can the United States remain stuck in the middle, with half the states deregulated and half regulated?
- Is there a phased schedule that would have benefits of its own, whereby the changes in regulation that offer intrinsic improvements in efficiency could be accomplished nationally, while leaving the final choice of deregulation to the states?

In the next chapter, we try to analyze these questions.

CHAPTER 20

Five Major Changes Revisited

The argument for competition is that it will increase efficiency, particularly in production. Four major changes are needed for competitive production markets, and a fifth for retail competition. Here they are again:

1. Demand responsiveness—hourly metering for most of the load, and rate designs that expose customers to the spot price for some of their consumption.
2. Trading arrangements based on an integrated model, with central dispatch and locational energy prices. System operations separate from traders.
3. Transmission business model—transmission ownership separate from traders; pricing and expansion arrangements; preference for profit making regulated Transcos incorporating the system operator.
4. Divestiture and break-up of utility generation if necessary; choice for large customers; deregulation of production markets. (At this point, there is production competition.)
5. Finally, when production markets are working, choice for all customers. This needs a settlement mechanism and customer education, and decisions about default provision. (At this point, there is retail competition.)

What is amazing is that the United States has done this almost entirely backwards—some states have instituted retail access without competition in production; there are no Transcos, no national trading arrangements, and even in the five competitive markets there is no requirement for hourly metering for demand response.

We now ask two questions:

1. What is the intrinsic value of the steps? Which of these changes can stand alone, and increase efficiency in the industry even if none of the others are done? Are these major changes helpful only as adjuncts to competition, or do they have some intrinsic contribution to efficiency that might be useful in themselves? Which of the things that are prerequisites for competition might simply be introduced to increase efficiency without deregulating production markets. Are the five steps a whole package, or can we pick and choose?
2. Which of the changes require a federal solution, and which can be left to the states? The states are suspicious[1] of federal legislation—what justification is there for it in each of these five areas? In particular, if a state does not wish to participate, are there external costs that this decision would impose on other states that did wish to become competitive.

In other words, how much does it matter if there is a checkerboard of competitive and noncompetitive states?

DEMAND RESPONSIVENESS

The Intrinsic Value of the Step

Hourly metering and changing the rate structures are required for competition because of the need for the demand side to participate in electricity markets. This, as we have explained, rations electricity when supplies are tight, prevents the price excursions we have seen in California, and limits market power.

But it will also increase conservation and efficiency even if nothing else is done at all, *even in the old regulatory regimes*. The efficiency implications of time-of-use metering are well known. If there is an hourly spot price, rather than prices set in advance, the efficiency becomes more dramatic, limiting the need for new peaking plant, and preventing blackouts. But even with time-of-use prices set in advance, if metering is cheap enough, there are

[1] These suspicions are not entirely unjustified; the history of federal legislation in this industry has not been exemplary. PURPA of 1978 was in many respects a disaster; the Fuel Use Act of the same year prohibited gas burning in utility plants and prevented the development of the new CCGT technology for a decade until it was repealed; it is nearly a decade since federal jurisdiction over access was granted under EPAct and the rules are still neither settled nor efficient.

substantial benefits. The reason it has not been done before is that metering was expensive—it is not any more, and will get less expensive if mandating it brings scale economies and competition in production of meters. This is clearly the best form of conservation, and lack of metering has created cross-subsidies and inefficiencies (Armani and the Gap) that need to be eliminated even if nothing else changes.

The current situation is that none of the competitive markets in the United States have adequate provision for demand response, and this is not even required as part of the many thousands of pages FERC has put out on trading arrangements.

The Jurisdictional Question

There is an authentic national interest in energy conservation which has justified federal energy-efficiency standards for appliances and automobiles. PURPA, the 1978 legislation, was based on a national need for conservation and efficiency, and required purchases by the utilities of the output of small non-utility generators, particularly those who did not use fossil fuels. *So there is precedent for federal legislation requiring the states to install hourly metering, in the name of conservation.* Metering and retail pricing are still in the hands of the states, and although the federal government presumably could preempt on the same conservation and efficiency grounds as it passed PURPA, the states might agree, through a national body such as NARUC, (the National Association of Regulatory Utility Commissioners) to go ahead with this.

TRADING ARRANGEMENTS

The Intrinsic Value of the Step

The integrated trading arrangements we propose can go into effect (with certain adjustments to the pricing rules) *before deregulating generation.* This is (more or less) how the tight pools in the United States worked *under the regulated regimes.* Regulated companies provided their own power, and traded at the margin through the tight pools. The trading arrangements of the tight pools effectively promoted economic dispatch and settled the marginal economy trades between regulated utilities, and between the utilities and the munis. The other form of trading arrangement in the United States under regulation was (and is) wheeling, where utilities do their own economic dispatch, and interutility trades are done bilaterally. However, wheeling is not suitable for scaling-up to competition, whereas the integrated model is.

What is clear is that the current wheeling arrangements are not working, and getting to the integrated model fast, with or without deregulation, would remove many of the current inefficiencies. The proposed integrated trading arrangements are much more suitable than the wheeling model currently in existence in the United States, even for marginal trading:

- They use the transmission much better, since there is no need for native load priority, and hence no over-reservation.
- They are more incentive-compatible than wheeling, with less need for policing, and less chance of mishaps.
- They provide congestion prices and hence real data about the need for transmission.
- They offer the opportunity to develop financial transmission rights.
- Independent generators selling to munis under EPAct can be accommodated.
- Small area problems with ancillary services and load pockets can be identified.
- They can be used for a dry run before competition in production takes over for real.

The Jurisdictional Question

FERC has jurisdiction over wholesale trading arrangements for wholesale access under EPAct 1992. Since all utilities buy and sell some power at wholesale (even in the still-regulated states) FERC could mandate an efficient set of trading arrangements, although its power to force consolidation of trading areas is in dispute, and without consolidation the arrangements we propose would not be workable. Utility-by-utility dispatch is just where we are now, and what creates many of the problems.

What needs to be done is for regional market areas (that would be suitable eventually for production competition) to be designated, system operations separated from generation and the trading arrangements consolidated. We propose that ideally the whole country have the same trading arrangements. (This means several separate control areas with the same rules, which makes interarea trading much simpler.) *The public generation and distribution entities should also participate*. Trading arrangements at a regional level, providing the regions were contiguous and large enough, would probably work. This is what FERC has been trying to do. FERC probably needs more legal authority to get this done, but it can clearly be done only at the federal level.

Provided the operations are separated from the generation, the integrated trading arrangements do not know or care whether the participants are regulated or deregulated.

THE TRANSMISSION BUSINESS MODEL

The Intrinsic Value of the Step

The United States already has a transmission business model, just not a good one. Generators are still permitted to own transmission, a situation that FERC has stated clearly and correctly, leads to conflicts and inhibits competition, but that it has no power to correct. Transmission is owned by over two hundred public and private entities, regulated by both FERC and the states, or in the case of the government by no one, planned on a company-by-company basis, and priced inefficiently.

The generation needs to be separated from the transmission to avoid conflicts of interest and exercise of market power, even with the current limited trading.

The transmission business arrangements need to be consolidation into wider areas, and the need for revised regulation—pricing, role of transmission contracts, regulation, governance and so on should be decided on a wider basis than the states.

The current pricing inhibits trade. The pricing should be based on marginal costs (congestion and losses) and integrated with the proposed trading arrangements. This would permit financial transmission contracts (or rights) to replace the current physical rights, which both limit the use of the transmission and enhance market power.

The regime for expansion needs to be settled. The United States has dismantled the old utility method of expanding transmission and has not replaced it with anything. This needs to be attended to urgently. Establishing regulated Transcos, with incentives to maintain and expand the system, would get the United States out of the current impasse.

These changes will be difficult, but they could also be made before any deregulation of the production markets, and would increase efficiency.

The Jurisdictional Question

FERC has jurisdiction over pricing transmission used for wholesale trading, but without further authority to consolidate existing transmission and impose a new regulatory regime, including the regime for expansion, FERC can do little to solve the problems. No one has the authority to require utilities to divest transmission into a Transco, or any other form of regional organization.

THE FIRST THREE STEPS SHOULD BE DONE ANYWAY

These three steps simply reorganize a regulated industry and create their own efficiencies, even if nothing is done about deregulating production. *They all have an independent contribution to efficiency, conservation, and national security in their own right.* Not only do these steps have independent benefits—they all have external costs that make them proper candidates for federal jurisdiction. Trading arrangements and a transmission business model have already been defined into federal jurisdiction, but without sufficient authority to do them properly. In these there areas, the externalities are fairly clear. The national benefits of requiring hourly metering and pricing (in the limited form we propose) are also clear. However, this is not necessarily true of deregulating production. Now we have to ask, what is wrong with a checkerboard of state decisions as to whether to deregulate generation and achieve competition in the production markets?

SUPPLY SIDE

The Intrinsic Value of the Step

Suppose we were now at the point where a cohesive set of trading arrangements were in place in a limited number of regional Transcos, and the states had efficient pricing and hourly metering. On the supply side, some major additional steps would need to be taken—stranded cost recovery (or the reverse), divestiture to control market power, contracting regimes that the Distcos should follow, and review of the retail regime to ensure that it is not antithetical to competition in the production markets. These are all major steps, and are potentially much more controversial in the United States than the three prior steps, but they need to be taken before production markets are deregulated. If all these things were done, competition should provide the lowest costs and the best value to consumers—there should not be any risk in going ahead and deregulating generation. But without them, as we have seen, there can be problems.

Deregulating existing utilities is where the risks to consumers lie. If the production markets turn out not to be competitive, then the consumers will be fleeced. California showed us two major things: The production markets cannot be competitive without demand and supply response; and if the continued regulation of the retail regime is not consistent with the deregulation of production, then utilities and producers can go bankrupt. (California also showed how bad trading arrangements can get when the parties are left to negotiate the rules.)

Nonetheless, production competition is the prize that is supposed to produce the big long run savings; it works everywhere else, and it only happens when generation is deregulated. Most countries make all the changes simultaneously, and deregulate with a big bang. But if they have to be done in steps, step 4 should follow steps 1, 2, and 3.

But markets are bigger than single states, and the states cannot go it alone. If the United States wants competition, this problem must be solved. The deregulation of the production markets is the big question mark in the jurisdictional issue in the United States today.

The Jurisdictional Question

It is presently in the jurisdiction of the states to propose deregulation of the utility generation. But since the remaining states are in market areas larger than a single state, and often containing government generation, no state can, by itself, create a competitive market as things stand.

Before competition can be introduced on the supply side, someone has to ensure that the production markets would have enough suppliers to prevent market power. This is now the task of FERC. FERC requires a showing that there is no market power before it grants market-based pricing authority. The tests it requires are rudimentary. What it has not done is to insist on systematic review that all the preconditions for competition are met before generating markets are deregulated. It does not review compatibility of the retail regime, the metering and the retail rates structures before approving the new markets.

But while FERC has the power to prevent bad designs going forward, it has no authority to impose good designs, no authority to require restructuring of generating companies that have too much of the market, no control at all over the government entities (and the big federal government generators are very large parts of their respective regions); and FERC cannot impose competition on states that have not proposed it.

The Case for Federal Intervention

Since this is an urgent issue in the United States, we have to ask whether there is a case for expanding federal jurisdiction. The rationale for any federal jurisdiction is the constitutional one of interstate commerce. Electricity clearly is in interstate commerce, but this is just the threshold question. The case for further federal involvement has to be based on detriment to commerce—"externalities" or external costs—if states have a checkerboard of rules, some deregulated and some not, some competitive and some still regulated.

Alcohol is clearly in interstate commerce, but is regulated by the states on the grounds there is no interstate impact if one state is dry and another is not. (Even though alcohol is state-regulated, the state laws that have made criminals of our 18-year-olds by preventing them from legally drinking alcohol have been passed by the states as a prerequisite for federal funding of the highways.)

The case for further federal jurisdiction in electricity would need to be that if one state does not go along with a beneficial reform, it either prevents others from doing so, or allows the nonreforming states to free-ride on those who do. This spillover effect on interstate commerce, which we call "externalities" or external costs, is the underlying constitutional reason for permitting federal action at all.

The question is: How important is it for all states in a region to deregulate at the same time? What are the problems if some states in a natural market want to deregulate and others do not? Can there be functioning, competitive, regional markets with some Distcos still retailing their own generation at regulated prices, and selling their excess at spot prices; while others deregulate, and make contracts and spot sales at market prices?

We have suggested that all the states in a region follow the same trading arrangements, along the lines of the decentralized model, whether or not they are deregulated (like the old tight pools). In the proposed trading arrangements there is explicit room for contracts, and in fact we have argued that contracts are necessary because they reduce market power. The utility's regulated prices act much like a contract—the power is sold forward at fixed (regulated) prices to the utility customers. It is important to understand that the trading arrangements do not care about the price of contracts; the transmission arrangements are also completely independent of whether the energy prices are regulated or not. These *rules* will work whether the players are regulated or not regulated. The critical question is: How different are regulated utility prices from any other forms of contract?

If we are right about the benefits of competition, the regulated utilities would not be as *efficient* as the free market generators—but that is not the point here. The point here is: If the states prefer to have their generators still regulated, what does it matter to the rest of the wider market area? What is wrong with a checkerboard? What are the externalities? How does it affect the remaining states going the deregulated route, if they wish to do so? Think here of a five-state market area. What happens in the production market if one state wants to be competitive, and the four others do not?

The effects will come through three prime causes:

1. Reduction in the size of the market;
2. Motivation of the players; and
3. Other externalities from regulation.

Reduction in the Size of the Market

Utility resources that are tied to their native load are not counted as part of the market supply. They are already married. Only the unmarried are in the market. Before deregulation, the relevant market is the amount of power available to be sold after the utilities have met their native load.[2] This is the test used in the old bulk power markets. After deregulation of the whole area, the relevant market would include all the power produced in the area[3]—this is the test used in the new markets.

We can only count the "uncontracted" generation (the deregulated generation, plus the marginal amounts available to trade after native load is met in the regulated states) as part of the market. A five-state market where a single state deregulated would be a relatively small "relevant market" and the two utilities in the would-be competitive state may have to be broken up. They would have been small competitors in the larger market, but they would loom as large competitors when the market is constricted by continued regulation. (Note that if one state were the lone holdout, it would have little or no impact. Vermont's continued regulation probably does not affect the New England market much.)

This is a real externality. The state that wants competition has to make substantial changes in the structure of its own companies that it would have avoided had the other states also deregulated.

Motivation of the Players

The motivation of regulated utilities and competitive players are subtly different. The unregulated players get all their revenues from the markets, while the regulated players have many of their costs met from a pot called "overhead," charged to their captive customers. Will the utilities play in the market for real, and if they do not, does it matter? One obvious thing that

---

[2] This is the formulation traditionally used by FERC to determine the relevant market for determinations of market-based rates—if generation is married to load by regulation, it is not in the market.

[3] This is the definition used after deregulation.

might happen is that the regulated utilities would sell their excess into the market below their true incremental cost, and might even keep building and selling into the neighboring states below cost—a form of *dumping*. The competitors might care, but the general economic approach to dumping is "dump on me, dump on me." The customers in the dumped-on state are better off, and if the regulated states want to keep subsidizing exports to its neighbors, well, let them.

The more subtle effect is on the prices in the competitive market. For example, the market price, especially in the peak hours, is critical to the success of an electric market. How might the incentives be different?

- A competitive generator, faced with running a plant flat-out at peak, would bid his plant taking account of the potential for it breaking down under such stress.
- A utility would probably not bid in this way—it may run the plant flat-out, but it will not reflect the cost of doing so in the bid it makes. It may not even not be allowed to do so under regulation.

However, if the utility plant breaks down, the costs of fixing it, or more likely, the cost of the insurance, will be charged to the customers; it just will not be reflected in the peak market price. So the utility's behavior can affect the market price. This then affects the revenues of competitive generators.

Since the market price is the competitive generators' only source of income, whereas the regulated utility has its regulated rates to fall back on, this puts the competitors at a disadvantage. The independent generators are deprived of the revenues they need to pay for the plants they have already built. When supplies get tight, the market price is supposed to rise. If it does not, the existing competitive generators lose money. If they know this is likely to happen, they will not come in the first place.

This example is repeated to a lesser degree in every hour:

- The utility's bids for hourly dispatch will almost certainly be lower than those of its competitors, even if the utility is required to bid its plant for dispatch "at its marginal cost."
- It is fairly clear that competitive entities have a wider view of their marginal costs—when the market has to provide all the revenues, independents cannot afford to ignore opportunity costs, or insurance costs, or environmental compliance costs in making their sales.
- But utilities can ignore these costs, and are often required to, since they get much of their money, under regulation, in an undifferentiated pot called *overhead*.

The costs, and the final prices to customers, are not lower under regulation, because they pay these overheads; but the market price may well be held down and become unremunerative to those who rely on it for all their revenues.

Some of these practices, if engaged in deliberately, might be classified as unfairly and inefficiently precluding generators in other states from competing. Therefore, the rules might require regulated generators to sell in these markets at "not below their incremental costs." But the history of regulation shows that when accountants get hold of "incremental costs" they completely ignore the sort of opportunity costs that truly are incremental, but are very hard to measure; and the marginal components of overhead costs is completely ignored. Regulated utilities will inevitably sell power at below incremental cost some of the time, if not all of it.

Other Regulatory Restrictions

Other regulatory restrictions that will affect the workings of the competitive market are the ones that affect the amount of capacity. Too much capacity results directly in lower market prices—markets are supposed to determine the price and the quantity at the same time.

Lower Cost of Capital If the utilities are allowed to build new plants at a regulated cost of capital, they can undercut the independents by their sales in the unregulated markets, especially in the contract markets. This is also true of the government entities. Regulated and government entities are financially less risky to lenders than competitive generators—therefore their cost of capital is lower. (They are financially less risky to lenders because under regulation the customers pick up the cost of failures. The total cost to customers is not lower, when the cost of capital is added to the failures.) Just as the market price of contracts appears to be getting high enough to justify new independent entrants, the utility or the government entity, following the old planning process, announces that it will build a new plant, probably adding that it will be cheaper. Independents cannot beat the low-risk regulated cost of capital, or the tax-free government bonds.

This is a recognized problem. So let us suppose that the utility and the government entities may build only enough for their own customers, and are prohibited from building more than this. There are still two other ways that regulation may induce excess capacity that keeps the market price from ever rising high enough to remunerate independents.

Excessive Reserves Regulators have typically permitted or required excessive reserves. If the utilities are required to build excess reserves, they can create constant excess capacity and destroy the functioning of the pricing, which is supposed to bring in new generators for the competitive part of the market.

Plant Closures Regulatory policies for recouping the cost of plants that close have often kept uneconomic plants open. If the utilities may not close plant that is uneconomic, they either hold it in reserve, or run it just enough to "keep it in the rate base," contributing excess capacity, with the same consequences as above.

There seem to be substantial, although subtle, externalities of having competitive generation and regulated generation in the same market, and helping to set the market prices. A small lone hold-out would have a *de minimis* impact, but a "market" mainly composed of regulated utilities might inhibit competitive entry in the states that want to deregulate.

The conclusion would seem to be that there really are externalities if some states do not deregulate. But whether these externalities are sufficiently compelling to persuade the states' Representatives and Senators to vote for such a change in Congress is an open question.

FEDERAL LEGISLATION?

To summarize, there is a strong case for getting ahead with demand response, trading arrangements and transmission reorganization for their own sake, to improve the efficiency of the current industry, even if states do not choose to deregulate. The trading arrangements, and the transmission organization can accept regulated and unregulated generators—regulation has the same economic effect as a contract, and the trading arrangements are constructed to accept contracts.

There is a strong case for federal legislation that would require all these items, since any state that desires competition would not be able to go ahead unless the other states cooperated. For the metering and tariff design issues, there is further precedent in the 1978 federal legislation PURPA, which mandated the states take certain actions, based on a national need to conserve energy.

However, when it comes to the deregulation of generation, there is a question. So what should be done? Here we examine two options for jurisdictional change:

1. One that takes federal jurisdiction over the first three of the big issues (up to but not including the changes needed on the supply side for

deregulation of production), but leaves deregulation of generation and retail access with the states;

2. The other that takes federal jurisdiction in addition over the supply side items, and deregulation of generation, so that the cut-off point is the decision for retail access, leaving the retail access issues with the states.

State Options for Deregulation of Generation

Many states, after California, are quite wary of deregulating generation. Deregulating generation in the United States has been an adjunct of retail access, but it can be (and in our view should be) done separately, with the Distcos initially purchasing in the competitive markets, and interim protection for customers until the trading arrangements are working well, and the market power issues are fully resolved. Then retail access can be introduced.

It is the deregulation of generation, not retail access per se, that has exposed customers to the risks we have seen in California. While we have argued that this is because it was done wrong—without demand response, with bad trading arrangements, and with a retail regime that was incompatible—it is quite simply true that if generation had not been deregulated, there would have been no problem. Yet there is no competition without deregulation of generation—it is the centerpiece of competitive production markets.

If steps 1 through 3 are in place, states that want to deregulate could do so. Some states might choose not to go ahead with deregulation, but for those that want to be gain the benefits of competition, the prerequisites would be in place, and they would be able to do so.[4]

[4] My own intuition is that competitive companies that have to earn all their revenues from the markets will find it hard to play in a game where not all the players are playing for real. But others are not convinced that my arguments present a sufficient case for preempting the states. Robert Marritz has suggested to me that the U.S. Constitution allows for interstate or federal-state compacts, which might offer a solution to the problem the states will have with relinquishing jurisdiction over transmission and the deregulation of generation. Government should play a role in the proper establishment, functioning, and oversight of logical regional trading areas, but perhaps Washington-based regulation is not the only alternative. Federal-state compacts have not been widely used in the United States, but there is precedent for them in the electric industry, and at least one has been set up and tested in the courts. The sort of solution he envisages would require federal legislation to set the ground rules, with clear mandates as to what the regional entities would have to accomplish. Federal authority would serve as a backstop if the regional entities were not formed or did not deliver.

State Options Only for Retail?

The alternative is a national policy of competition for all, which implies taking federal jurisdiction over the deregulation of generation as well. This actually requires only a relatively small change, because of the peculiar details of the jurisdictional arrangements under the Federal Power Act: If vertically integrated companies were required to put their generation into a subsidiary, in a holding company, and sell to the Distco as an affiliate, this would automatically become a FERC-regulated transaction.

FERC would be regulating all sales from generating plants—then the responsibility for deregulating wholesale sales from these plants would be FERCs. FERC would be able to require all generating plants to sell into an RTO with approved trading arrangements and could continue to regulate on the traditional cost of service basis, perhaps even delegating the task back to the states. The states would retain jurisdiction over retail access.

But short of this, the United States needs to complete the tasks it has started. It has permitted open access; it has encouraged independent generators. But it has not completed the essential underpinnings for competitive generating markets, which the states cannot do alone.

Ideally the United States would take three bold steps:

1. It should adopt a coherent national model of what it is trying to do; it needs an overall framework, a national model of trading arrangements, and a full checklist of requirements for competition.
2. It should accept the need for, and legislate to require, restructuring of privately owned companies.
3. It should revise the line between federal and state jurisdiction so that coherent regional decisions can be made and wholesale trading arrangements established, permitting generation to be deregulated at the wholesale level with some confidence that competition would be robust.

APPENDIX A

Electricity Restructuring in England and Wales

The Central Electricity Generating Board (CEGB), which owned 60,000 MW of generating capacity (as much as California), was privatized as part of the conservative government's widespread reforms of the U.K. public sector during the 1980s and 1990s. The reforms were driven in part by an ideological commitment to reducing the role of the state, and a desire to raise funds. At the time of the reform, energy sales were growing by only about 2 percent per year and peak demand was almost static. However, the CEGB had been demanding huge financial resources for a massive program of investment in nuclear power to displace British coal. The Government believed that the generation business, at least, could find more efficient ways to carry out its investments and operations, if given the right incentive.

By the time the Government White Paper setting out the new structure was published in 1988, both British Telecom and British Gas had been privatized as integrated monopolies. Although neither company had been privatized for long, the Prime Minister, Margaret Thatcher, already showed a dislike for regulated private monopolies. The new structure of the electricity industry was therefore driven by a strong desire to promote competition in order to provide good incentives for efficiency.

Prior to restructuring, the CEGB had a complete monopoly on generation and transmission. It produced, bought, sold, and delivered electricity to the 12 Area Boards, as shown in Figure A.1. The Area Boards in turn had a distribution and retailing monopoly over their customers. To create competition, the CEGB's generation was to be separated from its transmission business and broken up into more than one company.

THE REFORM

The process of reform has continued since 1988. Table A.1 lists the steps of the reform process to date.

FIGURE A.1 England and Wales structure prior to privatization.

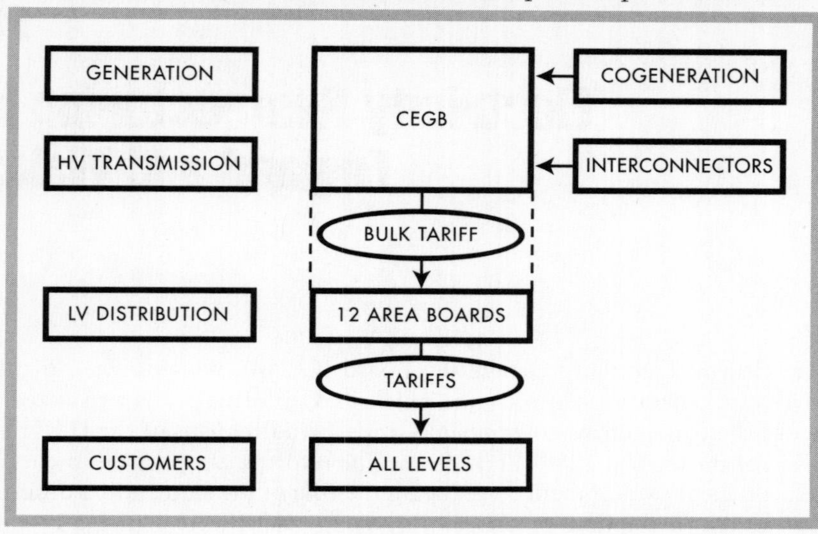

Industry Organization

The CEGB was broken up. Separate companies were formed for generation, transmission, and distribution, as shown in Figure A.2. The government used a new law to transfer assets and personnel from the CEGB to the new companies. The process of creating new companies is called *vesting*. Vesting Day was March 31, 1990, when all the contracts between the new companies were signed.

Generation

Three generating companies were formed: National Power, PowerGen, and Nuclear Electric. At vesting, these three companies accounted for 91 percent of total generation. The remainder came from independent power producers (IPPs), cogenerators, and interconnections with France and Scotland. Entry to the industry was made as simple as possible, and RECs were encouraged to contract with new generators; until 1993, the prices to small consumers were subject to price caps; after 1993 contract costs could be passed to customers, although after 1996 this pass-through was limited in some respects.

TABLE A.1 Timetable of Reforms in the United Kingdom

Date	Event
February 1988	Government publishes White paper outlining industry structure.
1989	Electricity Act passed to provide the legislative basis for industry restructuring.
September 1989	OFFER (Office of Electricity Regulation) established under the DGES (Director-General of Electricity Supply)—the independent regulator.
March 31, 1990	Vesting of the new companies: CEGB split into the National Grid Company (NGC), PowerGen, National Power, and Nuclear Electric. Hundreds of "Vesting Contracts" signed. 12 Regional Electricity Companies (RECs) formed from the 12 Area Electricity Boards. Ownership of NGC passed to the 12 RECs.
April 1, 1990	Pool operation commences. Retail competition opened to > 1 MW load.
December 1990	12 RECs privatized.
March 1991	60 percent privatization of National Power and PowerGen.
April 1994	Retail competition opened to 100 kW–1 MW load.
March 1995	40 percent privatization of National Power and PowerGen.
April 1995	Golden shares in RECs lapse, and takeovers/mergers begin.
December 1995	NGC privatized. NGC's pumped storage sold to Mission Energy (USA).
July 1996	Privatization of British Energy (modern nuclear plant, excluding Magnox).
1995–1996	First round of divestiture by National Power and Power Gen (to Eastern Electricity).
September 1998–June 1999	Staged opening of competition to under 100 kW customers.
1999–	Second round of divestiture by National Power and PowerGen (to a variety of owners).
2000	Utilities Act combines electricity and gas regulation under OFGEM (Office of Gas and Electricity Markets).
2001	Replacement of the Pool with the New Electricity Trading Arrangements (NETA).

FIGURE A.2 England and Wales structure at vesting.

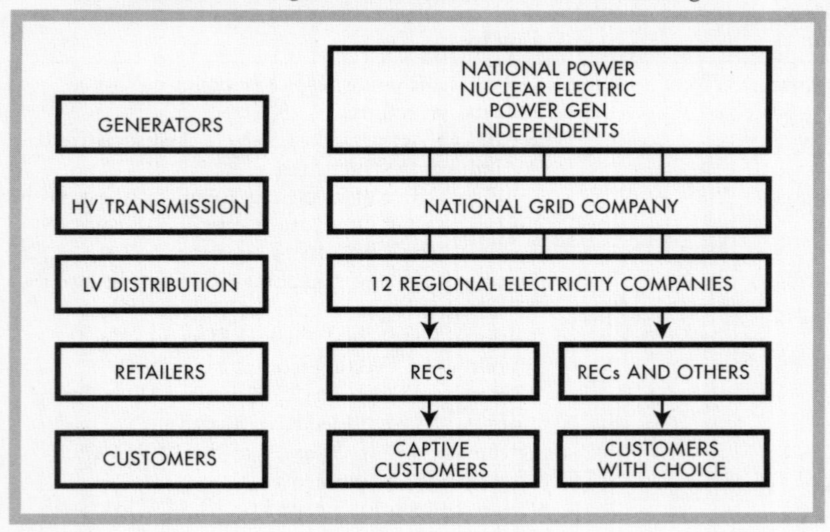

Transmission

National Grid Company (NGC) was formed to own and operate the transmission grid. It is the System Operator and the Transmission Owner, and in effect it also became the Market Operator, following rules established by the Pool, which was a separate organization. NGC is national in scope and although competing transmission companies are not prohibited, no license for such a company has ever been issued, so that NGC has a de facto monopoly on constructing new lines. (However, there is not much demand growth, and there is little need for new lines, so the scope of the monopoly has never been tested.) Initially NGC was given the pumped storage plant, which plays an important role in frequency control, but this was sold to Mission Energy of the United States in 1995.

Distribution

At vesting the 12 Area Electricity Boards were transformed into 12 regional electric companies (RECs). A study was done to decide how many RECs there should be, and concluded that the existing organizations should be kept just as they were. The RECs were privatized in December 1990 with the Government maintaining a *golden share* in each until April 1995. (A golden share prevented takeovers by other companies.) With the lapse of the golden shares, ownership of all 12 RECs has subsequently been the subject of mergers or acquisitions. Ownership of the RECs now includes multi-utilities, companies with major interests in generation, and foreign (U.S.) companies. The most significant change is the integration of some RECs with U.K. generators: ManWeb (Scottish Power), East Midlands (PowerGen), and Southern Electric (merged with Scottish Hydro). National Power took over MEB's retail business through a complex web of contracts. British Energy took over South Wales retail business but subsequently sold it to London Electricity (which in the meantime had been bought by EDF of France).

Trading Arrangements

In England and Wales, the Pool Rules provided the mechanisms for short-term trading of electricity, and a visible spot price. (The New Electricity Trading Arrangements, NETA, superceded the Pool Rules in March 2001; discussion of NETA is given later in this appendix.) Under the old Pool Rules, 80 percent to 90 percent of the traded electricity was hedged through medium- and long-term bilateral contracts. These contracts were structured as Contracts for Differences. (See Chapter 8.) Parties to such contracts settled outside the Pool's settlement procedures, usually between themselves rather than via any exchange.

There was just one market in England and Wales, and a single national price. (The England and Wales landmass is only 600 miles from end to end.) Locational differences were (and still are) taken into account in transmission charges, not in the Pool price. One useful reform in the rules was made in 1994 to improve incentives for efficiency. *Uplift* is a charge to users that comprises all the costs arising from transmission constraints, generation shortfall, and demand-forecast errors, plus specific payments for ancillary services. Uplift grew from 1990 because no one had any incentive to reduce the cost. Since 1994, NGC has had to pay a proportion itself, which reduced the cost of uplift, by making small investments in the transmission system, and improved management.

The initial design of the U.K. pool is well known, and in any event the trading arrangements have now been replaced by NETA.

Regulation

An independent regulator was established by law. It used to be called OFFER (the Office of Electricity Regulation) but it was combined with the gas regulator in 1998, and is now called OFGEM (Office of Gas and Electricity Markets). A visit to the Web site of OFGEM at www.ofgem.gov.uk will show how much work goes on there. No fewer than 78 public papers produced *in the period July to November 2000 alone* can be downloaded from the Web site.

Regulation is carried out via the licences under which the companies operate. Each company has a separate licence that governs their rights and obligations. For example, the price a regulated company may charge is a clause in the licence; when prices are changed, the licence condition changes. One of the duties of the regulator is to promote competition, and the current regulator recently tried, and failed, to control market power by changing the generators' licenses (see the next section). He failed because the companies can, and did, appeal to the Competition Commission, which supported their position.

The regulator also sets the prices for the monopoly transmission and distribution parts of the industry. The method for this is an RPI-X limit applied to average prices or total revenues, where RPI is the retail price index (a measure of inflation) and X is the specified level of real decrease (or increase if negative). There is also some provision for some costs to be shared with or passed through to consumers. X is set in advance in a review that happens every two to five years. The application of this methodology has been contentious, since, in the 1994 review at least, the regulator reduced prices far more than the companies felt was fair. Since then, the annual efficiency reduction, below inflation, has been 3 percent for all RECs. (See Figure A.3.)

Stranded Costs

In 1990, the energy market was expected, because of the excess capacity, to produce prices below the existing tariffs; this would have resulted in low valuations for the plants and low sale prices. In fact, the valuation of the generating plant was estimated at £5 billion, while it was carried on the accounting books at £25 billion. Although the government could have written off the excess book value (and did, to some extent), the U.K. Treasury used four tools to recoup its stranded costs:

1. Only the large customers could buy at the market price for the first 4 to 8 years; the smaller customers paid the old tariffs. The distribution companies signed vesting contracts with the generators. This paid for the coal subsidy until it was phased out.
2. Only 60 percent of the generating companies were sold initially at the low price justified by the low market prices—the other 40 percent was sold some years later at a much higher price, after the excess capacity was closed.
3. A levy (tax) of 10 percent was charged on all sales, to pay off some of the stranded costs of the nuclear plant.

FIGURE A.3 Average X-factors for distribution companies in England and Wales.

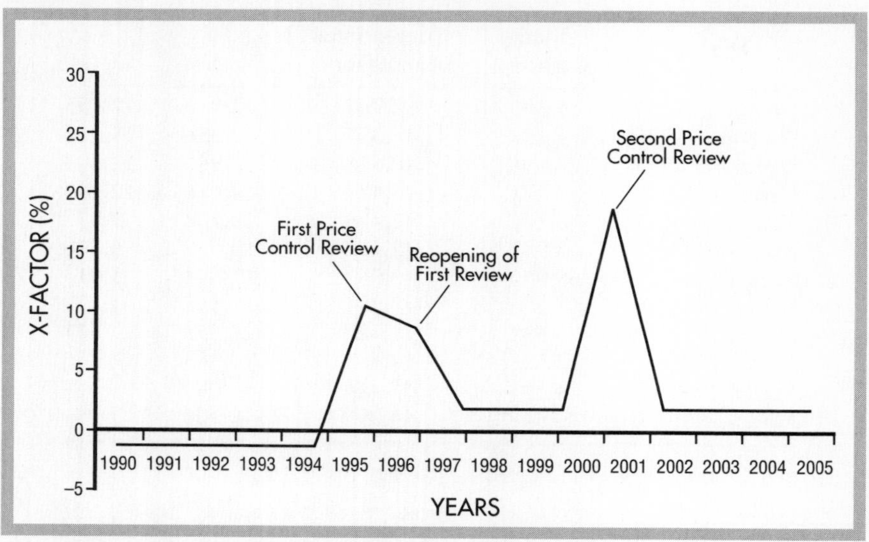

Note: A negative X means that prices are allowed to rise. A positive X implies a reduction. 2000–2001 is a one-time accounting change.

4. The distribution and transmission companies' charges were raised (and only reduced after several years).

RESULTS

New Investment in Generation

The CEGB had proposed to reduce its reliance on British coal by building a fleet of new nuclear power plants. One of the aims of the privatization was to subject this plan to a market test. In this it has been successful. Apart from the one nuclear plant already in construction in 1988, all the incremental investment has been in gas. A considerable amount of old capacity has been closed. Gas-fired generation in the form of CCGT capacity accounts for 85 percent of the 16,900 MW of new generating capacity added to the system between vesting and 1997/1998. One of the side effects has been a large reduction in the industry's emissions of sulfur oxides and carbon dioxide.

TABLE A.2 Generating Plant Capacity in England and Wales, 1989–1999 (MW, Month End)

	Total Capacity	Conventional Steam Stations	Nuclear	CCGT
December 1999	75,305	38,761	12,956	17,195
December 1998	73,153	38,327	12,956	15,418
December 1997	72,696	40,618	12,946	12,803
December 1996	73,271	41,422	12,916	12,462
March 1996	70,126	41,476	12,762	9,377
March 1995	68,937	42,152	12,019	8,540
March 1994	69,050	44,981	11,894	5,613
March 1993	67,506	47,841	11,353	1,279
March 1992	70,535	51,520	11,353	331
March 1991	73,525	54,644	11,353	76
March 1990	74,207	55,416	11,083	—
March 1989	70,348	54,397	8,308	—

Source: U.K. Energy Statistics, DTI (various years).

FIGURE A.4 Main changes to generating plant capacity in England and Wales, 1991–1998.

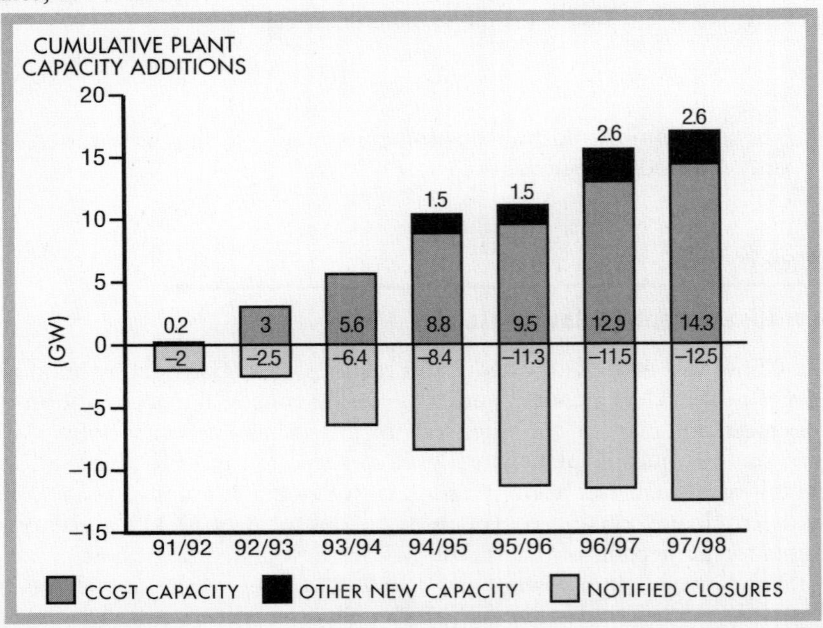

Source: National Grid Company.

Table A.2 shows the development in total electricity plant capacity since privatization. Also included is a breakdown of the capacity available from conventional steam stations, nuclear stations, and CCGT over the same period.

By 1999, CCGTs accounted for 17,000 MW or 23 percent of installed capacity. The additions to generation are offset by 12,500 MW of plant closures and a further 5,500 MW of mothballed plant. Changes in generating plant capacity over the period 1991 to 1998 can be seen in Figure A.4.

Market Power in Generation

Initially three generators controlled over 90 percent of the market; by March 2000 this figure was down to 49 percent, and still falling, boosted by the divestiture of 6,000 MW of coal-fired plant by National Power and PowerGen to Eastern Group in mid-1996 and further divestitures in 1998 to 2000. (See Figure A.5.) However, entrants have mainly built baseload plant, so that while the two big generators (National Power and PowerGen)

FIGURE A.5 Market shares in England and Wales.

YEAR	90/91	95/96	96/97	97/98	Oct 97- Sep 98	Apr 99- Mar 00
National Power	45.5	31.5	24.1	21.0	22.1	17.5
PowerGen	28.4	23.1	21.5	19.6	19.3	15.3
Nuclear Electric (BE & Magnox)	17.5	22.5	17.3	16.7	16.4	15.8
Others	8.7	22.9	37.1	42.7	42.2	51.4

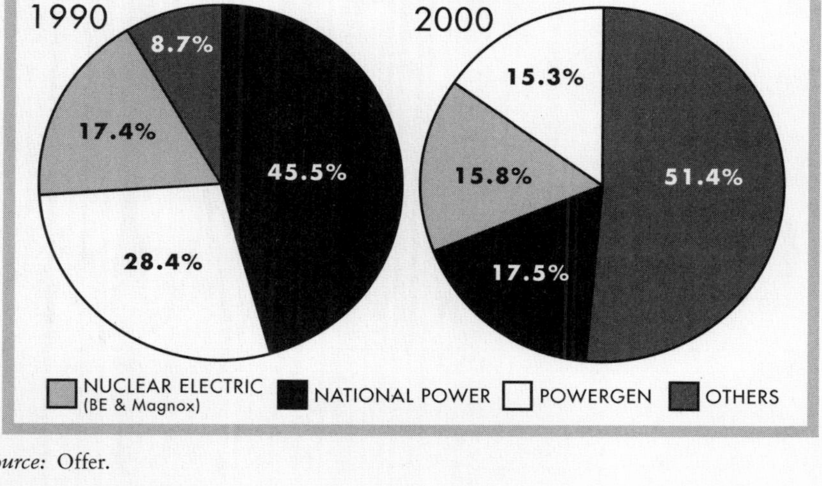

Source: Offer.

account for only 33 percent of the output, they still control most of the *mid merit* plants that set the market price—between them they set prices in 51 percent of the hours. This had led the regulator to propose more stringent rules for control of market power.

The aspect of the market that worries the regulator is that while costs have fallen, prices have not fallen as much. OFGEM claims that all input costs for generators have dropped significantly since privatization. Capital costs for new plants are down 40 percent, spot gas prices down 50 percent, and coal prices down 28 percent. There have also been dramatic improvements in labor productivity. In spite of this, the real decline in Pool prices was "only" 2.1 percent per year between 1993 and 2000.

When the Pool began, there was excess capacity in the industry and spot market prices were low as was to be expected. (Since virtually all sales were covered by vesting contracts, this did not result in a decline in prices to most consumers at the time.) It was expected that market prices would rise over the first few years as old plants was closed, and settle at the long run marginal cost or the "entry price," which was computed to be an annual average of about £29/MWh. The spot market price did indeed rise to an average of £29, and later fell back to £25. (See Figure A.6.) But the target has

FIGURE A.6 Wholesale electricity pool prices, 1990–2000 (pool purchase price, October 1997 prices).

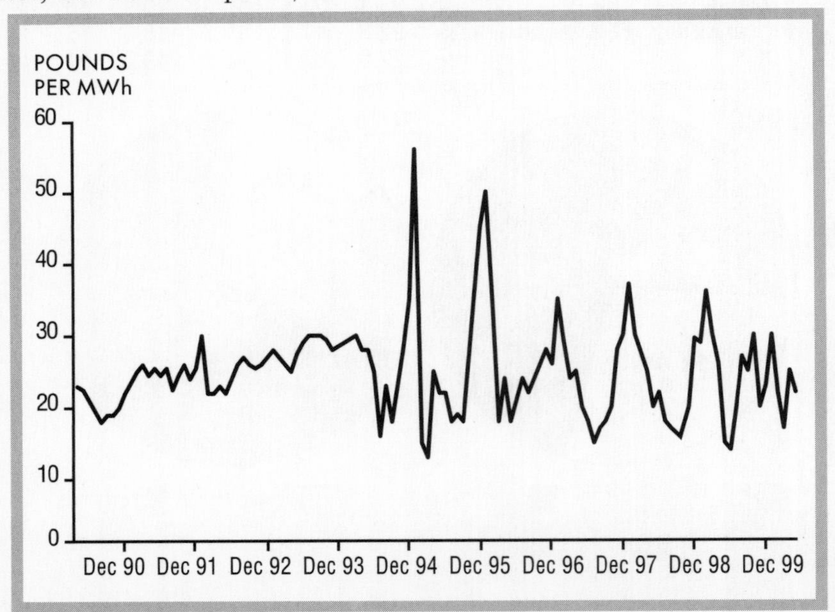

moved—the "entry price" has fallen to £21 or £22. The regulator believes that the excess of £3 to £4/MWh is due to the market power of the generators.

In April 2000, the regulator decided to introduce a "market abuse condition" into the licenses of seven generators (AES, British Energy, Edison Mission Energy, Magnox Electric plc, National Power, PowerGen, and TXU Europe). The condition would have allowed OFGEM to take action if a generator were found to be abusing a position of substantial market power. However, two of the seven generators (AES and British Energy) did not consent to the modification of their licence and their case was sent to the Competition Commission. In June, Edison was investigated under the market abuse condition because its decision to withdraw 500 MW of generating capacity. OFGEM calculated that Edison's action had raised Pool prices by 10 percent for nearly 60 days. In July, Edison agreed to restore the plant to the system. Even so, on December 11, the Competition Commission decided not to permit a market abuse licence condition to be included in the licences of the two companies. As a consequence, OFGEM will have to withdraw the market abuse licence condition from the licences of the generators who had previously accepted it.

Retail Electricity Prices

Overall, since vesting in 1990, delivered electricity prices have declined in real terms for all sectors, as shown in Figure A.7. Households faced the smallest decrease, 20 percent in real terms between 1990 and 1999, while small industrial customers received the largest reductions, 34 percent in real terms between 1990 and 1999. However, note that in 1989, the year before privatization, prices for large and medium industrial consumers were significantly reduced (by 7 to 8 percent), while those for small industrial users (and residential consumers) were increased.[1]

Customer Switching

In 1990, customers with maximum demand greater than 1 MW could choose their supplier. During the first year of competition, more than 25 percent switched from the RECs' default service to another supplier. As of 1998, more than 60 percent of the largest customers had switched. From April 1994, the right to choose a supplier was extended to sites with a

[1] Industrial prices are for Great Britain which includes Scotland. Industrial categories are defined as *Large:* greater than 8.8 TWh per year; *Medium:* between 0.8 TWh and 8.8 TWh per year; *Small:* less than 0.8 TWh per year. Domestic prices are for England and Wales and are based an annual consumption of 3,300 kWh, including VAT. Prices are in constant 2000 values (using the GDP-deflator).

FIGURE A.7 Average annual final electricity prices, 1988–2000.

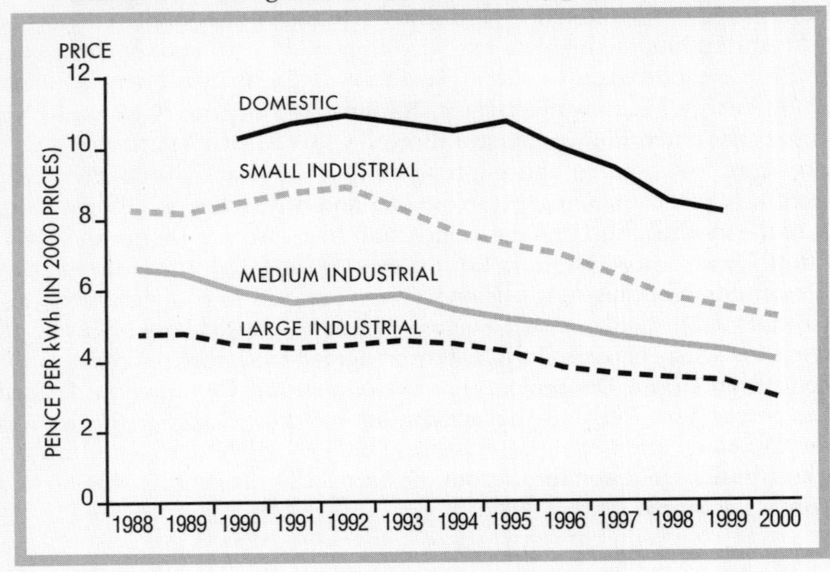

maximum demand of between 100 kW and 1 MW. By June 1999, all 24 million customers were able to choose their supplier. What is apparent from the switch rates (refer to Figure 3.6) is that as time goes on, more customers switch, and that the smaller customers are following the same pattern as the larger, but somewhat fewer are switching.

Metering Problems

Problems emerged in 1994 with the metering necessary to extend choice to smaller customers. Only 3,000 of the 9,000 sites registering for retail competition had the necessary meters installed in time. The remaining sites either did not have a time-of-use meter or the necessary communications links installed; in the short term, they have had to rely on load profiling in place of time-of-use meter readings. The total cost of introducing retail access for this group of customers was £24 million, rather than the expected £10 million.

The introduction of retail competition for smaller customers was delayed for 6 months to one year since the RECs did not have the necessary software and settlement systems in place. Rather than allowing all customers to begin switching suppliers on the same date, the process was phased in over a nine month period; even then, the costs of implementing the scheme has been estimated at over £800 million.

Quality of Service

With the introduction of competition came a new method of quality assurance—direct payment to customers for failing to meet service standards. Overall standards of performance have improved, with fewer payments made for failing to meet standards. More dramatic is the drop in the number of domestic disconnections, from 54,691 in 1992 to 383 in 1998. The RECs achieved this massive reduction by installing pre-payment meters, using modern "smart" technology, so that nonpaying customers effectively disconnected themselves. In addition, customer complaints and payments for missed appointments are down by 80 percent over the same time period.

CHANGES IN THE ENGLAND AND WALES POOL—NETA

In 1997 to 1998 the Pool was reviewed and recommendations made for significant changes. As described in Chapter 7, a new system called NETA subsequently replaced the Pool. These changes were planned for implementation by April 2000 but were not implemented until March 2001. (The original Pool was designed and put in place in about one year.)

The new system has been designed to permit generators and customers to schedule physical flows on the network, and although participants are able to make up shortfalls by paying for imbalances, *the aim was to make the imbalance market unappealing, so that participants are forced to contract. There is no transparent spot price, but there are two half-hourly imbalance prices, for buying and for selling.* These prices are set using an averaging of bids and offers (not at the marginal price, as in the Pool), and although there is no prohibition on making use of imbalances, the idea is that this system forces more traders into short-term bilateral contracts.

There are other more minor changes, but this is the central one. Interestingly, there was no proposal for locational energy prices, even though this had been introduced in most of the markets that were started after the United Kingdom.

The main complaint of the regulator, that triggered the changes, was that the Pool encouraged the abuse of market power (more often called "oligopoly power" in this context). Under the Pool, according to the regulator, all electricity had to be "sold on the spot market" which the large generators could influence; whereas, it was said, a system of physical contracting would remove the influence of the Pool price and reduce market power. In fact, under the Pool, forward contracts, written as Contracts for Differences, always covered what was reported to be 80 percent of the market, and had the same economic effect of restricting market power as any other forward contracts.[2]

There is no doubt that despite the complexity of the old Pool, the new system is even more complex, if only because the participants have to notify NGC of all their contracts, and because of the complex structure of half-hourly offers and bids. The old system was criticized for the complexity of its daily offers, but they simply reflected generator cost conditions. Under NETA, traders must submit up to 10 "bid-offer pairs" for deviations from the "final physical notification" that they submit 3.5 hours in advance. Each "bid-offer pair" specifies the quantity of the deviation (in MW), a price for making the deviation at NGC's request, and a different price for reversing this trade. The delays testify to the difficulties in arranging for secure information transfers between traders and the new market.

However, there seems to be some confusion about the intent. OFGEM was convinced that a real-time process of competing for short-term contracts on a pay-as-bid basis would *in itself* reduce oligopoly power, as compared to a single daily auction that named market-clearing prices.[3] No one presented analytical evidence for or against this proposition during the early discussion of NETA. However, during a Competition Commission procedure, OFGEM agreed that NETA would not remove the potential to exert market power. The first months of operation of NETA show buy prices that are much higher than market energy prices and sell prices that are near zero or even negative much of the time; the average difference between buy and sell prices was in the $50 to 70/MWh range. But this itself puts

[2] The U.K. Pool used gross settlement and contracts for differences—see the explanation of net and gross settlement in Part One. This is analytically exactly equivalent to using contracts for delivery and net settlement, as for example in PJM. However there was always a confusion that somehow everything in the old Pool was sold at spot prices, which was never true. Power passing over the grid was accounted for and settled by NGC at spot prices, and then 80 percent was immediately offset by the contracts, so that only 20 percent actually settled at spot prices. This is the main reason we propose net settlement—gross settlement is too confusing, if even the U.K. regulator is confused by it.

[3] It is easy to show that the *existence* of contracts does reduce the market power of those with contracts. And, in fact, most of the power in the United Kingdom has always been contracted in advance. However, OFGEM's argument was that the *process* of making short-term contracts for dispatch would limit oligopoly power.

more risks on small generators and forces them to consolidate to internalize their risks—increasing market power.

Since portfolio generators and large retailers (or large retailing divisions of distribution companies) are able to diversify away much of their risks of imbalances; *a dual cash out price artificially encourages large market participants at the expense of small participants.* In the early days of NETA, small companies closed down their windmills, because the penalties made continued operation uneconomic. Investment in combined heat and power plant has stalled, because the value of spilled power is so low, and the British Government is conducting a review of generation powered by renewable fuels, to see whether a special subsidy scheme is required. The owners of such plant have also submitted a proposed reform to NETA that would replace the current dual price system for imbalances with a single imbalance price—but only for renewable generators and other favored technologies.

The effect, particularly on the renewables sector, of having to buy really expensive replacement power when the wind does not blow or the sun does not shine, has led the old regulator, Stephen Littlechild, who supported the NETA changes, to suggest that perhaps single, market based, imbalance price would, after all be a good idea.[4] But for all the complicated software, the removal of the transparent spot price, and its replacement with two artificial imbalance prices was the only real change that was made in introducing NETA. What then was the point of NETA?

[4] Stephen Littlechild, *The Beesley Lectures on Regulation Series XI,* London England, October 9, 2001.

APPENDIX B

National Grid Company (U.K.)

The U.K.'s National Grid Company (NGC) is a possible model for a Transco type of operation that is recommended in the text—it is a private, regulated, profit-making entity that combines ISO functions with transmission ownership, regulated by OFGEM, the U.K. regulator of the gas and electricity industries.

Allocation of Main Functions

NGC, part of the National Grid Group (NGG), is responsible for system operation, transmission, and system planning for all of England and Wales (a single control area spanning about 60,000 MW).

The New Electricity Trading Arrangements (NETA) replaced the U.K. electricity Pool in March 2001. Under NETA, all licensed electricity companies must sign up to the Balancing and Settlement Code (BSC); other parties may choose to do so. The BSC sets out the rules for the balancing mechanism and the imbalance settlement process. The BSC is managed by a subsidiary of NGC called ELEXON.

NGC's three businesses (with separate accounts for regulatory purposes) are transmission, ancillary services, and interconnectors. The group also has telecoms interests. NGG established a telecoms subsidiary, Energis Communications Limited (Energis), in 1993. Energis builds and owns an optical fibre network and holds a public telecommunications operator licence. NGG floated Energis in 1997 and now owns 33 percent of the company.

NGG also has international interests in energy and telecoms. It has ongoing operations in Argentina, Brazil, Chile, the United States, and Zambia. It is currently involved in projects in Australia and India, as well as several interconnector projects around the United Kingdom.

Ownership

NGC is a stock exchange listed company. However, the Secretary of State for Trade and Industry holds a Special Share. Certain matters, notably alteration of the articles of association of the company, require the permission of the holder of the Special Share. In other words the U.K. government has a veto on certain matters.

DEGREE OF UNBUNDLING OF THE TRANSMISSION FUNCTION

NGC is completely separated from generation and distribution. Initially, NGC was owned by the Distcos and also owned some peaking generation plants, but these ties were broken by divestitures. NGC undertakes some trading, insofar as it is permitted to buy power in advance of balancing.

There is regulatory accounting separation between NGC's transmission business and its ancillary services and interconnector businesses.

Energis and other group companies are separate in legal and accounting terms from the transmission function, and have, in some cases, partial ownership separation.

REGULATION

NGC is regulated by the Office for Gas and Electricity Markets (OFGEM). Regulatory control is exercised through NGC's transmission licence, which specifies the prices it may charge. (In the United Kingdom, the company-specific "licence" is the regulatory mechanism. A licence review is the equivalent of a U.S. rate case.)

NGC's Regulatory Regime

NGC's roles as Transmission Asset Owner (TAO) and System Operator (SO) are subject to separate incentive schemes.

OFGEM sets a revenue cap for NGC's TAO role. Included within this cap are revenues from Transmission Network Use of System (TNUoS) charges and prevesting connection charges (those that were established before privatization). Post-vesting connection charges are restricted (under a license condition) to cost plus a reasonable rate of return, but since connection is a contestable activity these charges are not subject to formal rate of return regulation. Included within NGC's revenue formula is a year-on-year correction mechanism for the level of new connections.

OFGEM sets sliding scale incentive schemes for NGC's SO role, covering both external SO costs (e.g., all system and energy balancing costs) and internal SO costs (e.g., system management costs and central NGC overheads allocated to the SO).

NGC's Transmission Network Use of System (TNUoS) Charges

TNUoS charges are paid by generators and suppliers. NGC sets the charges using an Investment Cost Related Pricing (ICRP) transport model, that calculates the marginal cost of investment in the transmission system required as a consequence of an increase in demand or generation.

Charges vary across the 15 generation zones and 12 demand zones. Generators pay a £/kW charge on their Registered Capacity (i.e., the level of capacity for which NGC provides a connection). Retailers pay a £/kW charge on the three half hours (the triad) of maximum demand during each year.

GOVERNANCE

Operation of the balancing and settlement code (BSC) is overseen by the BSC Panel. The Panel has twelve members, composed of an independent Chairman (appointed by OFGEM); two independent members (appointed by the Chairman); two consumer representatives (appointed by Energywatch, the industry's consumer watchdog); five industry members (appointed by Trading Parties); a sixth industry member (appointed by the Chairman); and an appointee from NGC. A representative of Distribution System Operators, a representative from OFGEM, and the Chief Executive of ELEXON also attend the Panel.

The Panel has established Panel Committees to support it in exercising its various duties and delegates a number of its functions to such bodies. The Panel has established four Committees:

1. Imbalance Settlement Group;
2. Supplier Volume Allocation Group;
3. Performance Assurance Board; and
4. Trading Disputes Committee.

Any party can submit a proposed modification of the BSC to the panel. Modifications adopted by the panel must also be approved by OFGEM.

APPEAL MECHANISMS

Transmission Regulation: NGC can appeal to the Competition Commission over licence amendments imposed by OFGEM. OFGEM is expected to follow the Competition Commission's recommendations, although it is not obliged to do so. The Competition Commission has the power to block all or part of the licence amendments proposed by OFGEM, following a referral to the Commission, if the Commission believes that the proposed amendments exceed what is necessary.[1]

OFGEM is also subject to judicial review, which means that interested parties can take OFGEM to court for acting either unreasonably or outside the powers given to it under the legislation. In effect, it is only possible to prove that OFGEM acted unreasonably if it failed to follow the correct procedures in arriving at a decision, as the court will not query OFGEM's judgment. Such appeals are rare, but not unknown. The decisions of the BSC panel are also subject to judicial review.

SYSTEM EXPANSION

NGC has a licensed monopoly over the operation, planning, expansion, and maintenance of the 400 kV and 275 kV transmission system. Under the terms of its licence, NGC has a duty to operate an efficient and economical transmission system. It is obliged to publish an annual *Seven Year Statement*, which sets out its plans for the expansion of the system for each of the seven years from the time of the statement. The statement includes information on generation and demand, the characteristics of the existing and planned transmission system and its expected performance. It identifies opportunities for connection of further generation and demand and for increased power flows, and examines how system performance might change under different scenarios. It is not clear how NGC justifies expansion to OFGEM; in the last 10 years there has not been a lot of expansion.

The Connection Use of System Code sets out the terms and conditions of connection to and use of NGC's transmission system. Any parties requiring access to the transmission system are required to be party to the code.

---

[1] Utilities Act 2000, section 39/Electricity Act 1989, section 14A(1) 8(3).

APPENDIX C

The California Crisis 2000–2001

The California crisis was all over the U.S. newspapers for months and had a chilling effect on deregulation and reform in the rest of the United States and in many other places in the world. It began in June of 2000, was characterized by:

- Extraordinarily high spot market prices, raising total energy costs to up to 10 times historical levels;
- Shortages and subsequent rolling blackouts within the state; and
- The bankruptcy of the state's biggest utility, Pacific Gas and Electric (the utility, not the parent company), the Power Exchange, and a number of small power producers who were not paid for their power.

HIGH PRICES

High prices occurred mainly during peak hours in the summer of 2000. After November, prices were high in all hours. The total cost of energy (including energy and ancillary services) increased from an average of \$33/MWh in both 1998 and 1999 to \$317/MWh in December 2000. (See Figure C.1.) Wholesale power costs rose from \$7 billion in 1999 to \$27 billion in 2000.

SHORTAGES AND ROLLING BLACKOUTS

There were five episodes of rolling blackouts ordered by the ISO because of capacity shortages during 2001.[1] These occurred on January 17 and 18 in

[1] There had been a brief blackout in San Francisco in June 2000, due to a heat wave and local plant outages; but the outages in 2000 were different.

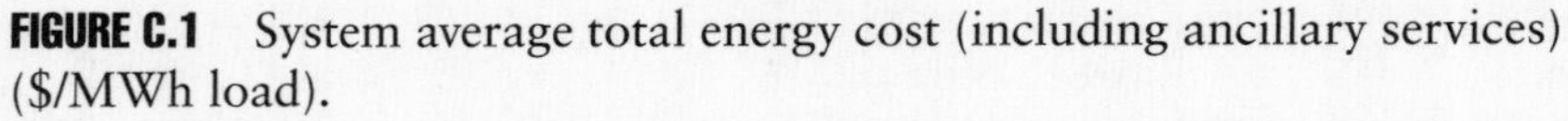

FIGURE C.1 System average total energy cost (including ancillary services) ($/MWh load).

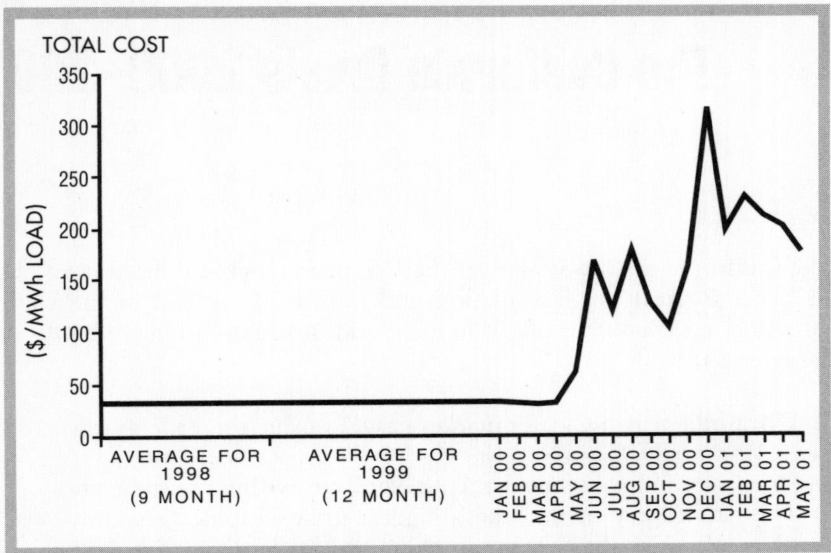

Source: California ISO, Market Analysis Report for June 2001, July 20, 2001, p. 10.

Northern California and on March 19 and 20 statewide. The last event occurred on May 7 and was due to an early hot spell during a time when many plants were down for maintenance. These episodes don't give a true picture of the kinds of problems the ISO was confronting. A more revealing indicator of shortages is the number of ISO-declared emergencies. These increased dramatically. In 1999, the ISO declared only *one* stage 2 emergency (reserves below 5 percent) and no stage 3 emergencies (reserves below 1.5 percent). In 2001, 55 stage 2 emergencies and 36 stage 3 emergencies had been called in the first 3½ months alone.

The crisis hit the national headlines for several months over the winter of 2000–2001 and it effectively stopped electricity restructuring in the U.S. dead in its tracks. The state of California appropriated some $12.5 billion in bond issues to relieve the crisis; the utilities incurred some $14 billion in debt.[2] With the summer approaching, all projections were that the crisis would get worse. Eventually three "solutions" (coupled with mild summer temperatures) brought the crisis to a halt: The state took over the purchasing of power on

---

[2] Developments in California's Power Crisis, *San Francisco Chronicle,* March 30, 2001.

behalf of the utilities and signed roughly $43 billion[3] in contracts, extending up to 20 years, at very high prices; FERC capped wholesale electricity prices for all sellers in the western interconnection; and California customer prices were raised by an average of 19 percent for residential customers.[4] Suddenly, the press announced in July 2001 that the crisis was over.

What is clear is that, while many people have been wise after the event, no one publicly predicted this set of outcomes,[5] even as late as early 2000. The system worked for over two years before the crisis and might have made it through to 2002 when the transitional arrangements would have ended (San Diego actually collected its stranded costs by 2000, and had moved beyond the transition arrangements, see below). In fact, but for bad luck in the form of a hot summer throughout the west, and a sudden increase in gas prices, California might well have emerged as a shining example of success. As it is, the spotlight focused on California has shown up a whole raft of problems in design that are potentially present in many other systems, except that they have not been subjected to the intense pressures that the California system faced in 2000–2001.

THE BACKGROUND

The California Public Utilities Commission (CPUC) initiated the process to restructure California's electricity industry in the early 1990s, after the passage of EPAct, by issuing a vision of a competitive market that went through several drafts, and was finally issued in April 1994 in what has become known as the Blue Book Proposal. The proposal said clearly that the utilities would be required to open their wires for retail access (customer choice) and that they would be allowed to collect their stranded costs.

The three state investor-owned utilities, Pacific Gas and Electric (PG&E), Southern California Edison (SCE), and San Diego Gas and Electric (SDG&E) quickly latched onto the restructuring process as a way to

[3] Mike Taugher, "California Regulators Issue Proposal to Deal with Power Crisis," *Contra Costa Times,* July 19, 2001.

[4] For some of the heaviest residential users the rate increased by as much as 71 percent and for other low-income ratepayers it did not increase at all. Industrial customers faced rate increases of about 50 percent, while commercial and agricultural ratepayers faced something less, *New York Times,* May 16, 2001.

[5] William Hogan predicted often, loudly, and correctly, that the trading arrangements would not survive. What no one predicted was that the interaction of the state law and the markets would lead to such enormous prices, the credit crunch, and the rolling blackouts.

recoup what they estimated were enormous stranded cost liabilities. But they became convinced that without legislation, the CPUC could not bind future Commissions to deliver on the stranded costs. The state legislature ultimately got involved and passed a law, AB 1890, in August 1996, putting into place several politically motivated provisions that did not necessarily fit into the envisioned market design. These transitional provisions would run out when the utilities had recouped their stranded costs, but no later than March 2002. The new system went in to operation on April 1, 1998.

We can divide the mistakes in California into two parts: the trading arrangements and the rest of the regulatory arrangements. The trading arrangements were developed separately from the rest of the regulatory arrangements, and were in FERC's jurisdiction. The rest of the deregulation and restructuring arrangements were in the jurisdiction of the state PUC, ultimately taken over by the legislature. The fact that the two sets of arrangements did not mesh well, particularly in the area of demand response, is part of the structural problem in the United States—regulatory jurisdiction is divided and no single agency is responsible for overseeing the whole change.

TRADING ARRANGEMENTS

The trading arrangements put in place in California are probably the worst set of arrangements that have ever been seriously suggested. The broad picture is this: The restructuring joined the transmission systems of the three investor owned utilities (PG&E, SCE, and SDG&E) into one control area and placed their operation under an independent system operator. A new control center was built in Folsom to house the new independent system operator (the CAISO—California ISO). (This is the good part of the story—the CAISO was the first of the ISOs proposed in the United States; what might have been a major battle over the need to separate and consolidate the system operators was quite easily solved.)

However, the municipal utilities of California, of which there are many, and some very large, did not join in the ISO. Therefore, significant portions of the transmission grid remained under the control of operators other than the California ISO.

Despite the agreement that there should be an ISO, there was a battle royal over the role of the ISO: should it or should it not run the spot market? The reader will be aware, from Part One, that this book is firmly for a system operator-run spot market and the integrated form of trading arrangements. Initially, Southern California Edison and San Diego Gas and Electric submitted a proposal to FERC for trading arrangements such as the ones proposed in this book; but the whole process of developing the trading arrangements became a political horse-trade—building the bridge by voting where the girders should go. Eventually a separate entity, the California Power Exchange (PX) was created, separate from the ISO, as one of many scheduling coordinators to run spot markets, and the CPUC required the utilities to trade through the PX, thus ensuring that it was first among equals in spot energy trading. The separation of the ISO and PX was opposed by a number of parties, on the grounds that there were serious coordination issues between the two entities, and duplication of functions. (Same energy, same time, same place should come to the same price—but of course it did not, creating immense inefficiency, and many opportunities for arbitrage.) However, those supporting separation (in particular Enron) won the day. The separation would ultimately prove to be a mistake—the PX suspended its daily markets in January 2001, and declared bankruptcy in March 2001.

The California trading arrangements—the specific rules governing scheduling, pricing of imbalances, congestion management, and management of reserves—were parodies of an efficient market. There was no provision for demand response, directly or by proxy, in setting the prices. The energy needed for congestion management, imbalances, and ancillary services were all priced in separate markets—in five separate markets for ancillary services alone. The contract was considered the fundamental unit of trade, so that if congestion was expected, a whole contract (rather than simply an export-constrained generator) was cut; the ISO was not permitted to make trades to resolve congestion at the scheduling stage, even where traders had given sufficient instructions of their intent. Customers had to scurry round to find a new supplier, using the new multiple "scheduling coordinators." (In real time the ISO was permitted to take more appropriate steps.)

One could be forgiven for thinking these rules were designed to give arbitrageurs the ability to make money off an inefficient market. There have been dozens of changes to the rules, and many interventions by the FERC to cap prices, and ultimately a thorough redesign of the trading rules was mandated. But the awful rules themselves were only bit players in the 2000–2001 crisis, with one exception: *If demand response had been built into the trading arrangements there would never have been a crisis*—the market prices could never have risen so high. And furthermore, the trading arrangements themselves were so inefficient that they could conceivably have been responsible for the 300 MW that the system was short when the first rolling blackouts had to be called.

THE REST OF THE REGULATORY ARRANGEMENTS

Certain elements of the legislation that was passed would also prove to be disastrous. The whole situation was highly politicized, especially with respect to stranded cost recovery. The utilities accepted some truly risky conditions in the deal that they made with the legislature—provisions that would later come back to haunt them.

Retail access was approved, but most retail prices were simultaneously reduced by 10 percent and frozen for a period not to extend beyond March 2002. This appears to have been a "quid pro quo" for the customers because they were paying for the stranded costs. Stranded costs were to be recovered by freezing prices to consumers.[6] All revenues that exceeded costs but fell below the frozen price level (called *head-room*) were applied to stranded cost recovery. This sort of method only works if wholesale energy prices remain low, and the retail prices exceed the wholesale prices. The wholesale prices did not remain low in California, thus the utilities found themselves in a position of purchasing wholesale energy at prices much above the fixed retail rate that they were allowed to charge their customers. The press has simplified this into the formulaic "supply was deregulated but retail prices were not"—and this is right, but there are three separate aspects of why it was such bad policy.

No Pass Through of Underlying Cost Increases

The utilities took the entire risk of increases in input prices—gas and other fuel prices and environmental permits. Their final prices to consumers were literally frozen. This type of regulatory mistake had not been made since 1974 when Con Edison nearly went bankrupt for a similar reason—delayed pass through of fuel costs to customers—in the oil price crisis of that year. After that virtually all state commissions permitted price adjustments for changes in fuel cost.

No Hedge against the Spot Price

At the same time that retail customers were insulated from market prices, the utilities were required to serve those customers choosing to stay with their traditional provider by purchasing all energy needs from the newly created PX on a daily basis. This would almost have worked if the utilities had been selling an equal amount of power from their own generating plants into the spot market—they would have had a natural hedge against high prices arising from shortages. If the spot prices had risen they would have bought and sold in the spot market at the same high prices, which would have been a wash.

[6] A top-down approach—see Part Two.

But the utilities were *required to divest about half of their fossil generation* to reduce market power and ultimately divested most of it.[7] More importantly—and an absolutely major mistake—they were *not allowed to enter into bilateral contracts* for the purchase of power. This mistake has not, as far as we know, been made elsewhere in the United States. Most utilities divesting plant have at least medium term contracts with the divested plant as a transition matter; nowhere else has the rule been "no contracting." The California utilities were taking a major risk—they were fully exposed to the volatility of spot markets, and they did not lock in forward energy hedges against gas prices.

No Demand Response

Under the frozen rate provision, retail customers were not exposed to the market price of energy. Most of them did not have metering equipment in place to allow them to respond to the high peak prices, but since they did not even see the *average* spot prices, their "conservation" was voluntary and in response to the exhortation of the governor.

California allowed itself to get into the dreadful position of designing its trading arrangements so as to rely on demand response, and then having customer prices frozen. There was no transition: It went cold turkey into a world of no installed reserve equipment, no demand response, no intelligent price caps, no anything. Because of the frozen retail prices, the demand bidding that had at one point been part of the design of the trading arrangements lost all meaning. This meant that the deregulated wholesale prices were virtually uncontrolled.

THE CALIFORNIA CRISIS: 2000–2001

The initial shock was perhaps due to bad luck. The failure to right the boat during the storm was due to bad design of the restructuring:

- There were numerous factors that pushed prices up—gas prices, environmental permit prices, increased demand, low hydro supply, lack of building;
- This in turn led to credit problems for the utilities because of the mismatch between the prices the utilities were paying and those they were allowed to charge;

[7] SCE kept its share of two coal plants (Four Corners and Mohave) and PG&E of one gas plant (Humbolt Bay). The utilities retained their nuclear and hydro assets, and their QF contracts.

- The credit problems themselves led to the bankruptcy of some small suppliers and withholding of supply by others; and
- This led to worse shortages, almost daily emergency conditions, and the five rolling blackouts.

Any one of the three things named above as faults in the regulatory design could have prevented these consequences:

- Pass through of cost increases;
- Adequate hedging of wholesale prices; and
- Demand response.

The High Prices in the Summer of 2000 Due to a Supply Shortage

At the outset of the crisis, high prices were caused by the classical situation of elevated demand and insufficient supply. No new significant generation had been built in California for over 10 years, increasing the state's *dependence on energy imports.*[8] It was hot all across the West in the summer of 2000, reducing available imports. To compensate, gas-fired generators within the state increased their output. These generators operate under strict environmental laws in southern California and are required to hold NO_X permits to operate. The increased output drove up the demand for NO_X permits *causing their prices to skyrocket.* The increased input costs found their way into electricity spot prices.

The high prices could have been managed, but for the flaws in the restructuring design. Most significant was the lack of demand response. There was no way for consumers to respond to prices by reducing consumption—and even a small reduction would have relieved the pressure on supply and brought prices in the market down. But the legislature had frozen retail rates, insulating consumers from the higher prices. Half of the market—the demand side—was not working.

The utility distribution companies were required to purchase almost all their energy needs in the short-term markets (day-ahead, hour-ahead, and real time). They were not allowed to hedge energy purchases. What could have been a minor or marginal problem—purchases of a small amount of

[8] The California Energy Commission has taken a lot of flak for having bottled up 6,000 MW of proposed new capacity in a slow approvals process, which was unbottled quite fast in 2001. But since there had been excess capacity for some years, the would-be generators had not been pressing very hard to speed the process along. The crisis took everyone by surprise.

spot energy at high prices, with the rest at contract prices—turned into a major problem—all purchases at high prices. The companies were buying energy at multiples of what they could charge their consumers. They began accumulating debt at a rapid rate.

High Prices during the Winter of 2001 Exacerbated by a Credit Crisis

The supply demand balance was expected to improve as the peak demand summer months concluded and the moderate fall and winter demand arrived. Unfortunately, this was not to be. In November and December, natural gas prices surged nationwide, but reached incredible levels in southern California, from $2/mmbtu in July to over $60/mmbtu briefly in some locations in early December, and an average of about $17/mmbtu for the months of November and December. (See Figure C.2.)

Hydro resources were much less abundant than expected. Generators that had been running full out over the summer had to come down for maintenance. There was a continued lack of supply and continued increases

FIGURE C.2 California border average gas spot prices, October 2000–January 2001.

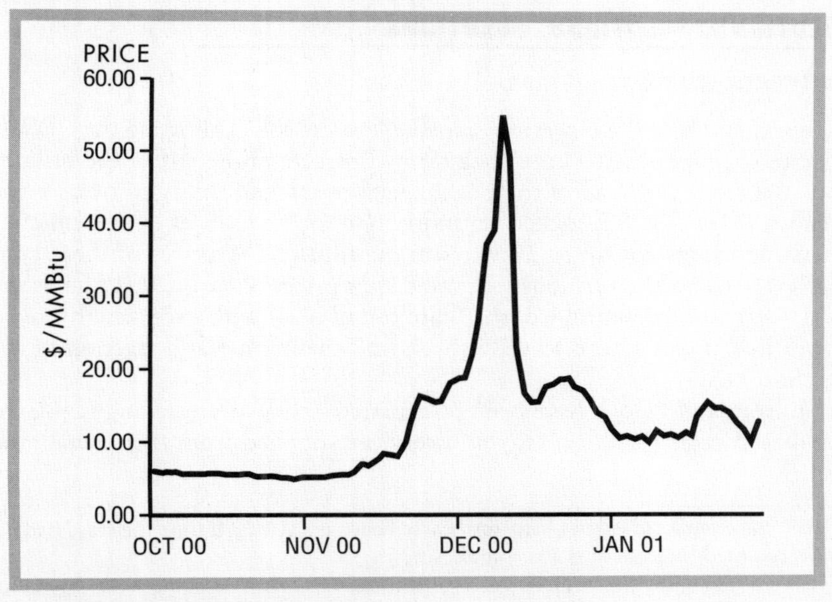

Source: Bloomberg Market Survey.

of input prices. By the end of the year, PG&E and Southern California Edison had accumulated over $12 billion in debt. The possibility of bankruptcy was now real. Suppliers withdrew energy to protect against nonpayment. This caused further deterioration in the supply demand balance and forced the federal government to intervene and require generators to supply energy to California.[9] Nonetheless, the ISO instituted rolling blackouts for two days in January and March increasing concern of more lengthy and widespread more blackouts in the spring and summer months.

Market Power?

A debate has raged in the academic literature over whether the high prices were due to market power. It is clear that there was no mechanism in the market for prices to be controlled by demand response. It is clear that many plants were withdrawn from service in the fall of 2000 and into 2001; the owners say they had been overstressed during the summer and were being repaired. It is clear that the owners had reason to worry about getting paid. What is at issue is whether there were deliberate withholdings *in order to* raise prices; or whether the withholding was a commercial reaction to potential bankruptcies of buyers, which had the undoubted *effect* of raising prices.

SOLUTIONS, SOLUTIONS, SOLUTIONS

Contracts with Generators

In February 2001, the Governor signed a law (ABX1 1) allowing the CDWR (a state agency) to enter into long-term contracts on behalf of the utilities and appointed the head of the Los Angeles municipal utility to oversee the process.[10] The CDWR locked up more than $43 billion in long-term contracts for energy for up to 20 years in the future. The prices of these contracts reflected the enormously elevated spot prices of early 2001 and as the mild 2001 summer unfolded, the State found itself with excess high priced power that it was forced to sell it back into the market at a fraction of the purchase costs.

Edison and PG&E have been reregulated—they are receiving regulated cost-based rates for the energy and services supplied from their remaining

[9] This requirement stayed in place until early February at which time the state had already assumed the role of power purchaser.

[10] ABX1 1 also authorized the issuance of revenue bonds for the long-term financing of these purchases.

generating plants. However, they still have the debt issue outstanding. As of August 2001, all California parties were involved in refund hearings at FERC scheduled to conclude sometime in March 2002. The State of California was demanding $8.9 billion in refunds from generators.

The five big independent generators in California: Duke, Dynegy, Reliant, Mirant, and AES/Williams, all ranked in Standard and Poors' top 10 for 2000. Their earnings for 2000 in some cases quadrupled. The Governor has accused these companies of gouging the state. The California ISO has calculated that the pure overcharges of these companies and PowerEx (the trading arm of BC Hydro), amounted to billions for the period May 2000 through February 2001:[11]

- British Columbia Power Exchange Corp.: $439 million.
- Duke Energy Corp.: $804 million.
- Dynegy Inc.: $530 million.
- Reliant Energy Inc.: $750 million.
- Mirant Corp. (formerly Southern Co.): $753 million.
- Williams Cos.: $860 million.

Demand Response

California still has not moved to hourly metering; but even the step of raising average prices caused a demand reduction. In the summer 2000 San Diego consumers clearly responded to the increase in prices by reducing demand—even though the increases were averaged and delayed in the monthly billing cycle.[12] In response to state-wide price increases and financial incentives to conserve put in place by Governor Davis, it has been estimated that in June 2001 alone, reductions in demand saved 5,570 MW which more than made up for the 5,000 predicted shortfall.[13]

Supply Response

The process for approvals was streamlined and five new plants came on line as of October 11, 2001, including:

---

[11] Leopold Jason, "Much California Power Price Gouging Beyond FERC's Reach," *Dow Jones,* Monday, June 25, 2001.

[12] San Diego Gas and Electric had completed its recovery of stranded costs and was thus allowed to start passing through wholesale prices to retail consumers. Due to the public outrage caused by the price increases, this policy was immediately reversed and caps were again placed on retail rates.

[13] "Energy Picture Brightens," *Orange County Register,* August 14, 2001.

- Kern County, 320 MW, Texas Global Gas & Power, 27 June 2001;
- Sutter County, 540 MW, Calpine, 2 July 2001; and
- Contra Costa County, 555 MW, Calpine, 9 July 2001.[14]

Price Caps

On June 19 2001, FERC instituted a price cap in the wholesale market to include all hours, and all sellers (including FERC nonjurisdictional municipalities and cooperatives) in California and ten additional western states. The caps remain in effect until September 2002. The cap is set at the marginal cost of the most expensive unit running inside California during a stage one emergency and is reset for each new stage one emergency. During nonemergency hours the cap is set at 85 percent of the stage one cap. Sellers (excluding marketers) may charge more than the cap, but those charges are subject to review and refund.

This set of actions appeared to have brought the crisis to a halt. The massive price increases due to the very expensive contracts signed by the state at the height of the panic ensure the generators very large profits, so they will never need to withhold again for fear of the utilities' credit situation. New plants are coming on. The customers are conserving (with up to 70 percent price increases, of course they are). The wholesale price caps are probably irrelevant, with contracts, new plants, and conservation relieving the supply-demand balance. Of all these fixes, we venture to suggest, the demand response is the most important, and it could have been there from the beginning. If hourly metering had enabled the customers of California to conserve at peak times, the spot prices would never have gotten so high, they would not have been locked in with long-term contracts in the middle of a panic, and things would have been back to normal in July of 2000, not 2001, at way less than the price the customers are currently paying.

CALIFORNIA TIMELINE

1978	PURPA requires IOUs to purchase power from QFs at "avoided cost." Introduces the first "free-market" principles to the electricity industry.
1992	National Energy Policy Act removes the barriers to IOU ownership in IPPs, and gives FERC the authority to order utilities to provide open access to their transmission system.

[14] California Energy Commission.

1994	CPUC issues "Blue Book" with plans to deregulate California's electricity industry.
1995	FERC allows the IOUs to *not* buy almost 1400 MW of QF power that was to be acquired through an auction.
August 1996	California Legislature approves AB 1890, restructuring the electricity industry.
March 31, 1998	Deregulation begins in California.
July 1999	SDG&E finishes its transition period under AB 1890, lifts the rate freeze for its customers, and begins passing on wholesale power costs. San Diego becomes the first area in California to complete the transition to retail deregulation.
May 2000	Wholesale electricity prices begin an unprecedented rise. PG&E and SCE begin to accumulate debts as the summer progresses.
June 2000	San Diego ratepayers start seeing dramatically higher bills.
June 14, 2000	Rolling blackouts in the Bay Area due to a heat wave and local power plant outages.
September 6, 2000	Legislature re-enacts retail rate freeze in San Diego for residential and small commercial customers retroactive to June 1, 2000.
December 5, 2000	ISO ask Californians to delay turning on holiday lights; Governor abides.
December 7, 2000	ISO issues first State III emergency.
December 13, 2000	Energy Secretary Richardson orders generating companies to sell power to PG&E and SCE.
December 15, 2000	FERC Order: ■ Eliminates requirement that utilities buy and sell through the PX, to allow for long-term bilateral contracts. ■ Implements a $150/MWh soft price cap. ■ Requires a new, independent ISO Board by January 29, 2001.
January 3, 2001	Legislature convenes an Extraordinary Session on energy.
January 4, 2001	CPUC approves emergency 90-day 1¢/kWh rate increase for PG&E and SCE customers.
January 17, 2001	PG&E and SCE's credit ratings downgraded to junk bond status. ISO orders rolling blackouts in California for the first time. Governor Davis declares a State of Emergency and orders the DWR to start buying power on behalf of PG&E and SCE.
January 18, 2001	Second day of rolling blackouts in Northern California.
January 19, 2001	Governor Davis signs legislation authorizing the DWR to purchase power for PG&E and SCE for a period of 12 days.
January 24, 2001	ISO Board replaced with a new, independent, 5-member Governor-appointed Board.

(continued)

January 30, 2001	PX suspends trading in its markets.
February 1, 2001	Governor signs AB1X, authorizing the DWR to enter into long-term contracts to buy and sell electricity, and authorizing the CPUC to suspend retail competition. The State begins to spend about $2 million per hour, and plans to issue $10 billion in bonds—the largest municipal bond issue ever. (Later increased to an estimate of over $20 billion).
February 16, 2001	Governor Davis announces plans to buy the utilities' transmission grids to restore them to financial viability.
March 1, 2001	ISO alleges that generators overcharged customers by $550 million in December and January, and requests FERC to refund the costs.
March 5, 2001	DWR secures the first round of long-term contracts.
March 9, 2001	FERC orders 13 generators to justify the high prices charged in January during State 3 alerts, or else refund $69 million for the month of January.
March 16, 2001	FERC orders generators to justify their prices or else refund $55 million for the month of February. Energy Secretary Abraham says the administration will not implement price caps.
March 19–20, 2001	First statewide rolling blackouts due in part to ~3,000 MW of QFs shutting down because they were not being paid by the utilities.
March 22, 2001	ISO estimates that power generators manipulated the market and overcharged $6.3 billion between May 2000 and February 2001.
March 27, 2001	CPUC Order: ■ Increases rates for PG&E and SCE customers by 3¢/kWh (for customers who use over 130 percent of baseline), and makes permanent the 1¢/kWh increase approved in January. ■ Requires the utilities to pay QFs within 15 days of power delivery (at a price indexed to the price of natural gas at the California-Oregon border), and to start paying DWR for its power purchases. ■ Requires accounting changes to effectively extend the transition period and rate control. Governor Davis calls the CPUC action premature.
April 3, 2001	CPUC orders an investigation into the money transfers between the utilities and their parent companies.
April 5, 2001	Legislature passes bills to increase conservation and efficiency programs, and caps the rates for all San Diego customers at 6.5¢/kWh. Gov. Davis addresses the State on the energy crisis by television and radio.

April 6, 2001	PG&E files for Chapter 11 bankruptcy, after awarding 6,000 employees more than $50 million in bonuses. Moody's Investors Service puts California on a negative credit watch.
April 9, 2001	SCE and Gov. Davis announce a deal for the sale of SCE's transmission lines to the State.
May 14, 2001	FERC announces regulatory actions to increase reliable energy supplies in California and other Western States. It streamlines regulatory procedures for wholesale power sales and for certification of natural gas projects. It also urges all hydroelectric licensees to assess the potential for increased generation capacity at their respective facilities.
May 16, 2001	Governor Davis signs SB 6X creating the "California Consumer Power and Conservation Financing Authority," which will have broad powers to construct, own, and operate electric power facilities, and finance energy conservation projects.
May 22, 2001	Governor Davis signs an emergency bill (SB 28X) to shorten the times for reviewing an application for a new power plant, and repowering (i.e., upgrading) an existing power plant.
May 28, 2001	U.S. Department of Energy Secretary Abraham orders the Western Area Power Administration (WAPA), a 15 State power marketing arm of the U.S. DOE, to complete planning and to seek outside financing for increasing California's transmission capacity. This action aims at reducing power transmission bottlenecks on Path 15, a high-voltage power line connecting northern and southern California.
June 2001	The PUC set a tiered rate structure for the 3-cent per kilowatt-hour increase adopted March 27, 2001. Residential customers of Pacific Gas & Electric and Southern California Edison will see rate increases of between zero and 80 percent, depending on their usage. Those using below 130 percent of the baseline amount and exempted or low-income consumers will see no increase. The tiered structure gradually increases the percentage of increase to 80 percent for customers who use over 300 percent of the baseline amount. Commercial rates will increase between 34 and 45 percent, industrial rates will increase an average of 50 percent, and agricultural rates will increase 15 to 20 percent. The new rates will begin June 1, 2001.
June 19, 2001	The Federal Energy Regulatory Commission extends and broadens its price mitigation and market monitoring plan (issued in April 2001). The price mitigation plan will now apply to spot market sales 24 hours a day, 7 days a week, in all 11 States in the Western Systems Coordinating Council. The formula to calculate the market clearing price is

(continued)

	changed to reflect the marginal cost of replacing gas used for generation, based on gas prices reported in Gas Daily for three spot market prices in California, adjust operating and maintenance expense upward, and eliminate the emission costs from the calculation (emission costs will be invoiced to the CA ISO and recovered separately). The price mitigation efforts will now apply to all spot market prices. When operating reserves are above 7 percent, the prices may not exceed 85 percent of the highest hourly price that was in effect during the most recent Stage 1 reserve deficiency period called by the ISO.
July 23, 2001	More than a dozen private investors turn in proposals for the expansion of Path 15 (the main bottleneck in California's electricity transmission grid).
July 24, 2001	San Diego is now aiming to create a regional public power. A bill is making its way through the Legislature—and being fought at every turn by the power industry—to make San Diego County one of the largest municipal utility districts in the nation.
July 27, 2001	Southern California Edison does not plan to file for voluntary bankruptcy protection as long as the Legislature is making progress on a plan that would restore it to creditworthiness.
August 6, 2001	Pacific Gas & Electric files a suit against the Public Utilities Commission on Monday in U.S. District Court in San Francisco and asked again a federal judge to allow it to pass on more than $9 billion in energy costs to ratepayers to recover money the utility spent buying power at prices far higher than it could legally charge customers.
August 8, 2001	U.S. West power prices fall as much as 3 percent because hydroelectric generation increases and temperatures are below normal. The average price of electricity in California from January to June almost quadruples from the same time in 2000.
August 13, 2001	California Gov. Gray Davis appoints his top energy adviser, S. David Freeman, as chair of the new California Consumer Power and Conservation Financing Authority. The Authority, with the right to issue as much as $5 billion in bonds, is charged with ensuring Californians have affordable power, boosting electricity reserves, and promoting conservation.
August 14, 2001	Federal Energy Regulatory Commission Judge Bruce Birchman is set to issue a recommendation to the commissioners by November 5 on how much, if any, California is owed in refunds for power it bought from October through mid-June.

REFERENCES: SELECT PAPERS RELATING TO THE CALIFORNIA CRISIS

Borenstein, Severin, James Bushnell, and Frank Wolak. *Diagnosing Market Power in California's Deregulated Wholesale Electricity Market,* POWER Working Paper PWP-067, University of California Energy Institute, August 2000.

Borenstein, Severin, James Bushnell, Christopher R. Knittel, and Catherine Wolfram. *Learning and Market Efficiency: Evidence from the Opening of California's Electricity Markets.* Mimeo November 7, 2000.

Borenstein, Severin, James Bushnell, Christopher Knittel, and Catherine Wolfram. *Trading Inefficiencies in California's Electricity Markets,* The University of California Energy Institute's Program on Workable Energy Regulation (POWER) PWP-086, October 2001.

Braithwait, Steven and Ahmad Faruqui. *Demand Response—The Forgotten Solution to California's Energy Crisis,* February 1, 2001.

Bushnell, James B. and Frank A. Wolak. *Regulation and the Leverage of Local MarketPower in the California Electricity Market,* POWER Working Paper PWP-070, University of California Energy Institute, September 1999.

California Energy Commission, "Market Clearing Prices Under Alternative Resource Scenarios 2000–2010," March 2000.

California Independent System Operator, "Annual Report on Market Issues and Performance," June 1999 ("CAISO Annual Report").

California Independent System Operator, "Report on Redesign of California Real-Time Energy and Ancillary Services Markets," Market Surveillance Committee, Frank A. Wolak, Chairman, October 18, 1999 ("CAISO MSC Report, October 1999").

California Independent System Operator, *Market Analysis Report,* December 20, 2000.

California Independent System Operator, "United States of America Before the Federal Energy Regulatory Commission." FERC Docket No. EL00-95-012, Comments of the California ISO Corporation on Staff's Recommendation on Prospective Market Monitoring and Mitigation for the California Wholesale Electric Power Market, circa March 2001.

California Independent System Operator, "Summer Assessment 2001," March 2001.

California Power Exchange Corporation Compliance Unit. "Price Movements in California Power Exchange Markets: Analysis of Price Activity: May–September 2000," *Power Exchange,* November 1, 2000.

Chandley, John D., Scott M. Harvey, and William W. Hogan. *Electricity Market Reform in California,* Working Paper, Harvard Electricity Policy Group, November 22, 2000.

Chao, Hung-Po and Robert Wilson. "Multi-Dimensional Procurement Auctions for Power Reserves: Incentive-Compatible Evaluation and Settlement Rules." Electric Power Research Institute, Stanford University, October 7, 1999.

Cook, Greg. "Memo to ISO Board of Governors Regarding Management Response to MSC June Price Spikes Opinion," California Independent System Operator, September 28, 2000.

Department of Market Analysis. California Independent System Operator, California ISO: Report on Real Time Supply Costs Above Single Price Auction Threshold: December 8, 2000–January 31, 2001, Final Draft, February 28, 2001.

European Federation of Energy Traders. "California Experience—Why the Market Failed." April 12, 2001.

Falk, Jonathan. "Empirical Assessment of Market Power in Electric Bid-Price Pools," *The Electricity Journal,* December 2000, pp. 2–4.

Falk, Jonathan. "How California Should Respond to High Electricity Prices." National Economic Research Associates, Energy Regulation Brief, September 2000.

FERC, Order on Rehearing of Monitoring and Mitigation Plan for the California Wholesale Electricity Markets, Establishing West-Wide Mitigation and Establishing Settlement Conference. FERC Docket EL00-95-031, June 19, 2001.

Harvey, Scott M. and William W. Hogan. *On the Exercise of Market Power Through Strategic Withholding in California,* Working Paper, AEI Brookings, April 24, 2001.

Harvey, Scott M. and William W. Hogan. *California Electricity Prices and Forward Market Hedging,* Working Paper, Harvard Electricity Policy Group, October 17, 2000.

Harvey, Scott and William W. Hogan. *Issues in the Analysis of Market Power in California,* Working Paper, Harvard Electricity Policy Group, October 27, 2000.

Hildebrandt, Eric. *Market Analysis Report,* Presentation to ISO Board. California Independent System Operator, Department of Market Analysis, November 30, 2000.

Hildebrandt, Eric. "Further Analysis of the Exercise and Cost Impacts of Market Power in California's Wholesale Energy Market." California Independent System Operator, Department of Market Analysis, March 2001.

Hildebrandt, Eric. "Potential Overpayments Due to Market Power in California's Wholesale Energy Market, May 2000–2001," California Independent System Operator, Department of Market Analysis, June 19, 2001.

Hogan, William W. *California Electricity Market: Policy Meltdown.* Presentation for KSG Faculty Seminar, February 14, 2001.

Hogan, William. *Designing Market Institutions for Electric Network Systems: Reforming the Reforms in New Zealand and the U.S.* Presentation at UTILICON Conference, Auckland, New Zealand, March 12, 2001.

Hogan, William. "The New Texas Electric Market and How It Compares to the California Market," Electricity Market Institutions, Texas and the California Meltdown Conference, The University of Texas at Austin, May 2, 2001.

Hogan, William. "Electricity Market Restructuring: Reforms of Reforms," 20th Annual Conference, Center for Research in Regulated Industries, Rutgers University, May 25, 2001.

Hogan, William. "Statement Before the Committee on Governmental Affairs," United States Senate, June 13, 2001.

Hogan, William. "Statement Before the Subcommittee on Energy Policy," Natural Resources and Regulatory Affairs United States House of Representatives, August 2, 2001.

Hogan, William. "The California Meltdown," Forum Article, *Harvard Magazine,* September–October 2001.

Joskow, Paul. "Deregulation and Regulatory Reform in the U.S. Electric Power Sector," in *Deregulation of Network Industries: The Next Steps* (S. Peltzman and Clifford Winston, Eds.), Washington, DC: Brookings Press, 2000.

Joskow, Paul. California's Electricity Market Meltdown, *New York Times,* Editorial, January 13, 2001.

Joskow, Paul and Edward Kahn. *A Quantitative Analysis of Pricing Behavior in California's Wholesale Electricity Market During Summer 2000,* Working Paper, MIT Department of Economics, January 15, 2001.

Joskow, Paul, Alfred Kahn, Severin Borenstein, et al. Letter to Bush on deep concern over the failure of the Federal Energy Regulatory Commission (FERC) to act effectively to enforce the provisions of the Federal Power Act that require it to set just and reasonable wholesale prices for electricity in California, May 2001.

Joskow, Paul. "Statement Before the Committee on Governmental Affairs," United States Senate, June 13, 2001.

Joskow, Paul and Edward Kahn. *Identifying the Exercise of Market Power: Refining the Estimates,* Working Paper, MIT Department of Economics, July 5, 2001.

Joskow, Paul. *California's Electricity Crisis,* Working Paper, MIT Department of Economics, July 21, 2001.

Kahn, Alfred E., Peter C. Cramton, Robert H. Porter, and Richard D. Tabors. *Pricing in the California Power Exchange Electricity Market: Should California Switch from Uniform Pricing to Pay-as-Bid Pricing?* Working Paper, MIT Department of Economics, January 23, 2001.

Kahn, Alfred E., Peter C. Cramton, Robert H. Porter, and Richard D. Tabors. "Uniform Pricing or Pay-as-Bid Pricing: A Dilemma for California and Beyond," *The Electricity Journal,* 14(6), 2001.

Kahn, Michael and Loretta Lynch. "CPUC Report to the Honorable Governor Gray Davis on California," *Electricity Conditions,* August 2, 2000.

Mount, T. D., W. D. Schulze, R. J. Thomas, and R. D. Zimmerman. *Testing the Performance of Uniform Price and Discriminative Auctions,* Revised Draft, June 6, 2001.

Puller, Steven. *Pricing and Firm Conduct in California's Deregulated Electricity Market,* POWER Working Paper PWP-067, University of California Energy Institute, November 2000.

Quan, Nguyen T. and Robert J. Michaels. Games or Opportunities? Bidding in the California Markets, *Electricity Journal,* 14(1), January 2001.

Sheffrin, Anjali. "Empirical Evidence of Strategic Bidding in California ISO Real Time Market," Independent System Operator, *Market Monitoring Unit,* March 21, 2001.

Sheffrin Anjali. *Preparing the California Market for Summer 2001,* EUCI Conference on Western Power Markets, May 2001.

Stoft, Steven. "Soft Price Caps and Underscheduling Penalties: How Would the FERC Plan Affect California Electricity Markets?" University of California, Program of Workable Energy Regulation, November 2000.

United States General Accounting Office (GAO). "Results of Studies Assessing High Electricity Prices in California," June 2001.

Wolak, Frank, Robert Nordhaus, and Carl Shapiro (MSC of the California ISO). "Preliminary Report on the Operation of the Ancillary Services Markets of the California Independent System Operator (ISO)." Preliminary Report in Compliance with the July 17, 1998 Order in Docket No. ER98-2843 et al., Market Surveillance Committee, California Independent System Operator, August 19, 1998.

Wolak, Frank A. (Chairman Market Surveillance Committee [MSC] of the California Independent System Operator [ISO]). *Proposed Market Monitoring and Mitigation Plan for California Electricity Market,* Market Surveillance Committee Presented to the California Independent System Operator Board, February 6, 2001.

APPENDIX D

The U.S. Gas Experience—A Comparison with Electricity

In this appendix, we look at the U.S. gas industry, which was deregulated quite successfully in the 1980s and 1990s—the production markets were deregulated, and open access was established for the pipelines, although retail access for small customers has not been instituted in many states to this day. The gas example has been cited in many different ways, but not in the most obvious way, which is that one solution to the problems of the electric industry would begin by asserting federal jurisdiction over production and transmission of electricity.

Gas also started as a local, vertically integrated industry, with "town gas" produced in smelly local plants. Then came "natural gas" from gas fields in Pennsylvania and Louisiana, Oklahoma, and Texas, and long distance pipelines owned mainly by the big producers. Local gas distribution companies stopped making their own gas and bought by contract from the pipelines. This arguably made the sales wholesale sales.

A series of cases in the 1950s and 1960s—most notably, a U.S. Supreme Court decision in 1954 called the Phillips decision,[1] which gave the FPC authority to control wellhead natural gas prices for sale in interstate commerce—gave FERC (then the Federal Power Commission or FPC) jurisdiction, under the Natural Gas Act of 1938, over the prices for sales from the field to the interstate pipelines, and over the price of interstate transport of natural gas. (Gas that never left Texas was never regulated—providing a comparison price for "free-market gas" from the fields as compared to the regulated price.) At first the FPC regulated prices well by well on a cost of service basis, then later it regulated prices on an area basis. When shortages

[1] *Phillips Petroleum Company v. Wisconsin*, 347 U.S. 672 (1954).

occurred (which many people attribute to the regulation of the field prices at below the cost of exploration and development) it developed a *two-tier* pricing system in 1978. This led to really high prices.

Then in 1984, FERC decided there was no need to regulate production—production was sufficiently competitive that prices could be left to market forces—and it deregulated the industry in a series of Orders—No. 380 (1984), No. 436 (1985), No. 500 (1987), and No. 636 (1992). In stages, these Orders unbundled gas from transport, and deregulated gas production, while keeping the pipelines regulated; and then effectively deregulated secondary markets for transport by permitting pipeline contracts to be traded, in Order No. 636. Order No. 436 required pipelines to provide "open access" to their lines.

There are eight things to note here with respect to electricity, four where the gas example might offer some solutions for electricity, and four where there are clear differences. But one major lesson from the gas example is that *if FERC comes up with a solution, it actually has (or certainly had in gas) enormous powers to put it into practice.* The courts have backed the Orders, and Congress eventually legislated to tidy up the whole process.

1. FERC (the FPC as it then was) asserted *jurisdiction* over field prices of natural gas sold in interstate commerce; it regulated and was then able to deregulate. Intrastate prices were deregulated. Congress imposed a comprehensive scheme of price controls at the wellhead in 1978, which worked very badly, leading to eventual deregulation in 1985.
2. Pipelines were *unbundled* from production, into separate companies. But gas companies were not vertically integrated into distribution and retailing to small customers, so the restructuring required was much less than would be required in electricity.
3. FERC determined that *production markets could be competitive* and deregulated them.
4. FERC did not order *retail access* in gas and neither did the states, except for the largest customers. The distribution companies purchased from the producers for small consumers. Only much later did the states open up choice to small consumers.
5. *Consumer response:* This was not an issue in gas. Gas customers do respond to price, but do not need complex metering to do so, since the price varies mostly by season or by year. In electricity wholesale prices vary hourly. Consumer response in electricity requires much more complex metering.
6. One place the example of gas is frequently, and erroneously, cited as an example to follow is in the *trading arrangements*. But electric transmission is a complex network, not a pipeline, and the pipeline model does not work here.

7. *Transmission:* The arrangements in gas are exemplary, but hard to emulate in electricity.
8. *Locational prices for energy:* These have developed in gas to the same end-point that we recommend in electricity, although the method of getting there will be different in electricity.

JURISDICTION

FERC asserted *jurisdiction* over sales of gas to interstate pipelines. It was effectively regulating the price of production in the fields. Having regulated it, it had the power to deregulate it. This is despite the 1938 statutory language, which appears not to extend FERC jurisdiction to "the production and gathering of natural gas." The U.S. Supreme Court reviewed the FPC's regulatory regime in 1954, and concluded that the Commission must regulate gas sales at the wellhead.

FERC has never attempted to assert jurisdiction over all electricity generation and transmission, although it is clearly in interstate commerce. FERC has jurisdiction over wholesale sales, not retail sales. With gas, the *production* had moved, making the sales to the pipelines clearly wholesale sales. With electricity, it is the *transmission* that has expanded, which, while it puts electricity clearly in interstate commerce, does not change the nature of retail sales. For a vertically integrated utility whose generation is in the same operating company (which it is in almost all cases), there is no wholesale sale—all sales to the captive customers are retail. Electric generation is therefore effectively regulated by the states.

In the few cases where electricity companies have production in a separate subsidiary from distribution (NEES in the 1970s, Illinois Power and some others more recently), *the sales from the generating arm to the distribution arm become wholesale sales,* and FERC has jurisdiction over the price of sales from the generating company to the distribution company. In these cases, the state PUCs are required to pass the federally determined prices though to customers under the so-called *filed rate doctrine.*

If all generation were put into subsidiaries, FERC would acquire jurisdiction to regulate sales to the distribution companies, and also the authority to deregulate when the markets were competitive. But FERC has no obvious authority to require this.

UNBUNDLING OF PRODUCTION AND TRANSPORT

Gas pipelines were *unbundled* from production, into separate companies. Gas companies were not vertically integrated from production through distribution, so the restructuring effort required was smaller than it would be in electricity. Pipelines and producers are permitted to remain as affiliates, but FERC ordered the unbundling in Order No. 636.

In gas the pipelines were permitted to remain affiliates of the production companies but the nature of pipeline contracts, and the rules FERC introduced to allow these contracts to be tradable, removed much of the conflict between production and transport in gas (see below). FERC has no obvious authority to require electric companies to restructure in this way.

The additional problem in electricity is the fragmented nature of the transmission ownership, so that it also needs to be consolidated into regions. No one appears to have the authority to require this either.

PRODUCTION COMPETITION

The regulation of the price of wellhead gas had produced serious distortions. Rather than improve regulation, FERC determined that *gas production markets could be competitive* and deregulated them. Production in gas was deemed to be competitive (and has proven to be). But this is unlikely to be the case in electricity without some serious changes. There is a difference between observing that markets have the characteristics to be competitive, and requiring the changes to achieve these characteristics.

FERC simply deregulated (stopped setting regulated prices for) gas production when it thought the markets were sufficiently competitive. In electricity the markets would not be competitive without some major changes, such as demand responsiveness, more competitors and perhaps incremental transmission. The natural markets are bigger than a single state and no one has the authority to order all the changes necessary for wholesale competition to work in multistate areas.

RETAIL ACCESS

FERC did not order *retail access* in gas and neither did the states, except for the largest customers, who were already purchasing from the pipelines directly. The distribution companies purchased from the pipelines for small consumers. Only much later did the states open up choice to small consumers.

The electric industry might consider the gas example, and phase retail access over a long enough period that the infrastructure of settlement is in place to work well. There was a very limited amount of retail access in gas until recently, and it was not part of the deregulation. The major purchasers were the local distribution companies, and only the large customers had the ability to purchase direct from the pipelines. This is changing gradually by order of the states.

TRADING ARRANGEMENTS

One place the example of gas is frequently, and erroneously, cited is the *trading arrangements*. The gas market traders naturally thought of the local spot markets that operate in gas, and thought they could be translated to the electric industry, keeping the ISO out of the spot markets. But electric transmission is a complex network, not a pipeline, and the pipeline model does not work here.

The trading arrangements for electricity have to be much more complex because of the network characteristics and the need for operational control. Electricity travels at 22 million times the speed of gas, and gas can be stored. Pipelines go from the gas field to the distribution company and it is unambiguous where the gas went. The gas pipelines were built specifically to get all the gas from the fields to the customers. There is little or no congestion—the pipelines are large enough, and anyway gas can be stored.

Short-term trading arrangements for gas are irrelevant to electricity.

TRANSMISSION BUSINESS MODEL

Although the gas trading arrangements are irrelevant to electricity, the arrangements for pricing and expanding pipelines are exemplary in gas, and rudimentary in electric. Most of the effort in gas regulation has been to price the pipeline service and introduce tradable contacts, issues that electricity has yet to get to.

Gas pipeline contract prices are regulated at cost of service by the FERC, but the contracts are renewable virtually in perpetuity, and the capacity can be sublet on competitive terms, so the pipeline market is very competitive. The holders of the contracts essentially have a property right in the pipeline capacity. They pay the (minimal) usage fees for pumping. To restrain any potential monopolization of the pipeline by holders of contracts, the pipeline company can sell the space if the contract holder is not using it. There are no such tradable contracts in electricity.

However, the pipeline contracts are not complicated—they are for point-to-point transport on a given system—a contract path. In electricity, the transmission system is a grid; the laws of physics mean that electricity does not flow over the designated contract path. (In other words, point-to-point in gas is equivalent to contract path, whereas in electric, point-to-point is different from contract path.) What this means is that the physical laws governing flows of electricity on the grid make it extremely difficult to create a system of tradable property rights in transmission capacity that can facilitate trading power. Rights are both difficult to define and to enforce.

Users pay for gas pipeline expansion, and get tradable contracts to use the expansion they paid for; but what they paid for and what they use is unambiguous in gas, and is not in electricity. The regulated pipeline prices are based on the incremental cost of the expansion, and are not rolled into an existing rate base. By contrast, except in unusual circumstances the beneficiaries of an electric transmission expansion are difficult to identify, since expansion benefits all the users to some extent by increasing the capacity of the network.

One solution in electricity is financial transmission rights (FTRs) that have been described as "gas pipeline contracts at the speed of light." These are described in Part One.

Consumer Response

Consumer response was not an issue in gas. Gas customers do respond to price, but do not need complex metering to do so, since the price varies mostly by season or by year. In electricity wholesale prices vary hourly. Consumer response requires much more complex metering. As we have said earlier, this is an area where there are still many unsolved problems in electricity.

Locational Prices in Gas

The arrangements for secondary markets in gas pipeline capacity in Order Nos. 636 and 637 have resulted in simultaneous determination of competitive prices for transportation and product all over the United States. When we described locational electricity prices in the first part of this book, we replicated a map, produced by FERC, of April 1996 gas spot price differences between various points in the United States (Figure D.1). FERC described the importance of this information:[2]

> *What is important about this information is the fact that the developing natural gas market produced a situation where the differences in prices*

[2] State of the Markets 2000, Measuring Performance in Energy Market Regulation, Federal Energy Regulatory Commission, March 2000.

FIGURE D.1 Implicit price of transportation from South Louisiana to New York, average weekly new York spot price minus average weekly South Louisiana spot price.

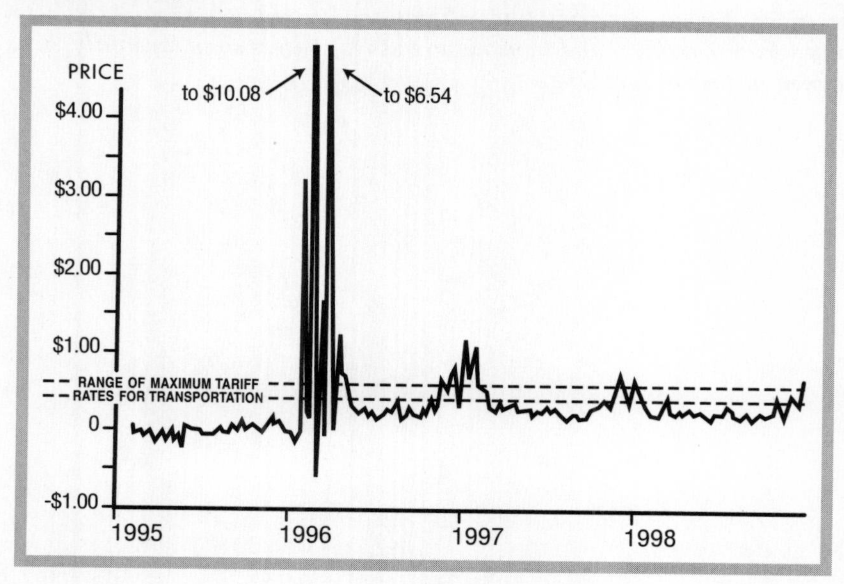

between *distant regions created powerful market forces which dramatically changed the implicit price of gas transportation. This is shown in the graph above, which presents the implicit price of transportation service between New York and South Louisiana, compared to the regulated rate caps placed on that service.*

The inter-regional spot price disparity created a value for transportation which was at times far in excess of what pipeline companies could charge for the service. This implicit value of pipeline transportation, which could not be recovered through flat rates, led to efforts by market participants to recover this value through other means. Through the use of informed analysis such as this, the Commission determined the need for a major rulemaking on short-term natural gas transportation services, culminating in the issuance of Order No. 637.

This form of locational pricing, determining the transport prices and the product prices simultaneously, is exactly what we suggest should be accomplished in electricity. In gas it is accomplished by trading transmission contracts and gas in multiple bilateral negotiations. Because of the speed of light factor, and because there are so many more price points in electricity, waiting for bilateral trading to come to this result simply will not work in electricity. *We suggest using traders' bids and a computer program to determine locational prices and transmission usage charges simultaneously, as explained further in Part One.*

APPENDIX E

Building New Generators—When, Where, and How

This appendix describes how decisions were made to build generating plant in the old world of vertical integration, and how those decisions should be made in restructured electricity markets.[1] In summary:

- In the old world, utility planners were required by regulators or governments to build enough generating plant so that all load was almost always met (the rule was one day of partial outage in ten years). They were required to choose the location and type of the required generating plant, and when to build them, so as to minimize total cost.
- Under the new system, the role of markets and an active demand side should ultimately replace the central planning role, and in theory the decision should be very similar (although many issues remain).

In the explanations that follow we assume that costs and demands for electricity are known in advance with certainty (i.e., the decision processes we describe are *deterministic*). In reality, of course, nothing can be predicted with certainty, and the decision process has to take account of this (i.e., be *stochastic*). We describe the deterministic versions because they are easier to describe, and are good enough to make the basic point. The stochastic decision-making processes are extensions of the deterministic ones.

---

[1] Much of this appendix is extracted from Hamish Fraser, "The Importance of an Active Demand Side," *Electricity Journal,* November 2001. Refer also to R. Turvey and D. Anderson, *Electricity Economics: Essays and Case Studies,* The Johns Hopkins University Press, Baltimore, 1977.

CENTRAL PLANNING

When it comes to generation planning in the old world of central planning, the keyword is *quantity.* A system planner decides what quantity of different types of generating capacity to build by working out what it takes to minimize the cost of meeting future demand. This planning is done within large-scale computer programs that calculate what combination of different types of plants is the least cost option and where to site plants.

The analysis used to determine which types of plants to build model can be illustrated with the following load duration curve (Figure E.1). If load is represented over a year by this curve (sorted by high-load hours to low-load hours)[2] then some plants will run to meet load almost constantly (C = base-load), others will run about half the time (B = mid-load) and others will run only in the highest load hours (A = peakers).

It follows that it may be cheapest to have a combination of generating technologies combining to meet the total load requirements:

- Peaking plants like GT or jet units tend to have low fixed costs, but high running costs; they are the cheapest option if the plant only runs for a few hours, but their average cost would be too high if the plant was run all year (plant type A).
- Base-load plants like large nuclear and coal-fired units tend to have high fixed costs, but low running costs, so they can have the cheapest average cost when they run for much of the year (plant type C).
- Mid-load plants are somewhere in the middle (plant type B). Often these are existing older plants whose "fixed costs" are the costs of keeping them maintained.

It also stands to reason that there might be an hour or two per year when the cost of serving *all* demand would be prohibitive. If, for example, all load is served on the peak hour of the year and the peak hour has ten MW more demand than the second-to-peak hour, then 10 MW of generation might be built to run for only *one* hour per year. Of course, it is quite likely that of all the customers consuming in the peak hour, there are 10 MW worth of "low value-added" ones who wouldn't be terribly inconvenienced if they stopped consuming—but they would need incentives to do so. That is why we emphasized earlier in this book that time-of-use pricing and metering are essential components of reform (and not just for the peak

[2] A load duration curve is the demand of all hours of the year, sorted from highest to lowest.

FIGURE E.1 Load duration curve.

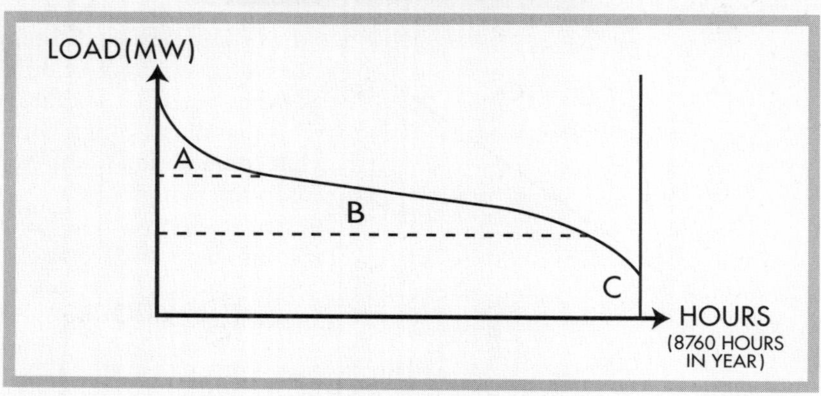

hour, for all hours). But even in the vertically integrated world, where low value-added consumers have no incentive to identify themselves because all prices fixed at regulated levels, it is still probably the case that there is an hour or two when we're better off if *someone* doesn't consume.

To solve the problem of exactly how much of each type of plant to build, and in how many hours to allow an outage, central planners use complicated optimization software. Conceptually though, the solution is simple to find (at least while other factors are held constant). Assume for example that the three competing technologies have fixed costs of F_A, F_B, and F_C, and variable costs of V_A, V_B, and V_C dollars per MWh, respectively,[3] and that you can build these plants in any small increments you want:

Step 1—Start with the decision of how many hours of outage to allow: The most efficient number of hours of outage to allow is a function of the Value of Lost Load (VOLL) and the fixed and variable costs of a peaker. The answer to the question "How many hours of outage should I allow?" is derived from a straightforward cost analysis: Load should be unserved in hours when the cost of serving it would exceed VOLL. Put algebraically, outage makes sense so long as VOLL × (Outage Hours) < F_A + (V_A × (Outage Hours)), and solving this gives us the answer. Visually, this can be represented as the simple cross-over chart in Figure E.2.

Where does VOLL come from? In the vertically integrated world with regulated prices, customers have no reason to reveal their individual

[3] A represents the peaker plant, B represents the mid-load plant, and C represents the base-load plant.

FIGURE E.2 Economic outage hours to allow.

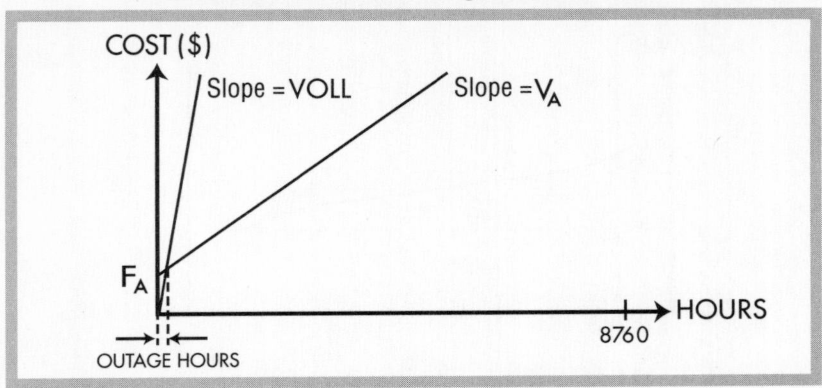

VOLLs, so central planners have to make an estimate. The correct value to estimate is the average value to all consumers, if disconnections will be random, or the marginal value to those who will be cut off, if disconnections will be specified. Its value can be estimated from the value-added in each industry using electricity, and also from other methods.

Step 2—The next question is how much peaking capacity to build: The answer to the question "How many MW of the peaker do I build?" is derived from a straight-forward cost analysis of peakers versus mid-load plants: Peakers are the least cost option so long as $F_A + XV_A < F_B + XV_B$, and solving for X gives us the number of hours that the last peaker built runs. Visually, this can also be represented as the simple cross-over chart in Figure E.3.

If a generator has to run for less than X hours, then the cheapest alternative is a peaker. If it must run for more than X hours, then a mid-load plant is cheaper.

It remains, therefore, to determine how much peaking *capacity* is required. If the marginal peaker runs for X hours, we can extrapolate to the load-duration curve to determine how much load must be met by generating plant that run for less than or equal to X hours, how much load is unserved in peak hours, and thus the necessary MW of peaker capacity. See Figure E.4.

Step 3—The next question is how much mid-load capacity to build: In this case, the answer is derived from a cost analysis of mid-load plants versus base-load ones. Mid-load plants are the least-cost option so long as

FIGURE E.3 Run-time of last peaker built.

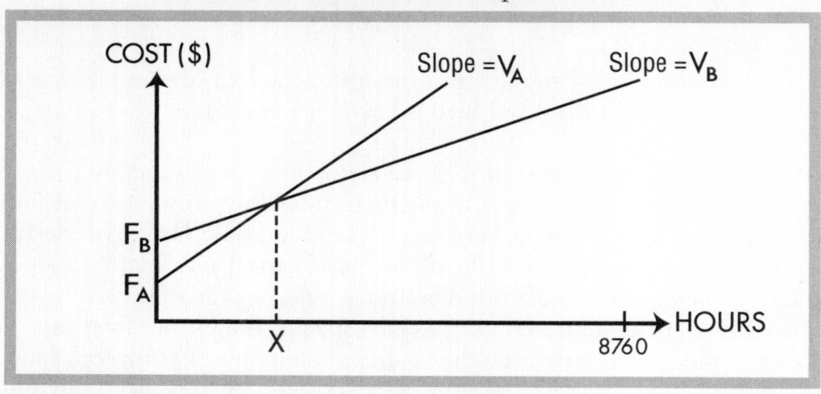

FIGURE E.4 Calculation of required peaking capacity.

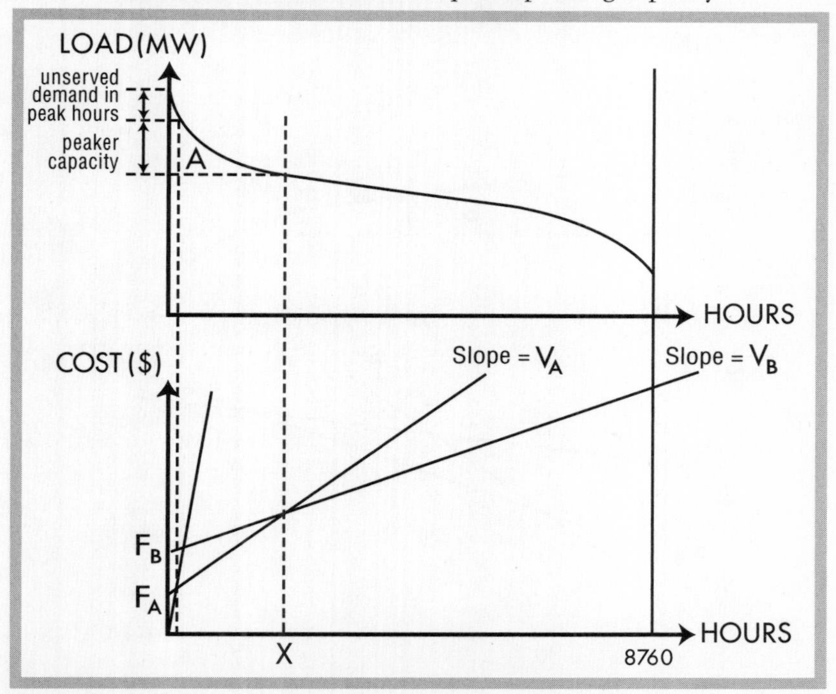

$F_B + YV_B < F_C + YV_C$, where Y is the number of hours that the last mid-load plant built runs. Visually, the cross-over chart looks like the one in Figure E.5.

Following the same process of look-up to the load duration curve, we can see how many MW of mid-load capacity are necessary.

Step 4—The final question is how much base-load capacity to build: Since there are only three types of plants in this illustration, it follows that any capacity not built as peakers or mid-load must be built as base-load. The required and least-cost MW of base-load capacity to build under this old model method of calculation therefore equals peak load minus unserved demand in the peak hour, minus peaking capacity, minus mid-load capacity. (The example in the cross-over charts uses three types of plant, but in general the conceptual framework of this analysis can be applied to any number of different types of plant.)

FIGURE E.5 Calculation of required mid-load capacity.

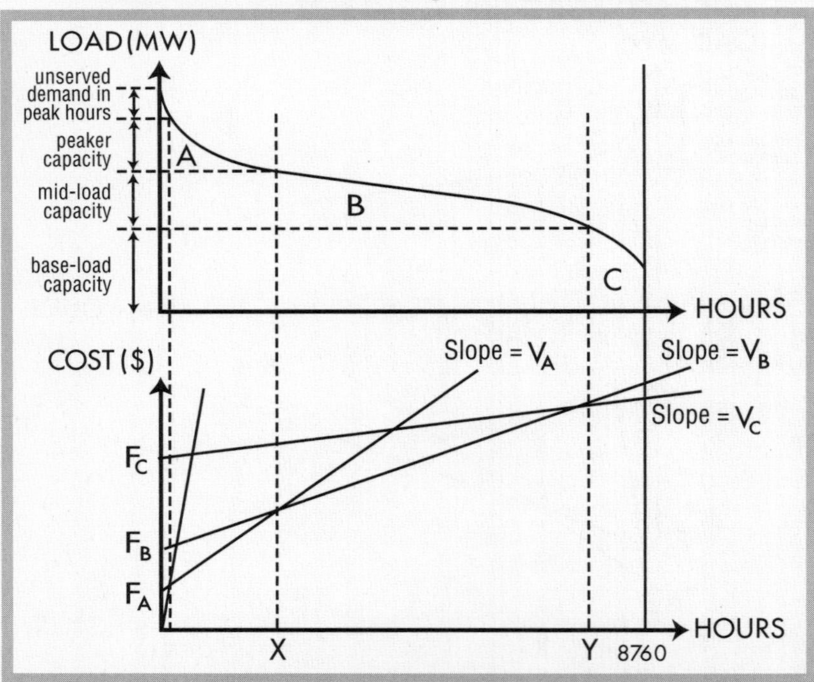

It can be shown that in a system planned this way, if everything turned out as planned and if prices are set at marginal cost, then all generators will recover all their cost. If the charges to customers are set at V_C for the hours when the baseload plant is marginal, at V_B when the mid-level plant is marginal, at V_A when the peaking plant is marginal, and at VOLL when outages occur, *then all the plants will make enough to cover their running costs and their fixed costs.* This theorem has been used for setting electric tariffs in many countries and many states of the United States. If you plan for minimum cost investment and set prices at marginal cost you get an efficient solution in both the short term and the long term. But competitive markets are supposed also to deliver minimum cost investment and marginal cost prices. They should come to much the same solution as a central planner would have done. To see how this works, we now turn to the competitive situation.

COMPETITIVE ELECTRICITY MARKETS

In generation planning under the new (market-based) model of industry organization, the keyword is *price.* Market participants plan generation investments on the basis of their expectation of future energy prices. (Market participants also take into account ancillary services prices and perhaps capacity prices, where capacity markets exist. For simplicity these are ignored in this appendix.) They build new plant when energy prices are high and do not build when prices are low.[4]

Because the market model relies so heavily on price signals, it is very important that the pricing rules are right. Prices should not only signal how much total capacity to build and thus how many hours of unserved energy there will be,[5] but also how much of each type of capacity to build. Prices during peak hours should signal the profitability of peakers up to and no further than the point at which mid-load plants are a more efficient choice. Likewise for base-load plants. Prices should signal that new capacity is

[4] Market participants will make sensitivity (stochastic) analyses of their price forecasts. In particular, they make careful projections of the factors that can alter the future supply/demand balance because when capacity is expected to be tight, prices should be high, and when surplus capacity is expected, prices should be low. But again, we ignore these stochastic analyses in this appendix, for simplicity.

[5] As we have said elsewhere, it is the lack of an active demand side, and the reluctance of politicians and regulators to "let the market decide" how many hours there will be of unserved energy, that has led to the capacity credit obligations and capacity markets in the Northeast United States.

more valuable in some locations than in others. The distribution of prices should adjust and the market should self-correct if wrong decisions are made; for example if too much base-load plant is built, then off-peak prices should drop. If there is too little capacity in a transmission-constrained region, then prices there should rise.

The pricing rules, which we have described in the trading arrangements sections of this book, should encourage generators to offer energy to the system operator at marginal cost by setting the price of energy at the offer of the most expensive generator taken. If demand is curtailed, the price should be able to go higher; in the case of an active demand side with demand bidding, up to the level of the last demand bid accepted by the system operator; it should go higher still in the event of an outage, potentially to some estimate of VOLL.

It is not intuitively obvious how these market prices will provide the right incentives in a competitive market for development of an optimal amount of capacity, and capacity of the right type, as the old industry model did. The theory is, however, rather simple: Markets push producers to minimize costs. Decentralized market participants should in theory have incentives to build the same amount and type of capacity as central planners who followed minimum cost rules. The same basic economic principles apply to market investment decisions as did to centralized ones—the difference is that centralization relies on *internalizing* quantity decisions and competitive electricity markets rely on *external* price signals and profit incentives.

The best way to illustrate the theoretical equivalence is to return to the central-planning cross-over charts:

Step 1—Start with the evaluation of how many hours of outage will result: The answer to the question "How many outage hours will result?" is determined by a profitability analysis of peakers: Peakers will be enticed into the market, and will limit outages, at the level of output where they can first recover all their costs, fixed and variable, such as when they first make an excess profit of zero. This occurs where $P \times (\text{Outage Hours}) \geq F_A + (V_A \times (\text{Outage Hours}))$, where P is price.

(The term *excess profit* refers to profits in addition to those necessary to remain in business—an excess profit of zero doesn't mean that the generator will go bankrupt.)

The price that energy is set to when there is an outage is therefore the driver that determines how many hours of outage will result. If the pricing rule says that price goes to the customers valuation, VOLL, in the event of an outage, the cross-over point between outage and peakers is defined by the function $\text{VOLL} \times (\text{Outage Hours}) \geq F_A + (V_A \times (\text{Outage Hours}))$. (See Figure E.6.)

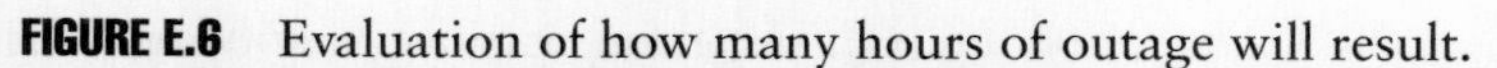

FIGURE E.6 Evaluation of how many hours of outage will result.

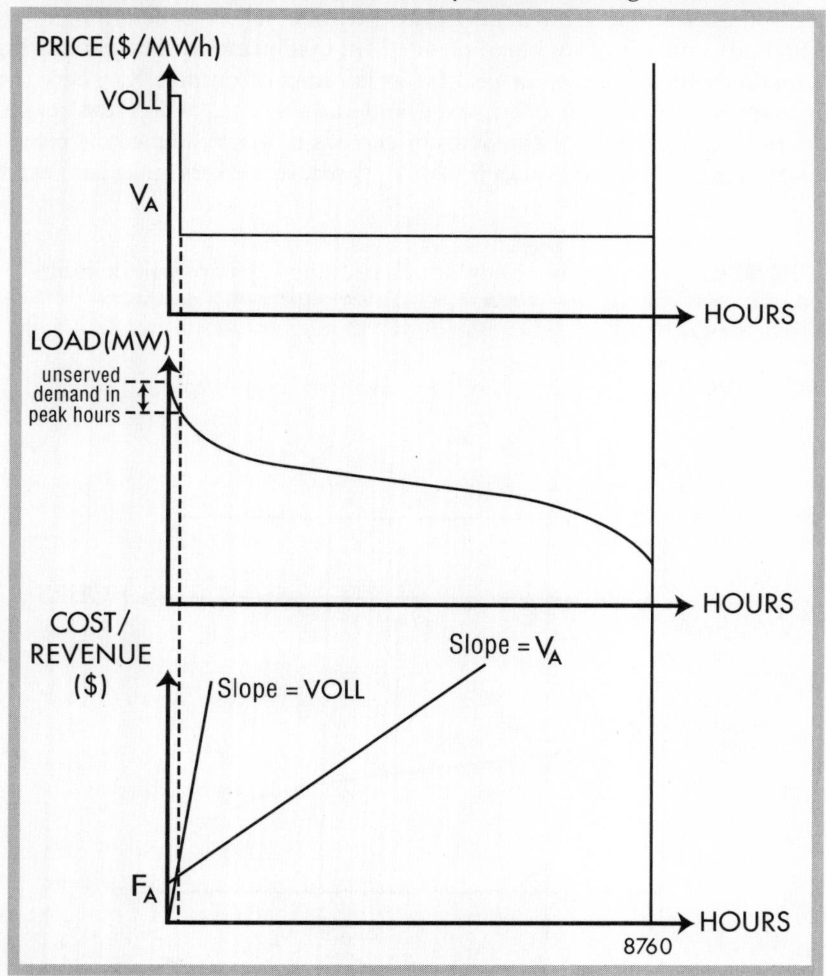

What excess profits do the peakers that enter make? The first MW of peaker built makes just enough margin above its variable cost in the outage hours to exactly offset its fixed cost since P × (Outage Hours) = $F_A + V_A \times$ (Outage Hours). Every other MW of peaker that is built and runs recovers its fixed costs from running in the same hours. In each additional hour that these units run, they are price-setters and thus receive a price equal to their marginal cost (V_A). Excess profits therefore remain at zero.

Step 2—Evaluation of how much peaking capacity will be built: The answer to the question "How many peakers will be built?" is determined by a profitability analysis of mid-load plants: Mid-load plants will be enticed into the market and will undercut peakers at the level of output, X, where they can first recover all their costs, fixed and variable (i.e., where the revenue from running in X hours first equals or exceeds $F_B + XV_B$). Since the revenue from running in X hours equals $F_A + XV_A$ (because peakers make zero excess

FIGURE E.7 Evaluation of how much peaking capacity will be built.

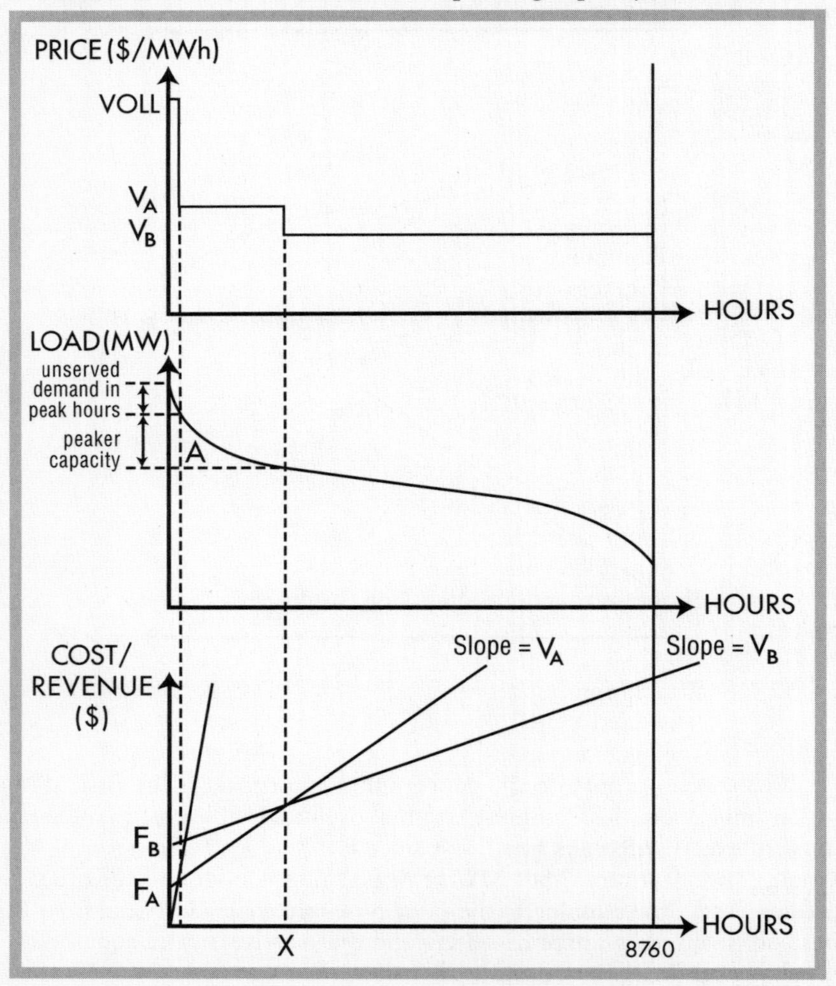

profits) the cross-over point is defined by the point where $F_A + XV_A = F_B + XV_B$. (See Figure E.7.)

What excess profits do mid-load plants that enter make? The first MW of mid-load plant built makes just enough margin above its variable cost in the first X hours to exactly offset its fixed cost since the revenue from running in X hours equals $F_B + XV_B$. Every other MW of base-load plant that is built and runs recovers its fixed costs from running in the same hours. In each additional hour that these units run beyond X, they are price-setters and thus receive a price equal to their marginal cost (V_B). Excess profits therefore remain at zero. Since no peaker runs beyond X hours, the excess profit of peakers stays at zero.

Step 3—Evaluation of how much mid-load capacity will be built: The answer to the question "How many mid-load plants will be built?" is determined by a profitability analysis of Base-load plants: Base-load plants will be enticed into the market and will undercut mid-load plants at the level of output, Y, where they can recover all their costs, fixed and variable, such as when the revenue from running in Y hours first equals or exceeds $F_C + YV_C$. Since the revenue from running in Y hours equals $F_B + YV_B$ (because mid-load plants make zero excess profits), the cross-over point between mid-load plants and base-load plants is defined by the point where $F_B + YV_B = F_C + YV_C$. (See Figure E.8.)

What excess profits do base-load plants that enter make? The first MW of base-load plant built makes just enough margin above its variable cost in the first Y hours to exactly offset its fixed cost since the revenue from running in Y hours equals $F_C + YV_C$. Every other MW of base-load plant that is built and runs recovers its fixed costs from running in the same hours. In each additional hour that these units run beyond Y, they are price-setters and thus receive a price equal to their marginal cost (V_C). Excess profits therefore remain at zero, and hence the excess profit of all generating plant built is zero.

Step 4—Evaluation of how much base-load capacity will be built: Like in the old, centralized model, base-load plants will meet all the remaining capacity requirements not met by peakers and mid-load plants.

THEORETICAL EQUIVALENCE

To summarize, the cross-over chart analyses indicate that the most efficient mix of plant types and the most efficient number of hours to allow outage are arrived at in a market much like the process under central planning,

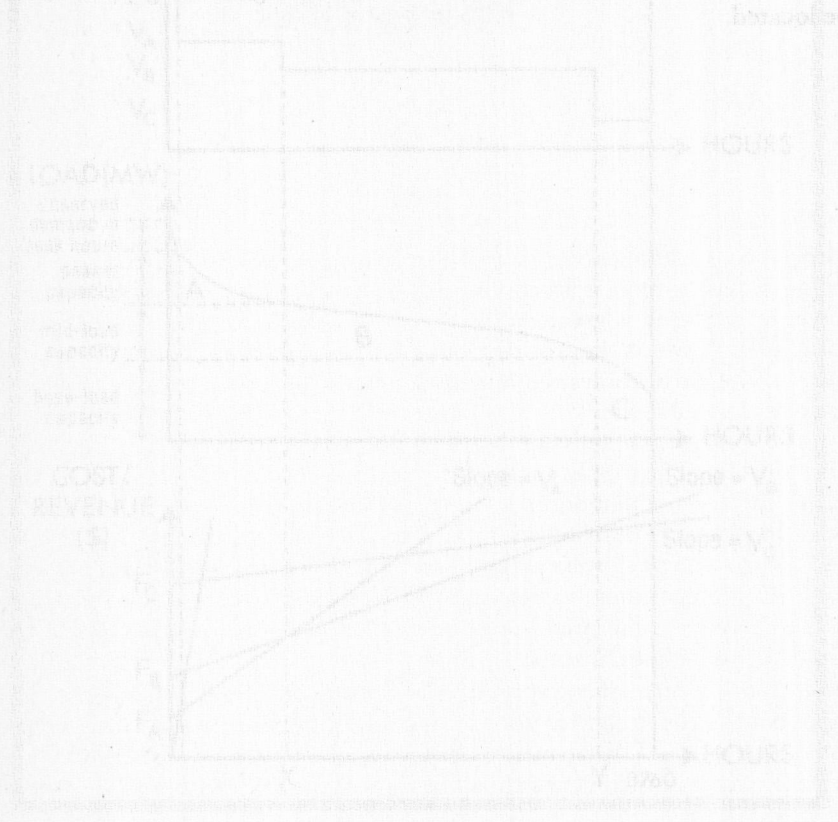

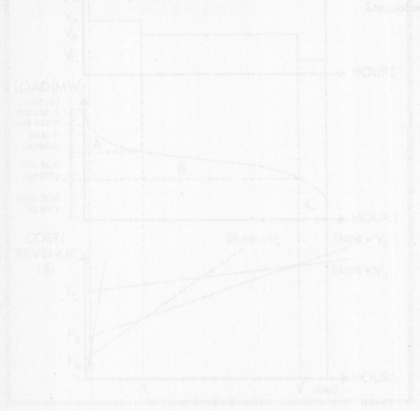

APPENDIX F

Building New Transmission—When, Where, and How

Stripped of complicating factors the central feature in evaluating a new line is quite simple: it is economic to build a line if the value of additional power transported is greater than the cost of the line.[1] The value of transporting the power is the cost difference between generating at A and generating at B. This is always the fundamental cost-benefit analysis that should be done for a new line.[2]

The value of transmission between two zones, A and B, is illustrated in this appendix. The supply curves for each zone are shown in Figures F.1 and F.2. In each zone the marginal cost of generation increases as more expensive generators are dispatched: that is, the supply curves are upwards sloping. If the two zones were unconnected, the marginal costs of generation would define economic values of $14/MWh in zone A and $23/MWh in zone B. These are the prices at which the supply curves intersect with the level of demand in each zone.

Figure F.3 turns the graph for zone B through 180 degrees and superimposes it on the graph for zone A. Figure F.3 shows the total demand for both zones as X + Y, to be met by generation in one zone or the other. In the absence of transmission constraints, transportation would be costless (if we

[1] Much of this appendix is extracted from the authors' work with the Mexican Ministry of Energy, published as: Secretaría de Energía, Propuesta de Cambio Estructural de la Industria Eléctrica en México, México 1999, and from Sally Hunt and Graham Shuttleworth, *Competition and Choice in Electricity,* John Wiley, 1996.

[2] Complicating factors include the value of extra transmission to (1) enlarge marketplaces to reduce potential market power and (2) provide backup in the event of hostile attack. For market-based transmission investment, distortions caused by electricity price caps are also a complication.

FIGURE F.1 Zone A.

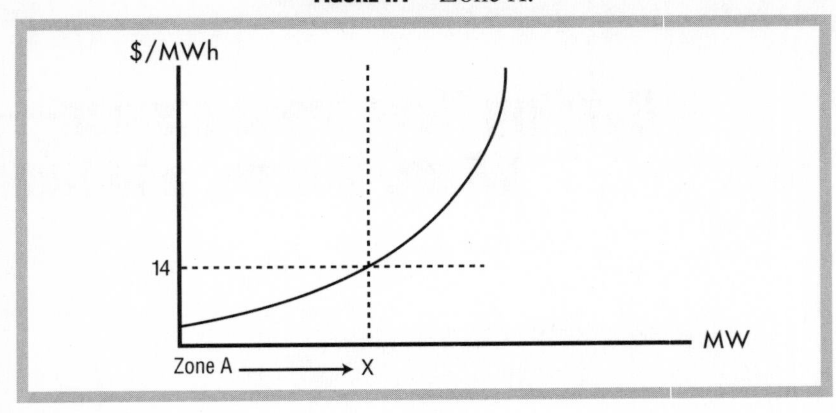

assume no losses) and the least cost solution would require marginal costs to be equal in both zones. This happens at the intersection of the two supply curves, where generation is X + T in zone A and Y – T in zone B. Line flow from A to B, in MW, would be T and the marginal cost of generation would be $20/MWh in each zone.

However, if there is a constraint on transmission between the two zones it is not possible to reach this position. For example, if the capacity of the link between A and B (L) is less than the unconstrained level of transmission between them (T), the level of generation in zone A will need to be pulled back to X + L. Figure F.3 shows that this would reduce the price of generation in zone A from $20/MWh to $17/MWh. Generation in zone A would

FIGURE F.2 Zone B.

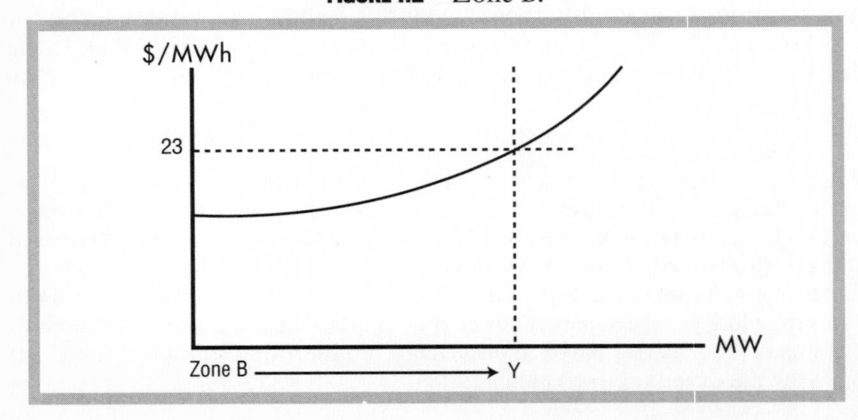

FIGURE F.3 Zones A and B.

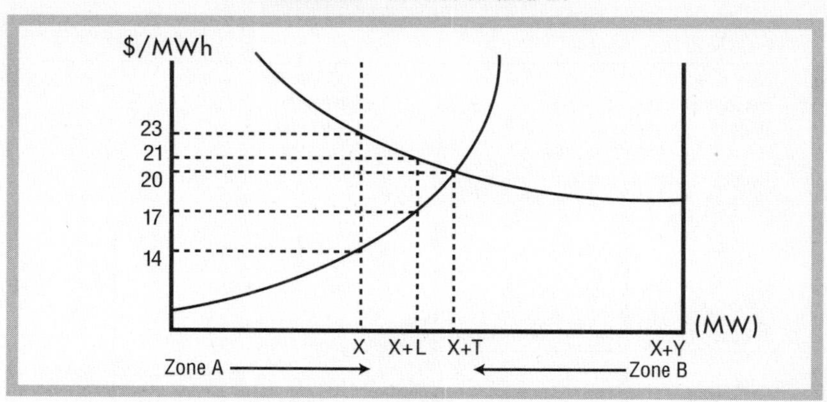

need to be replaced by more expensive generators on the other side of the constraint. The marginal cost of generation in zone B would increase to \$21/MWh, and the total cost of generation in the two zones together would be higher. In this example, the short-run marginal value of transmission from A to B is \$4/MWh. It is calculated as the difference between the marginal costs of generation in the two zones (that is, \$21/MWh minus \$17/MWh).

JUSTIFICATION OF TRANSMISSION EXPANSION

Transmission expansion is justified when the discounted present value of dispatch savings integrated over all hours of future system use, rises above the cost of expansion. The economic rules for system expansion are:

- Only build additional capacity if total savings in the cost of generation (and load management) exceed the total expansion costs; and
- Add capacity until the marginal generation savings equal the marginal cost of building additional capacity.

If these rules are followed, the value of any project exceeds its cost and the sum of future short-run costs equals the long-run marginal cost of future expansion.

Suppose that there is initially no line from A to B. Suppose further that the annual costs for a new line from A to B is \$32,000/MW/year, and that the line will carry 8000MWh/year per MW built. Then the average cost of

FIGURE F.4 700 MW line.

EXAMPLE:

Line size	700 MW
Average line cost	$4/MWh
Price difference before new line	$9/MWh
Price difference after new line	$4/MWh
Average value of new line	(9+4)/2=$6.50/MWh

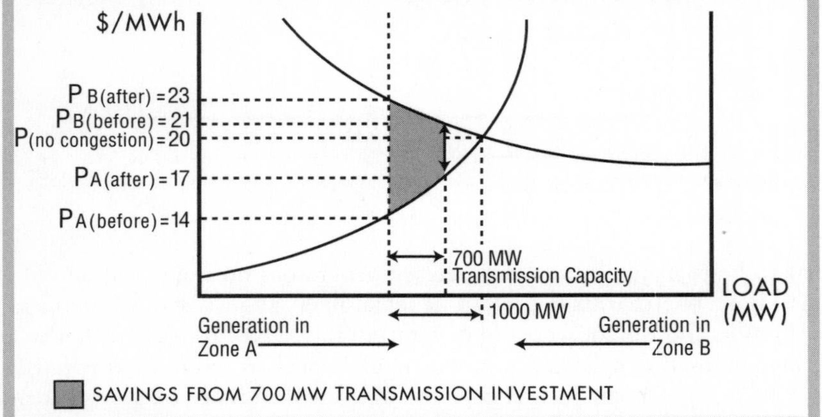

$/MWh
P B(after) = 23
P B(before) = 21
P(no congestion) = 20
P A(after) = 17
P A(before) = 14
700 MW Transmission Capacity
1000 MW
LOAD (MW)
Generation in Zone A
Generation in Zone B
SAVINGS FROM 700 MW TRANSMISSION INVESTMENT

the line is $4/MWh. The marginal value of transmission before the expansion is represented by the energy price at B minus the energy price at A, or 23 – 14 = $9/MWh. The marginal value of transmission between A and B after a 700 MW line is built is $4/MWh ($21/MWh minus $17/MWh). Figure F.4 shows that the average value of a 700 MW transmission expansion is therefore approximately $6.50/MWh ((9 + 4)/2) and it is economic to build the line.

Note that the line is economic, but does not relieve congestion entirely. If there are no scale economies (none are assumed in Figure F.4), the marginal costs of additional expansion beyond 700 MW would exceed the benefits. Building less capacity would forgo opportunities to make economic transactions. The transmission capacity of 700 MW would be optimal.

ECONOMICS OF SCALE AND FTRS

More generally, transmission investment will involve nondivisibilities and economies of scale. Capacity is therefore added at infrequent intervals. This might mean that it is not practical to build exactly 700 MW of transmission. However, the same principles apply. Actual expansion proposals might be for K MW, and K might be either greater or less than 700. If K is less than 700, and the cost of transmission is still $4/MWh, then the proposal will be cost effective since the marginal value of transmission will be higher than $4. If K is greater than 700, the marginal value of transmission will be less than $4, but it is still possible that the proposal is cost effective if the average value of the new transmission built is greater than $4. This is illustrated in Table F.1 where K = 1,000 MW, but the line is still cost effective. In this instance, the average value of the new line is $4.50/MWh.

If this line was funded by market participants in exchange for FTRs (see Chapter 9), they would receive FTRs for 1,000 MW between A and B. Collection of FTR payments gives market participants funding the new line the guarantee that if it becomes congested (and the price of transmission usage rises again) they still receive the benefits of the line. For instance, in this example before the line is built, the price difference between A and B is $9/MWh ($23/MWh minus $14/MWh). A generator at A funds the line and gets FTRs for 1,000 MW from A to B. These FTRs entitle it to the price difference between A and B multiplied by 1,000 MW. Immediately after the link is built, the prices are equalized in each location since all congestion is relieved. The value of the line shows up in the price of electricity at A ($20/MWh vs. $14/MWh). The generator who paid for the line gets a higher local price, which justifies having put in the line. He "sells in a higher priced market."

But this situation may not be permanent. Continuing with the example, another generator (generator 2) builds a 1,000 MW plant at A. The line is now congested again. Generator 2 bids energy into the market at a lower price than generator 1 (who built the line). Generator 1's output is reduced to the level it was before the transmission expansion and the price at B is reduced to the price before the expansion ($14/MWh). But what the FTR does is assign the value of the transmission—the energy price at B minus the energy price at A, reflecting the new level of congestion after the new line

TABLE F.1 1,000 MW Line

EXAMPLE	
Line size	1,000 MW
Line cost	$4/MWh
Price difference before new line	$9/MWh
Price difference after new line	$0/MWh (refer to Figure F.4)
Average value of new line	(9 + 0)/2 = $4.50/MWh

and new generator—to generator 1 for 1,000 MW. Generator 1 continues to receive the value of the right he paid for, even though someone else is using the line.

It is as if he sold the right temporarily to generator 2 for its value. *FTRs act as tradable transmission rights that are in fact traded but the trading is automatic. Generator 1 receives the rents without having to sell his FTR, irrespective of who uses the line and when the line is used.*

INDEPENDENT APPROVAL OF ALL PROPOSED EXPANSIONS

The regulator and/or ISO must verify that privately funded transmission expansions are for the public good. In evaluating the economic merit of individual transmission expansion proposals, it/they should compare the total present value of the generation savings to the total cost of the expansion. This comparison is illustrated in Figure F.5.

If the dispatch savings are greater than the expansion cost, then the investment is economic and it should proceed (like the 700 and 1,000 MW examples given earlier).

It is possible that market participants will support transmission expansion, when the expansion is not of net economic benefit. This could occur, for example, if other generators at A would benefit from a higher price from the X MW they are already producing at that location. The amount of this benefit is illustrated in Figure F.6.

FIGURE F.5 Investment with indivisibilities.

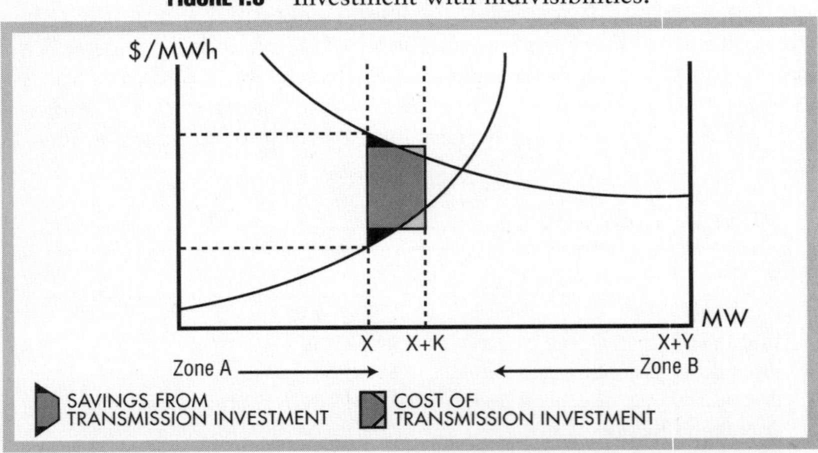

FIGURE F.6 Rent transfer to other generators.

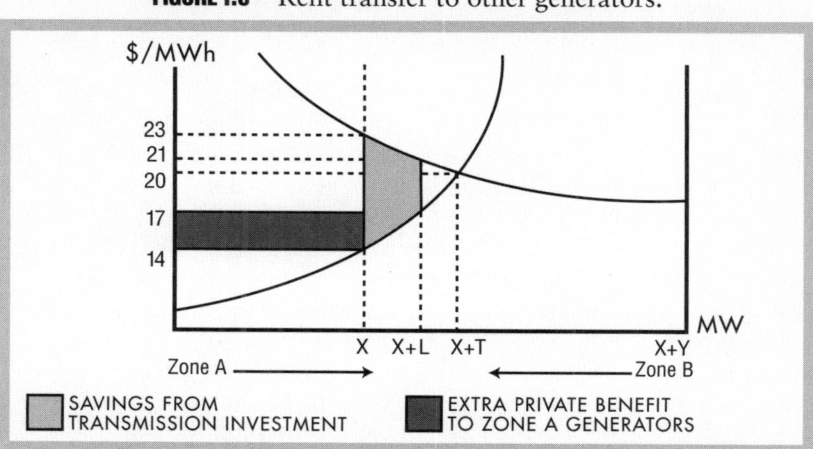

This gain is not an economic benefit. It is a transfer of "economic rent" from local consumers to local generators. This transfer of economic rent may make an expansion of transmission capacity appear to be cost-effective, when in fact it is not. But note: It is still possible that the expansion is for the public good on the grounds of national security, of reducing potential market power problems, or if price caps in power markets are distorting the value of transmission; this is for the regulator/ISO to determine.

glossary

ancillary services Those services required to deliver electricity to end-users at stable frequencies and voltages; includes frequency regulation or control, spinning reserves, non-spinning reserves, and reactive supply/voltage control.

bilateral contract A contract between two named parties. The common forms used in electricity are the physical bilateral contract; and the financial equivalent, the contract for differences (CfD).

bottom-up pricing A method of setting retail rates based on unbundled prices.

bundled price A combined charge for generation, transmission, and distribution service in customer rates.

capacity The maximum electric power output, usually measured in MW, for which a generating system or plant is rated.

capacity payment A payment for making generation capacity available to the system.

cap-and-trade An environmental management policy in which some aggregate capacity of emissions is established and translated into permits to produce emissions up to that level. Initial endowments of permits are allocated which can then be freely traded.

cogeneration The use of an energy source to produce electricity as well as another product, such as steam for heating.

combined cycle gas turbine (CCGT) An electric generating plant that uses one source of energy to drive two types of turbines: a combustion turbine and a steam turbine.

congestion The event of one or more transmission lines being filled to maximum capacity.

congestion management The process of managing the use of the transmission system so transmission capacity constraints are not violated.

contract path The path over the transmission system that an individual electricity transaction is assumed to follow (used in the wheeling trading model).

contracts for differences (CfDs) Bilateral contracts in the form of financial agreements to pay the difference between the contract price and and some specified market prices.

cost of service regulation A method of regulation that allows companies to recover their actual (or prudently-incurred) costs, including the cost of capital.

customer choice *See* retail competition.

customer switching The process of customers leaving the regulated service of a utility to be served by a competitive energy provider.

decentralized trading model A form of trading arrangements in which the aim is to minimize the system operator's role in the operation of spot markets.

default provider The provider of default service.

default service Service, under customer choice, to end-use customers who do not wish to choose.

deregulation The process of ceasing to regulate.

dispatch The process of precisely matching generation with load in real time. This role is carried out centrally by the system operator.

dispatchable A generator that is willing and able to have its output controlled in real time by the system operator, in response to market prices.

Distco The term used in this book for a distribution division/company under competition.

distribution The transport of electricity over medium- and low-voltage lines to end-use customers.

distribution division/company The commercial entity that runs the distribution system and interfaces with customers.

distribution system The low voltage system of lines, cables, transformers, and other equipment used to transport electricity to end-use customers, usually within a local region.

divestiture The requirement that utilities sell off assets as part of the restructuring process.

eligible customer A customer who is allowed (by a regulator) to switch to a competitive energy provider.

end-use customer The ultimate (final) consumer of electrical power. (Normally a residence, commercial business or industrial facility.)

Energy Policy Act of 1992 (EPAct) The law that permitted the U.S. federal regulator to order open access to the transmission, and removed constraints on entry of generators.

Federal Energy Regulatory Commission (FERC) The federal regulator of energy matters in the United States.

financial transmission right (FTR) A right (denominated in MW) to receive the price difference arising from congestion between one defined point on the transmission system and another.

flexible *See* dispatchable.

forward market A market where delivery is at some point in the future.

generation The electric power output, usually measured in MWh, from a generator.
generator Refers to a power plant (although technically it means a component within a power plant).
green power Power from renewable resources; power from windmills, solar cells, and so on.
grid Transmission system.
Gridco In this book, a company that owns only transmission assets.
hydro plant A plant in which the turbine-generators are driven by falling water.
imbalance The differences between an amount contracted, and the amounts actually sent out by a supplier and consumed by a customer in real time.
imbalance price The price paid or received per MWh for imbalances. *See also* spot price.
incentive-compatible rule A rule that makes the people who have to obey it do so voluntarily because it is in their own interest to do so.
independent power producer (IPP) Generating companies who sell output under contracts, often life-of-plant contracts. They do not serve a designated service territory.
independent system operator (ISO) A system operator independent from control by any single market participant or group of participants.
inflexible *See* nondispatchable.
installed generating capacity The amount of generation capacity (usually denominated in MW) that is connected to the transmission system.
integrated trading model A form of trading arrangements in which operational arrangements (including congestion, imbalance, and ancillary services management) and commercial arrangements (including spot markets) are highly integrated and carried out by the system operator.
intelligent price caps Price caps that approximate the demand/supply intersection.
interconnector A transmission line connecting two transmission systems.
interruptible service A service (tariff) to an end-use customer in which the customer has agreed to be cut off by the system operator, if necessary, under certain infrequent conditions. It is most likely to be used by industrial customers.
kW; MW; GW Units of capacity kilowatt (=10^3W), megawatt (=10^6W), gigawatt (=10^9W).
kWh; MWh; GWh Units of electric energy: kilowatt-hour, megawatt-hour, gigawatt-hour.
load The amount of electric power delivered or required instantaneously. Also referred to as demand. Usually measured in MW. (The term is sometimes used to mean all customers collectively.)

load profiling An estimation technique used to assign hourly consumption to customers who do not have time-of-use meters.

locational prices Prices for electricity that differ by location for reasons of congestion and marginal losses in transmission. Locational prices are either zonal prices or nodal prices.

loop flow A term used to describe the fact that electricity takes the path of least resistance (according to Kirchoff's law) and that electricity moves across many parallel lines instead of only one.

losses Loss of electrical energy incurred during transmission or distribution (mainly due to the heating of wires).

loss of load probability (LOLP) The probability that the electricity system will have a service interruption due to a lack of generating capacity.

market operator The institution responsible for operating the spot market.

market power The ability of a seller to reduce the output supplied to the market so as to raise the market price, and do so profitably.

merchant generator A privately financed generating company or generating plant; generally used to mean one not dependent on life-of-plant contracts, in contrast to Independent Power Producers (IPPs).

merit order The principle by which generators are ranked by order of short-run cost to establish economic precedence and lowest overall cost of dispatch.

municipality (muni) A type of utility, which is owned and operated by a city.

National Grid Company (NGC) The company formed at vesting to own and operate the U.K. transmission grid.

native load The retail load of the customers served by a vertically integrated utility.

New Electricity Trading Arrangements (NETA) The trading arrangements put in place in 2001 in England and Wales.

nodal pricing A method of locational pricing in which there is a unique price at each node.

node A point on the transmission system, normally used to define prices for delivery of energy to or from the grid. (Typically it is the busbar at the end-terminal of a branch of the transmission system.)

nondispatchable A generator that is not willing and/or able to have its output controlled in real time by the system operator.

North American Electric Reliability Council (NERC) A voluntary organization promoting electric system reliability and security in North America.

open access Access to the transmission grid for all transmission users.

Order No. 2000 The order put out by FERC in 1999 initiating RTOs.

Order No. 888 The order put out by FERC in 1996 that dictates much of the way energy is traded today in the United States.

pancaking The stacking up of transmission fees when a transaction is deemed to cross two or more areas.

peak demand The maximum load during a specific time period. Usually it is measured in MW.

performance-based regulation (PBR) A form of regulation that provides incentives for utilities to cut costs and make efficient investment decisions. A utility's return on investment is linked to its performance according to specific performance criteria.

physical bilateral contract A bilateral contract specifying physical delivery of power that requires the contract to be scheduled with the system operator.

physical transmission right (PTR) A transmission right that is needed, under the wheeling trading model, in order for an independent generator to be able to schedule an energy transaction (over an assumed contract path).

PJM The Pennsylvania–New Jersey–Maryland Interconnection, L.L.C., a limited liability company. This company is responsible for the operation and control of the electric power system throughout major portions of five Mid-Atlantic states and the District of Columbia in the United States.

power pool (pool) Term used for an organization coordinating dispatch between different companies.

Power Purchase Agreement (PPA) A contract, usually long-term, between parties for the sale of power at predetermined prices or price formulae.

price cap An administratively imposed maximum price in a market.

privatization The sale of government-owned generation, transmission, or distribution assets to private investors.

provider of last resort (POLR) The provider of service to end-use customers that no retailer wants (e.g., because they are credit risks), or to those whose retailers have gone out of business.

Public Utility Commissions (PUC) The state regulators of electricity matters in the United States.

Public Utility Holding Company Act of 1935 (PUHCA) The U.S. law that caused the break up of large interstate holding companies. (The break up was by divestiture, until each became a single consolidated system serving a circumscribed geographic area.) Another feature of the law permitted holding companies to engage only in business that was essential and appropriate for the operation of a single integrated utility.

Public Utility Regulatory Policies Act of 1978 (PURPA) The U.S. law that requires, among other things, a program providing for increased conservation of electric energy, increased efficiency in the use of facilities and resources by electric utilities, and equitable retail rates for electric consumers. It also requires electric utilities to interconnect with and buy whatever amount of capacity and energy is offered from any facility meeting the criteria for a QF, and further requires that the utility pay for that power at the utility's own incremental or avoided cost of production.

qualifying facility (QF) A cogeneration or small power production facility that meets certain ownership, operating, and efficiency criteria established by FERC pursuant to PURPA.

rate Price. *See also* tariff.

Regional Transmission Organization (RTO) A term used in FERC's Order No. 2000 to describe new entities arising from regional consolidation of transmission systems.

restructuring Changing existing companies; separating some functions and combining others, and sometimes creating new companies.

retail access *See* retail competition.

retail competition The ability of different energy providers (retailers) to compete in the electricity market to sell residential, commercial or industrial customers power at unregulated rates.

retailer A firm that sells electricity to end-use customers.

RPI-X A formula used in price-cap regulation to adjust tariffs by the amount of inflation minus an efficiency coefficient (X factor) based on expected productivity improvements.

settlement The process of accounting for electricity that generators produce and customers consume.

settlement software The suite of computer programs used by the market operator to calculate market charges and payments.

shopping credit The "price to beat" that consumers under customer choice use to compare retailers.

spot market A market where delivery is immediate.

spot price The price for spot transactions.

stranded costs Costs that result from investments, contracts, and regulatory decisions made before the reform of the electricity industry, which cannot be recovered from market prices.

system operator The entity responsible for operation of the transmission grid, including resolving congestion, and dispatching generation.

tariff The set of approved electricity prices (varying by class of customers, season, time of day, etc). Can also be used to refer to nonprice terms and conditions of a regulated service such as quality standards, disconnection rules, and credit requirements. ("Tariff" generally implies official governmental or regulatory approval, as opposed to a competitive offering.)

tight pool A U.S. term applying to one of the three power pools in the Northeastern United States (New York, New England, and PJM) that existed under regulation and arranged central dispatch in their respective areas. (The U.K. Pool was the first set of trading arrangements in the United Kingdom, superceded by NETA.)

top-down pricing A method of setting retail rates based on the concept that the current regulated (and bundled) prices are recovering stranded costs.

trading arrangements The rules that govern the marketplace, encompassing the legal agreements covering all aspects of the traders' relation to the system operator and to the transmission owner.

transco In this book, a combined ISO and Gridco.

transmission network or transmission system The high voltage network of lines, cables, transformers, and other equipment used to transport electricity.

transmission The transport of electricity over high voltage lines from generators to local distribution networks, or direct to high-voltage large industrial customers.

unbundled prices Separate charges for generation, transmission, and distribution service in consumer rates.

unit As used in this book, several units at the same site make up a power plant.

value of lost load (VOLL) The cost to end-use customers if power is cut off.

vertical integration The provision of transmission, distribution, and generation by a single utility.

vesting contract A contract endowed upon a company at the time of its restructuring, usually designed so as to be in effect during the transaction to a deregulated market.

virtual direct access A pass-through of the wholesale spot price to consumers under retail access.

wheeling trading model A form of trading arrangements in which an integrated utility with its own generation runs system operations and provides access to its transmission by scheduling contracts at the request of traders, after it has scheduled its own resources for its native load.

wholesale market A market that facilitates trades between large buyers (retail companies and sometimes industrial customers) and sellers (generators) of electricity.

zonal pricing A method of locational pricing in which there is a unique price at each zone, where a zone is a group of nodes.

index